# The GIFT of the BLESSING

---

# The GIFT of HONOR

# The GIFT of the BLESSING

## The GIFT of HONOR

*Two Bestselling Works Complete in One Volume*

### GARY SMALLEY
### JOHN TRENT, PH.D.

## INSPIRATIONAL PRESS

NEW YORK

Previously published as two separate volumes:

THE GIFT OF THE BLESSING
Copyright © 1993 by Gary Smalley and John Trent. All rights reserved. Original
copyright of *The Blessing* 1986

THE GIFT OF HONOR
Copyright © 1987 by Gary Smalley and John Trent.

First Inspirational Press edition published in 1998.

Inspirational Press
A division of BBS Publishing Corporation
386 Park Avenue South
New York, NY 10016

Inspirational Press is a registered trademark of BBS Publishing Corporation.

Published by arrangement with Thomas Nelson, Inc.

Library of Congress Catalog Card Number: 98-72398

ISBN: 0-88486-216-X

Printed in the United States of America.

# Contents

The Gift of the Blessing      1

The Gift of Honor      267

# The GIFT of the
# BLESSING

# *Dedication*

*This book is dedicated to our wives, Norma and Cynthia, for their loving support and encouragement, and to four couples who have been a tremendous source of blessing to us in making this book possible: David and Karen Cavan, Doug and Judie Childress, Jerry and Judy LaBrasca, and Steve and Barbara Uhlmann.*

# Contents

|  |  | The Birth of the Blessing | 9 |
|---|---|---|---|
| *Chapter* | *1* | In Search of the Blessing | 11 |
| *Chapter* | *2* | The Blessing: *Yesterday and Today* | 22 |
| *Chapter* | *3* | The First Element of the Blessing: *Meaningful Touch* | 37 |
| *Chapter* | *4* | The Second Element of the Blessing: *Spoken Words* | 55 |
| *Chapter* | *5* | The Third Element of the Blessing: *Expressing High Value* | 70 |
| *Chapter* | *6* | The Fourth Element of the Blessing: *Picturing a Special Future* | 86 |
| *Chapter* | *7* | The Fifth Element of the Blessing: *An Active Commitment* | 100 |
| *Chapter* | *8* | Homes That Withhold the Blessing: Part 1 | 119 |
| *Chapter* | *9* | Homes That Withhold the Blessing: Part 2 | 131 |
| *Chapter* | *10* | Learning to Live Apart from the Blessing. | 149 |
| *Chapter* | *11* | When You Know You Will Never Receive a Parent's Blessing | 172 |
| *Chapter* | *12* | Giving the Blessing to Your Spouse and Friends | 183 |
| *Chapter* | *13* | Giving the Blessing to Your Parents | 201 |
| *Chapter* | *14* | Giving the Blessing to Your Older Children | 214 |
| *Chapter* | *15* | A Church That Gives the Blessing | 228 |
| *Chapter* | *16* | A Final Blessing | 238 |
| *Appendix A* |  | Evenings of Blessing to Apply with Your Loved Ones | 246 |
| *Appendix B* |  | Sample Blessings Based on the Scriptures | 257 |
| Notes |  |  | 260 |

# *Acknowledgments*

We would like to express our deepest thanks to the following people:

To the hundreds of people who have written and spoken to us over the years about the positive difference this book has made in their lives. This revised and expanded edition gratefully shares some of their insight, applications, and encouragement;

To Janet Thoma, Susan Salmon Trotman, and Laurie Clark, for their encouragement and hard work in this revision;

To Diana Trent, for the hours she put into proofreading the manuscript;

To Larry Weeden and Bruce Nygren, our editors at Thomas Nelson on the original version of *The Blessing,* for their encouragement and expertise;

To our teammate in ministry, Terry Brown, for his careful reading of the manuscript and helpful suggestions;

To the many individuals and small groups who were willing to offer their comments and suggestions to help us refine the concepts found in the book, especially to the following people: Randy Vogel, Pat Dixon, Richard and Donna Alverson, Chuck and Jane Beuerlein, Rick and Denita Ryan, Don and Nancy Schlander, and Rick and Angie Wonder.

# The Birth of the Blessing

*T*he writing of every book has its own history.

Nearly fifteen years ago, God used two experiences to show me (John) the power of the blessing. I was leading a Bible study at Northwest Bible Church in Dallas, Texas, working through the book of Genesis. I was also completing my doctorate in counseling and working with many couples and individuals in therapy. Day after day, I saw people in deep depression and emotional distress over pain from their past. And, one day, while working on my Bible study, I ran into Genesis 27 and Esau's bitter cry, "Bless me, even me also, O my father"! (Gen. 27:34 NASB).

Suddenly, I saw echoed in the lives of those I counseled all the heartache and unfulfilled longing that Esau felt. What's more, stripped bare and laid before me was my own lack of receiving the blessing from my father.

Because of this profound revelation, the concept of the blessing became the subject of my doctoral dissertation. And then, several years after teaming up with Gary Smalley, we molded my research into an earlier version of the book you hold in your hand, *The Blessing* (Nashville: Thomas Nelson Publishers, 1986). Gary, too, missed receiving the blessing from his father. Together, in sharing and writing about the heartache we both felt, this book became our personal journey, not just an academic one.

Today, the blessing has become a life-message that I teach at "Blessing" seminars across North America and overseas, and at our "Love is a Decision" seminars. Each time I bring up Esau's lament, I look into the eyes of people who have felt that anguish. And I look into the eyes of people who want to make sure their own children never know that pain.

In this revised, expanded edition of *The Blessing* we have tried to maintain the basic content and structure of our first book. Yet after eight years we've gained new insights that we want to share with our readers.

While our original book focused on giving the blessing to young children, in this version you'll discover eight ways to give the blessing to your older children and grandchildren. You'll also learn more about the dark side of the blessing from those who have lived under a "curse." And you'll see how to personally deal with the loss of a parent who never blessed you.

We are convinced that the blessing is perhaps the most powerful parenting concept in the Scriptures. As you read this book (again, or for the first time), we hope it will be a source of great encouragement to you as a parent, and to you as an adult child. May it make your heavenly Father's love more real to you and within easier reach than ever before.

# Chapter One

## In Search of the Blessing

**A**ll of us long to be accepted by others. While we may say out loud, "I don't care what other people think about me," on the inside we all yearn for intimacy and affection. This yearning is especially true in our relationship with our parents. Gaining or missing out on parental approval has a tremendous effect on us, even if it has been years since we have had any regular contact with them. In fact, what happens in our relationship with our parents can greatly affect all our present and future relationships. While this may sound like an exaggeration, our office has been filled with people struggling with this very issue, people just like Brian and Nancy.

### THE CRUSHING OF BRIAN'S DREAM

*"Please say that you love me, please!"* Brian's words trailed off into tears as he leaned over the now still form of his father. It was late at night in a large metropolitan hospital. Only the cold, white walls and the humming of a heart monitor kept Brian company. His tears revealed a deep inner pain and sensitivity that had tormented him for years, emotional wounds that now seemed beyond repair.

Brian had flown nearly halfway across the country to be at his father's side in one last attempt to try to reconcile years of misunderstanding and resentment. All his life, Brian had been searching for his father's acceptance and approval, but they always seemed just out of reach.

Brian's father had been a career Marine officer. His sole desire for Brian was that when he grew up he would follow in his father's footsteps. With that in mind, Brian's father took every opportunity to instill in his son discipline and the backbone he would need when one day he too was an officer.

Words of love or tenderness were forbidden in their home. It was almost as if any slip into a display of warmth might crack the tough exterior Brian's father was trying to create in his son.

Brian's father drove him to participate in sports and to take elective classes that would best equip him to be an officer. Brian's only praise for scoring a touchdown or doing well in a class was a lecture on how he could and should have done even better.

After graduating from high school, Brian did enlist in the Marine Corps. It was the happiest day of his father's life. However, his joy was short-lived. Cited for attitude problems and a disrespect for orders, his son was soon on report. After weeks of such reports (which included getting into a vicious fight with his drill instructor), Brian was dishonorably discharged from the service as incorrigible.

The news of Brian's dismissal from the Marines dealt a death blow to his relationship with his father. He was no longer welcome in his father's home, and for years there was no contact between them.

During those years, Brian struggled with feelings of inferiority and lacked self-confidence. Even though he was above average in intelligence, he worked at various jobs far below his abilities. Three times he had been engaged—only to break the engagement just weeks before the wedding. Somehow he just didn't believe that another person could really love him.

Although Brian was unaware of it at the time, he was experiencing common symptoms of growing up without a sense of the family blessing, a missing element in his life that finally led him to seek professional help.

We began counseling with Brian after he had broken his third engagement. As he peeled away the layers of his past, Brian began to see both his need for his family's blessing and his responsibility for dealing honestly with his parents. That is when the call came from his mother saying that his father was dying from a heart attack.

Brian went immediately to the hospital to see his father. The entire flight he was filled with hope that now, at long last, they could talk and reconcile their relationship. "I'm sure he'll listen to me. I've learned *so* much. I know things are going to change between us." Brian repeated these phrases over and over to himself during the flight. But it was not to be.

Brian's father slipped into a coma a few hours before he arrived. The words that Brian longed to hear for the first time— words of love and acceptance—now would never be spoken. Four hours after Brian arrived at the hospital, his father died without regaining consciousness.

"Dad, please wake up!" Brian's heartbreaking sobs echoed down the hospital corridor. His cries spoke of an incredible sense of loss: not only the physical loss of his father, but, like many others, also the emotional sense of losing any chance of his father's blessing.

## NANCY RELIVES A PAINFUL PAST

Nancy's loss was a different sort, but the hurt and pain she received from missing out on the blessing stung her just as deeply. In fact, living apart from the blessing had caused problems not only with her parents, but with her husband and children as well.

Nancy grew up in an affluent suburb outside a major city. During Nancy's early years, her mother loved to socialize with other women at the club and at frequent civic activities. In fact, with a marriage that was less than fulfilling, these social gatherings became of paramount importance to Nancy's mother.

When Nancy was very young, her mother would dress her up in elegant clothes (the kind you had to sit still in, not play in) and take her and her older sister to the club. But as Nancy grew older, this practice began to change.

Unlike her mother and older sister, Nancy was not petite. In fact, she was quite large and big-boned. Nor was Nancy a model of tranquility. She was a tomboy who loved outdoor games, swinging on fences, and animals of all kinds.

As you might imagine, such behavior from a daughter who was being groomed to be a debutante caused real problems. Nancy's mother tried desperately to mend her daughter's erring ways. Nancy was constantly scolded about being "awkward" and "clumsy." During shopping sprees, Nancy was often subjected to verbal barbs designed to motivate her to lose weight. "All the really nice clothes are two sizes too small for you. They're your *sister's* size," her mother would taunt. Nancy was finally forced on a strict diet to try to make her physically presentable to others.

Nancy tried hard to stick to her diet and be all her mother wanted. However, more and more often Nancy's mother and sister would go to social events and leave Nancy at home. Soon all invitations to join these functions stopped. After all, her mother told her, "You don't want to be embarrassed because of the way you look with all the other children around, do you?"

When Nancy first came in for counseling, she was in her thirties, married, and the mother of two children. For years she had struggled with her weight and with feelings of inferiority. Her marriage had been a constant struggle for her as well.

Nancy's husband loved her and was deeply committed to her, but her inability to feel acceptable left her constantly insecure and defensive. As a result of this hypersensitivity, every time she and her husband began to draw close, Nancy would feel threatened. Invariably, some small thing her husband did would set her off, and her marriage was back at arm's length.

Frankly, because of her lack of acceptance in the past, being at arm's length was the only place Nancy felt comfortable in a relationship. Her marriage was certainly of concern to her. Yet where Nancy struggled most was with her children, and with one child in particular.

Nancy had two daughters. The older girl was big-boned and looked very much like Nancy, but the younger daughter was a beautiful, petite child. What was causing Nancy incredible pain was the relationship between her mother and this younger child and the effect of that relationship on Nancy's feelings and behavior.

Just as in Nancy's childhood, her mother catered to the younger "pretty" daughter, while the older daughter was left out and ignored. Old hurts and wounds that Nancy thought were hidden in her past were now being relived through watching her own children. The heartache and loneliness that her older daughter was feeling was an echo of Nancy's unhappiness.

In spite of herself, Nancy's attitude toward her younger daughter began to change. The slightest annoying thing this child did brought an explosion of anger. Bitterness and resentment began to replace genuine affection.

In her heart of hearts, Nancy was also angry at God. In spite of her prayers, she felt He had changed neither her relationship with her mother nor her present circumstances. She seemed doomed to repeat vicariously through her daughters her own painful past. As a result of this barrage of feelings, she stopped going to her Bible study group, calling Christian friends, and even praying to God.

For Nancy, her relationship with her husband, her children, and God had all been affected by missing out on the blessing that she had tried for years to grasp, but that never quite came within reach.

## OUR NEED FOR ACCEPTANCE

For Brian and for Nancy, the absence of parental acceptance held serious consequences. For Brian, the lack of the blessing was a major reason for his broken engagements and for keeping him from getting close enough to another person to become genuinely committed. For Nancy, an inability to feel acceptable as a person was destroying her most important relationships. Without realizing it, Brian and Nancy were searching for the same thing—their family's blessing.

Brian and Nancy typify people who are searching for their family's blessing. For years after they had moved away from home *physically,* they still remained chained to the past *emotionally.* Their lack of approval from their parents in the past kept a feeling of genuine acceptance from others in the present from taking root in their lives. In Nancy's case, this lack of approval even kept her from believing that her heavenly Father truly accepted her.

Some people are driven toward workaholism as they search for the blessing they never received at home. Always striving for acceptance, they never feel satisfied that they are measuring up. Others get mired in withdrawal and apathy as they give up hope of ever truly being blessed. Unfortunately, this withdrawal can become so severe that it can lead to chronic depression and even suicide. For almost all children who miss out on their parents' blessing, at some level this lack of acceptance sets off a life-long search.

This search for the blessing is not just a modern-day phenomenon. It is actually centuries old. In fact, we can find a graphic picture in the Old Testament of a person who missed out on his family's blessing. This person was a confused and angry man named Esau. As we look at this man's life, we will also begin to learn about the blessing and what it can mean to grow up with or without it.

## "BLESS ME, EVEN ME ALSO, O MY FATHER!"

Esau was beside himself. *Could this really be happening?* he may have thought. Perhaps his mind went back to the events of that day. Just hours before, his father had called him to his side and made a special request. If Esau, the older son, would go and bring in fresh game for a savory meal, his father's long-awaited blessing would be given to him.

What was this blessing that Esau had waited for over the years? For sons or daughters in biblical times, receiving their father's blessing was a momentous event. We will discover that it gave these children a tremendous sense of being highly valued by their parents and even pictured a special future for them. At a specific point in their lives they would hear words of encouragement, love, and acceptance from their parents.

We will see that some aspects of this Old Testament blessing were unique to that time. However, the *relationship elements* of this blessing are still applicable today. In Old Testament times, this blessing was primarily reserved for one special occasion. In contrast, parents today can decide to build these elements of blessing into their children's lives daily.

For Esau, his father, Isaac, followed the custom of waiting until a specific day to give his son the blessing. Now at long last, Esau's waiting was over. His time of blessing would begin as soon as he could catch and prepare a special meal.

With all the skill and abilities of an experienced hunter, Esau had quickly and efficiently gone about his work. In almost no time a delicious stew was prepared as only one familiar with the art of cooking in the field could do.

All had been done just as he was told. Why, then, had his father trembled so when Esau stood before him? As if in a dream, the scene played over and over in Esau's mind. He had just entered his father's tent and greeted him:

> *"Let my father arise and eat of his son's game, that your soul may bless me." And his father Isaac said to him, "Who are you?" So he said, "I am your son, your firstborn, Esau."*
>
> *Then Isaac trembled exceedingly, and said, "Who? Where is the one who hunted game and brought it to me? I ate all of it before you came, and I have blessed him—and indeed he shall be blessed."*
>
> *When Esau heard the words of his father, he cried with an exceedingly great and bitter cry, and said to his father, "Bless me—me also, O my father!"*
> *(Gen. 27:31–34, italics added)*

Little did Esau know that when his aged and nearly blind father had called him to his side, another had been listening. Rebekah, the mother of Esau and his twin brother, Jacob, was also in the tent. As soon as Esau went out into the fields to hunt fresh game, she ran to her favorite son, Jacob, with a cunning plan.

If they hurried, they could kill a young kid from the flock and prepare a savory meal. What's more, they could dress Jacob in his brother's clothing and put animal skins on him to simulate Esau's rough and hairy arms, hands, and neck.

Putting on Esau's clothes did not present a problem, but one thing they couldn't counterfeit was Esau's voice. That almost blew the whistle on them (Gen. 27:22). But even though Isaac was a little skeptical, ultimately their plan worked just as they had hoped it would. We read in Genesis 27:22–23, "So Jacob went near to Isaac his father. . . . And he did not recognize him, because his hands were hairy like his brother Esau's hands; so he blessed him." The blessing meant for the older son went to the younger.

Jacob should not have had to trick his way into receiving the blessing. God Himself had told Isaac that regarding his twin sons, the "older shall serve the younger" (Gen. 25:23). Yet while Esau went out to hunt for food, an even more cunning hunter stole into his father's tent, and came out with a priceless treasure.

When Esau returned and discovered that he had lost the blessing to his brother Jacob, he was devastated. Was Esau crying over losing his inheritance? As we will see later, the oldest son's inheritance was something that came with his birthright, and entitled him to a double share in his father's wealth. Yet years before, Esau had already *sold* his birthright to his brother for a pot of red stew! (Gen. 25:29–34)

Esau wasn't lamenting the fact that he lost the cattle and sheep—he had already despised that gift. What ripped at his heart was something much more personal . . . his father's blessing. In Old Testament times a father's blessing was irretrievable, and irretractable once it was given, and now Isaac's blessing was forever outside Esau's reach.

Filled with hurt, he cried out a *second* time, "Do you have only one blessing, my father? Bless me, even me also, O my father." So Esau lifted his voice and wept (Gen. 27:38 NASB). In response to his pitiful cries, Esau did receive a blessing of sorts from his father (Gen. 27:39–40), but it was not the words of high value and acceptance that he had longed to hear.

Can you feel the anguish in Esau's cry, "Bless me, even me also, O my father"? This same painful cry and unfulfilled longing is being echoed today by many people who are searching for their family's blessing, men and women whose parents, for whatever reason, have failed to bless them with words of love and acceptance. People just like Brian and Nancy. People you rub shoulders with every day. Perhaps even you.

## THE IMPORTANCE OF THE BLESSING TODAY

Genuine acceptance; an unmet need in Brian, Nancy, and Esau's lives; a need that goes unmet in thousands of lives today—perhaps you have this need or a loved one is struggling with it, a need that the blessing helps to meet. Yet, the family blessing not only provides people a much needed sense of personal acceptance, it also plays an important part in protecting and even freeing them to develop intimate relationships.

Today, as in centuries past, orthodox Jewish homes bestow a special family blessing on their children. This blessing is much like the patriarchal blessing we were introduced to in the story of Esau. This blessing has been an important part of providing a sense of acceptance for generations of children. But recently, it has also provided an important source of protection to those children.

All across the country, cults are holding out a counterfeit blessing to our children. Cult leaders have mastered the elements of the blessing we will describe in the pages that follow. Providing a sense of family and holding out (at least initially) the promise of personal attention, affection, and affirmation is an important drawing card for many of these cults.

Children who grow up without a sense of parental acceptance are especially susceptible to being drawn into cults. In fact, thousands are drawn in every year. However, like beckoning hungry children to an imaginary dinner, the smell and aroma may draw them to the table; but after eating they are left hungrier than before.

If you are a parent, learning about the family blessing can help you provide your child or children with a protective tool. The best defense against a child's longing for imaginary acceptance is to provide him or her with genuine acceptance. By providing a child with genuine acceptance and affirmation at home, you can greatly reduce the likelihood that he or she will seek acceptance in the arms of a cult member or with someone in an immoral relationship. Genuine acceptance radiates from the concept of the blessing.

However, the blessing is not just an important tool for parents to use. The blessing is also of critical importance for anyone who desires to cleave, or draw close, to another person in an intimate relationship. One of the most familiar verses in the Bible is Genesis 2:24: "For this cause a man shall leave his father and his mother, and shall cleave to his wife" (NASB).

Many books and tapes talk about the need to cleave to our spouse. However, very few talk about the tremendous need people have to "leave" home. Perhaps this is because people have often thought of leaving home as simply moving away physically.

In reality, leaving home has always meant much more than putting physical distance between our parents and ourselves. In the Old Testament, for example, the farthest most people would actually move away from their parents was across the campfire and into another tent! Leaving home carries with it not only the idea of physical separation but also of *emotional* separation.

The terrible fact is that most people who have missed out on their parents' blessing have great emotional difficulty leaving home. It may have been years since they have seen their parents, but unmet needs for personal acceptance can keep a person emotionally chained to his or her parents' home, unable to genuinely cleave to another person in a lasting relationship. For this reason many couples never get off the ground in terms of marital intimacy. This is what happened to Brian and Nancy. You or a loved one may be facing this problem. Understanding the concept of the blessing is crucial to defeating the problem and freeing people to build healthy relationships.

## A JOURNEY OF HOPE AND HEALING

In a world awash with insecurity and in search of acceptance, we need biblical anchors to hold on to. The search for acceptance that Brian and Nancy and so many others go through often leads people to accept a cure that is worse than the problem itself. Finding oneself through traumatic re-creations of the past or losing oneself through hypnosis or a similar psychological technique seldom, if ever, offers lasting change. On the other hand, God's Word and His principles do offer a changeless blue-print for constructing or reconstructing relationships.

In the pages that follow, you will discover more about the blessing. If you are a parent, you will see how to give your children, young and old, the blessing and how to discern if they have it now. You can also evaluate whether your parents received the blessing and how that may have affected their attitudes toward you. For those of you who grew up with the blessing, you will see how your parents communicated it to you and you will be encouraged to express your thanks to them.

We also offer help if you had to grow up without your parents' blessing. You will gain insight into common patterns of those who grow up without the blessing. You can discover practical lessons on living apart from an earthly family blessing. And you will be exposed to God's spiritual family blessing that is offered to each of His children. There is hope for ending the search for personal acceptance you may have been on for years.

If you are a teacher, discovering the blessing can help you better understand your students. If you counsel others, it can provide a helpful framework for understanding many problems and offering practical solutions. If you are involved in ministering to others, it can help you understand a crucial need every person has and give you resources to meet that need.

Our prayer is that in the pages that follow, you will take the time and have the courage to journey into the past, a journey that can lead to hope and healing. Even more, we pray that you will be willing to look honestly at the present and apply the things you will discover.

These pages may end a lifelong search for you or begin a new relationship with your children, your spouse, your parents, or a close friend. Our deepest desire is that this book will enrich your relationship with your heavenly Father as you learn more about the source of blessing He is to each believer. All this as we look at the family blessing—yesterday and today.

# Chapter Two

## The Blessing: Yesterday and Today

**O**ver the years we have heard countless stories of people who have, and have not received their parents' blessing. Both of us have experienced the pain of living *without* all or part of our fathers' blessings. Though we understand, firsthand, all the difficulties missing our fathers' blessings has brought into our lives, it still amazes us to see the devastating effect on a child when the blessing is withheld. It also amazes us to see the immeasurable, invaluable impact when a child truly receives the blessing. For me (John), I can still remember the effects of receiving the blessing from the most important man in my early life.

When I was young, my grandparents came to live with us for several years to "help out" with three very rambunctious boys! My grandfather was a wonderful man, but a stern disciplinarian. He had rules for everything—and swats to go along with all his rules! But there was one iron-clad rule that we hated because it carried two automatic swats. *"Be home before the street light comes on!"*

There was no "grading on the curve" in my home. With the street light planted right in our yard, all he had to do was look out the kitchen window and see if we'd made it home in time. And one night, my twin brother, Jeff, and I, didn't.

Never one to delay punishment, I shuffled down the hallway to Grandfather's room, and received my two swats. But little did I know that I was also about to receive one of the greatest blessings in my life.

After my spanking, my grandmother told me to go back down the hall and call my grandfather for dinner. I didn't feel much like being polite to him at the time, but I didn't want to risk another spanking either. So off I went to his room.

While many children grow up with open access to the grandparent or parent's room, we didn't. We were to knock on his door, ask permission to enter, and call him "Grandfather" or "Sir" when we addressed him.

I meant to knock on the door, but I noticed it was already slightly ajar. That's when I broke the cardinal rule and gently pushed it open to look inside.

What I saw shocked me. My grandfather, a man who rarely showed any emotion, was sitting on the end of the bed, crying. I stood at the door in confusion. I had *never* seen him cry, and I didn't know what to say. Suddenly, he looked up and saw me, and I froze where I was. *I hope catching him crying isn't a 60 swat offense!* I thought to myself!

Yet instead of another spanking, my grandfather said to me, "Come here, John," his voice full of emotion.

When I reached him, he reached out and hugged me closely, and in tears, he told me how much he loved me, and how deeply it hurt for him to have to spank me. "John," he told me, seating me on the bed next to him and putting his big arms around me, "I want more than anything in life for you and your brothers to grow up to become godly young men. I hope you know how much I love you, and how proud I am of you."

I can't explain it, but when I left his room that night, I was a different person because of his blessing. As I look back today, that evening provided me with a meaningful rite of passage from childhood to young adulthood. For years afterwards, recalling that clear picture of my grandfather's blessing helped to shape my attitudes and actions.

A few months later, in that same room, my grandfather died instantly and unexpectedly of a cerebral aneurysm. I know now that the Lord allowed me, for that one and only time, to hear and receive the blessing from him. While I would never receive the blessing from my own father, I did receive it that day from my grandfather.

Just what is this blessing that seems to be so important? Does it really apply to us today, or was it just something for Old Testament times? What are the elements of which it consists? How can I know whether I have received it or whether my children are experiencing it now?

These questions commonly surface when we introduce people to the blessing. In answering them, we will discover five powerful relationship elements that the Old Testament blessing contains. The presence or absence of these elements can help us determine whether our home is, or our parents' home was, a place of blessing. In this chapter, we will also look at how orthodox Jewish homes have bestowed a blessing on their children and why they have done so down through the centuries.

A study of the blessing always begins in the context of parental acceptance. However, in studying the blessing in the Scriptures, we found that its principles can be used in any intimate relationship.

Husbands can apply these principles in blessing their wives, and wives their husbands. Friendships can be deepened and strengthened by including each element of the blessing. These key ingredients when applied in a church family can bring warmth, healing, and hope to our brothers and sisters in Christ, many who never received an earthly blessing from their parents. As we will see in a later chapter, they are the very relationship elements God uses in blessing His children.

Is the blessing we build into a person's life today exactly like the blessing in the Old Testament? Certainly not. While the basic relationship elements of blessing remain the same, the Scriptures contain several spiritual aspects of the blessing that were unique to that time.

## UNIQUE ASPECTS OF THE
## BLESSING IN THE OLD TESTAMENT

The Hebrew word for *blessing* in the Old Testament is one of the most important words in the Bible. It was used over 640 times in the Old Testament alone, and held four crucial functions.

First, the word for blessing pictured God's original plan for mankind. Do you know the very first thing God did after creating us? In Genesis 1:27-28, we read, "So God created man in His own image; in the image of God He created him; male and female He created them. *Then God blessed them . . .*" (italics added).

What an encouraging truth to know that we were created for blessing! That is God's design for us. Yet, as we'll see later, some of us have grown up under a "curse," not a blessing. In Old Testament thought, there was nothing worse than being under a curse. But as powerful as a curse might be, there was one thing stronger . . . *a blessing.*[1]

In Genesis 12:3 God tells Abraham that through his descendants (pointing to Christ), ". . . All the families of the earth shall be blessed." When we experience God's blessing, and learn to bless others, we are connected to the major purpose for our creation.

Second, the blessing was a time to pull together a group. In the Old Testament, many examples exist of a blessing being given to unite a group of people. Melchizedek has Abraham gather his family and blesses them as a group (Gen. 14:19, 20); Moses assembles the entire Nation of Israel in the wilderness to bless them (Deut. 33:1–5), as do Aaron, David, and Solomon after him (Num. 6:23–27; 2 Sam. 8; 1 Kings 8:15–61).

There is tremendous strength and unity when we gather people together for a blessing. Many pastors call their congregations to rise, and bless them as a group. In orthodox Jewish homes, every Friday night finds a father calling the entire family together for a time of blessing. We even know of one flight leader during Desert Storm who would gather the six pilots he led, and their ground crews, and pronounce a blessing on them before they headed out on a mission. Blessing a group can increase the unity each member feels for that group and it can do much more.

Third, the blessing was a time to call upon God's protection. For those living in the days of the patriarchs, the blessing was a time to call on God's protection for a loved one. So important was this blessing, that if a family member was to travel beyond the horizon, they received a blessing before they set out. (See Genesis 28:1 where Isaac blesses Jacob before sending him to seek a wife.)

Travel in Bible times was even more dangerous than today, and no one ever wanted a loved one to go "beyond their sight" without words of blessing resting upon the traveler.

And fourth, the blessing was used to mark an important rite of passage. Whether it was at a birth (Ruth 4:14–15), a marriage (Gen. 24:60), or on the passing of leadership from an older generation to a younger (Gen. 27:1; 48:1), a blessing was used to mark significant milestones in one's life.

The Rabbinic tradition remains today with the *Bar Mitsva* at the coming of age of a son, and the *Bat Mitsva* for a daughter. These milestones of physical maturity are times when specific blessings are given from a father and mother to their child. They almost always become treasured memories.

These four functions of the Old Testament blessing: tying us to God's creative purpose, uniting a group, invoking God's protection, and providing a rite of passage, were common practices in Bible times. Unfortunately, today they're absent in many homes and churches.

While there were unique spiritual and prophetic aspects of the blessing, which lay with the patriarchs alone, orthodox Jewish homes have continued to practice blessing children. The basic relational elements of the blessing provide powerful tools to communicate acceptance, protection, and affirmation that still apply to men and women today.

## THE BASIC ELEMENTS OF THE BLESSING

What are these basic elements, and how do they work together? While neither of the authors admits to being an expert gardener, an elementary understanding of how a flower grows can help us picture the way the basic components of the blessing work together.

A flower cannot grow unless it has the necessary elements of life. Every flower needs soil, air, water, light, and a secure place to grow (one where its roots are not constantly being pulled out). When these five basic ingredients are present, it is almost impossible to keep a flower from growing. The same thing is true of the basic elements of the blessing.

Like the flower's basic needs, the blessing has five key elements. These five elements, blended together, can cause personal acceptance to blossom and grow in our homes today. Each individual part provides a unique contribution. Each is needed in giving the blessing.

In later chapters, we will look in detail at each of these five elements. But for now, we will introduce them briefly.

A definition of the family blessing that contains its five major elements reads:

> *A family blessing begins with meaningful touching. It continues with a spoken message of high value, a message that pictures a special future for the individual being blessed, and one that is based on an active commitment to see the blessing come to pass.*

Here is another way to look at the five basic parts of the blessing.

## THE FAMILY BLESSING INCLUDES:

- Meaningful Touch
- A Spoken Message
- Attaching "High Value" to the One Being Blessed
- Picturing a Special Future for the One Being Blessed
- An Active Commitment to Fulfill the Blessing

Let's look a little closer at each of these.

### Meaningful Touch

Meaningful touch was an essential element in bestowing the blessing in Old Testament homes. So it was with Isaac when he went to bless his son. We read in Genesis 27:26 that Isaac said, "Come near now and kiss me, my son." This incident was not an isolated one. Each time the blessing was given in the Scriptures, meaningful touching provided a caring background to the words that would be spoken. Kissing, hugging, or the laying on of hands were all a part of bestowing the blessing.

Meaningful touch has many beneficial effects. As we will see in the next chapter, the act of touch is a key to communicating warmth, personal acceptance, affirmation—even physical health! For Isaac, as well as for any person who wishes to see the blessing grow and develop in a child, spouse, or friend, touch is an integral part of the blessing.

## A Spoken Message

The second element of our definition is based on a spoken message. In many homes today, words of love and acceptance are seldom heard. A tragic misconception parents in these homes share is that simply being present communicates the blessing. Nothing could be further from the truth. A blessing becomes so only when it is spoken.

For a child in search of the blessing, the major thing silence communicates is confusion. Children who are left to fill in the blanks when it comes to what their parents think about them will often fail the test when it comes to feeling valuable and secure. Spoken words at least give the hearer an indication that he or she is worthy of some attention. I (John) learned this lesson on the football field.

When I began playing football in high school, one particular coach thought I was filled with raw talent (emphasis on "raw"!). He was constantly chewing me out. And he even took extra time after practice to point out mistakes I was making. After I missed an important block in practice one day (a frequent occurrence), this coach stood right in my face and chewed me out six ways from Sunday.

When he finally finished, he had me go over to the sidelines with the other players who were not a part of the scrimmage. Standing next to me was a third-string player who rarely got into the game. I can remember leaning over to him and saying, "Boy, I wish he would get off my case." "Don't say that," my teammate replied. "At least he's talking to you. If he ever *stops* talking to you, that means he's given up on you."

Many adults we see in counseling interpret their parents' silence in exactly the same way. They feel as though they are "third-string" children to their parents. Their parents may have provided a roof over their heads (or even a Porsche to drive), but without spoken words of blessing, they are left unsure of their personal worth and acceptance.

Abraham spoke his blessing to his son Isaac. Isaac spoke a blessing to his son Jacob. Jacob gave a verbal blessing to each of his twelve sons and to two of his grandchildren. When God blessed us with the gift of His Son, it was His *Word* that "became flesh and dwelt among us" (John 1:14). God has always been a God of the spoken word.

"But I don't yell at my children or cut them down like some parents," some may say. Unfortunately, even a lack of negative words does not translate into a spoken blessing. We will see this lack illustrated in several painful examples in a later chapter.

To see the blessing bloom and grow in the life of a child, spouse, or friend, we need to verbalize our message. Good intentions aside, good *words* are necessary to provide genuine acceptance.

## Attaching High Value

Meaningful touch and a spoken message. These first two elements lead up to the words of blessing themselves, words of high value.

To value something means to attach honor to it. In fact, this is the meaning of the verb "to bless." In Hebrew, the word *bless* literally means "to bow the knee."[2] This word was used in showing reverence, even awe, to an important person. Now, this doesn't mean that in order to bless a person we are to stand back, fall to our knees, and bow before that person in awe! Nonetheless, words of blessing should carry with them the recognition that this person is valuable and has redeeming qualities. In the Scriptures, recognition is based on who they are, not simply on their performance.

In blessing his son, Isaac says, "Surely, the smell of my son/Is like the smell of a field/Which the LORD has blessed. . . . Let peoples serve you,/And nations bow down to you" (Gen. 27:27–29).

That pictures a very valuable person! Not just anybody merits having nations bow down to him!

As you may have noticed, Isaac uses a word picture to describe how valuable his son is to him. ("The smell of my son is like the smell of a field which the LORD has blessed.") Word pictures are a powerful way of communicating acceptance. Later, we will look not only at the use of these word pictures, but we will also learn how to use them in giving a blessing. In the Old Testament, they were a key to communicating to a child, a spouse, or a friend a message of high value—the third element of the family blessing.

## Picturing a Special Future

A fourth element of the blessing is the way it pictures a special future for the person being blessed. Isaac says to his son Jacob, "May God give you/Of the dew of heaven,/Of the fatness of the earth. . . . Let peoples serve you,/And nations bow down to you" (Gen. 27:28–29). Even today, Jewish homes are noted for picturing a special future for their children. One story we heard illustrates this activity very well.

Sidel, a young Jewish mother, was proudly walking down the street pushing a stroller with her infant twins. As she rounded the corner, she saw her neighbor, Sarah. "My, what beautiful children," Sarah cooed. "What are their names?" Pointing to each child, Sidel replied, "This is Bennie, the doctor, and Reuben, the lawyer." This woman believed her children had a special future and great potential before them! Isaac believed that about his son, and we should communicate this message to those we seek to bless.

One distinction should be made between Isaac's blessing and picturing a special future for a person today. Because of Isaac's unique position as a patriarch (God's appointed leader and a father of the nation of Israel), his words to Jacob carried with them the weight of biblical prophecy. This position was also true of Jacob later in the book of Genesis. His blessing to each of his sons pictured their future exactly as it would unfold for them.

As parents or loved ones today, we cannot predict another person's future with biblical accuracy. We can, however, encourage and help them to set meaningful goals. We can also convey to them that the gifts and character traits they have right now are attributes that God can bless and use in the future.

Psychological visualization and picturing grandiose accomplishments in the future will not give a person the blessing. If anything, such practices pile up unattainable expectations that can move the person further away from genuine acceptance.[3] However, as we will see in a later chapter, our Lord Himself speaks quite often about our future. In fact, He goes to great lengths to assure us of our present relationship with Him and of the ocean full of blessings in store for us as His children in the future.

We can use a healthy, biblical way to picture a special future for our children. With this fourth element of the blessing, a child can gain a sense of security in the present and grow in confidence to serve God and others in the future.

## An Active Commitment

The last element of the blessing pictures the *responsibility* that goes with giving the blessing. For the patriarchs, not only their words, but God Himself stood behind the blessing they bestowed on their children. Several times, God spoke directly through the angel of the Lord to the patriarchs confirming His active commitment to their family line.

Parents today, in particular, need to rely on the Lord to give them the strength and staying power to confirm their children's blessing. They too have God's Word through the Scriptures as a guide, plus the power of the indwelling Holy Spirit.

Why is active commitment so important when it comes to bestowing the blessing? Words alone cannot communicate the blessing; they need to be backed with a commitment to do everything possible to help the one blessed be successful. We can tell a child, "You have the talent to be a very good pianist." But, if we neglect to provide a piano for that child to practice on, our lack of commitment has undermined our message.

When it comes to spending time with our children or helping them develop a certain skill, some children hear, "Wait until the weekend." Then it becomes "wait until *another* weekend" so many times that they no longer believe our commitments match our words.

The fifth element of the blessing, an active commitment, is crucial to seeing the blessing communicated in our homes.

Provide a flower with the essential elements it needs, and watch it grow! Provide the five basic ingredients of the blessing—meaningful touch, a spoken message, attaching high value to the one being blessed, picturing a special future for them, and confirming the blessing by an active commitment—and personal acceptance can thrive and bloom in a home.

To further understand the blessing in the Scriptures, let's turn our attention to the way it has been used in Jewish homes. For centuries, the blessing of children has been an important part of Jewish family life. In terms of communicating acceptance and affirmation, they have much to teach us about providing a blessing for important people in our lives.

## THE BLESSING AND JEWISH FAMILY LIFE

> *Before the children can walk, they should be carried on the Sabbath and on the Holy Days to their father and mother to receive their blessing.*
>
> *After they are able to walk, they should go to them of their own accord, with body bent and with head bowed, to receive the blessing.*
>
> *(From the Brantshpiegal, a book on Jewish family life and practices written in 1602.)*

From Old Testament times to today, the blessing has been an important gift offered to Jewish children. In fact, it has been a *duty* of parents to their children.[4] It has also been a regular part of the rabbis' duties toward children on *Shabat* (the Sabbath) and on feast and holy days.[5]

The earliest Jewish families we see are, of course, recorded in the Scriptures. The practice of blessing children was probably familiar to Abraham, even before God called him out from Ur of the Chaldees. All across Egypt and the Middle East, the practice of giving a blessing to children was common.[6]

In Old Testament times, each child in the family was given a general blessing as well as a special blessing for the firstborn. Esau, whom we saw in the first chapter, looked forward to receiving his blessing as the firstborn son in his family. In Genesis 49, not only the oldest, but also each of Jacob's twelve sons, received a blessing from their father. While there were additional *privileges* that went to the firstborn, the essential *elements* of both blessings were the same as those we listed above. What were some of the special additional privileges the firstborn child might enjoy?

Firstborn daughters had the right to be married before a younger sister. Laban observed this custom in arranging for Jacob to marry his older daughter, Leah. Only after she was married was Jacob allowed to marry Laban's younger daughter, Rachel (Gen. 29:21-30). (That certainly wasn't the way Jacob had planned it, by the way!) In addition, ancient tablets found in Syria spoke of special rights of inheritance that belonged to the firstborn daughter.[7]

Firstborn sons made out even better. For one thing, their blessing bequeathed to them *twice* the inheritance of any other brother (2 Kings 2:9). Now, perhaps you can see how much Esau lost when he acted on impulse in selling his birthright. By allowing hunger pangs to dictate his actions, he became a negative example for all time. In the book of Hebrews, God lists the greatest heroes of the faith in Chapter 11. But in Chapter 12, in contrast to the heroes, the writer says of Esau, "[See to it that . . .] . . . there be no immoral or godless person like Esau, who sold his own birthright for a single meal" (Heb. 12:16 NASB).

There were other aspects of the firstborn son's blessing. The firstborn son was designated as the leader of the family when the father died. It would become his responsibility to be the spiritual leader in the home. All in all, firstborn children received many special privileges.

An Old Testament law prohibited arbitrarily bypassing the eldest son to give the firstborn's blessing to another child (Deut. 21:15-17), but it certainly could happen and was done. This even happened in Jacob's family. Reuben was the firstborn son of twelve brothers, but it was Joseph, the next to the youngest, who actually received the firstborn's blessing (Gen. 48:22). Many ancient tablets mentioned that the shifting of the blessing from one child to the other—whether sons or daughters—was common during this period.[8]

As we have seen in our look at Old Testament times, parents gave a *general blessing* to each child and sometimes reserved a *special blessing* for the firstborn. While the firstborn could receive certain privileges a younger child did not, the basic elements of both blessings remained the same.

The next stop in our look at how Jewish families adopted the blessing comes during New Testament times, the time of the Pharisees. During this period there were rules and regulations for nearly every event—the blessing of children not excluded. Around the time of Christ's birth, Rabbi Jesus ben Sirach wrote, "The blessing of the father builds houses for the sons; the blessing of the mother fills them with good things."[9]

While there remained a general blessing for children during this time, a definite trend to favor blessing sons instead of daughters developed. This tendency is seen in many of the Hebrew commentaries on the law that sprang up during that day.

In an explanation of the priestly benediction, "The LORD bless thee, and keep thee" (Num. 6:24 KJV), one rabbi wrote, "May the Lord bless thee with sons, and keep thee from daughters because they need careful guarding!"[10] In even stronger language, another rabbi wrote, "What is the interpretation of the words 'all things' in the Scripture, 'The Lord blessed Abraham in all things'? That he had no daughter!"[11] His words may have been humorous—as long as you weren't a daughter.

While the tendency to bless only sons was present, exceptions to the rule were made in some Jewish homes with some religious leaders. In fact, another man some called rabbi during this same period welcomed both sons *and* daughters to receive His blessing. We read in Mark 10:13–16:

> *Then they brought little children to Him, that He might touch them; but the disciples rebuked those who brought them. But when Jesus saw it, He was greatly displeased and said to them, "Let the little children come to Me, and do not forbid them. . . ." And He took them up in His arms, laid His hands on them, and blessed them.*
>
> *(Mark 10:13–16, italics added)*

Jesus knew that both little boys *and* little girls needed the elements of the blessing.[12] In a later chapter, we will see that in almost every detail, His blessing of children parallels the important elements of the family blessing.

Looking to modern-day Jewish homes and practices, the blessing is still an important concept in many orthodox families. At many Shabat (Sabbath) services, the parents are to bring their children for a special blessing. There the rabbi will call the children in the congregation forward to receive their blessing. Acting on behalf of the parents, the rabbi will lay his hand on the head of each child and recite words like these, "May God bless you and make you as Ephraim and Manasseh."

This blessing originally comes from Genesis 48:20, where Jacob was blessing Joseph's two sons—Jacob's *grandchildren*. Listen to the blessing this aging patriarch bestows on these two young boys: "So he blessed them that day, saying, 'By you Israel will bless, saying, "May God make you as Ephraim and as Manasseh!"'" What a blessing! Even today, centuries later, in synagogues and in Jewish homes, this blessing is a favorite for parents to use with their children.

While studying how the blessing is given in modern Jewish homes, I (John) had the privilege of speaking with several rabbis. In those interviews, I discovered that bestowing a family blessing was still very much alive. The family blessing is considered an important vehicle for communicating a sense of identity, meaning, love, and acceptance. In fact, in many orthodox homes, a weekly blessing is given by the father to each of his children. With the ceremonial candles lit, a time of blessing begins.

Sharing special meals; kissing, hugging, or the laying on of hands; creating a word picture or using one in the Scriptures to praise a child; even asking God to provide a special future for each child are common elements of blessing children in orthodox homes today.

While the blessing is an ancient practice, it still holds important keys to granting genuine acceptance. From a blessing to the firstborn to special words of love and acceptance for each child, the blessing remains a part of Jewish family life today. *For Christian parents who have the hope and reality of Jesus, the Messiah, and His love, their blessing can be even more powerful.*

## AT HOME WITH THE FAMILY BLESSING

We have looked at the basic elements of the blessing and at how it has been carried on for centuries in Jewish homes. Our aim now is to become very practical as we look closely at each of the five key elements of the blessing. Learning more about these powerful tools for communicating personal and parental approval can help us become a source of blessing to our children, spouse, brothers and sisters in Christ, and others.

Some of you who are reading this book may already feel a little discouraged. In reading about the key elements of the blessing, perhaps you realized for the first time that you never got the blessing from your parents, or that it is not an active part of your relationship with your children. Please don't lose heart. As we look closely at the five basic elements of the blessing, you can gain practical skills to become a source of blessing to others. Later, you will also discover how to deal effectively with missing out on the blessing in your life.

Together, we will stop in several of the most common homes we see in counseling that *withhold* the blessing from their children. And we will look at God's provision for dealing with the loss of an earthly family blessing. We will also look at several modern-day homes that are models for bestowing the blessing on children, spouse, church family, and friends.

With that in mind, let's turn our attention to the first element of the blessing, meaningful touch. Harnessed within this first key to communicating personal acceptance is an incredible power to bless, right at our fingertips.

# Chapter Three

## The First Element of the Blessing: Meaningful Touch

*I*sabel was a sensitive young woman, suffering greatly in a diabetic/medical-surgical unit. She was in so much pain, she would cry regularly to the nursing staff, pleading for pain killing injections. Yet the medicine therapy she was on and her own physical condition precluded her from receiving the shots in spite of her cries. The risk for infection and internal bleeding was simply too great.

Finally, after Isabel's continual badgering of the nurses on every shift, the senior nurse in charge went to talk to Isabel.

Nurse Heath was a thirty-year veteran of the wards and a reserved, capable teacher. She explained to Isabel, logically and practically, the potential dangers if they gave her a shot. She also assured Isabel that the other nurses were trying to protect her, rather than harm her, by administering the injections. Isabel listened intently, and even nodded understanding.

Her mission accomplished, Nurse Heath was preparing to leave when Isabel stopped her. "If I can't have my shot . . . *can you give me a hug?*"

Not thinking she had heard right, she asked, "Excuse me?"

Isabel repeated, "Could you give me a hug for the pain . . . *please?*"

Caught off guard, the stately nurse said, "Well, OK," and put her arm around Isabel's shoulder. But then, it was as if God spoke to her and said, "For goodness sake, Ida, that's not what she asked for!" Then Nurse Heath put her arms around Isabel and really gave her a hug.

Isabel burst into tears.

"All this time I thought the nurses hated me. I'm just hurting so badly. Whenever I need a pain shot, can I call you and get a hug instead?"

Nurse Heath assured Isabel that she could get her hug whenever she needed it, and even wrote it down on her medical Kardex under the medication section, "Pain hugs" for Isabel upon request.

Isabel died a few months later at the age of thirty-four. But before her death, whenever she was admitted to a different ward in the hospital, or when the nights became too long, she'd call Nurse Heath for her "pain hug."

A hug can't wipe away all our pain, but it can help. And while meaningful touch can't chase away all our fears, it can cure most of them.

A little four-year-old girl became frightened late one night during a thunderstorm. After one particularly loud clap of thunder, she jumped up from her bed, ran down the hall, and burst into her parents' room. Jumping right in the middle of the bed, she sought out her parents' arms for comfort and assurance. "Don't worry, Honey," her father said, trying to calm her fears. "The Lord will protect you." The little girl snuggled closer to her father and said, "I know that, Daddy, but right now I need someone with skin on!"

The honesty of some children! This little one did not doubt her heavenly Father's ability to protect her, but she was also aware that He had given her an earthly father she could run to: someone whom God had entrusted with a special gift that could bring her comfort, security, and personal acceptance—the blessing of meaningful touch.

This little girl was fortunate. Her father was willing to share this important aspect of the blessing with his daughter. Not all children are as fortunate. Even in caring homes, most parents (particularly fathers) will stop touching their children once the children reach the grade school years.[1] When they do stop touching them, an important part of giving their children the blessing stops as well.

For a four-year-old, being held and touched is permissible in most homes. But what about the need a fourteen-year-old has to be meaningfully touched by his mother or father? (Even if the teenager outwardly cringes every time he or she is hugged.) Or a thirty-four-year-old? Or your spouse or a close friend?

Your spouse and others need meaningful touch. However, children are particularly affected by touch deprivation. Sometimes the absence of touch can so affect a child that he or she spends a lifetime reaching out for arms that will never embrace him or her.

"I wish. . . . I wish. . . ." Lisa had slumped down in her chair, hugging herself and rocking backward and forward as she repeated these words. Lisa was a new adolescent patient in the psychiatric ward where I (John) was a seminary intern. Whenever she felt afraid or sad, she would wrap herself in her arms and rock back and forth.

We found that Lisa had behaved this way since she was seven years old. That was when her mother had abandoned her at an orphanage.

Lisa was trying to escape the hurt and pain she was feeling by holding herself. Lisa had no one else to hold her; all she had was the wish her mother would return. She needed meaningful touch so much that she would wrap her arms around *herself* and try to hug away the hurt.

## THE BLESSING: MEANINGFUL TOUCH

In the Scriptures, touch played an important part in the bestowal of the family blessing. When Isaac blessed Jacob, an embrace and a kiss were involved. We read, "Then his father Isaac said to him, 'Please come close and kiss me, my son'" (Gen. 27:26 NASB).

The Hebrew word for "come close" is very descriptive. It is used of armies drawn together in battle. It is even used to picture the overlapping scales on a crocodile's skin.[2] It may have been a while since you last saw a battle or a crocodile, but these word pictures still call up in our minds a picture of a very close connection.

Isaac wasn't asking his son to give him an "Aunt Ethel hug." (Remember Aunt Ethel—the one who pinched your cheek and then repeatedly patted you on the back when she hugged you like she was bringing up gas?) Free of the current taboos our culture sets on a man embracing his son, Isaac was calling Jacob close to give him a bear hug.

For fathers in North America, there is strong correlation between the age of a son, and whether his father will touch him.[3] Yet with Isaac, his grown son was at least forty years old when he said, "Come close and kiss me, my son."[4]

Children of all ages need meaningful touch, particularly from a father. Studies show that mothers touch their children in more nurturing ways, and fathers in more playful ways. But when the children were interviewed, perhaps because it didn't happen as often, they perceived their father's touch as more nurturing.[5]

As we have seen with Lisa, our need for meaningful touch does not go away when we enter grade school. Isaac modeled someone who didn't set up barriers around the need to be touched. He was a model that parents, husbands and wives, and even friends at church need to follow in giving the blessing.

I (John) deeply appreciated my mother's commitment to meaningfully touch us when we were children, even when we didn't show her how we appreciated it!

As a single parent, my mother had to work full-time to support three hungry, healthy boys. In the morning, she'd get us all up, get herself ready, and then we'd all pile in the car, us off to school and her to work.

While her driving saved us the long walk, there was one thing about the taxi service that my twin brother and I hated. Before we were allowed to get out of the car, we had to give Mom a hug.

As you can imagine, hugging your mom in front of all your school friends was not tops on the list of two aspiring football players. In fact, each year, we'd make our mother drop us further and further from school—just in case someone saw us hugging her!

Her pattern of hugging us was so regular, even when we'd say, "Oh, Mom!," or, "I can't stand it!" I can remember only one time when it didn't happen, and it got me in major trouble!

On one particular morning, we were all in a rush to get the day launched. We were anxious to get to school to shoot some hoops before the morning bell, and my mother had a major presentation at work. Distracted by her busy day, she let us out of the car without forcing us to give her a hug.

As she drove away, Jeff and I just looked at each other. She hadn't even *mentioned* hugging us— and I instantly thought the worse.

"She must know something," I told Jeff. "I *know* she knows something!"

Unfortunately, at the time there were a number of things she could have found out that could have resulted in our being grounded until we were in our mid-thirties.

All day, we brooded over "what" she'd discovered that caused her to be so angry that she'd chosen not to hug us. And finally, the day was over and we were all sitting around the dinner table—in silence. While dinner time was normally filled with enthusiastic conversation, that night there was dead silence as we waited for the storm to break. While Jeff could have waited all night, the silence quickly got to me and I broke down and blurted out, "OK, Mom. We're sorry. I can't believe you found out, but we are *really* sorry." I wasn't ready for the confused look that came across my mother's face.

"What are you talking about John?" she asked.

"Well, this morning," I told her. "When we got out of the car . . . You know . . . You didn't hug us!"

Laughing, she said, "Oh, I'm sorry. I guess I was so busy thinking about the presentation I had to make, I just forgot." But then her smile vanished, and she said, "But what was it you were confessing to?"

As Jeff glared at me, I realized I had just gotten us both in big trouble, all because I'd missed the hug I always said I hated!

What a contrast with my father, however. If I could count on my mother's touch, I could rely on his being off-limits. When we finally began a relationship with our father after nearly fifteen years of his absence, it was obvious that meaningful touch wasn't something he was comfortable with.

Of course, during my teenage years I didn't mind the absence of public displays of touch. But as the years went on, I found myself wishing that even once, my father and I could stand and hug each other. At my wedding. Or when Kari was born. Or Laura. Or at Christmas time, or anytime.

The handful of occasions when I held my father's hand were when he was so seriously ill he couldn't object, and each time stands out like a beacon. A memory of closeness that was pushed away from me any time he had the strength.

In the Scriptures, we find another clear example of including meaningful touch in bestowing the blessing. This time the blessing involves a grandfather who wanted to make sure his grandchildren received this special gift of personal acceptance. Let's look in on this "touching" scene:

> *And Joseph said to his father, "They are my sons, whom God has given me in this place." And he said, "Please bring them to me, and I will bless them." Now the eyes of Israel were dim with age, so that he could not see. Then Joseph brought them near him, and he kissed them and embraced them.*
>
> *Then Israel stretched out his right hand and laid it on Ephraim's head . . . and his left hand on Manasseh's head.*
> *(Gen. 48:9–10, 14)*

Jacob (whose name had now been changed to Israel) not only kissed them and held them close, but he also placed his hands on each grandson's head.[6] This practice of laying on of hands was an important part of many of the religious rituals for the patriarchs and for Israel. There are at least two important reasons why placing our hands on someone as a part of the blessing is so special. First, there is a symbolic meaning attached to touching, and, second, there are tremendous physical benefits to the laying on of hands.

## THE SYMBOLIC MEANING
## PICTURED BY TOUCHING

In the Old Testament, the symbolic picture of the laying on of hands was important. In this touch was a graphic picture of transferring power or blessing from one person to another.[7] For example, in the Old Testament book of Leviticus Aaron was instructed to use this practice in his priestly duties. During the Day of Atonement, he was to place his hands on the head of a goat that was then sent into the wilderness. This picture is of Aaron symbolically transferring the sins of Israel onto that animal. (It is also a prophetic picture of how Christ, like that spotless animal, would take on our sins at the Cross.) In another example, Elijah passed along his role as God's prophet to Elisha by the laying on of hands.

Even today the symbolic meaning of touch is powerful. While we may not be consciously aware of it, the way we touch can carry tremendous symbolic meaning.

A young woman holding hands with a new boyfriend can signal "I'm taken" to other would-be suitors. Two men shaking hands can seal an important business transaction. A minister at a wedding says to a couple, "If you then have freely and lawfully chosen one another as husband and wife, please *join your hands* as you repeat these vows."

Near the end of the Desert Storm campaign, Gary and I witnessed an example of the symbolic meaning of touch at one of our favorite places to watch human behavior—the airport.

A young, Japanese-American soldier was on our plane coming into Ontario airport in Los Angeles. He was on his way home from almost six months in the Gulf, and had ridden a tank through the heaviest fighting. He told of firefights at night, burning oil wells, the jubilant Kuwaitis, and of missing home. Then our plane touched down.

At the Ontario airport, a glass wall separates the passengers who have cleared the metal detectors from family and friends who have come to meet them. As we rounded the corner, we heard cries of joy.

There, pounding on the glass wall were the soldier's wife, two sets of parents, and two young children. While many orientals may be characterized by their reserve, there was nothing reserved about this young hero's reception. He ran through the exit doors and into his family's arms to be smothered with hugs, kisses, smiles, and tears. All of us in the waiting area were caught up in this wonderful reunion. Total strangers spontaneously burst into applause, and many had tears in their eyes as we all shared in the happiness of this homecoming.

Just a few months later, I (John) saw a different type of homecoming, which captured many of those same powerful emotions. The network television program, "20/20" chronicled the story of two Vietnamese orphans who had been evacuated when Saigon fell. While they were too young to realize it at the time, their parents were alive! Shelling from the advancing North Vietnamese army had separated this five- and four-year-old boy and girl from their parents. But instead of being casualties, their mother and father were desperately searching for them as they feared the worst.

Now, twenty years later, "20/20" cameramen went to Vietnam with two grown children. While each had grown up in loving American homes, with caring adoptive parents, now they were going to the home of their birth.

The orphaned boy was a United States Army second lieutenant, and his sister, a married mother of three. They had kept in touch with each other over the years, and in high school began the painstaking research and writing that would one day lead them to discover that their parents were alive.

With relationships beginning to soften between Vietnam and the United States, the two children were finally granted visas to return and be reunited with their parents and the brothers and sisters they had never seen.

The emotion captured by the cameramen was incredible. Half a world separated this family. So too, a terrible war, over twenty years, and even now, language. Yet they still had one thing in common. When they saw each other for the first time, they ran and fell into each other's arms with sobs, hugs, and kisses that said, in a language they all understood, "We love you. . . . We missed you. . . . We're so glad you're home."

They may have needed a translator to talk with each other in *words*, but as they sat and held hands, they clearly communicated the warmth and love that even a war couldn't kill.

While great symbolism accompanies our touch, this is not the only reason God made it a part of the blessing.

## MEANINGFUL TOUCH BLESSES US PHYSICALLY

For one thing, over one-third of our five million touch receptors are centered in our hands![8] Our hands are so sensitive that some blind people are being taught to read without Braille, by seeing through their fingertips! At Princeton University's Cutaneous Communication Laboratory, "vibratese" is an experimental procedure through which blind people are able to read a printed page by translating the words into vibrations on their fingertips.[9]

Interestingly enough, the act of laying on of hands has become the focus of a great deal of modern-day interest and research. Dr. Dolores Krieger, professor of nursing at New York University, has made numerous studies on the effects of laying on of hands. What she found is that both the toucher and the one being touched receive a physiological benefit.[10] How is that possible?

Inside our bodies is hemoglobin, the pigment of the red blood cells, which carries oxygen to the tissues. Repeatedly, Dr. Krieger has found that hemoglobin levels in *both* people's bloodstreams go up during the act of the laying on of hands. As hemoglobin levels are invigorated, body tissues receive more oxygen. This increase of oxygen energizes a person and can even aid in the regenerative process if he or she is ill.

We are sure that Ephraim and Manasseh were not thinking, "Wow, our hemoglobin levels are going up!" when their grandfather laid his hands on them. However, one of the things that certainly stayed with them as they looked back on their day of blessing was the old patriarch's gentle touch.

Hugs and kisses were also a part of meaningful touching pictured in the Scriptures. So healthy is meaningful touch, we ought to listen to the words of Ralph Waldo Emerson: "I never like the giving of the hand, unless the entire body accompanies it!" Let's look further at the physical benefits of touching and the deep emotional needs that can be met by this first element of the family blessing.

How would you like to lower your husband's or wife's blood pressure? Protect your grade-school child from being involved in an immoral relationship later in life? Even add up to two years to your own life? (Almost sounds like an insurance commercial, doesn't it?) Actually, these are all findings in recent studies on the incredible power to bless found in meaningful touching.

## More Reasons Why Meaningful Touch Blesses Us Physically

Every day, researchers are discovering more and more information about the importance of touch. If we are serious about being a source of blessing to others, we must consider putting these important points into practice. As we saw in the studies of the laying on of hands, a number of physical changes take place when we reach out and touch. Let's look at a few recent examples:

In a study at UCLA, it was found that just to maintain emotional and physical health, men and women need eight to ten meaningful touches each day![11]

At a marriage seminar I (Gary) was conducting, I told the couples that an important part of the blessing was given through meaningful touch. When I cited this UCLA study, I noticed a man in the second row reach over and begin patting his wife on the shoulder and counting, "One, two, three . . ." That is not meaningful touching! These researchers defined meaningful touch as a gentle touch, stroke, kiss, or hug given by significant people in our lives (a husband or wife, parent, close friend, and so on).

This study estimated that if some "type A driven" men would hug their wives several times each day, it would increase their life span by almost two years! (Not to mention the way it would improve their marriages.) Obviously, we can physically bless those around us (and even ourselves) with meaningful touch. But touching does much more than that.

Do you have a newborn in your home? Newborns make tremendous gains if provided with meaningful touch—and may be at risk if they don't.

Researchers at the University of Miami Medical School's Touch Research Institute began giving premature babies forty-five minutes of massage each day. Within ten days, the massaged babies showed 47 percent greater weight gain than those children who were not regularly touched.[12] In a second study, actual bone growth of young children who had been deprived of parental touching was half that of the bone growth of children who received adequate physical attention.[13] And in groundbreaking studies, Drs. Schanberg and Butler at Duke University Medical School found that without maternal touch, rat pups do not produce a type of protein crucial to their growth and development. When these rat pups were separated and unable to feel their mother's touch, they responded by slowly shutting down production of an enzyme crucial to the development of major organs. As soon as the pups were reunited with their mother, however, enzyme production returned to normal.[14]

Even the smallest act of touch can help a child who is unable to move. One group of physically handicapped children were placed on a smooth surface (like smooth Naugahyde) and a second group on a highly textured surface (like a rubber floor mat). EMG studies showed marked differences between the two groups, including increases in muscle tone, simply by having them lie on a textured surface![15] You can't get away from it. Overwhelming evidence shows that physical touch benefits and blesses children. But how about adults?

Are your parents getting up in years? Meaningful touch can be an important part of maintaining health and positive attitude with older persons. In a practice that has become commonplace now, residents in nursing homes were brought together with pets from a neighboring animal shelter. At first it was thought to be just a good recreational activity. Upon further study more significant results began to surface. Those residents who had a pet to touch and hold not only lived longer than those without a pet, they also had a more positive attitude about life![16]

Elderly patients with more serious problems have also demonstrated a number of tremendous benefits from regular, meaningful touching. For those suffering with dementia, a regimen of regular meaningful touch significantly increased their nutritional intake, helping them gain needed weight.[17] In addition, with Alzheimer's patients, physical touch decreased strange movements, picking up things, and repetitious mannerisms.[18]

But perhaps the most powerful study to come out of aging research is how touch may actually help preserve a healthy person's brain as it ages! Robert M. Stapolsky of Stanford University found that with even a small amount of extra stimulation soon after birth, there was a lasting effect on rats' brains. Meaningful touch in infancy caused their brains to put a brake on the development of glucocorticoids, stress hormones that are "a disaster to have in the bloodstream." By limiting their action, over time when these rats became old, they didn't lose any of the 10-to-20 percent of memory-critical gray matter that older rats, monkeys, and humans normally tend to lose.[19]

While meaningful touch may not be the "fountain of youth," it certainly does provide a clear stream of physical benefits for young and old alike. And what's more, people who regularly give and receive meaningful touch consistently feel better about themselves and have higher self worth![20]

## Meaningful Touch Blesses Our Relationships

An interesting study done at Purdue University demonstrates how important touch is in determining how we view someone else. Librarians at the school were asked by researchers to alternately touch and not touch the hands of students as they handed back their library cards. The experimenters then interviewed the students. Do you know what they found? You guessed it. Those who had been touched reported far greater positive feelings about both the library and the librarian than those who were not touched![21]

A doctor we know, a noted neurosurgeon, did his own study on the effects of brief times of touch. With half his patients in the hospital, he would sit on their bed and touch them on the arm or leg when he came in to see how they were doing. With his remaining patients, he would simply stand near the bed to conduct his interview of how they were feeling.

Before the patients went home from the hospital, the nurses gave each patient a short questionnaire evaluating the treatment they received. They were especially asked to comment on the amount of time they felt the doctor had spent with them.

While in actuality he had spent the same amount of time in each patient's room, those people he had sat down near and touched felt he had been in their room nearly twice as long as those he had not touched!

In similar studies, shoppers in a Kansas City, Missouri, supermarket were asked to sample a new brand of pizza. Those who were touched for only a fraction of a second during the sales pitch were more likely to buy the new product.[22] Even flight attendants who "accidentally" touched people on a long distance flight saw similar results. Those who were touched rated the attendant as more qualified, the airline as more professional, and the plane trip as *safer* than those who were not touched![23]

*Come on, Trent. Get serious, Smalley,* you may be thinking. Do we really mean that a touch lasting a few seconds or less can help build better relationships? Actually, we hope you touch your loved ones much more than that, but even small acts of touch can indeed leave a lasting memory.

Touching a child on the shoulder when he or she walks in front of you; holding hands with your spouse when you wait in line; stopping for a moment to ruffle someone's hair—all these small acts can change how you are viewed by others. A ten-minute bear hug is not the only way to give another person the blessing. At times, the *smallest* act of touch can be a vehicle to communicating love and personal acceptance.

A free-lance reporter from the *New York Times* was interviewing Marilyn Monroe years ago. She was aware of Marilyn's past and the fact that during her early years Marilyn had been shuffled from one foster home to another. The reporter asked Marilyn, "Did you ever feel loved by any of the foster families with whom you lived?"

"Once," Marilyn replied, "when I was about seven or eight. The woman I was living with was putting on makeup, and I was watching her. She was in a happy mood, so she reached over and patted my cheeks with her rouge puff. . . . For that moment, I felt loved by her."[24]

Marilyn Monroe had tears in her eyes when she remembered this event. Why? The touch lasted only a few seconds, and it happened years before. It was even done in a casual, playful way, not in an attempt to communicate great warmth or meaning. But as small an act as it was, it was like pouring buckets of love and security on the parched life of a little girl starved for affection.

Parents, in particular, need to know that neglecting to meaningfully touch their children starves them of genuine acceptance—so much so that it can drive them into the arms of someone else who is all too willing to touch them. Analyzing why some young people are drawn to cults, one author writes:

> *Cults and related movements offer a new family. They provide the follower with new people to worry about him, to offer him advice, to cry with him, and importantly, to hold him and touch him. Those can be unbeatable attractions.*[25]

They certainly can, especially if meaningful touch has not been a part of the blessing a child receives. Even if a child is not lured into a cult to make up for years of touch deprivation, he or she can be drawn into the arms of an immoral relationship.

Promiscuous men and women, women who work as prostitutes, and women who repeatedly have unwanted pregnancies have told researchers that their sexual activity is merely a way of satisfying yearnings to be touched and held. Dr. Marc Hollender, a noted psychiatrist, interviewed scores of women who have had three or more unwanted pregnancies. Overwhelmingly, these women said that they were "consciously aware that sexual activity was a price to be paid for being cuddled and held." Touching before intercourse was more pleasurable than intercourse itself, "which was merely something to be tolerated."[26]

In a similar study with homosexual men, a common characteristic they shared was the absence of meaningful touching by their fathers early in life.[27] Dr. Ross Campbell, in his excellent book, *How to Really Love Your Child*, comes to a similar conclusion. He writes, "In all my reading and experience, I have never known of one sexually disoriented person who had a warm, loving, and affectionate father."[28]

Touch from both a mother and father is important. In a later chapter, we will look at how a single parent can help to make up for the lack of touch from a missing spouse. However, in any case, meaningful touching can protect a child from looking to meet this need in all the wrong places.

If we ignore the physical and emotional needs our children, spouse, or close friends have for meaningful touch, we deny them an important part of the blessing. What's more, we shatter a biblical guideline that our Lord Jesus Himself set in blessing others.

## JESUS AND THE BLESSING OF MEANINGFUL TOUCH

As we mentioned in an earlier chapter, Jesus was a model of someone who communicated the blessing to others. Let's look at these verses again that speak of His touching the children.

> *Then they brought little children to Him, that He might touch them; but the disciples rebuked those who brought them. But when Jesus saw it, He was greatly displeased and said to them, "Let the little children come to Me, and do not forbid them; for of such is the kingdom of God. . . ." And He took them up in His arms, laid His hands on them, and blessed them.*
>
> *(Mark 10:13–14, 16)*

Meaningful touching was certainly a part of Christ's blessing children. Mobbed by onlookers and protected by His disciples, Jesus could have easily waved to the children from a distance or just ignored them altogether. But He did neither. Jesus would not even settle for the politicians' "chuck under the chin" routine; He "took them up in His arms, laid His hands on them, and blessed them."

Jesus was not simply communicating a spiritual lesson to the crowds. If He was, He could have done so by simply placing one child in the center of the group as He did on another occasion (Matt. 18:2). Jesus was demonstrating His knowledge of a child's genuine need.

For children, things become real when they are touched. Have you ever been to Disneyland and seen the look on a little child's face when he or she comes face to face with a person dressed like Goofy or Donald Duck? Even if the child is initially fearful, soon he or she will want to reach out and touch the Disney character. This same principle allows children to stand in line for hours to see Santa Claus (the same children who normally can't sit still for five minutes).

Jesus was a master of communicating love and personal acceptance. He did so when He blessed and held these little children. But another time His sensitivity to touch someone was even more graphic. This was when Jesus met a grown man's need for meaningful touch, a man who was barred by law from ever touching anyone again. We read about this in Mark 1:40-42:

> And a leper came to Him, beseeching Him and falling on his knees before Him, and saying to Him, "If You are willing, You can make me clean."
> And moved with compassion, He stretched out His hand and touched him, and said to him, "I am willing; be cleansed." And immediately the leprosy left him and he was cleansed (NASB, italics added).

To touch a leper was unthinkable. Banishing lepers from society, people would not get within a stone's throw of them. (In fact, they would throw stones at them if they did come close![29]) In a parallel passage in Luke, we are told that this man was "covered with leprosy." With their open sores covered by dirty bandages, lepers were the last persons anyone would want to touch. Yet the first thing Christ did for this man was touch him.

Even before Jesus spoke to him, He reached out His hand and *touched* him. Can you imagine what that scene must have looked like? Think how this man must have longed for someone to touch him, not throw stones at him to drive him away. Jesus could have healed him first and then touched him. But recognizing his deepest need, Jesus stretched out His hand even before He spoke words of physical and spiritual healing.

We know of one person who could understand the pain of not being touched. Her name was Dorothy, and she spent years of her life longing for meaningful touch.

We learned about Dorothy through a speech teacher at a large, secular university, a man in his early sixties who is an outstanding Christian. For nearly twenty-five years, this man had been a source of encouragement to students inside and outside of class. Many young men and women have trusted Christ as their Savior through his quiet modeling of godly principles. However, what changed Dorothy's life was neither his ability to communicate nor his stirring class lectures, but one act of touch.

During the first day of an introductory speech class, this teacher was going around the room, having the students introduce themselves. Each student was to respond to the questions "What do I like about myself?" and "What don't I like about myself?"

Nearly hiding at the back of the room was Dorothy. Her long, red hair hung down around her face, almost obscuring it from view. When it was Dorothy's turn to introduce herself, there was only silence in the room. Thinking perhaps she had not heard the question, the teacher moved his chair over near hers and gently repeated the question. Again, there was only silence.

Finally, with a deep sigh, Dorothy sat up in her chair, pulled back her hair, and in the process revealed her face. Covering nearly all of one side of her face was a large, irregularly shaped birthmark—nearly as red as her hair. "That," she said, "should show you what I don't like about myself."

Moved with compassion, this godly professor did something he'd never done before in a classroom. Prompted by God's spirit, he leaned over and gave her a hug. Then he kissed her on her cheek where the birthmark was and said, "That's OK, Honey, God and I still think you're beautiful."

Dorothy cried uncontrollably for almost twenty minutes. Soon other students had gathered around her and were offering their comfort as well. When she finally could talk, dabbing the tears from her eyes she said to the professor, "I've wanted so much for someone to hug me and say what you said. Why couldn't my parents do that? My mother won't even touch my face."

Dorothy, just like the leper in Christ's time, had a layer of inner pain trapped beneath the outward scars. This one act of meaningful touching began to heal years of heartache and loneliness for Dorothy and opened the door that drew her to the Savior.

We know that for many people, meaningful touch simply wasn't a natural part of growing up. For me, (John), growing up in Arizona, the cultural norm was, "It's OK to hug your horse, but not your kids!"

Wherever you live across the United States, you may not come from a warm, affectionate background. Sociologist Sidney Jourand studied the touch behavior of pairs of people in coffee shops around the world. The difference between cultures was staggering. In San Juan, Puerto Rico, people touched on average 180 times per hour. In Paris, France, it was 110 times per hour. In Gainesville, Florida, 2 times per hour. And in London, England, *0* times per hour.[30]

We aren't known as a country of huggers, and with all the media reports of child abuse and inappropriate touching, we've backed away from touch even more. We need to realize, however, that avoiding healthy, appropriate, meaningful touch sacrifices physical and emotional health in our lives and the lives of our loved ones.

If we want to be people who give the blessing to others, one thing is clear. Just like Isaac, Jacob, Jesus, and even the professor, we must include meaningful touch in our contacts with loved ones. This element of the blessing can lay the groundwork for the second key aspect of the blessing—a spoken message.

# ─── *Chapter Four* ───

## *The Second Element of the Blessing: Spoken Words*

*M*ost of us grew up reciting clever sayings like, "Early to bed, early to rise, makes a man healthy, wealthy, and wise." "A bird in the hand is worth two in the bush." And "A stitch in time saves nine." But unlike all these words of wisdom, one saying we memorized is an absolute lie.

Do you remember the lines, "Sticks and stones may break my bones, but words will never hurt me"? All too quickly we learn that words *do* hurt. They can cut a person deeply, destroy a friendship, or rip apart a home or marriage.

Words have incredible power to build us up or tear us down emotionally. This is particularly true when it comes to giving or gaining family approval. Many people can clearly remember words of praise their parents spoke years ago. Others can remember negative words they heard—and what their parents were wearing when they spoke them!

We should not be surprised, then, that the family blessing hinges on being a *spoken* message. Abraham *spoke* a blessing to Isaac. Isaac *spoke* it to his son Jacob. Jacob *spoke* it to each of his twelve sons and to two of his grandchildren. Esau was so excited when he was called in to receive his blessing because, after years of waiting, he would finally *hear* the blessing. In the Scriptures, a blessing is not a blessing unless it is spoken.

## THE POWER OF SPOKEN WORDS

If you are a parent, your children desperately need to *hear* a spoken blessing from you. If you are married, your wife or husband needs to *hear* words of love and acceptance on a regular basis. This very week with a friend, a coworker, or someone at your church, you will rub shoulders with someone who needs to hear a word of encouragement.

Throughout the Scriptures, we find a keen recognition of the power and importance of spoken words. In the very beginning, God "spoke" and the world came into being (Gen. 1:3). When He sent us His Son to communicate His love and complete His plan of salvation, it was His Word which "became flesh and dwelt among us" (John 1:14). God has always been a God who communicates His blessings through spoken words.

In the book of James, three word pictures grab our attention and point out the power and importance of spoken words. All three illustrate the ability the tongue has to build up or break down relationships, the ability to bless or to curse.

First, our tongue is pictured as a "bit" used to direct a horse (James 3:3). If you control a horse's mouth by means of a small bit, the entire animal will move in the direction you choose. (We have ridden a few horses who seem to be exceptions, but the general rule is certainly true.) The second picture illustrates this same principle in a different way. Here a "small rudder" is used to turn a great ship (3:4). These analogies point out the way spoken words can direct and control a person or a relationship.

A parent, spouse, or friend can use this power of the tongue for good. He or she can steer a child away from trouble or provide guidance to a friend who is making an important decision. He or she can minister words of encouragement or lift up words of praise. But this power can also be misused, sometimes with tragic results.

That is what the third word picture shows us. It illustrates all too clearly that spoken words can burn deeply into a person's life, often setting the course that person's future will take. Listen to the awesome power a spoken message can have:

> *The tongue is a small part of the body, and yet it boasts of great things. Behold, how great a forest is set aflame by such a small fire! And the tongue is a fire, the very world of iniquity; . . . and sets on fire the course of our life.*
> *(James 3:5–6 NASB, italics added)*

Just like a forest fire, what we say to others can burn deeply into their hearts. In fact, I (John) saw a living picture of the darkness that can result from fiery words.

I first met Lynda on a blistering summer's day in Arizona. The temperature outside was over 105 degrees and most people wore shorts or cool cotton clothing—but not Lynda. A tall, attractive twenty-year-old, she had on a heavy, long-sleeve *black* dress. (In Arizona, people avoid wearing black during the summer because it soaks up the already scorching heat. Yet in talking with her in counseling over several weeks, I found out that summer or winter, day or night, black was the only color Lynda would wear.)

Lynda grew up with a cruel, abusive father, who was addicted to alcohol and watching horror movies. As early as age five, Lynda was forced to stay in the family room and watch gruesome films. Then her father would laugh hysterically when she cried in fear. As the years passed, he continued exposing her to other aspects of the occult. Finally, when Lynda was in high school, he died and the horror stopped, in part.

As we talked, it wasn't the pictures of terror that had covered Lynda's heart with such darkness. They were terrible without question. But it was his *words* that had done the most damage. For all the hurtful things he did, what haunted her most was his favorite nickname for her. It came right out of his horror films: "demon daughter." That nickname burned its way into her heart, and even affected the way she dressed on a summer's day.

In the Scriptures, there is tremendous power in a name. Before Moses went to Egypt to confront Pharaoh, he asked to know God's "name." God changed Abram's name to Abraham, father of nations. Jesus changed Simon's name to Peter, His rock. But leave it to an angry, evil father to change Lynda's name to one that represented darkness and death.

Thankfully the ending to Lynda's story is one of great hope, not hurt. Through counseling and a loving church, she came to know Christ personally and traded in her old nickname for a new one "child of God." Like Jesus promised in the book of Revelation, "I will write on him [believers] the name of My God . . . My *new* name" (Rev. 3:12, italics added). God's love broke through to Lynda's heart in a dramatic way. Today, Lynda is married to an outstanding Christian man, wears a radiant smile, and has a wardrobe full of beautiful, pastel colored clothes.

Perhaps you still stumble over hurtful words your parents, spouse, or a close friend spoke to you (or negative words we have spoken to ourselves), words that come to memory time and again and point you in a direction in life you don't want to go. If so, don't lose hope. As you learn more about the blessing, you can begin to hear and speak words that can lead to a new course of life.

Each of us should be keenly aware of the power of spoken words. We should also be aware of how powerful the *absence* of spoken words can be.

## "I'LL TELL THEM TOMORROW": TODAY'S MOST COMMON CHOICE

In homes like Lynda's, negative words can shatter children emotionally rather than shape them positively. But that is not the most common choice of parents. Most parents genuinely love their children and want the best for them. However, when it comes to speaking words of love and acceptance—words of blessing—they are up against an even more formidable foe than the temptation to speak negative words.

A thief is loose in many homes today who masquerades as "fulfillment," "accomplishment," and "success." Actually, this thief steals the precious gift of genuine acceptance from our children and leaves confusion and emptiness in its place. That villain's name is *over-activity*, and it can keep parents so busy that the blessing is never spoken. Even with parents who dearly love their children, as one woman we talked to said, "Who has time to stop and *tell* them?"

In many homes today, both parents are working overtime, and a "family night" makes an appearance about as often as Halley's comet. The result is that instead of Dad and Mom taking the time to communicate a spoken blessing, a babysitter named *silence* is left to mold a child's self-perception. Life is so hectic that for many parents, that "just right" time to communicate a spoken blessing never quite comes around. What is the result?

- A father tries to corner his son to communicate "how he feels about him" before he goes away to college, but now his son is too busy to listen.
- A mother tries to communicate a spoken blessing to her daughter in the bride's room just before the wedding, but the photographer has to take her away to get that "perfect" shot.

Spoken words of blessing should start in the delivery room and continue throughout life. Yet the "lack of time" and the thief's motto, "I'll have time to tell them tomorrow," rob children of a needed blessing today.

"Oh, it's not that big a deal," you may say. "They know I love them and that they're special *without* my having to say it." *Really?* We wish that explanation worked with many of the people we counsel. To them, their parents' silence has communicated something far different from love and acceptance.

Let's look at what commonly happens in homes where spoken words of blessing are withheld. What we will see is that silence does communicate a message; and like an eloquent speech, silence too can set a course for a person's life. But it's not the path most parents would like their children to take. In fact, for many, silence affects their every relationship and leaves them wandering between workaholism and extreme withdrawal.

# WHAT HAPPENS WHEN WE WITHHOLD WORDS OF BLESSING?

Both people and relationships suffer in the absence of spoken words of love, encouragement, and support—words of blessing. Take a marriage, for example.

Dr. Howard Hendricks, a noted Christian educator, is fond of telling the story of a couple he counseled several years ago. This couple had been married over twenty years, but their problems had become so acute they were now considering divorce. Dr. Hendricks asked the husband, "When was the last time you told your wife you loved her?" The man glared at him, crossed his arms, and said, "I told my wife I loved her on our wedding day, and it stands until I revoke it!"

Take a guess what was destroying their marriage. When a spoken blessing is withheld in a marriage, unmet needs for security and acceptance act like sulfuric acid and eat away at a relationship.

Not only marriages, but individuals—particularly children—suffer from the lack of a spoken blessing. Without words of love, acceptance, and encouragement, children often grow up traveling one of two roads that lead to unhealthy extremes. Take Dan, for example. He took the road marked, "Try a little harder, maybe that will get you the blessing."

## Taking the Road to Workaholism

Dan grew up in a home where nothing positive was ever said. In fact, little of *anything* was ever said. His parents seemed too busy with their careers or too preoccupied with constantly "remodeling" the house to do much talking. There came, however, an exception to the general rule of indifference when Dan was just a boy.

At the end of one semester in grade school, Dan received an excellent report card with nearly all *A*'s. For the first time in memory, his parents openly spoke words of praise. At last, he felt like a somebody.

Like a starving man who stumbles across a loaf of bread, Dan thought he had learned the key to hearing words of acceptance:

*overachieve.* Acceptance was worth the hours spent inside studying (with the neighbor kids playing right outside his window) just to hear a few words of affirmation at the end of a semester. This working to overachieve lasted right through college.

The only problem Dan had was that his need for words of acceptance outlasted the years he spent in school. As a result, he took his motivation to "show them I'm somebody" right into the marketplace. Naturally, Dan became a "perfect" junior executive (which translated means he was a committed workaholic, always driven to achieve more and more regardless of the personal or relationship costs).

Why the intense drive and the insatiable need to achieve? Just look back at Dan's home, where no spoken blessing was given—except for some spectacular achievement. While Dan would never admit it (but inside he always knew it), pulling into his parents' driveway in a new car said he was still a somebody—didn't it? Getting that corner office would show them—wouldn't it?

Dan met every qualification of a "driven" man. He had fallen into the trap many men and women do who never received the blessing. Like Moses' fading glory, accomplishments could not sustain a missing sense of personal acceptance. Dan was forever having to make one more deal, sell one more product, attend one more motivational seminar. Spoken words of love and acceptance went unsaid early in Dan's life; as a result, his search for acceptance left him at the door of the driven.

Dan finally came to grips with missing out on the blessing. Until then, his search for personal acceptance kept him on the barren road to success and away from the pathway of life.

## Taking the Road of Withdrawal

Many people who missed out on hearing words of blessing take another road. These people head in the opposite direction. Convinced they can do nothing to hear words of love and acceptance, they give up and travel down the road of apathy, depression, and withdrawal. At the end of the road of withdrawal can be a terrifying, yet beckoning, cliff.

A classic example of a child who took this road is found in a film that circulated several years ago. As the movie begins, we see several children waiting for their school bus. The sun is out on a cold January morning. Snow covers the rural countryside like a beautiful, white blanket.

All bundled up for winter weather, a few of the children are making snowballs and throwing them at a fence. Others laugh and talk and stomp their feet trying to stay warm. All except Roger.

Standing by himself at the edge of the group, Roger stares down at the ground. In the next few moments, you almost get the feeling that Roger is invisible. Several children run right by him in excited conversation; others crowd around him when the bus finally comes. But Roger never looks up, and the other children never speak to him or acknowledge his existence.

The children rush to see who gets on the school bus first. Glad to be in out of the cold, the children happily take their seats—that is, all except Roger. The last one on the bus, he wearily mounts the steps as if climbing each one requires a monumental effort. He stops briefly and looks up expectantly into the faces of the other children, but no one beckons him to join them. Heaving a sigh, he slumps into a seat behind the driver.

The sound of compressed air is heard being released from the bus's hydraulic system, and the door slams shut. With one look behind him to make sure everything is in order, the bus driver pulls slowly away from the curb and onto the country lane.

They have traveled only a few miles when suddenly Roger drops his books and staggers to his feet. Standing next to the bus driver, steadying himself on a metal pole, Roger has a wild and distant look in his eyes. Shocked by his sudden ill appearance, the bus driver asks, "Are you all right? Are you sick or something? *Kid, what's the matter?*" Roger never answers, and half out of frustration, half out of concern, the bus driver pulls over to the side of the road and opens the door.

As Roger begins to walk down the steps of the bus, he pitches forward and crumples into the snow. As the opening scene ends, we see the bus driver standing over Roger's body, trying to discover what has happened. As the camera pulls away, we hear an ambulance siren begin to whine in the distance, but somehow you know its coming will be too late.

This scene is from the excellent educational film *A Cipher in the Snow*, a film designed for teachers but that speaks to anyone concerned about giving the blessing to others. The movie is a true story of a young boy who actually died on the way to school one day and the resulting confusion over the reasons.

Medical records indicated no history of problems in either Roger or his family. Even the autopsy shed no light on his death. Only after an interested teacher looked into his school and family background were the reasons for his death discovered.

This teacher found that Roger's life had been systematically erased like a blackboard. In his first few years at school, he had done well, up until problems began at home. His parents' marriage had disintegrated, and a new, preoccupied stepfather never had time to fill any of the missing gaps. Resentful of any attention his new wife gave Roger, the stepfather would limit their time together. His mother loved Roger dearly, but soon she was either too busy or too intimidated by her new husband to give Roger any attention at all. Like being pushed away from a seat near the fireplace, Roger was now left with only the cold ache of indifference.

As a reaction to his home life, Roger's school work began to suffer. Homework assignments were either turned in late or not at all. Tired of his apparent apathy, his teachers gave up on him and left him to work alone. He also began to withdraw from the other children at school, and he lost the few friends he once had. Roger would not begin a conversation, and soon other children wouldn't bother to try. Slowly but surely he was retreating into a world of silence.

In only a few months, everything and everyone of value to Roger had either been lost or taken from him. With no place of shelter and no words of encouragement, he felt like a cipher—an empty zero. This sensitive child was unable to stand the pain for long.

Roger was not killed by an infirmity nor a wound. He was killed by a lack of words of love and acceptance. Roger withstood the painful silence as long as he could. Ultimately, however, the lack of a spoken blessing from family and friends acted like a deadly cancer. After months of pursuing its course, it finally ate away his will to live. He died a cipher in the snow, believing he was totally alone and unwanted.

Are words or their absence *really* that powerful? Solomon thought so. Like throwing ice water in our faces, he shocks us into reality with his words, "Death and life are in the power of the tongue" (Prov. 18:21).

If we struggle with speaking words of love and acceptance to our family or friends, another proverb should encourage us. Again, it is Solomon writing:

> *Do not withhold good from those to whom it is due/ When it is in the power of your hand to do so./Do not say, . . . "Go, and come back,/And tomorrow I will give it,"/When you have it with you. (Prov. 3:27–28)*

If we can open our mouths to talk, we have the ability to communicate the blessing by spoken words. By deciding to communicate words of love and acceptance verbally, we do not have to send away a child, spouse, or friend in need.

## WHY IS IT SO HARD TO SPEAK WORDS OF BLESSING?

The damage of withholding words of blessing should be obvious in the examples of Mike, Dan, and Roger. But if spoken words of love and acceptance are so important, why are they offered so infrequently? Here are a few reasons we have gathered from people we have counseled:

> *"I don't want to inflate my child's ego."*
> *"I'm afraid if I praise them, they'll take advantage of me and won't finish their work."*
> *"Communication is too much like work. I work all day, then she expects me to work all night talking to her."*
> *"I just don't know what to say."*
> *"They know I love them without my having to say it."*
> *"If I get started, I'll have to make a habit of it."*

Our favorite reason is this one:

> *"Telling children their good points is like putting on perfume. A little is OK; but put on too much and it stinks."*

If the truth be known, the reason many people hesitate to bless their children or others with spoken words of love and acceptance is that their parents never gave them this part of the blessing.

## BEWARE OF SOME FAMILY RULES

Both praise and criticism seem to trickle down through generations. If you never heard words of love and acceptance, expect to struggle with speaking them yourself. Why? If your family had a "rule" that loving words were best left unsaid, you may find it very difficult to break this rule.

Every family operates by certain "rules." These rules make up "the way our family does things." Some families have a rule that "people who know anything about anything" open Christmas presents on *Christmas morning.* Other families follow the rule that "truly civilized people" open Christmas presents on *Christmas Eve.* (Both our wives, Cindy and Norma, just groaned when we wrote this!) Conflicting family rules often meet in a marriage. Many an argument has gone fifteen rounds to see whose family rule will win out in a new marriage.

Families set all kinds of rules: What we will eat in this family, and what we won't eat. What television programs we can watch, and which are dull or off limits. What is safe to talk about, and what subjects should never be brought up. Whom we invite over to the house, and who doesn't get an invitation.

In some cases family rules can be very helpful. For example, families can adopt biblical rules like "not letting the sun go down on our anger" and "being kind, one to another." Another way of setting positive family rules is by using "contracts" that can help build communication and encourage your children.[1] These types of family guidelines can be safely passed down generation after generation.

But not all family rules are worth retaining. Some family rules—written or unwritten—can devastate a family. Like words cast in steel, a destructive family rule can hammer away at a family, from parent to son or daughter, until at last someone breaks this painful pattern, someone like Cherryl.

When Cherryl was growing up, a simple plaque hung in the family room. The plaque had belonged to Cherryl's grandfather and had become a kind of unspoken "family motto." The plaque was not impressive looking, and it carried only two hand-painted words: STAND UP. Just two words—yet these two words had written volumes of hurt into three generations of Cherryl's family.

The words were originally part of a longer sentence, a motto that went something like this: "Don't take anything off anyone. Stand up and fight." This slogan may have been a helpful frontier slogan, but it did nothing but damage to personal relationships in Cherryl's family. Just look at Cherryl's father.

Cherryl's father had been infected with the "never give an inch" attitude of *his* father. "I'm sorry," or "You're right" were not in the vocabulary of someone who based his life on the words "Stand up and fight." Also absent were words that were not useful in a fight. Words like "I love you," "Will you forgive me?" and "You're important to me." While following this family rule of "never give an inch" pushed Cherryl's father ahead in business, it pushed him back into a corner with his wife and children.

Cherryl's mother and father fought constantly, each an expert on the other's faults, neither willing to give an inch in an argument. When each of Cherryl's four brothers and sisters grew old enough to dislike "taking orders" from their father, they joined the battle too. Soon there were seven people under the same roof following the family rule of "Stand up and fight" and its corollary principles, "Fight for my rights" and "Death before saying I'm sorry." This situation was true until Cherryl became a Christian.

Cherryl went away to a Young Life camp and trusted Christ as her Lord and Savior. The first thing Cherryl noticed when she came back home were those two words, "Stand Up." She thought about how Jesus had laid down His life and how tired she was of following this family rule. Little by little, and at the painful cost of constant ridicule from her brothers and sisters, Cherryl began to break several family rules.

Right in the middle of a fight, Cherryl would say, "I'm sorry; you're right. Would you forgive me?" and end the argument. She even began saying, "Love you, Mom, love you, Dad," and then giving them a hug as she left for school.

Cherryl's father had never gotten the blessing from his parents, only a plaque that almost destroyed his marriage and family. But over the next two years, he received the blessing from Cherryl. Meaningful touch, spoken words of high value, the picture of a future filled with hope, and the commitment to love him, no matter the cost—all these were relationship tools that chipped away at their existing family structure.

Family rules die hard, but they can be broken. Cherryl's younger sister was so taken with Cherryl's changed life that she also trusted Christ. Soon Cherryl's older brother followed, and the plaque on the wall was beginning to shake. Last Christmas, as a baby Christian, her father took down the plaque.

What a testimony to God's power to break even the most difficult family rule! And what a help to Cherryl's family to have a new family rule to follow! They are now free to "speak up" and share words of blessing with each other—because of one child's courage to go to battle with a hurtful rule of silence.

## PUTTING WORDS OF BLESSING INTO PRACTICE

We put spoken words of blessing into practice in our homes and relationships by deciding to speak up rather than clam up. Good intentions aside, good words are needed to bestow the blessing on a child, spouse, or friend.

*We are not simply saying talk more to your children or others.* While that is normally a good idea, sometimes if you don't know how to communicate in a positive way, you can say less by saying more. As we will see in the next chapter, it is not just *any* words, but words of high value, that attach themselves to a person and communicate the blessing. These are the kinds of words you often hear in the final hours before a family reunion ends.

Almost all of us have had the opportunity to attend a family reunion. A common phenomenon at these gatherings is that during the first two days, everyone is busy talking up a storm about this recipe, that football team, this book they've read, or that movie to attend. But something happens the last afternoon of the reunion. Suddenly with only an hour left before family members say their good-byes, meaningful words will begin to be spoken.

A brother will say in private to his sister, "I know things will work out in your marriage. I'll be praying for you." An aunt will say to her niece, "You've always made me proud. I know school is hard, but I know you can do it. I believe in you." Or a daughter will say to a parent, "Look around you, Mom. We didn't turn out half bad, did we? We have you and Dad to thank."

Spoken words—many times we have to be facing the pressure of time before we say the things closest to our hearts. What we have tried to communicate in this chapter is that with your children, your spouse, your close friends, even with your parents, it's later than you think. In some relationships, it is already late afternoon in your opportunity to talk to them.

In 1986 a tragic airplane crash in Japan took the lives of over five hundred people. Four people survived the crash, and they told authorities and reporters the story of the tragic last half hour of their doomed flight. For thirty-four minutes, the plane was without a rear tail stabilizer to control their descent. As a result, the erratic descent of the airplane was a time of panic and horror for all on board. While some passengers cried in fear and others took the time to don life jackets, one middle-aged Japanese man, Hirotsugu Kawaguchi, took his last few moments of life to write a note to his family. His note was found on his body by rescuers at the wreckage site, and it finally made its way to his wife and three children.

Listen to the last words of this man who deeply loved his family. They picture his desire for his wife and children to have a special future, even now that they would be physically separated in this life.

*I'm very sad, but I'm sure I won't make it. The plane is rolling around and descending rapidly. There was something like an explosion that has triggered smoke. . . . Ysuyoshi [his oldest son], I'm counting on you. You and the other children be good to each other, and work hard. Remember to help your mother. . . . Keiko [his wife], please take good care of yourself and the children. To think our dinner last night was our last. I am grateful for the truly happy life I have enjoyed. . . .²*

This man's wife and children no longer have him to hold and love. Hirotsugu Kawaguchi died when the plane crashed. But they do have his final words to them, words that pictured his hopes for their future, and words that will echo in their lives in a positive way in the years to come.

In the next chapter, you can learn about the kind of words—words of high value—that can especially bless people, but don't delay. Time passes so quickly. Please don't let that important person leave your life without hearing the second element of the blessing—spoken words.

# Chapter Five

## The Third Element of the Blessing:
## Expressing High Value

Diane's parents had tried unsuccessfully for years to have children. Perhaps that is one reason why their joy was unbounded when they learned that they were expecting their first child. Everything seemed normal during the pregnancy and delivery, until they saw the doctor's reactions. When Diane was given to them for the first time they saw that her left arm had never developed below the elbow.

There were tears in the delivery room and deep concern as test after test was performed on Diane. As doctors and specialists sought to determine the extent of her physical problems, Diane's parents didn't know how they should handle the anxious questions from relatives and friends.

Two days later, the doctors told Diane's parents some encouraging news. In all their tests, they had not picked up any other signs of medical or physical problems. Diane appeared to be a normal, healthy baby girl, with the exception of her left arm.

After the doctors had gone, Diane's parents bowed together in prayer. They thanked God that their daughter had no other serious problems. But they prayed something else that proved to be of tremendous benefit to their daughter. In that hospital room, with Diane nestled in her mother's arms, her parents prayed that their love for her would make up for any lack of physical abilities she possessed. They decided that morning that they would encourage Diane to become all that God would have her be, in spite of the problems they and Diane would have to face along the way.

Years have gone by since Diane's parents prayed for her in that hospital room. In fact, Diane is nineteen now and attending a major university. However, something special about Diane draws your attention away from her empty sleeve, particularly when you listen to her play a beautiful melody on the piano—with only one hand.

Diane has had to deal with tremendous obstacles in her nineteen years. The stares, giggles, and tactless questions of her peers in grade school; the fears and uncomfortable feelings of whether to go to a dance in junior high; the questions and worry that perhaps she would never date in high school, just to name a few. On the other hand, throughout the real-life struggles of being born handicapped, Diane received a precious and powerful gift from her parents—the security of knowing she was highly valued and unconditionally accepted.

"My parents didn't try to hide from me the fact that I was different," Diane told us. "They have been very realistic with me. But I always knew, and they have told me over and over that 'I am their greatest claim to fame.' Whether I was trying out for softball or my dad was teaching me how to drive, they have been my biggest fans. They have prayed for me and thought the best, even when I've pouted and gotten angry at God because of my handicap. Without question, my parents deserve a lot of credit for helping me accomplish the things I have."

They certainly do. Credit for deciding, in spite of a physical deformity, to value their daughter as whole and complete. Diane's parents are realists. They have not sugar-coated the very real problems their daughter has faced. But for nineteen years, they have communicated the blessing to her by showering her with meaningful touch and spoken words of high value and unconditional acceptance.

## WORDS OF HIGH VALUE

What do we mean by "high value"? Let's look at the word *value* to see the part it plays in the blessing.

As we mentioned in an earlier chapter, to "value" something means to attach great importance to it.[1] This is at the very heart of the concept of "blessing." In Hebrew, to "bow the knee" is the root meaning of blessing.[2] This root word is used of a man who had his camel bend its knees so he could get on (Gen. 24:11). In relationship to God the word came to mean "to adore with bended knees."[3] Bowing before someone is a graphic picture of valuing that person. Notice the important principle here: Anytime we bless someone, we are attaching high value to him or her. Let's illustrate this by an example in my (Gary's) home.

In my life, I want God to be of utmost value to me. He is my best friend and the source of my life. If I were to chart this on a 1-to-10 scale, I would value the Lord at "10," of highest value. Right beneath my relationship with the Lord would come my relationship with Norma, my wife. Humanly speaking, she is my best friend, and I love and value her right beneath my love for the Lord, maybe a "9.5." Then come my children. I love each of them dearly, and while neither they nor Norma are aware that I love them at a different level, I would value them at about a "9.4," right behind Norma. I do not love them less; but in attaching value to them, they come right behind my relationship with my Lord and with my wife.

Now I need to be honest with you. Emotionally, there are times with the kids when my feelings for them might drop to a "6.4" or even a "4.2." Particularly if we are camping in our minimobile home, and it has been raining all week. But, because I want to love and value them at a "9.4," I continually try to push their value back where it belongs. The same thing is true with Norma. I don't want to hurt or devalue her in any way. That is why if I do offend her, I immediately decide to raise her value to just beneath where I value the Lord. How does this apply to the blessing?

This principle is so important, let's repeat it. When we bless someone, we are deciding that he or she is of high value. This is what the psalmist is telling us in Psalm 103 when he says, "Bless the LORD, O my soul;/And all that is within me, bless His holy name." When we "bless the Lord," we are actually recognizing God's intrinsic worth and attaching high value to Him. He is worthy of our "bowing the knee" to Him.[4]

In the Scriptures, we are often called on to bless or value the Lord; but the Scriptures also give many examples of men blessing other men (Deut. 33:1, 2; Josh. 14:13; 2 Sam. 6:18) and others. When they did, they were attaching high value to the person they were blessing. They were recognizing him or her as a very special individual.

This valuing is exactly what the patriarchs in the Old Testament did in blessing their children with the family blessing. They were attaching high value to them. We do the same thing when we bless our children, spouse, or friends, and every person today needs the blessing to feel truly loved and secure about himself or herself. This concept of valuing another person is so important that we believe it can be found at the heart of every healthy relationship.

## WORDS OF HIGH VALUE IN OLD TESTAMENT HOMES

In the Old Testament, shining threads of love and value run throughout the fabric of the blessing. We can see this in the words Isaac spoke to Jacob: "Surely, the smell of my son/Is like the smell of a field/Which the LORD has blessed. . . ./Let peoples serve you,/ And nations bow down to you" (Gen. 27:27-28).

Telling your children today that they "smell like a field" would probably not be seen as a compliment! But Jacob knew what his father meant. So can you if you remember driving through the country when hay or wheat has been harvested recently. Particularly with the morning dew on the ground, or after a rain shower, the smell of a newly cut field is as fresh and refreshing as a mountain spring.

Isaac also pictured his son as someone who other people, including his own family, should greatly respect. He was even someone who deserved to be "bowed down to" by nations because he was valuable.

In the United States, no premium is placed on bowing before dignitaries. About the only people who know how to bow anymore are orchestra conductors and high school debutantes. Most of us would have to practice for hours to properly bow if we were going to meet a visiting king or queen. In Isaac's day, to bow the knee was a mark of respect and honor, something that was expected in the presence of an important person.

We can't miss the idea in these two pictures of praise that Jacob's father thought he was very valuable, someone who had great worth. This message is exactly what modern-day children need to hear from their parents. This message is what Diane received and what caused her life to blossom and grow, in spite of her physical deformity.

## WORD PICTURES: HELPFUL TOOLS FOR COMMUNICATING VALUES TO OTHERS

Telling children they are valuable can be difficult for many parents. As we saw in the last chapter, that just right time to say such important words can get crowded out by the urgent demands of a busy schedule. Some parents do struggle through the obligatory "I love you" during holidays or at the airport; but it seems stiff and out of place.

Other children may hear an occasional word of praise, but only if they perform well on a task (like Dan's story in the previous chapter). When words of value are only linked to a child's performance, they lose much of their impact. Children who have to perform to get a blessing retain a nagging uncertainty about whether they ever really received it. If their performance ever drops even a small amount, they can ask and re-ask, "Am I loved for 'who I am' or only for 'what I can do'?"

We need to find a better way to communicate a message of high value and acceptance, a way to picture a person's valuable qualities and character traits apart from his or her performance. Hidden inside the family blessing is a key to communicating such feelings to our children, spouse, friends, or church family, a key we can perfect with only a little practice, and one that even gets around the walls a defensive adult or child can set up. This key is found in the way word pictures are used throughout the Scriptures.

We may not be aware of it, but we use word pictures all the time. Let me give you one example of a word picture that I (John) remember vividly.

I was at lunch some time ago with a close friend in Dallas, Texas. We were eating at a quaint little basement restaurant where you walk down a steep flight of steps to reach the front door. The hostess seated us, and from our table we had a view of the stairs leading down to the restaurant. That is when it happened.

While we were waiting for our meal, we noticed at the top of the stairs a little girl of about two. She was holding on to someone's hand who as yet we could not completely see. In fact, all we could see were two huge tennis shoes and a massive hand holding on to this little girl. As these two came down the stairs, we were able to see more and more of this very large man helping his little daughter down the stairs.

When they reached the foot of the stairs and the door to the restaurant opened, in walked a football player for the Dallas Cowboys. At 6'4" and 265 pounds, this huge defensive tackle took up nearly the whole doorway! As he and his daughter walked by our table (the ground shaking and plates rattling on our table as he walked by), my friend leaned over to me and said, "Boy, what a moose!"

Calling this man a moose is using a word picture. Randy White does not have antlers and fur; and while he is very large as far as human beings go, he does not outweigh even a baby moose. Yet by picturing him as a moose (when he couldn't hear us do it of course), I instantly knew what my friend was talking about: a very large individual was walking by our table!

Some men have called attractive women chicks down through the years. Obviously, they do not refer to the fact that they scratch around in the dirt. A junior high school girl who tells her girlfriends that her latest boyfriend is a "dream" at a slumber party does not mean he will evaporate when she wakes up (even if it frequently happens!). Each of these "word pictures" captures an emotional feeling apart from the literal meaning of the words.

Now, let's look at the Scriptures and the blessing Jacob used with three of his sons. Each is a beautiful example of how this communication tool can be used to communicate high value to a child.

Jacob used a different word picture with each of his sons to bestow the blessing. We read, "And this is what their father said to them when he blessed them. He blessed them, every one with the blessing appropriate to him" (Gen. 49:28 NASB).

> *Judah is a lion's [cub] . . ./And as a lion, who dares rouse him up?*
>
> (*Gen. 49:9 NASB*)

Judah was depicted as a "lion's cub." In the Scriptures, a lion portrayed strength and was also a symbol of royalty in the ancient Near East.[5] The leadership qualities and strength of character Judah possessed were illustrated by this word picture.

> *Naphtali is a doe let loose,/He gives beautiful words.*
> (*Gen. 49:21 NASB*)

Jacob pictured Naphtali as a "doe." The grace and beauty of this gentle animal were used to show the artistic qualities this son possessed. He was the one who spoke and wrote beautiful words.

> *Joseph is a fruitful bough,/A fruitful bough by a spring.*
> (*Gen. 49:22 NASB*)

Joseph was called a "fruitful bough by a spring." This word picture illustrated how Joseph's unfailing trust in the Lord resulted in his providing a place of refuge for his family. Jacob's word picture carries a similar message to one used first of Jesus in Psalm 1:3: "And he will be like a tree firmly planted by streams of water,/Which yields its fruit in its season,/And its leaf does not wither;/And in whatever he does, he prospers" (NASB).

Each of Jacob's sons was an individual, and each of them received a blessing that depicted his value to his father in the form of a word picture he could remember always.

Before we rush off to call our child or spouse a lion, doe, or someone filled with fruit, we need to learn a little more about word pictures. To do so, let's turn to a book in the Old Testament that is filled with them. Word pictures can be used in any relationship to communicate words of high value. While this book pictures a marriage relationship, the same principles are used in giving children the blessing. Let's look in on how this couple communicated words of love, acceptance, and praise. In doing so, we will discover four keys to communicating high value.

## WORD PICTURES: FOUR KEYS TO COMMUNICATING HIGH VALUE

In the Song of Solomon, God's picture of an ideal courtship and marriage, this loving couple praise each other using word pictures over eighty times in eight short chapters. That's a lot! But they had a lot they wanted to communicate about how highly they valued each other and their relationship.

Let's begin our look at how they used these descriptive words with each other by looking in on their wedding night. Not often is someone's wedding night written up for posterity, but this one is worth remembering. It is a loving record of a godly relationship.[6]

Seven times (the biblical number of perfection) Solomon praises his bride. She was altogether beautiful to him. He begins his praise of her by saying, "Behold, you are fair, my love!/Behold, you are fair!/You have dove's eyes behind your veil" (Song 4:1).

### The First Key: Use an Everyday Object

What Solomon does with his word picture (and what a wise parent does in blessing his or her child) is to try to capture a character trait or physical attribute of his beloved in an everyday object. In this case, he pictures her eyes as dove's. The gentle, shy, and tender nature of these creatures would be familiar to his bride. By using a familiar object, Solomon is able to communicate far more meaning using a picture than he could by using mere words. Spoken words are often one-dimensional, but a word picture can be multidimensional. Plus, an added feature is that each time she saw a dove thereafter, it would remind her of how her husband viewed her and valued her.

Let's look at how one young woman's parents used an everyday object in a blessing to their daughter and how it ministered to her life. While Christmas doesn't come every day, their choice of an object was familiar to their loved one.

Nancy was born in late December, near Christmas day. As she grew older, her parents would repeatedly say to her, "Just remember, you're God's special Christmas gift to us, a gift of great price because you're so special to us." As a way of illustrating their feelings, each Christmas (now for almost thirty-five years), a small package is placed under the Christmas tree addressed from Jesus to Nancy's parents. Each year, Nancy is given the honor of opening this package. Inside the package is her baby picture! Listen to Nancy's thoughts about how being called a Christmas gift over the years has ministered to her.

"There have been many times when I haven't felt very special. I can remember one time in particular. It was my thirtieth birthday, and I was really struggling with growing older. When I was at my lowest point, I received a package in the mail from my parents. In the package was a brightly wrapped box, and inside was my baby picture and a note from my parents. I've always known I was special to them. But I *needed* to know I was special that day. It wasn't even Christmas, but reading again that I was their special 'Christmas gift' and very special to them—even on my thirtieth birthday—filled my heart with love and warmth."

## The Second Key: Match the Emotional Meaning of the Trait You Are Praising with the Object You've Picked

Over and over Solomon uses everyday objects that capture the emotional meaning behind the trait he wants to praise. These objects may not be familiar to us, but they were familiar to his bride. Take, for example, his praise for his beloved just a few verses later.

Solomon looks at his bride and says, "Your neck is like the tower of David,/Built for an armory,/On which hang a thousand bucklers,/All shields of mighty men" (4:4). Was Solomon trying to end his marriage before it began? Certainly not. Let's look at just how meaningful this analogy would have been to an insecure, blushing bride on her wedding night.

High above the old city of Jerusalem stood the Tower of David. A farmer working outside the city walls could look up from his work and see this imposing structure. However, what would impress him even more than the height of this tower was what was hanging on it.

Hanging on this tower during times of peace were the war shields of David's "mighty men." The mighty men were King David's greatest warriors and the leaders of his armies. Looking up at the sun shining off their shields would be a reassuring sight for one outside the protection of the city walls. By the same token, if that farmer looked up and the shields of the mighty men had been taken off the tower, he would know it was time to hightail it inside the city walls! Danger was in the land.

Solomon's comparing David's tower to his bride's neck now begins to make more sense. In Old Testament times a person's neck stood for his or her appearance *and* attitude. That is why the Lord would call a disobedient Israel a "stiff-necked people" (Ex. 33:5). For Solomon, the peace and security represented in David's tower provided a powerful illustration to express his love for his bride. He was praising the way she carried herself; with serenity and security.[7]

Let's give a modern-day example to reinforce what we have discovered about word pictures, something that took place right in my (John's) home.

For four years before her sister was born, our oldest daughter, Kari, had our undivided attention. So it's understandable that there were adjustments for all of us when a precious baby named Laura came home with Cindy from the hospital.

With all the demands of a newborn, Kari was trying her best to be the perfect big sister. She'd run to get a diaper for Mommy; or tiptoe down the hall on those rare occasions when the baby was napping; or she'd simply sit next to Cindy when she was feeding the baby, stroking Laura's little head or holding her dainty little fingers.

While there were times when she felt envious of all the attention Laura demanded, her love and care for her sister didn't go unnoticed by Cindy. So Cindy decided to think of a creative way to communicate words of high value to our daughter. She looked around for an object that represented some of the same characteristics that Kari displayed. She found that object one day while they were watching television.

While feeding the baby, Cindy and Kari were watching a National Geographic afternoon special on the educational channel, a program about eagles in Alaska. The footage was breathtaking! During the show, there was a long scene where a beautiful mother eagle helped to feed, protect, and shelter her young. There was the picture that Cindy had been looking for. On a trip by a local toy store, she bought a small, inexpensive stuffed eagle and waited for a quiet time to talk with Kari.

"Sweetheart," she said. "Do you remember watching that television program about the eagles?"

Instantly Kari recalled many of the details and talked about how much she'd liked the program.

"Well, Honey, I want you to know that you remind me of that mommy eagle. You've helped take such good care of your little sister since she's come home—even when it hasn't been easy—and I want you to know how proud I am of you."

For *days*, Kari never let that stuffed eagle out of her arms. It was the first thing I saw when I got home that night, and the only stuffed animal she allowed to sleep with her at bedtime.

By using an object familiar to Kari to praise her, Cindy wisely communicated much more than a simple compliment. She gave our daughter a living (or at least a stuffed) illustration of one way she was so valuable to her mother.

## A Third Key: Word Pictures Unravel Our Defenses

Solomon gained a third thing by using word pictures that a parent, spouse, or friend can also use today. What he gained is the ability word pictures have to get around the defenses of insecure or defensive people and to get across a message of high value. Let's look first at how a word picture can encourage an insecure person. We can see this with Solomon's bride herself, and it can be a valuable lesson to anyone who has a loved one who struggles with accepting herself or himself.

Like most young women who would unexpectedly meet a dashing young king, the Shulamite woman was insecure about her appearance. When she first meets Solomon she says, "Do not look upon me, because I am dark,/Because the sun has tanned me" (1:6). But after she had been around Solomon for only a short time, she calls herself, "The rose of Sharon,/And the lily of the valleys" (2:1). That is quite a change of perspective! How did it happen?

In spite of herself, Solomon's word pictures made their way around his bride's defenses. If Solomon had simply said, "You're cute," her insecurity could have thrown up a dozen reasons why this matter-of-fact statement could not be true: "Maybe his eyesight is bad." "I bet he's been hunting for three months, and I'm the first woman he's seen." "Maybe my father paid him to say that." These same kinds of reasons are used by insecure people today to ward off any compliments they hear about themselves. But word pictures capture our attention in spite of our defenses.

We will listen to praise more intently when it comes packaged in a word picture. That is one reason why our Lord used word pictures to communicate both praise and condemnation through the parables. These extended object lessons kept his audience's attention, even if, like the Pharisees, they really didn't want to hear what He was saying!

Jesus knew the importance of using word pictures with those who were timid of heart. He would talk about being the Good Shepherd who watched over the flock; the true vine that could bring spiritual sustenance; and the bread of life that would provide spiritual nourishment. By using everyday objects, He was able to penetrate the walls of insecurity and mistrust these people had put up, because stories hold a key to our hearts that simple words do not.

How do we know word pictures really got through to Solomon's bride in their marriage? Just look at how her attitude changed over the course of their married life.

During their courtship, she viewed their relationship with a certain insecurity and possessiveness. These feelings are evident in the way she talks about their relationship saying, *"My beloved is mine, and I am his"* (2:16, italics added).

As their story continues after their wedding—and as she grows more secure in his love—watch the subtle but powerful change in how she views their relationship. Once they are married, in speaking to the ladies of the court she says, *"I am my beloved's,/And my beloved is mine"* (6:3, italics added). This statement shows a little more security.

Then, as their story draws to a close, she even says, *"I am my beloved's,/And his desire is toward me"* (7:10, italics added). This final statement shows a lot more security than her view of their relationship just before their wedding night. Why? The major reason is the way word pictures of praise and great value have brought security to an insecure woman's heart. Repeatedly (over fifty times), Solomon expressed his high value for his bride by using word pictures, something parents and even friends can effectively use today in praising an insecure person.

As we mentioned above, word pictures can also be used with people who may not be insecure, but are defensive when it comes to what we want to tell them. Let us illustrate how one word picture got around the defenses of a couple that was struggling in their marriage and literally changed their relationship for the better.

I (Gary) was counseling a young couple who had been having heated arguments for a long period of time. Things had become so strained between Bill and Barb that they had even considered separating. They were angry and defensive when they walked into the office. Sitting with their arms crossed looking straight ahead, each of their nonverbals was saying "You just try and say something to change my mind. I'm walking out of this marriage."

Bill was a rugged outdoorsman who had moved his family outside the city limits so he would be closer to the hunting and fishing he loved. He didn't mind the thirty-five-mile drive to work each day as long as he could live in the wilderness. At first, his wife had liked joining him on his backpacking trips; but with two young children, now he did all his camping alone.

Barb was a petite, city girl who enjoyed socializing. With the move out of town, she was now an hour from her closest friend. The only socializing she did during the day was with two toddlers. While Barb loved her children deeply, being isolated from her friends and having a husband who hunted or fished every spare minute was leading her to become bitter and resentful.

After listening to them talk for more than an hour about how insensitive the other person was, I shared with them this word picture that opened their eyes to a completely new way of viewing each other.

"Let me close our time together by telling you two a word picture that comes to my mind as I have listened to you talk. Bill, I could see you as a picture, hanging on a wall, of a mighty stag with a huge rack of antlers. You are standing proudly near a mountain stream, looking over the forest, with your doe and newborn fawns in the background. The square frame around the picture is heavy and made out of antique wood.

"Barb, I see you as a picture of a delicate, beautiful wildflower with dazzling colors and fine brush strokes. Your picture has a lovely matting around the oval picture, and the frame is narrow and classy looking with white glossy paint.

"Both of you are beautiful pictures even though you look so different. However, you're not seeing the beauty in the other person's picture. In fact, you keep trying to repaint the picture to make it look more like your own. This week I'd like you to look for the beauty that is a part of each of your pictures, just the way you are. And let's get back together next week and talk about it."

What a difference a week can make. Using that one word picture communicated volumes to this couple. Instead of trying to change each other into their own image, they actually began looking at the beauty in each other's life and rediscovered the attraction that had drawn them together in the first place. Instead of dishonoring each other in anger, they began to be more patient with each other by recognizing the other person's uniqueness.

Whether we are dealing with defensive people, or those who battle with insecurity, using a word picture can help us get around their defenses and help us attach high value to them.

## The Fourth Key: Word Pictures Point Out a Person's Potential

A fourth reason for using word pictures is to illustrate the undeveloped traits of a person. Jesus did this in changing Simon's name to Peter (literally "rock" in Greek). Peter certainly didn't act like a rock of strength and stability when he tried to talk Jesus out of going to the cross, when he went to sleep in the garden, or when he denied Jesus three times. But Jesus knew Peter's heart; and after the Resurrection, Peter became the rock he was pictured to be. In a modern-day instance, we saw this happen with a young lady in our church.

Several years ago, this young woman's husband divorced her to pursue an immoral relationship. Left with two young children under three, and no marketable skills or experience in the work force, she faced one struggle after another. Today, six years later, she has a good job that allows her time to spend with her children and still to provide for their basic financial needs. When we asked her what was the greatest source of help to her during those first, difficult years, she said:

"The Lord was certainly the greatest source of help to us when Jack first left; but from a human perspective, I would have to point to my father. Every time I wanted to quit school or just give up, he would say to me, 'You'll make it, Jenny. You're my rock of Gibraltar. I know you'll make it.' I didn't feel like a rock at the time. My whole world seemed to be caving in. But it helped me so much to know that he pictured me this way. It gave me the hope that maybe I could make it." We can give this same hope to others when we use a word picture to describe their abilities, abilities they might not acknowledge or even be aware of.

To review, we have discovered four keys to using word pictures in communicating words of high value:

- Use an everyday object.
- Match the emotional meaning of the trait you are praising with the object you've picked.
- Word pictures unravel our defenses.
- Word pictures can point out a person's potential.

A well-known saying tells us that one picture is worth a thousand words. When we link a word picture with a message of high value, we multiply our message a thousand times.

In the next chapter, we will look at the fourth major element of the blessing. Closely tied with words of high value is a message of a special future in store for the person being blessed.

# Chapter Six

## The Fourth Element of the Blessing:
## Picturing a Special Future

*H*ow could anyone as dumb and ugly as you have such a good-looking child?" Mark's mother was grinning as she cuddled her grandson in her arms. To most observers, her words might have been brushed aside as a bad joke; but almost instantly, they brought tears to Mark's eyes.

"Stop it!" Mark said emphatically. "That's all I've ever heard from you. It's taken me years to believe I'm not ugly and dumb. Why do you think I haven't been home in so long? I don't ever want you to call me dumb again."

Mark's mother sat in stunned silence. Tears came to her eyes. After all, she really had meant her words as a joke. But for the first time, one of her children had had the courage to confront her. For years, without realizing the impact of her words, this mother had constantly kidded her children about being stupid, fat, or ugly. After all, she had been kidded unmercifully by *her* mother when she was growing up. . . .

### WHAT KIND OF FUTURE
### DO OUR WORDS PICTURE?

When it comes to predictions about their future, children are literalists—particularly when they hear predictions from their parents, the most important people from an earthly perspective, in their lives. For this reason, communicating a special future to a child is such an important part of giving the blessing. When a person feels in his or her heart that the future is hopeful and something to look forward to, it can greatly affect his or her attitude on life. In this way we are providing our children, spouse, or friends with a clear light for their path in life.

Have you ever been camping in the woods on a dark night? If you have, you probably remember what it's like to walk away from your campfire into the night. In only a few steps, darkness can seem to swallow you up. Turning around and walking back toward the fire is a great deal more reassuring than groping around in the dark.

Words that picture a special future act like a campfire on a dark night. They can draw a person toward the warmth of genuine concern and fulfilled potential. Instead of leaving a child to head into a dark unknown, they can illuminate a pathway lined with hope and purpose.

Children begin to take steps down the positive pathway pictured for them when they hear words like these: "God has given you such a sensitive heart. I wouldn't be surprised if you end up helping a great many people when you grow older," or "You are such a good helper. When you grow up and marry someday, you're going to be such a help to your wife (or husband) and family." On the other hand, just the opposite is true as well.

If children hear only words that predict relationship problems or personal inadequacies, they can turn and travel down a hurtful path that has been pictured for them. This can happen if they hear statements like: "You'd better hope you can find someone who can take care of you when you're older. You're so irresponsible you'll never be able to do anything for yourself," or "Why bother to study so much? You'll just get married and drop out of school anyway." Let's look back at Mark's family to see how this happened in his home.

Over the years, Mark's mother had repeatedly given her children a negative picture of their future. "Nobody's going to want to date a fat mess like you!" she would say with a resounding laugh (and her daughter would ache inside). "You might as well drop geometry now; that's for smart kids," she would remark (and her youngest son would throw down his pencil and quit trying to understand the math problem in front of him, hating himself for giving up).

These were just playful words from the mother's perspective. Unfortunately, for her children, these words robbed them of an important part of the blessing, the critical need every child has to have a special future pictured for him or her.

In Mark's family, facing the future as dumb, ugly, or unappealing—even if such words were spoken in jest—eroded each child's self-confidence. The youngest son dropped out of high school after flunking his junior year. After all, he "never was intelligent" anyway. Mark's older sister neglected her appearance so much that no boys were interested in dating her. After all, she knew she was "ugly" anyway.

Mark had taken just the opposite approach to the negative future pictured for him. He became the family "overachiever." His entire lifestyle bordered on extreme workaholism in his need to be successful—all in an attempt to try to prove to his mother that her predictions were wrong.

If you add up the incredible costs exacted from the children in this family, you can see how devastating picturing a negative future can be. You can also see why the blessing in the Scriptures puts such a high priority on providing a special future for each child.

## PICTURING A SPECIAL FUTURE IN PATRIARCHAL HOMES

In the Old Testament, the fourth element of the blessing pictured a special future for children. We can see this by looking at the words Isaac spoke to Jacob.

> *"Therefore may God give you*
> *Of the dew of heaven,*
> *Of the fatness of the earth,*
> *And plenty of grain and wine.*
> *Let peoples serve you,*
> *And nations bow down to you.*

> *Be master over your brethren,*
> *And let your mother's sons bow down to you.*
> *Cursed be everyone who curses you,*
> *And blessed be those who bless you!"*
> *(Gen. 27:28–29)*

When Isaac spoke these words, much of his son's blessing lay in the future. Jacob was not swamped with people wanting to bow down to him, and he had no land or flocks of his own that God could bless. Yet the picture of a fulfilling future was a powerful gift. The picture gave him the security of knowing he had something to look forward to.

One generation later, Jacob's son, Judah, received a blessing that pictured a special future for him. Jacob blessed him with these words: "Judah, you are he whom your brothers shall praise;/Your hand shall be on the neck of your enemies;/Your father's children shall bow down before you" (Gen. 49:8).

Like father, like son—Jacob passed down this part of the blessing. This blessing pictured a special future that would take years to become reality, but offered Judah a special hope as each year unfolded.

As we noted in Chapter Two, these patriarchs' words had a prophetic nature that is not a part of the blessing today. We as parents cannot predict our children's future with biblical accuracy, but we can provide them with the hope and direction that is part of picturing meaningful goals. Our children can begin to live up to these goals and so will gain added security in an insecure world, the kind of personal goals still pictured in many Jewish homes.

In orthodox Jewish homes and services, the wish for a special future for each child is constantly present. At the synagogue, the rabbi often says to young boys:

> *May this little child grow to manhood. Even as he has entered into the Covenant, so may he enter into the study of Torah, into the wedding-canopy and into a life of good deeds.*[1]

In orthodox Jewish homes, blessing children is also interlaced with words that picture a special future. I (John) saw this blessing with a special future in a Jewish home I was invited to visit one Thanksgiving. By the time I arrived, almost forty people were preparing or waiting patiently for a scrumptious dinner. With the grandparents, parents, and their children, three generations had assembled for this special occasion.

When the meal was prepared and before it could be served, the patriarch of the family (the grandfather in this case) gathered all the family together. He had all the men and their sons stand on one side of the living room, and all the women and their daughters stand on the other side. He then went around, placing his hands on the head of every person in the room saying to each man, "May God richly bless you, and may He make thee as Ephraim and Manasseh" and to each woman, "May God richly bless you, and may you grow to be like Rebekah and Sarah."

From the oldest child, to the youngest grandchild, this time of blessing pictured a special future for each person in the room—even me, a stranger to him. Far from being a meaningless ritual, the blessing provided everyone with a warm wish for a fulfilling life in the years to come.

## BRINGING OUT THE BEST IN THOSE WE BLESS

Picturing a special future for a child, spouse, or friend can help bring out the best in their lives. It gives them a positive direction to strive toward and surrounds them with hope. We can see this very thing in our relationship with the Lord. Listen to the beautiful way in which the prophet Jeremiah assures us of the special future we have in our relationship with the Lord: "For I know the thoughts that I think toward you, says the LORD, thoughts of peace and not of evil, to give you a future and a hope" (29:11).

Jesus also went to great lengths to assure His insecure disciples that they had a special future with Him. During their last Passover meal together, Jesus made sure they knew their future together would not end at His death. In John 14:2–3 we read:

> *"In My Father's house are many mansions; if it were not*
> *so, I would have told you. I go to prepare a place for you.*
> *And if I go and prepare a place for you, I will come again*

*and receive you to Myself; that where I am, there you may be also."*

Time and time again, God gives us a picture of our special future with Him in His Word. However, His written Word is not the only way God communicates this message to us. Scattered throughout nature are a number of physical pictures of spiritual truths, pictures that illustrate the importance of providing a special future for the ones we love.

Anyone who has ever watched a caterpillar emerge from its cocoon as a butterfly has seen such a picture. The caterpillar is probably not on anyone's list of the world's "ten most beautiful creatures." Yet a caterpillar has the potential to be transformed into a list-topping, beautiful butterfly. What does this have to do with the blessing? Words that picture a special future for a child, spouse, or friend can act as agents of transformation in their lives.

Words really do have that kind of transforming power. The apostle Paul certainly thought so.

The actual term for the transformation of a caterpillar to a butterfly is the Greek word *metamorphosis*. Paul used this same Greek word in the book of Romans, which we translate as "transformed." In writing to the church in Rome, Paul was aware that the world had tremendous power to squeeze and mold these saints into a godless image. To counter this, he tells these young believers to "be transformed by the renewing of your mind, that you may prove what is that good and acceptable and perfect will of God" (Rom. 12:2).

What does it mean to be "transformed by the renewing of your mind"? One excellent New Testament commentator explains the concept this way: "Since men are transformed by the action of the mind, transformed by what they think, how important to have the organ of thought renewed!"[2] In other words, godly thoughts and thinking patterns have the ability to transform us into godly men or women, rather than leaving us to be squeezed into the imperfect mold of the world. Let's see how this works with regard to the blessing.

Children are filled with the potential to be all God intended them to be. It is as if the Lord places them on our doorstep one day, and we as parents are left as stewards of their abilities. During the years we have children in our home, the words we speak to them can wrap themselves around them like a cocoon. What we say shapes and develops their thoughts and thinking patterns. Loving words that picture a special future help children change and develop in a positive way. In the previous chapter we saw how this picture of the future helped Diane.

In spite of her physical handicap, Diane's parents provided emotional support and words of a special future that lay before her. When she "emerged from the cocoon" of her parents' home and went off into the world, her love for the Lord and other people shone as brightly as the colors on a Monarch butterfly's wings.

In other homes, the words that wrap around developing children actually restrict growth and positive change, rather than promote it. This restriction was true in Barry's home.

"You're a bum. You'll always be a bum." Barry's father said these words to him on his way to his college graduation—a ceremony his father did not even attend. This was not the first time, nor the last, that Barry would hear these words. In fact, up until his father's death, they were the only comments Barry received about his future.

When we saw Barry in counseling, he had just lost an important position in a major insurance company. At first glance, it seemed hard to believe. Barry was extremely intelligent and gifted. He was an eloquent speaker and had that charisma that marks many successful businessmen. However, in less than a year after he had been given an important position in this company he had self-destructed.

Barry demonstrated all the motivation in the world in the way he worked to land his job; but all that motivation seemed to evaporate once he was hired. He became irresponsible in handling projects and people, and within six months he was looking for work.

What was it that acted like an anchor in holding Barry back from reaching his God-given potential? Three words: "You're a bum." Repeated over and over in Barry's mind (even eight years after his father's death), they wrapped themselves around him like a cocoon; and he emerged an insecure, irresponsible, and defeated man. Barry was searching for the acceptance found in the blessing he missed.

A law of physics says that water cannot rise above its source. A similar principle could be applied to Barry and many people like him. If a parent pictures for a child that his or her value in life is low, that child will find it difficult to rise above these words. In one insightful study of fathers and their daughters, it was found that these women's achievements in life were directly related to the level of their father's acceptance of them.[3] Those who truly desire to give their children the blessing will provide the room for these boys and girls to grow by encouraging their potential and by picturing a special future for them.

Let's look at another important picture in nature that mirrors what happens when we bless our children with words of a special future. This picture, explained to me (John) by my twin brother Jeff, a medical scientist, is of something that happens in every cell in our body.[4]

Imagine a typical cell in our body by thinking of a circle. Attached to the outside of this circle are a number of receptor points. We could picture these receptor points as little squares that almost look like gears on a wheel. To make things easier for us to understand, let's picture these receptor sites as little square people.

Floating around near the cell are "Harry" hormone and "Ethyl" enzyme. They would each love to shake hands with (or activate) these little receptor sites. In fact a great number of these hormones and enzymes could grasp hold of a receptor site, but some have a special ability to stimulate a cell's activity. We can picture this special ability as someone coming up to you and shaking your hand up and down so vigorously that your whole body shakes! This stimulation is called "positive cooperativity"; and not only does this one receptor site get to shaking (and working harder as a result), but all the other receptor sites around it get to shaking and working harder as well!

Other hormones and enzymes act in a negative way when they "shake hands" with a receptor site (called "negative cooperativity"). Have you ever had your hand squeezed so hard that you almost crumpled over in pain? That's the kind of thing that happens when these hormones and enzymes grab hold of a receptor site. In fact, not only does this one receptor site shut down and stop working because its "hand" is being squeezed, but all the receptor sites around it stop too.

Words that picture a special future for a child act like positive hormones that attach themselves to a child. In fact, they stimulate all kinds of positive feelings and decisions within a child that can help him or her grow and develop. With words of a special future, a child can begin to work on a particular talent, have the confidence to try out for a school office, or even share his or her faith with other children. But just like the negative hormones that shut down cell activity, a critical, negative picture of the future can pinch off healthy growth in a child. Emotional, physical, and even spiritual growth in a child can be stunted because of the stifling effect of a negative picture of the future.

## PUTTING WORDS OF A
## SPECIAL FUTURE INTO PRACTICE

No more pictures of butterflies or cells shaking hands! Now we *know* how important it is to provide our children with words that point out a special future for them. However, to make sure we not only understand this principle, but also know how to apply it in our homes, let's look at two practical ways to make sure our message gets across to those we want to bless. We'll begin by taking two steps back to make sure our past actions do not undermine our words about the future.

### Consistency in the Past

Inconsistency in the past can make a person unwilling to believe our words in the present. If we are serious about offering a message of a special future to our children, we need to follow the example the Lord sets. His consistency in the past acts like a solid footing on which words of a special future can stand.

Throughout the Scriptures, the basis for believing God's Word in the future lies in His consistency in fulfilling His Word in the past. In Psalm 105:5 we read: "Remember His marvelous works which He has done,/His wonders, and the judgments of His mouth." And in Psalm 33:9 the psalmist wrote: "He spoke, and it was done;/He commanded, and it stood fast."

Because God has been reliable in the past, His words of a special future for us in the present have credence. The same principle is true in our desire to provide a special future for those we wish to bless. Our credibility in the past will directly affect how our words are received in the present. Just as it did for Ted.

Ted was a sales manager for a national marketing chain. His job responsibilities meant that he was in town one week and out the next. In an average year (adding in an occasional "back to back" trip and sales conferences and subtracting major holidays), Ted was gone thirty-one weeks a year. His schedule ate away at the credibility of his words that his children had a special future.

Ted had two young children at home, and they loved their daddy dearly. All week they would besiege their mother with the question, "Is Daddy coming home today?" When Daddy finally did come home, he was so tired from "jet-lag" and his demanding schedule that he didn't have the energy to spend meaningful time with the children.

Ted did a good job of "picturing" a special future for his children. The only problem was that he never followed through on his word. He had noticed his daughter's deep love for animals, and he would say, "Samantha, we're going to get a horse for you so you can ride it and take care of it. You might even become a veterinarian someday." His son was very athletic for his age, and he would say to him, "Bobby, you're pro shortstop material. Just give me a little time to rest up, and we'll go down to the park and I'll hit you some grounders." However, a few days would pass and then it was time for Ted to go back on the road. Somehow there was never enough time to settle all the details on what kind of pony Sam should get and where they would stable it; nor a free afternoon to hit grounders to Bobby, a potential shortstop.

After nine years of being on the road, Ted finally realized that he needed to greatly reduce his traveling schedule if he was ever going to build a secure marriage and family life.

Ted even took a cut in pay to move to a position in the company where he could stay at home. One of the first things he did was to surprise his daughter with a new pony—only now, nine years later, Samantha wasn't interested in horses anymore. Neither was Bobby interested in going with his father to a pro base-ball game. His children had listened to the empty promise of a special future for them so long that Ted's words carried as much weight as the air used to speak them. They had their friends, their relationship with their mother, a new set of interests, and a deep-set impression that any future they had would not in-clude their father's being involved in it.

This story has a happy ending, however. Ted truly loved his wife and children, and he persevered in trying to regain lost ground with his family. As the weeks turned into months, Ted was beginning to build up a track record of honored commit-ments. It took nearly two years, but Ted finally built up a "past" with his children that assured them he really did want the best for their future. Interestingly, Samantha even began to rekindle an interest in animals, and Bobby dug his baseball glove out of the bottom of the closet.

Perhaps your past has been anything but consistent with those you want to bless. Today really *is* the first day of the rest of your life. And you can begin to build the kind of "past" that words of a special future need to rest on by honoring commit-ments to your children today. Remember, there is no such thing as inconsistent "quality" time that makes up for consistency in our relationships. We need to have a track record of daily deci-sions that demonstrate our commitment to our children, our spouse, or anyone we would bless. Only then will our words of a special future really find their mark.

## COMMITMENT IN THE PRESENT

As we mentioned above, if our words of a special future are to take hold and grow, we need to demonstrate commitment in the present. This idea of commitment is so important, we will spend the entire next chapter looking at it. Commitment is the fifth el-ement of the blessing. However, one aspect of a present com-mitment applies directly to our look at picturing a special fu-ture. That aspect is the degree of certainty our children have in whether we will be around long enough to see our predictions come to pass. I (Gary) saw this clearly one night at the dinner table in something my grade-school daughter said.

We were all sitting around the table, enjoying a meal my wife, Norma, had prepared. We were all talking about our day and having a nice conversation, when out of the blue Kari turned to her mother and said, "Mom, do you think you'll ever divorce Dad?" Everyone got quiet the moment she asked the question, and Norma nearly choked on her dinner. "Kari!" she said in shock, "you know that I would never divorce your dad." Then stopping to think about it a little more, Norma added with a twinkle in her eye, "Murder maybe, but never divorce!"

After we stopped laughing, we found out why Kari had asked her question. We were only two months into the school year, and already the parents of two of her classmates had gotten a divorce. What Kari was asking that night was the same thing every child asks (whether out loud to parents or in the silence of his or her heart) about his parents: "Will you be here in the future as I grow up, or will one of you leave me?"

Recently, I (John) counseled a husband and wife who were constantly fighting. I had asked the entire family to come in to try to get a better picture of what was happening with the couple. That meant that I had an eleven-year-old boy and a six-year-old girl join us for our counseling session. I began the session by addressing my first question to this six-year-old young lady (children are *soooooo* honest, even when their parents hesitate to be too specific).

"What bothers you the most about your parents' arguing?" I asked. What was causing her the greatest pain and insecurity wasn't their loud voices or even what they said. What concerned her most was the surprising answer she gave me. "Every time my daddy gets mad at my mom, he takes off his wedding ring and throws it away."

Children are incredibly perceptive, and this little girl was no exception. While her father said it was "no big deal," his habit of pulling his wedding ring off his finger and throwing it somewhere in the house sent out a message loud and clear. Every time he "threw away" his wedding ring, this little girl saw her future with her parents (the greatest source of security a child has) go sailing right along with it.

Words of a special future for a child can dissolve into ashes when a husband or wife walks out on a relationship. In a later chapter, we will see just how difficult it is for some children to feel blessed who have lost a parent due to divorce or death (and also how a single parent can help correct this). For those of you who are married, an important part of picturing a special future for your children is keeping your present commitment to your spouse strong and intact.

## A GUIDING LIGHT TO FOLLOW

Thankfully, many people realize the importance of providing their children, spouse, or friends with a picture of a special future. These people know how to use words of blessing to help mold, shape, and guide others into the full potential God has in store for them. Even when that person was labeled a "slow learner" like Marcia.

Marcia struggled throughout her years in school. If it took her classmates a half hour to do an assignment, you can bet Marcia would only be halfway through the same project an hour later. Her parents even received the disturbing news from her teacher that she was being placed in the "slow learners" group. However even this news did not discourage Marcia's parents from picturing a special future for her. While they knew she was struggling in school, they also knew that their daughter had many positive characteristics.

Rather than pushing Marcia to "hurry up" or read faster, her parents would praise her for being methodical and for staying with an assignment until she finished it. They also noticed that Marcia had an obvious gift for verbally encouraging her younger sisters and the neighbor children and for explaining things to them in a way they could understand. They began to encourage her to use these talents by letting her help them teach the young children in Sunday school and use her gifts in serving these little ones.

After Sunday school one morning, Marcia announced to her parents that she wanted to be a teacher when she grew up. Her comments could have been met with a chuckle, a "What'll you want to be next week," or even the pious words, "Now Marcia, let's be realistic" (particularly when the quarter's grades had just come out and Marcia was still at the bottom of her class). However, Marcia's parents looked beyond her sagging test scores and saw the God-given talents Marcia had.

Instead of laughing at her, they pointed out these gifts and encouraged her. They said that if she was willing to stay with it, one day she could become a teacher. This picture is of a future few "slow learners" would ever dream of painting for themselves or ever hear pictured for them by their parents.

Marcia struggled through every year of school. Her parents had to provide and pay for tutors in grade school and special reading classes in high school. When Marcia decided to go to college, it took her six and a half years to graduate from a four-year program because she could not handle taking a full load of classes. Nonetheless, on a beautiful Saturday afternoon in May, Marcia graduated from college with an elementary education teaching degree.

While graduation day meant that many of her classmates were just beginning to look for a job, Marcia already had one. She had done such a magnificent job of student-teaching at an elementary school in a fine school district that the principal had asked her to return the next year and take over a first grade teaching position.

Actually, three people deserved to be honored that graduation day. Marcia certainly deserved a great deal of credit for plodding forward day by day to reach her goal of being an elementary school teacher. Yet her parents also deserved high praise for encouraging her to reach her dream. Even more, they deserved acclaim for encouraging their daughter's dream by picturing a special future for her—even when years' worth of grade school report cards had branded Marcia a "slow learner."

Are you providing your children, spouse, or intimate friends with a blessing that pictures a special future for them? Did your parents take the time and effort to provide you with the hope of a bright tomorrow as you grew up? Wherever the blessing is given or received words that picture a special future are always spoken, words that represent the fourth element of the blessing.

# Chapter Seven

## The Fifth Element of the Blessing:
## An Active Commitment

*M*ost children have at least one subject in school that they particularly dread. Whether it is history, English, geography, or in my (Gary's) case, geometry, that course represents the worst hour of their school day.

Mathematics was always the subject I dreaded the most. In grade school it was my poorest subject, and that continued to be true during my first two years of high school. In fact, when I had to repeat geometry my senior year I was sure after only a month that I was going to flunk the course. One reason I had such a difficult time getting into the subject was because my teacher felt sure I was going to flunk the course. My only solace was the fact that more than half the class was flunking with me. Our teacher would constantly remind us of this fact by arranging our chairs according to our current grade. Those of us who were failing lined the back wall.

One Monday morning when we dragged ourselves into the classroom all that changed. Sitting behind the teacher's desk was a substitute teacher. That was good news in itself! Then when we found out that our regular teacher had been reassigned to a different district, we felt like the people in Paris during World War II who had just been liberated! The only problem that remained was that half of us were still failing the course. I was particularly discouraged. A new teacher might bring some relief, I reasoned, but I still felt I was below average when it came to mathematics.

Something that teacher said that morning literally changed my life. In fact, it motivated me so much that I ended up minoring in mathematics in college! While I didn't realize it at the time, he actually blessed me and the other students in the class. He did this by providing us with a clear picture of an active commitment—the fifth element of the blessing.

Standing before the class that morning, our new teacher told us, "If anyone fails this class, then I have failed." He made a commitment that morning to do whatever it took to see that we all passed the course. He pledged himself to see that we learned and enjoyed the subject to the best of our abilities. Whether that meant his staying after school to tutor us or even coming in for a special session on the weekend, he dedicated himself to seeing that each of us made it through the course. Nearly every Saturday morning he would help several of us with our homework, and then he played a little volleyball with us for fun.

Imagine the turnaround that took place in that class. Where once we dreaded coming, now it became something we looked forward to. Even better was what happened at the end of the school year. When our teacher posted our grades the last day of class, we all passed! I even received my first *A* in math! You should have seen it. We were all jumping around and hugging each other. All because one man committed himself to a struggling bunch of students.

In the school of life, children desperately need parents who will make that same type of active commitment to them. In the area in which they are weak, they need to be encouraged and built up. They need to be hugged and verbally praised for their strengths. When they are hurting, their parents' arms need to be around them giving them assurance and helping them back on their feet. Undeveloped potential needs to be brought out into the open and developed—even if it takes our weekends. These actions and attitudes are a part of bestowing the blessing.

In the past four chapters we have looked at the first four elements of the blessing.

- Meaningful touch
- Spoken words
- Expressing high value
- Picturing a special future

These four elements are the building blocks of the blessing. But the mortar that holds them together is an active commitment—the fifth element of the blessing.

## TWO WAYS TO EXPRESS AN ACTIVE COMMITMENT

What do we mean by "active commitment," and why is it such an important part of the blessing? Commitment is important because as we have seen in earlier chapters, words of blessing alone are not enough. They need to be backed by the commitment of a person to see the blessing come to pass. This principle is what the apostle James wants us to understand in his letter. There we read:

> *If a brother or sister is naked and destitute of daily food, and one of you says to them, "Depart in peace, be warmed and filled," but you do not give them the things which are needed for the body, what does it profit?*
>
> *(James 2:15–16)*

To answer his question, such words are about as useful as a crooked politician's shouting promises on election eve. Children of all ages need the daily "food and clothing" of love and acceptance that the blessing can provide. Yet like the verse we have just read, mere words of blessing are not enough.

We need to take action if we are to give the blessing. If we "talk the talk" but then fail to put the elements of the blessing into practice in our home, we leave our children undernourished and ill-clothed in their need for love and acceptance.

In strong contrast to speaking empty words to our loved ones is the blessing in the Scriptures. It pictures two ways we can make sure we have an active commitment to our children, spouse, or others. These steps begin by asking the Lord to be the one who confirms their blessing.

## The First Step:
## Commit the Person Being Blessed to the Lord

When you look at the blessing in the Old Testament, something that stands out is the way the patriarchs committed their children to the Lord. When Isaac blessed Jacob, we read: "May *God* give you/Of the dew of heaven,/Of the fatness of the earth" (Gen. 27:28, italics added). Years later, when Jacob blessed his sons and grandchildren, he began by saying, "The *God* who has been my shepherd all my life to this day/ . . . Bless these lads" (Gen. 48:15–16 NASB, italics added). One reason why they called on God to confirm their child's blessing was because they were sure of His commitment to them. We can see this clearly with Isaac and Jacob.

In Genesis 26, Isaac was facing real problems. Living in the desert, he knew that his most precious commodities were the wells he dug for fresh water. Twice Isaac had been driven from wells his father had dug. Finally, he had to dig a third well to provide water for his flocks and his family. As if to assure Isaac of his future in this land, we read: "And the Lord appeared to him the same night and said, 'I am the *God* of your father Abraham; do not fear, for I am with you. I will bless you and multiply your descendants'" (Gen. 26:24, italics added).

Isaac had been driven away from two wells that rightfully belonged to him. Hearing his heavenly Father declare His commitment to him must have been like drinking cool refreshing water on a hot summer's day.

God echoed His words of commitment to Jacob at a difficult time in his life. Fleeing his brother Esau's anger, he stopped one night to sleep out in the desert. It was there that God spoke to him and said:

> *"I am the LORD God of Abraham your father and the God of Isaac. . . . Behold, I am with you and will keep you wherever you go, and will bring you back to this land; for I will not leave you until I have done what I have spoken to you."*
>
> *(Gen. 28:13–15)*

Isaac and Jacob were sure of their relationship with God. A natural extension of that certainty was to ask the Lord to bless their children through them. This is something we frequently see in churches today.

This past Sunday, in churches all across the country, the pastor closed the service with the words, "May the Lord bless you, and keep you." By linking God's name to the blessing he spoke, the pastor was asking God Himself to be the one to confirm it with His power and might, the very thing Isaac and Jacob did with their children.

We also see this in a "children's dedication" at the church. Often the pastor will lay his hands on a child and bless the child, a picture of the desire the parents and the entire congregation have in asking God to bless this little one.

Wise parents will model this practice in bestowing the blessing on their children. When they say, "May the Lord bless you," they are first recognizing and acknowledging that any strength they have to bestow the blessing comes from an all-powerful God. Even the very breath of life they have to speak words of blessing comes from Him.

We are all prone to be inconsistent, and we stumble occasionally in providing the elements of the blessing for our children. In contrast, God remains changeless in His ability to give us strength to love our spouse and children in the way we should.

A second important reason to commit our children to the Lord when we bless them is that this teaches them that God is personally concerned with their life and welfare. Stressing the fact that the Lord is interested in their being blessed is like introducing them to someone who can be their best friend, a personal encourager they can draw close to throughout their lives.

When the Lord is brought into our words of blessing, it provides a sense of security for a child that we as frail humans cannot convey. We saw this in the way the children in one family reacted after the unexpected death of their father.

Karen and Nichole were still in grade school when their father died. He was only forty-one years old when he died of a massive heart attack. These children no longer had his arms to comfort them or his encouraging words to bless them. But they did have a certain knowledge that Papa was with the Lord, and that Jesus would confirm their blessing. Why such certainty? Because a wise father and mother had reassured them of this fact over and over. Listen to the words of his widow, Lisa, who also could draw comfort from her husband's words.

"Before Ray died, he used to gather us all together right before dinner. We would all get in a little circle, holding each other's hands. Then Papa would pray and thank the Lord for our day and for the food. He would end each prayer by squeezing my hand and saying, 'Lord Jesus, thank You that You are Karen's, and Nichole's, and Lisa's, and my shepherd. Thank You that You will never leave us or forsake us. Amen.' It's been rough this past year without Ray, but it has helped so much to be able to remind the children that Jesus is still their shepherd as well as their father's."

Children need the certainty and security that comes from our committing them and their blessing to the Lord. That does not mean that we do not participate in the blessing. Rather, it means that we recognize and acknowledge that only by God's strength and might will we ever be able to truly bless our children.

## The Second Step:
## Commit Our Lives to Their Best Interests

How do we begin committing ourselves to our children's best interest? First, as we have noted throughout the book, it takes a commitment of our time, energy, and resources. However, Jacob observed another important principle in blessing his children. He recognized that every one of his children was unique.

In Genesis 48 and 49, Jacob (now called Israel) pronounced a blessing for each of his twelve sons and two of his grandchildren. After he had finished blessing each child, we read: "This is what their father [Jacob] said to them when he blessed them. He blessed them, *every one* with the blessing appropriate to him" (Gen. 49:28 NASB, italics added).

In Hebrew, the end of this verse reads, "He blessed them, every one with his own blessing." While the elements of the blessing might remain the same, how they are applied in blessing a child is an individual concern. One daughter might need a dozen "hugs and kisses" at night before going to bed, while her sister does well with two. One son might feel secure with hearing encouraging words only once, while his brother may need to hear "You can do it" over and over again in approaching the same activity.

Wise parents will realize that each child has his or her own unique set of needs. The book of Proverbs shows us this.

Most of us are familiar with the verse, "Train up a child in the way he should go,/And when he is old he will not depart from it" (Prov. 22:6). However, another helpful way to view this verse would be to translate it, "Train up a child according to his bent. . . ."[1] In training (or blessing) a child, we need to take a personal interest in each child. The better we know our children and their unique set of needs, the better we will be able to give them their own unique blessing.

Please pay close attention to this next statement: Physical proximity does not equal personal knowledge. We can spend years under the same roof with our spouse and children and still be intimate strangers. Many people feel as though they "know" another person's interests and opinions because they took an active interest in their lives in the past. However, people's thoughts, dreams, and desires can change over the years. Doctors tell us that every cell in our body wears out and is replaced by new cells within a few years. We are constantly changing physically and emotionally.

In our homes, we can be people who are close in terms of proximity to each other, but far away in terms of understanding the other person's real desires, needs, goals, hopes, and fears. However, we can combat this by taking the time to understand the unique aspects of those we wish to bless.

Blessing our children involves understanding their unique bent. In addition, it means being willing to do what is best for that person—even if it means having to correct them when they are wrong.

## BLESSING OUR CHILDREN ALSO INVOLVES
## DISCIPLINING THEM

We want to show you a second way we can actively commit ourselves to our children's best interest. While it may seem the very opposite of "blessing" another person, in actuality we bless our children by providing them with appropriate discipline. We see this when we look back at the individual blessings Jacob gave to each of his children.

Genesis 49 records a blessing for each son. We are told this very clearly in verse 28, "He [Jacob] blessed them, every one with the blessing appropriate to him" (NASB). However, at first glance the blessing that Reuben, the oldest son, received looks more like a curse than a blessing. However, Jacob dealt with each son individually, and in Reuben's case his blessing included discipline as well as praise:

> *"Reuben, you are my firstborn,*
> *My might and the beginning of my strength,*
> *The excellency of dignity and the excellency of power.*
> *Unstable as water, you shall not excel,*
> *Because you went up to your father's bed;*
> *Then you defiled it."*
>
> *(Gen. 49:3–4)*

If we look closely at these verses, Jacob balances words of praise with words of correction. Reuben had several positive qualities his father praised (his might, strength, dignity, and power). However he also had a glaring lack of discipline in his life. His unbridled passions led him to the bed of one of his father's concubines. As a result he now was being disciplined for his actions.

It should not surprise us that blessing and discipline go hand in hand. If we genuinely love someone, we will not allow him or her to stray into sin or be hurt in some way without trying to correct our loved one. This lesson the writer of Hebrews explains to us when he says, "My son, do not regard lightly the discipline of the Lord/ . . . for those whom the Lord loves He disciplines" (Heb. 12:5–6 NASB).

God actively deals with us as children rather than merely ignoring our wrong behavior. With other people's children, many earthly parents couldn't care less about their actions. However, like a loving parent with a highly valued child, God does care about our behavior.

Our sons' and daughters' actions will also concern us if we are going to be a person who truly blesses them. We should not shy away from including loving discipline when it is appropriate and in their best interest.[2]

Initially, disciplining another person can seem painful for both parties. Yet being willing to take that risk can help bring out the best in that person's life by training that person and guiding him or her to a place of peace and righteousness (Heb. 12:11). Discipline is an important way of actively committing ourselves to a person's best interest.

We have already looked at two ways in which we can demonstrate an active commitment in blessing others. We can commit them to the Lord and we can seek their best interest. A third way we can demonstrate an active commitment to them is to become a student of those we wish to bless. This is something I (John) have seen modeled before me all my life.

## Third Step:
## Become a Student of Those We Wish to Bless

Nestled away in a modest condominium in southern Arizona lives a seventy-two-year-old woman. Seven major operations due to rheumatoid arthritis have slowed her down a bit; but she is still busy, active, and lots of fun to visit.

If you were to drop in on her some day, you would see something in her home that pictures what it means to be a "student of your children." While it might not catch your eye right off, whenever I walk into my mother's home, it flashes at me like a neon light. What is it? It is a nondescript-looking bookshelf, but it carries special meaning for my two brothers and me.

One rack of the bookshelf is filled with theology and psychology books, and a second is filled with medical journals and books on genetics. The third shelf seems even more out of place for a seventy-two-year-old, arthritic woman. Lining this shelf are past issues of *Heavy Equipment Digest* and "How to" books on driving heavy equipment.

These seemingly unrelated books and magazines might lead a person to think this woman is an "eccentric" who reads anything, or perhaps even has a touch of schizophrenia that causes her to jump from one topic to the next. Neither of these explanations would be close to the truth. This collection is actually a beautiful picture of the active commitment our mother has made in giving us the blessing.

Over the years, in my studies in seminary and in my doctoral program, my mother has asked for and read numerous popular books and textbooks on theology and psychology. They are in her bookcase because she has taken an interest in my interests.

My twin brother, Jeff, is a medical doctor who specializes in genetic research in the battle against cancer. To try to understand his field of interest and to be able to converse with him about it, she has read (or tried to read) medical and genetics books. At the age of sixty, she even enrolled in a beginning genetics class at a local university!

To be truthful, she ended up dropping the course after failing the first two major exams. However, sitting proudly on the shelf with other highly technical books is the slightly worn textbook she struggled to understand. Each book is a trophy of her willingness to learn and her desire to communicate with my brother in his areas of interest.

What about the magazines and books on operating road construction equipment? My older brother, Joe, is now Director for Dealer Support for a national company; but for several years he excelled as a heavy equipment operator. Because my mother was also interested in what this son was involved in, she subscribed to *Heavy Equipment Digest* just so she would know about the latest bulldozer or earth mover.

This magazine does not get many subscription requests from seventy-two-year-old, grey-haired, arthritic women—but they did from this one. All because she made a commitment to become a student of each son and of his individual interests.

## First Steps Toward Becoming a Student of Your Children

We would like to give you some practical help in how you can become a student of your children, spouse, or others. One thing that can greatly help is to be lovingly persistent in communicating with them. I (Gary) learned this lesson from my oldest son, Greg, when we were both on a television talk show.

We were on a talk show discussing my parenting book, *The Key to Your Child's Heart*. Because my children actually helped me write the book, I had brought Greg on the show with me to share his perspective on parent/child communication. I learned a great deal about my son, and about children in general, by listening to one of his answers to a question.

The show's host asked Greg what one thing he would urge parents to do to communicate with their children. Without hesitation Greg said, "Don't believe it when your son or daughter tells you they 'Don't want to talk.' Sometimes I'll say that to my dad and mom when they ask me how I'm doing, but I don't mean it. I'm really hoping they will be persistent and help me talk about it."

Particularly if we have struggled in our relationship with our children or we haven't been close to them in the past we must be lovingly persistent in encouraging them to talk. That doesn't mean badgering them or trying to pry the words out of their mouths. We must consistently set up times with them when meaningful communication can develop.

In our parenting book, we talk about a second step toward becoming a student of those we wish to bless—the importance of sharing activities.[3] Not only do they draw us closer together, but sharing activities with our children offers tremendous opportunities to learn about our children.

My younger son, Mike, and I went hunting together recently. With deadlines to face in writing books and with a busy traveling schedule, I was not too thrilled about taking a week to walk up and down steep mountains. However, I knew it would be a tremendous time to spend with my son.

Sitting next to each other on the flight, walking in the woods, sitting by the campfire—these are the kinds of "unguarded" moments when meaningful conversation can take place. Without having to "manufacture" conversation, we ended up talking about some of his dreams, his girlfriend situation, and on and on. In some ways, I felt as though I had been re-introduced to my son.

"But I don't know what to ask them about themselves or how to get started!" For those parents who want to become a student of their children, but need some questions to get them started in conversation, here are several that you can begin to ask in those unguarded times at the hamburger place, at the ball game, or just taking a walk. Taking the initiative in asking questions can be a third important way to become a student of our children.

### Do I Know the Following Things About My Children?

1. *What do they most often daydream about?*
2. *When they think of their years as a young adult (twenty to thirty), what would they really enjoy doing?*
3. *Of all the people they have studied in the Bible, who is the person they would most like to be like, and why?*
4. *What do they believe God wants them to do for humankind?*
5. *What type of boyfriend or girlfriend are they most attracted to, and why?*
6. *What is the best part of their school day, and what is the worst?*

Let's look a little closer at each of these.

These are just a few questions that can help us become a student of our children. We can and should ask our children many more to help us learn about them and so to value them for who they really are.

A fourth practical way to get started in becoming a student of those we wish to bless is to listen to them with our full attention. We actually bless our children by being emotionally present when they talk to us rather than by being preoccupied with something else.

Many of us at some time or another have carried on an entire conversation with our children while we were absorbed in the evening news or in reading the paper. "Uh, huh" and "That sounds good, Honey" uttered with our head in the newspaper does not communicate acceptance to our children; nor does it help us become a student of what they want to share.

One way to remind ourselves to actively listen to our children, spouse, or others is found in the book of Proverbs: "Bright eyes gladden the heart" (Prov. 15:30 NASB).

Most of us have had the experience of walking into a room and seeing somebody's eyes "light up" when he or she sees us. That sparkle in another person's eyes communicates to us that that person is really interested in us and in what we have to say. An interesting research study was done based on this very verse.

In this study, a number of college men were given ten pictures of college-aged women who were nearly equally attractive. Each student was then asked to rate the pictures from "most attractive" to "least attractive."

What these young men did not know was that five of the women had been given an eye-drop solution just before their picture was taken. This solution dilated the pupils in their eyes, the same thing that happens naturally when we are really glad to see someone! The results of the study were just as we might expect. The girls with "bright eyes" were chosen hands down as the five most attractive women in the pictures!

Do our eyes "light up" when we listen to those we wish to bless? Our children or our spouse will notice if they do or don't. We can decide to put down the newspaper or turn off the television to talk to our loved ones as we take an active interest in their interests. Active listening is an important part of communicating acceptance and blessing to our loved ones.

Those of us who are parents need to realize that our children are incredibly complicated people. So are our wives or husbands. If we would begin today to list all their wishes, opinions, goals, and dreams, it would take us a lifetime to complete the task. That is just the right amount of time needed to finish the course entitled, "Becoming a Student of Your Loved Ones," a class men and women will enroll in if they are serious about bestowing an appropriate blessing to each person in their life. All it takes to register is a decision to actively commit ourselves to others and a pair of "bright eyes."

## A KEY TO CONTINUED COMMITMENT

Many of us have shelves of notebooks from various marriage or parenting seminars, and pages of notes from the pastor's sermons. Typically, we will get excited about a certain principle we have read or a tape we have listened to, and it can make a dramatic difference in our lives. However, let a few weeks go by, and that book or tape usually finds its way to a dusty bookshelf with the other inspirational material.

In teaching people about blessing their children, we have seen dramatic changes in their lives. For the first time many people have come to grips with whether they ever received the blessing themselves and with how well they are doing in providing it for their children. We hope you have already seen your parents' home and your own in a new and challenging light. Yet like any other call to commitment, that inner voice that encourages us to bless our children can be heard less and less as time wears on.

How can we establish a pattern of commitment that can make each element of the blessing a permanent resident in our homes? The best thing we know of is found in a single word—accountability.

For some reason we don't fully understand, genuine commitment to provide the blessing for our loved ones grows best in small groups. When three or four couples take the time, week by week, to go through a book or tape series together, lasting changes can take place.

Imagine someone asking us how we did in terms of providing meaningful touching for our spouse or children that week; what encouraging words we spoke that attached high value to a son or daughter; or even asking on a "one-to-ten" scale, how high was our commitment to bless our family this week?

Even better, imagine a place where you can admit your struggles and learn from other people's insights (and mistakes). Does this description sound challenging and inspiring? It can happen during Sunday school at your church or in your home on a weeknight. All it takes is the courage to ask honest questions and a loving spirit to share God's truth and your own personal insights. And you need one more thing: the nerve to pick up the phone and call three or four other couples.

Even if you are not part of a small group, you can stop right now and ask your spouse or a close friend how well you are doing in being a source of blessing to them. If your children are old enough, you can even ask them how they think you're doing in terms of giving them the blessing. Children will usually be honest with you, and you can learn valuable lessons from them—if you will take the time to talk and listen to them. On the next page we have included an evaluation sheet that you can photocopy and use with your children, with your spouse, or in a group to help you get started in the accountability process.

We know that asking questions, and even more, being willing to answer them, can be threatening to some people. Even so, small groups or one-on-one conversations are a tremendous way to evaluate where we are at the present. These meetings also give us an added incentive to work on an area we are struggling with. Left on our own, most of us will tend to forget or sidestep these important areas. Faithful friends can help us face things and help us grow as a result. Their love and emotional support can share our sorrow and double our joy.

Accountability can help train us in how we can become even better vessels of blessing for those we love. It can also give us an edge in developing continued commitment as we seek to bestow the blessing.

# Personal Evaluation Sheet

On a scale of 1–to–10, how well am I doing in bestowing the blessing on my loved ones?

Circle your response.

1. Do I meaningfully touch them?

   1  2  3  4  5  6  7  8  9  10

   RARELY              FREQUENTLY

2. Do I verbally speak words of blessing?

   1  2  3  4  5  6  7  8  9  10

   SELDOM              OFTEN

3. Am I attaching "high value" to the people I'm blessing?

   1  2  3  4  5  6  7  8  9  10

   LOW VALUE          HIGH VALUE

4. Have I pictured a special future for their life?

   1  2  3  4  5  6  7  8  9  10

   SELDOM              OFTEN

5. Overall, my commitment level to fulfill my words of blessing is:

   1  2  3  4  5  6  7  8  9  10

   VERY LOW            VERY HIGH

## ONE FINAL LOOK AT THE COST OF COMMITMENT

No doubt about it, commitment is costly. If you are serious about committing yourself to blessing those you love, expect to pay a price. Not in monetary terms necessarily. A spouse and even small children are far too wise to be bought off with presents for very long. Rather think in terms of the time, energy, and effort you will need to invest to see the blessing become a reality in their lives. Is the price worth it? The book of Proverbs certainly seems to show us that it is.

The final chapter of Proverbs describes a woman who blesses her family in many ways. She is industrious and loving, has a positive outlook on the future, and is committed to her husband and children. Of equal importance are her words to her family that are filled with wisdom and kindness.

Did she just happen to be born this way? Certainly not. Each of these qualities was developed at a price. What is often skipped over when this passage is taught is how often this woman was up at dawn and how hard she worked to bless her family with her actions and words. She used the same kind of energy that gets parents out of bed on the weekend to take their children camping or that is needed to stay up late helping a husband or wife complete a project.

Was it really worth all that effort? It was for this woman. Read what her family has to say about her and her decision to make a genuine commitment to them; "Her children rise up and call her blessed;/Her husband also, and he praises her:/'Many daughters have done well,/But you excel them all'" (Prov. 31:28–29).

It takes hard work, wrapped in the words "active commitment," to provide the blessing to another person. It takes time to meaningfully touch and hug our children when they come home from school or before they go to bed. It takes courage to put into a spoken message those words of love for our spouse that have been on the tip of our tongue. It takes wisdom and boldness to "bow our knees" to highly value those we love. It takes creativity to picture a future for them filled with hope and with God's best for their lives. But all this effort is worthwhile.

One day, perhaps years later, that blessing will return. Your children will rise up and bless you. What's more, your joy at seeing another person's life bloom and grow because you have been committed to their best is a blessing in itself. Just ask one couple who took the time early in their only son's life to provide him with the blessing. When he grew up, he would provide words of blessing to his parents—in a most unusual way.

"Bubs" Roussel was only seventeen on that infamous Sunday morning in 1941 when Pearl Harbor was bombed. Later that day, he told his father and mother the shocking news of the Japanese attack.

Not long after, Bubs was called into the Army and ended up serving in the Army Air Corps (now called the Air Force). After special training in communications in Kansas, he was assigned as a radio operator in a B-29 bomber. The youngest in his crew, Bubs and many young men like him had to grow up fast. In only a few months he was stationed on the island of Saipan in the western Pacific.

From this tiny island, B-29s were making bomber runs on Japan. The work was dangerous and deadly. On the morning of December 13, 1944, eighteen bombers soared out over the Pacific to make a bomb run on factories at Nagoya, Japan. Four of the planes that left Saipan that morning never returned. Bubs's plane was among them.

Official word came from the War Department saying their son had been killed in action. Family members of each of Bubs's crew received along with the telegram a small white flag, bordered with red and trimmed with blue and gold. The flag had one small gold star in the middle—the symbol of a son who has fallen in battle.

Bubs's parents received something else. Almost a month after his plane went down, they received a letter Bubs had placed on his pillow before his last mission.

> *Dear Folks:*
> *I have left this with instructions to send it on to you if anything happens to me. I send you my love and blessings. My life has been a full one. I have been loved like very few persons ever. I love you all with the best that is in me. It*

*hasn't been hard for me, knowing you believe in me, trust me, and stand behind me in fair or foul. Knowing this has made me strong.*[4]

Would our children be able to write a letter like this to us? They could in homes committed to being a source of blessing, homes like the one in which Bubs grew up. The words might be different, but the sentiment would be the same. Giving our children the blessing is like casting bread upon the waters. In years to come, they too will rise up and bless us.

Our prayer for every person who reads this book is that you will become a person of blessing. The cost is genuine commitment, but the rewards can last a lifetime and beyond.

For five chapters we have looked at homes that bestow that blessing on children. Unfortunately, not all children receive a blessing they can give back to their parents. Let's look now at the homes we see most commonly in counseling that withhold the blessing—and the consequences on their children and later generations as a result.

# Chapter Eight

## Homes That Withhold the Blessing: Part 1

*F*ew people see themselves as struggling with missing out on their family's blessing, but people around them see it. Whether it is reflected in an underlying sense of insecurity, or, more blatantly obvious, in an angry, hostile spirit, we can hide very little from those who know us well.

As we have noted all along in looking at the blessing, living for years with our family leaves a profound mark on us. In most cases, this mark is a positive one, issuing from a family that deeply cares for us. Yet some have struggled in homes where the blessing was never given. Often, the parents who withhold the blessing lack the knowledge or skill to pass on the blessing. But some homes have serious problems that can deeply scar a man or woman. These homes can cause an individual to wear the mark of his or her family like the mark of shame God put on Cain.

Such people can spend years struggling to free themselves from their past and as a result are never free to enjoy a commitment relationship in the present. If hurtful patterns from the past are not broken, they are likely to repeat themselves in the next generation. Unfortunately, this is where the terrible truth found in Exodus 20:5 comes true, a home where "the iniquity of the fathers" is passed down to the third and fourth generations.

In a later chapter, we will look at how these hurtful patterns from the past can be broken. We will also discover God's spiritual family blessing that can provide healing to those living apart from their parents' blessing. However in the next two chapters, we want to introduce you to the six most common homes we see in counseling that withhold the blessing.

We recognize that there may be more homes than these; but in counseling couples and individuals all over the country, these six patterns have continued to surface time and time again. We also want to share with you seven characteristics of those we see who have never come to grips with living apart from the blessing. These characteristics will help us identify and better understand someone who has grown up apart from the blessing.

Before we begin our tour of these homes and common characteristics, we want to make one thing clear. In no way do we want this chapter to become ammunition to dishonor a parent or to become an excuse to blame all present problems on the past. In fact, just the opposite is true. We hope that speaking truthfully and honestly about these homes and patterns will lead us to honor our parents (perhaps for the first time) and take responsibility for how we behave today.

Only when we can honestly look at our parents and our past are we ever truly free to "leave" them in a healthy way and "cleave" to others in present relationships (Gen. 2:24). If we are carrying around anger or resentment from the past, we are not free to "leave." Rather, we are chained to the past and are likely to repeat it.

In gaining a better understanding of these homes that withhold the blessing and the characteristics they produce, we may also find we better understand our parents' backgrounds. Our parents were greatly influenced by growing up with their parents, and that experience reflects on us. By looking at the type of home our parents grew up in, we can often find answers to difficult questions about our parents that may have plagued us for years.

Our aim in the pages that follow is to inspire comparison, not heap criticism on horrible parents. Most horrible parents are people who truly love their children (even if they do not know how to show it) and have tried their best with the information they had. Even with those who have not, we can still decide to value them and forgive them just as God, in Christ, has forgiven us. To reinforce this desire, we will share in the pages that follow the stories of people who have actually worked through having missed out on the blessing—by applying the information we will make available in a later chapter.

God's Word gives help and hope to deal with the lack of the family blessing, hope that doesn't come from dishonoring our parents or burying our heads in the sand and ignoring the past. Yet before we can look at a remedy, we need to understand the problems that exist. Only then can we be free to move forward in the present and to receive help not to repeat a painful past.

With this important caution in mind, let's look at the first home that commonly withholds the blessing. In our first example, one child is showered with the blessing and the other children are not.

## THE FIRST HOME: FACING A FLOOD OR A DROUGHT

In the springtime, the Seattle area is particularly beautiful, lush, and green. Almost every day, clouds will roll in and drench the land with refreshing rain showers. However, if you leave the city and travel only a few hours east, up and over the mountains that are set in from the coastline, you will see a far different scene. These mountains do such an effective job in halting the rains that very few clouds get past them. As a result, the land on the east side of the mountains is actually semi-arid.

We can see a picture of a similar phenomenon in many homes today. One child, for what can be a number of reasons, will be drenched with lush showers of blessing from his or her parents. As a result, outwardly this child thrives and grows.

Unfortunately, sitting "just east" of him or her at the dinner table can be one or more siblings whose emotional lives are like parched ground. So few drops of blessing have fallen on the soil of their lives that emotional cracks begin to form. This very thing happened in one Old Testament patriarch's home.

We are already familiar with the patriarch Jacob and the fact that at the end of his life he gave each son a special blessing. However, the Scriptures paint real life, not Hollywood fiction; and the facts are that Jacob showered only one son with the blessing when his children were young. We read about this in Genesis 37:3–4:

> *Now Israel loved Joseph more than all his children, because he was the son of his old age. Also he made him a tunic of many colors. But when his brothers saw that their father loved him more than all his brothers, they hated him and could not speak peaceably to him.*
> *(Gen. 37:3–4)*

That beautiful tunic may have spelled special acceptance to one son, but it brought out hatred from eleven brothers. Each one knew at that time that he was living apart from the blessing. This anger reached such proportions that Joseph's brother came close to putting him to death (Gen. 37:18–22).

Anger, resentment, and insecurity are often emotions that children carry who grow up without the blessing. Particularly when that blessing was so close, yet so far away. Like a thirsty man looking at rain falling at a distance, discouragement and depression can well up inside a child who is left out of the blessing. In such people's lives, emotional cracks and pain can result in persistent anger or resentment.

We normally think that only Joseph's brothers, or those like them, face all the problems in this type of home; but that is far from the truth. Both the children who miss out on the blessing and the one being showered with it can experience significant problems. We have seen this regularly in the one child who gained the blessing in a family but who feels guilty and defensive about receiving it.

Pro athletes commonly have this feeling. Often, because of their outstanding physical abilities, they are singled out for special praise far beyond any brother or sister. We talked to one athlete who feels this extra attention was a curse, not a blessing! He desperately wanted to have a close relationship with his brothers, but his parents' excessive attention to him kept his brothers at arm's length and left him aching with loneliness and feeling rejected inside.

Please don't misunderstand. Each child needs to be singled out sometimes for special praise or recognition. But if the elements of the blessing fall exclusively on one child, serious problems can develop for each child in the family. Just ask Joyce. Her story is perhaps the most dramatic we've ever heard when it comes to the damage that favoritism can wreak on a home and it clearly shows the potential damage that can be done in this all-too-common home.

Joyce's parents were well-to-do educators at an outstanding university. After growing their careers for years, they finally decided that they had room in their lives to grow a family as well. That is, a home for *one* child.

When Joyce's mother became pregnant, ultrasound technology or heartbeat "microphones" weren't as popular as they are today. And that's why her parents were so shocked when several months into the pregnancy, the two heartbeats that had been linked as one finally separated. Joyce wasn't alone! There would be a surprise guest, a twin sister, on the day Joyce was born. Double the joy? Not for this couple. In their well ordered, well coordinated lives, there wasn't room for *two*. They only wanted one child, and they would express their disappointment and anger in subtle and obvious ways throughout the girls' growing up years.

Twins are difficult. As a twin, I (John) can attest to that fact personally! But to have one twin, Joyce, come into the world and be verbally praised and appreciated by her parents, and the younger twin, Janice, to be scorned, brought resounding heartache to both children.

When children don't receive positive attention, they'll look for it any way they can. And so Janice began, even in early grade school, to live up to her "unwanted" label. She did poorly in school, received even worse marks in conduct, and brought home the kind of notes and comments from her teachers that made her "educator" parents livid.

Things deteriorated until finally, at age seventeen, Janice ran away from home with her latest boyfriend. "Good riddance!" were her parents' only publicly printable comments, and they went back to "blessing" their oldest daughter. Little did they know that it would be over twelve years before they saw their daughter again. Neither could they guess the circumstances that would lead to that reunion.

I (John) first met Joyce at a conference on the Blessing I did at a large, metropolitan church. For two days, I had taught on this subject, and during each break I talked and counseled with many people who came from homes that withheld the blessing. It was then that Joyce came up and told me her story—and how it ended.

Joyce had gone on to college, and her parents had even paid for her to complete a two-year master's degree in music. She then married, and two beautiful grandchildren sported their mother's and grandparents' red hair. But a terrible sorrow and sadness lay behind all the joy in Joyce's life. All because of her sister.

The hurts the neglected child faced in a home with extreme favoritism, are obvious. But for Joyce, the pain of being the one who received the blessing had been magnified 100 times. That happened on the day that her parents received a call from an AIDS clinic in New York. Her sister had just died there—a prostitute who had contracted the deadly disease. After several days the clinic had finally traced her back to her hometown through old letters, and confirmed her identity through dental records. Janice was so hurt and alienated from her family, that even in her dying days, she would not pick up the phone and call home.

Her parents refuse to talk about what happened, but Joyce can't forget it. The joy of watching her own children grow up, the education she received that her sister never did, the husband who loves her, and the church she enjoys so much—suddenly all those positive things seemed to be a product of a terrible home, not gifts from a loving God. And all because she'd been born $7\frac{1}{2}$ minutes before Janice.

While this story is the most dramatic we've heard, we've seen literally hundreds of examples of people who have suffered in a home that plays unfair favorites. Yet as we'll see, honestly coming to grips with this fact can be the first step towards freeing us from a home where the blessing falls on only one side of the mountain.

## THE SECOND HOME: WHERE THE BLESSING IS PLACED JUST OUT OF REACH

Craig looked strangely out of place in the psychiatric ward where I (John) was a seminary intern. He was tall, athletic looking, and quite handsome. With his preppie clothes, he looked as if he belonged back on his university campus, not in the hospital; that is, until you looked at his wrists and saw the thick bandages wrapped around them.

Craig had been admitted to the hospital for attempting suicide. If his roommate had not unexpectedly come back to the dorm and found him, Craig would have succeeded. What was it that caused this young man so much pain that he felt he could no longer face the future? He grew up in a home where the blessing was always placed just out of reach.

Craig's father was a petroleum engineer who was considered a genius in his field. He demanded excellence from himself and expected nothing less from his family. As a result of his critical attitude and incredibly high expectations from his son, his blessing became like the mechanical rabbit at a dog race—running slow enough to excite the chase, but fast enough not to be caught.

Nothing Craig accomplished ever quite measured up to his father's standards. That was particularly true when it came to Craig's academic abilities. Craig had done well in school. He even received a partial scholarship to a good engineering school in the state. His father's only remark on this achievement was that it "wasn't a full scholarship" and that there were "better schools out of state he didn't hear from." What finally caused Craig to attempt to take his life was that for the first time in his three years at college, he was going to receive a *B* in a class.

Craig wanted his father's blessing so badly that he had studied diligently to be an *A* student, just like his father. And receiving his first *B* meant more to him than losing a perfect grade point. That *B* meant losing any chance at his father's blessing. This "failure" discouraged Craig so badly that the future was not worth facing.

When the blessing is held just out of reach, it can create tremendous problems for a child. While most people will not come to the point of trying to take their lives as Craig did, almost every child who grows up in this type of home will be lured into a futile chase for his or her parents' blessing.

Robin was an example of someone who spent her life in pursuit of her parents' love and acceptance.

Robin's parents were both demanding. Her father was a successful businessman, and her mother was a leader in social circles. "Success" was a motto in their home and had something to do with every magazine they subscribed to. They demanded excellence from Robin and would only award praise or hugs upon a spectacular achievement. What these parents didn't realize by placing the blessing way up on the top shelf was that their daughter grew up in a terrible "double bind."

To try to please her father, Robin had majored in marketing in college, just as he had. She did quite well in school and landed a job with prestige and the chance for further advancement. Robin spent many extra hours at her job, and her father was quite pleased with her achievements.

Then Robin fell in love and married a junior partner in the company. After a few years, children were born to the couple. Immediately their two boys became the apple of their grandmother's eye. Robin's mother expected her daughter to do all the things with the children that she had done (forgetting that she had never worked during her marriage) and told Robin this constantly.

Soon Robin was being mercilessly pulled in two directions. To try to capture her father's blessing, she tried to keep the same pace at work that had won his praise in the past. But she didn't have two preschool children then. To try to reach her mother's blessing, Robin tried to be "supermom" and do everything with her children that a nonworking mother could do. After several years of a killing schedule, one day the pressure became too much. Like pressing too hard against a glass window, her emotional life shattered around her.

In the United States we live in a culture that is so "fast paced" that it makes it easy to be "driven" to the breaking point. Unfortunately, people who have missed out on the blessing are often susceptible to this kind of frenzied activity. In reaching for parental acceptance, they can become workaholics.

Workaholics seeking the blessing are found in the Christian community, and not just among those sitting in the pews. Many church leaders today are driven to do more and more to serve others. However, what is really driving them may be an attempt to gain acceptance from other people that they never received at home from their parents.

Forgetting about God's sovereignty and biblical passages concerning our need for a "Sabbath rest,"[1] many modern-day pastors will work themselves until they drop. In the process of helping so many people, they often receive "buckets" of praise and appreciation that are poured on their lives. However, instead of this praise fulfilling their missing blessing from the past, it actually creates the need to help even more people in order to somehow feel acceptable. This is exactly what happened to a friend of ours in the ministry who never received the blessing from his parents.

Pastor Rick was what many considered a model pastor. He had majored in Hebrew and theology in seminary and had still managed to win the preaching award for his class. He began his pastoral ministry working at a small church that had not grown at all in over fifteen years. Within two years he had tripled the attendance and had moved on to another church. Great success followed this move up the church growth ladder, and he was pushed even further into the Christian limelight. After four years at his second church, working day and night to minister to the congregation, he was offered the senior pastorate at a "mega-church" with a membership of several thousand people. For a pastor in his denomination, he was on top of the mountain of success looking down.

Everywhere Pastor Rick went, more and more people would tell him how great he was. And he would feel more and more empty when they did. Television appearances and making the "conference circuit" could not fill his real needs, though. At the peak of his profession, at only forty-six years of age, he had a nervous breakdown and had to leave his church.

One major reason this happened was that crowds of people could never fill the lack of acceptance this man felt from his parents. His parents were not believers, and nothing he ever accomplished brought words of blessing from their lips. He had tried harder and harder to be the perfect minister, trying to prove to his parents that he was worth blessing; but their blessing never quite came within reach. His drive to fill that missing blessing with the praise of others left him emotionally broken and his life in ruins.

This man needed to deal honestly with the underlying forces that shaped him. Fortunately, he did. After four months of honestly looking at his life and of taking the time to re-introduce himself to the God who says, "My yoke is easy, and my burden is light," he was able to go back into the ministry with a whole new perspective. Because he was no longer driven to try to fill this need for personal acceptance through other people, for the first time in his years of ministry he was truly free to serve his congregation. He could finally enjoy God's acceptance for just breathing, not for trying to meet all the thousands of needs around him. His ministry, his wife, and his family blossomed as a result.

Through applying the same principles we will discover in a later chapter, this pastor discovered how to live a fulfilling life apart from his parents' blessing. He learned to drink from his heavenly Father's overflowing cup of blessing, rather than from his parents' empty cup. But he only did this by honestly coming to grips with his past, a past that included growing up in a home where the blessing was always just out of reach.

## THE THIRD HOME: WHERE THE BLESSING IS EXCHANGED FOR A BURDEN

In some homes, a form of the blessing is given to a child, but at a terrible price. Read the words of one woman who wrote a letter to a national columnist. Her words speak of an incredible cost associated with gaining only a small part of the blessing:

> *Ever since I was a little girl, my mother made me feel guilty if I did not do exactly as she wanted. Dozens of times she has said, "You will be sorry when I am in my coffin." I*

*was never a bad girl! I always did everything she requested me to do. . . .*

*Both my parents are eighty-two. One of these days my mother will die, and I am terrified of what it will do to me.*[2]

This poor woman has paid a tremendous price for her blessing—her very life. A blessing she is not even sure she has received. One certainly can't say she didn't try hard enough. Did you catch her words? "I was never a bad girl. I always did everything she requested me to do." In spite of all her efforts, she received a burden instead of a blessing.

In this third home that withholds the blessing, a terrible transaction takes place. A child is coaxed by guilt or fear into giving up all rights to his or her goals and desires. In return, the child gets a blessing that lasts only until the parent's next selfish desire beckons to be met. So it was with Nicole, a woman who had to carry around a terrible secret in order to keep her blessing.

When Nicole was only nine years old, her parents divorced. After a whirlwind romance, her mother remarried in less than six months; and a stepfather moved into the house. While Nicole's mother was away at work one evening, her stepfather came into her room. What started out in his words to be "playing" became an evening of shame and horror for Nicole. Like thousands of young girls her age, she became the victim of sexual abuse.

The next morning, her stepfather pulled Nicole aside and told her that if she ever mentioned what had happened to anyone, he would divorce her mother, beat her within an inch of her life, and leave her and her mother to "starve on the street." On the other hand, if she told no one, he would accept her and be nice to her and her mother.

The fear of what would happen to her mother, added to her own feelings of shame, kept her quiet. Because Nicole never mentioned to her mother what happened, her stepfather kept his part of the bargain. He went on with his life and marriage as though nothing had ever happened. He even treated her decently after that one event.

In remaining quiet to keep her stepfather's favor, Nicole paid a terrible price. Over the years, she was emotionally held hostage in her own home. In error, she believed her silence would buy her stepfather's blessing for her and her mother. Only later did she realize a man like her stepfather gives only a curse.

When we first met Nicole, she was married and the mother of three children. For years she had been living in another state and only infrequently saw her mother and stepfather. To keep her parents together, she had paid a terrible price. Unable to share her deepest hurt and pain out loud, her painful memories shouted to her day and night to right this wrong. Only when she broke down and shared her secret with her loving husband did she begin to find freedom from this past burden.

Parents who hold out the elements of the blessing to their child with such strings attached do them a grave disservice. They are using one of the most powerful needs in the human heart to lure a child to the web of their own selfish needs.

Nicole and others like her can receive a genuine blessing. Nicole first saw this in the patient, loving attitude of her husband. Then she believed it when she discovered for the first time her heavenly Father's love, with no strings attached.

If we are carrying a great burden to gain our parents' blessing, or if we are expecting it of our children, we need to understand that we are giving or receiving a counterfeit blessing. The blessing we saw in the Old Testament was not purchased at such a terrible cost. The blessing was a gift that was given, not something that was earned. Like God's love, it is an act of unmerited favor and unconditional acceptance and is bestowed upon a person of high value.

In spite of the problems that were a part of their homes, Joyce, Jim, Craig, Robin, Pastor Rick, and even Nicole were able to work through missing out on the blessing. They discovered, as we all will in a later chapter, that help and hope are available for anyone who grew up in a similar situation. However, we still need to visit three more homes that commonly withhold the blessing. Then we will look at the help these people discovered. In our first stop, we will see a home that is more like a "minefield" than a place of rest and safety.

# Chapter Nine

## Homes That Withhold the Blessing: Part 2

*I*t was 1969, and my twin brother and I (John) were sitting down with my father for lunch. This was a first! My father left home when my twin and I were just three months old. We rarely spent time with him and we had *never* been asked by our father to go to lunch.

But Jeff and I were facing something the next day, that my father had gone through himself when he was our age—the draft. So he called and asked to take us to lunch. "If your draft number is picked tomorrow," he said with deep concern, "you've got to know what you're going to face if you must go and fight." So for the next two hours, for the first and only time, I heard my father speak in detail about his war experiences.

A young marine with the Third Division, he fought and was wounded on an island called Guadalcanal. I still vividly remember many of the stories he shared that day, but in particular I remember his talking about the one thing he hated most about that campaign: "having to walk on point."

Picture the scene. You're deep in the jungle, on patrol with a squad of soldiers. You're the "point man," the first one in line, and it's your job to scout for enemy soldiers and snipers—and to watch for any booby-traps they left behind. You never know if your foot will come down on a camouflaged mine or if you'll trip over a wire that sets off an explosion that could cripple or kill you and those behind you.

Imagine the stress of each footfall. Imagine the tension never leaving you, the fear gripping your heart. And no matter what your feelings, you have no choice but to keep walking forward, knowing that the next step might be your last.

Now realize that many people grow up in a home that puts children through a similar experience emotionally. The fourth home that can rob a child of the blessing often reminds me of my father's story that day. It's a home with "emotional minefields," unseen booby-traps that can blow up in a child's face, and leave him or her with an inner tension, stress, and fear that runs counter to healthy relationships.

## THE FOURTH HOME: A PLACE WHERE THERE ARE "EMOTIONAL MINEFIELDS"

Growing up in an explosive, emotional environment can leave a child openly fearful of connecting with others, or inwardly afraid of genuine commitment. In 1 John 4:18, we read that "perfect love casts out fear." Yet for children who grow up in an emotional minefield their fear can reverse the equation and make them *less* loving. Often these are ACA (Adult Children of Alcoholics) homes, and they commonly leave scars that are felt for a lifetime, just like they did for Steven.

Steven considered himself a typical teenage boy. When he got home from school, the first door he'd hit (after the front door) was the refrigerator door! In counseling, Steven recounted a typical occurrence in his minefield home.

On most days, his father would be sitting at the kitchen table when he walked in. One day, Steven could open the refrigerator and eat or drink anything he wanted. (Even drink right from the milk carton!) But then the next day, if he even *reached* to open the refrigerator door, there was an explosion of anger! His father would rant and rave about "eating him out of house and home," and slam shut the door, pushing Steven out of the way.

Steven learned that home was never safe. You never knew *when*. You could never be sure what would set it off. In a home with such explosions, you don't invite friends over—because of the minefield. And you don't walk into the house with an unguarded heart—because on the day you do, all the mines explode. Such homes bequeath an unsettling legacy, leaving children confused, fearful, and often feeling powerless.

It's not only a father who can create such a home. In his inspiring, and very honest autobiography, General H. Norman Schwarzkopf tells of what it was like growing up in a home with an alcoholic mother. While he avoided many of his mother's "explosions," his sisters walked into an emotional minefield almost every night.

> I used to dread coming home at night. I'd go around the side of the house, where there was a window that looked into the kitchen. I'd stand in the dark and look inside and try to judge what kind of night it was going to be. Mom had a Jekyll and Hyde personality. When she was sober, she was the sweetest, most sensitive, loving and intelligent person you ever met. But when she was drunk she was a holy terror.

That terror was often vented on General Schwarzkopf's sisters.

> When Mom was drunk, a terrible meanness would come out, mostly in the form of personal attacks on my sisters. She might look at Sally and say, "Sit up straight! Why are you always slouching? Why don't you sit up straight at the table?" Then it would be "Just look at you. You're such a mess. Look at that hair." The small jabs would go on until she sensed she'd hit on something my sister was particularly sensitive about, and then she'd bore in until my sister broke down in tears.[1]

There is an innate unfairness in homes like this that withhold the blessing. A mixed message that can say to a child one day, "I love you. I care. I'm sorry." And the next day those words are blown away with explosive actions that say, "I hate you. You're ruining my life. You're the reason for my unhappiness."

While growing up in an emotional minefield can cause lasting scars, these homes are in neck-to-neck competition with a fifth home that also robs a child of the blessing.

## THE FIFTH HOME: WHERE UNFAIR FAMILY "ROLES" RULE

Jim was confused and brokenhearted. At nineteen he had been ordered out of his parents' home by his father, and he didn't know where to turn. What was the problem? Was it open rebelllion? Lying? Stealing?

Actually, for Jim's father, it was something even worse. Jim had a role he was expected to fulfill in his family, and Jim had decided it was a mold he did not fit. Such an attitude is an unpardonable sin in homes that fly the banner, "Unyielding Traditions Live Here." In this home the blessing is only given when these traditions are met.

Jim's father was a minister. His grandfather was a minister. Even his great-grandfather was a minister! Three generations of Smiths had heard the call to the ministry early in life and unquestioningly responded to it. Now it was the fourth generation's turn. Jim's older brother had decided to go into the ministry and was attending the seminary his father had attended. However, with Jim the pattern was about to be broken.

Jim had trusted Christ as his Lord and Savior early in life, and he had grown in his love for the Lord over the years. He was attending a Christian college in his hometown and dating another minister's daughter. Up to this point, Jim had fulfilled the prescribed plan for a Smith. Seminary would certainly be right around the corner, and then a small pastorate to continue his family's tradition.

Then Jim told his parents of a decision that left them angry and upset. When Jim had to declare his major in college, he had chosen marketing over missions.

Jim's father was mortified. Having three generations of Smiths in the ministry and both his sons in seminary or pre-seminary training had been such a good illustration in sermons and at conferences. Now he was in jeopardy of losing his bragging rights. All because a rebellious son dared to question the unquestionable, something that Smiths could not do.

At first, his girlfriend was suspected of luring Jim away from his calling; but that proved to be false. His closest friends were all believers, and little evidence could be amassed that a conspiracy had been launched from that direction. No, it came down to Jim himself. In an angry session in the living room after dinner one night, he and his father exchanged angry words. When Jim would not admit that it was sin in his life that had led him astray, his father "invoked discipline" on his erring son. Jim was ordered to separate himself from his family until he had repented of the error of his ways.

Sound incredible? This separation happens every day to a son or daughter who breaks an unbreakable family tradition. We have seen it with a son who refused to take over his father's garage and with a daughter who didn't marry into the right social class. This type of separation has surfaced with someone else's son who dared to vote Republican and with another daughter who turned down a bid to join her mother's sorority.

In each of the examples above, the parents felt cheated out of something they expected from their children. As a result, they have withheld or taken back their blessing from that child as punishment.

This fifth home that withholds the blessing, like the other homes we have looked at, causes problems for each child in the family. This home can force a brother to "choose sides" with his parents against another brother and force one sister to sneak out at night to visit another. For erring sons or daughters, it can ruin every holiday and special family event because of the layer of ice that forms the moment they walk in the door.

We need to be clear about what kind of parents we are looking at who foster such actions. We are not talking about the kind of parents who grieve over a son or daughter who has strayed into legitimate error and who are, for that reason, forced to keep the child at arm's length—parents like Eddie and Belle.

Eddie and Belle's oldest son, Don, was an alcoholic. He had started drinking in Vietnam by turning to the bottle to try to deaden the horrors of war. When he returned home, he had continued to drink as an escape from facing the struggles of re-entry into civilian life.

Don met and married a young lady in less than four months, and within a year she had given birth to their first child. Unable to keep a decent job over the years and drinking more than ever, Don began to take out his frustrations on his wife and children. At one point things became so bad that his wife had to get a restraining order against him to protect herself and the children.

Don's destructive behavior broke his parents' hearts. They prayed for him daily and tried to be both counselors and encouragers. They had bailed him out financially innumerable times, and they had even bailed him out of jail on two occasions.

Throughout his struggles, Don's parents had never withheld their blessing. They never approved of his behavior, and they had told him so; but he was their son, and they loved him deeply. Yet when he began physically abusing his family, they made the painful decision to withhold financial support from Don, unless he attended an alcoholic treatment program.

Eddie and Belle shared their decision with their son in love, and he exploded in anger. Calling them every name under the sun, he said they had betrayed him. He threatened to get even and stormed out of the house.

Don's parents did not stop loving their son. Yet because they loved him and wanted the best for him as a person even more than they loved their relationship with him, they were willing to confront him and risk losing him for a season. They withheld one aspect of the blessing from their son because of the destructive problems he faced. Both biblically and relationally they were on firm ground to withhold that portion of their blessing from their son.

Such parents do not qualify to have the banner "Unyielding Family Traditions" raised over their home. Their tough love displays too much maturity, personal integrity, and courage. The kind of house that deserves this banner is reserved for people like Jerry and Helen who withheld every bit of their blessing from their daughter for reasons as solid as quicksand.

Brenda was a charming, intelligent young lady who deeply loved her parents. They cared for her too and had the material resources to express that affection in tangible ways—new clothes, new cars, the finest schools. These were hers until she met and fell in love with Brent.

Brent was attending the same distinguished school that Brenda was. But Brent was paying his own way. He was doing extremely well and had a bright future ahead of him.

Brent and Brenda met the first day of school at the sorority house where Brent was "hashing" (cooking and cleaning up) to pay for his meals. Both Brenda and Brent were new believers in Christ, and they found out they had many interests in common. Their relationship began as a close friendship, but by the end of school it had developed into a deep love for each other.

They were each sure that a summer off from dating would end their infatuation with each other; but after dozens of letters back and forth and phone bills so high that they could have provided the money to add two new stories to the Southwestern Bell office, they knew they had been smitten with the real thing. By December of the next year they were talking engagement, and it was time for Brent to meet Brenda's parents.

Brent's mother lived near the college, and Brenda had seen her numerous times. Already, a deep affection was growing between these two. Brent's father had died in an automobile accident when Brent was just a boy, and his mother had raised him by working in a local grade school cafeteria. Brenda felt at home with Brent's mother, and she just knew her parents would welcome Brent with open arms. Nothing could have been further from the truth.

Brenda was so in love with Brent that she had failed to see the hardening attitude of her parents regarding their relationship. Not wanting to push her further into the relationship by forbidding it, they had hoped by hosting parties and taking her to the club where all the "nice boys" were she would break off the relationship on her own. The little they had heard about Brent's background had been more than enough. He would never, under any circumstances, enter their home much less become their son-in-law. Her parents had too much at stake when it came to their daughter's social standing, and their own.

Brenda was shattered when she received this message. Brent was sitting right in the room with her when she called her parents. She and Brent had been so excited to "break the news" that he was coming home with her to ask for her hand in marriage. However, in only a few minutes this couple's hopes had turned to ashes. Brenda could *not* bring him home, and she was to stop seeing him or lose her parents' financial backing at school.

Brent and Brenda tried to pick up the pieces of their shattered dreams. Brenda made a trip home to see if she could change her parents' attitude. She could not. They only repeated the firm warning that too much was at stake for her to throw it all away on someone who "didn't deserve" her or her family.

Brent and Brenda sought counsel from their pastor and close friends, and even called on Brenda's family's pastor to ask his advice. Yet heaven and earth were not sufficient to move her parents' ultimatum one inch.

Brenda explained to her parents that she felt the Lord had brought Brent and her together. Like everyone at the club, Brenda's parents went to church; but the God they knew would never approve of such a social outcast. If being poor were not enough, he was even a Yankee to top it off. In their minds, God's blessing, as well as their own, would never rest on such a person.

To try to honor Brenda's parents, Brent and Brenda put off their engagement and marriage for a year and a half. Still, any attempt for Brent to meet her parents face to face or to discuss the issue was stopped before it began.

With a semester of school left, Brenda made the most difficult decision in her life, a decision she is still paying for almost seven years later. She and Brent were married at a lovely service in a small university chapel, with only Brent's mother representing their parents. Brenda took a part-time job at the school bookstore to help pay for her final semester and graduation.

Brenda's parents have been out to see Brenda and Brent two times over the past seven years. Each time they have come to see a new grandchild for a few days. Yet their bitter rejection has never let up. By withholding their blessing on Brenda's marriage—even years after the wedding itself—they have won a hollow victory. They lost the battle when it came to whom their daughter married, but they win the war every lonely day and unhappy holiday that Brenda faces without their love and support.

It could be debated that Brent and Brenda should never have married in the first place, especially without her parents' blessing. However, to remain bitter, resentful, and unwilling to make contact with their daughter or her husband—even seven years after their wedding—shows a desire to punish, not to stand on principle.

Without question, one of the greatest gifts parents can give their child is their blessing when it comes to that child's marriage. When parents withhold the blessing from their children for cheating them out of a "high church" wedding, or for marrying a Greek instead of a Czech, a German instead of an Italian, or for choosing to attend First Presbyterian rather than Second Baptist, they hit below the belt.

We are not talking about parents who agonize over their believing son who is set on marrying an unbelieving woman or the parents who face the possibility that their never-married daughter may marry a man fresh from his fifth divorce. Yet even in these situations parents can still demonstrate love for their child in spite of disapproving his or her actions.

Homes that wave the banner "Unyielding Traditions Live Here" do not consider right and wrong—only tradition. They know full well the impact of their punitive decision to withhold their blessing—and that is exactly why they do it. Their pride has been hurt, now their children will hurt as well. As the years go by, the parents' position can harden. They are unwilling to give an inch, as if doing so meant giving a mile. They can sit through sermon after sermon about forgiveness in church, never once misunderstanding what the pastor says, but still refuse to put their son's or daughter's picture back on the mantle.

In these homes, fulfill every expectation, and the blessing will be given. Travel a different road, and expect to wander far from the shelter of acceptance. This is the fifth home that commonly withholds the blessing, and it can leave a child emotionally in a place where it is always winter, never spring.

# THE SIXTH HOME: RECEIVING ONLY A PART OF THE BLESSING

In this final home, a child does receive the blessing, but only in part. There are several ways in which this can happen, and each has the power to leave a child feeling only half-blessed. We will look at three common situations where a part of the blessing can be withheld: divorce, desertion, and adoption.

## When Parents Divorce

In previous chapters, we have discussed the effects that an "emotional divorce" can have on a child. This situation happens when one parent withholds the blessing from a child or spouse, yet the marriage stays together. It is equally difficult for children to handle when the parents actually do divorce, regardless of the age of the children when the divorce takes place.

In the typical scenario that surrounds a divorce, the wife will retain custody of the children and the father will move out. Studies have shown that during the first year following a divorce, many fathers see their children on a regular schedule. In fact, the "Sugardaddy" syndrome appears quite frequently.

This syndrome occurs when the father smothers the children with gifts and attention right after the divorce. As a result, the children may feel closer to him than they have in years. (The one who usually has difficulty during this time is the mother who is struggling to make ends meet and has to compete with lavish gifts and trips for the children, which she cannot afford.)

Unfortunately, such attention is usually temporary, and typically after one year the contact between father and child will begin to decrease. By the time three years have gone by, many fathers will see their son or daughter once a month or less.

Many of these children grow up experiencing only part of the blessing. They have the consistency of their mother's blessing and also the constant longing for the missing blessing of their father. When the flood of initial attention from their father slows down to only a trickle, anger, insecurity, and misbehavior can often result.

The blessing a father gives his child is just as important as the blessing the child's mother extends. When it is absent, there is going to be a vacuum present in that child's life, a vacuum that needs to be filled.

We want to stress one important point to the parent remaining at home who consistently gives his or her child the blessing. (This point is also important to consider for parents of children who were deserted or adopted.) Children will naturally long for the blessing of the absent parent, regardless of the situation surrounding the divorce. Their desire for that missing element does not negate or point out any flaws in the way they are loved by their custodial parent. Almost all children have an emotional need to re-establish connection with the other person responsible for their birth.

I (John) found this to be true in my life. My mother and father divorced when I was a little over thirteen months old. My mother retained custody of my older brother, my twin brother, and me, which gave her three children under three years of age to raise.

As I have had the opportunity later in life to look through "How to" books on single parenting, I discovered that my mother could have been on the cover. To this day, I cannot remember her running down my father verbally or erecting walls that would keep us from contacting him. This was true even in the first years after the divorce when she had to go to work.

My mother worked full time as an executive at a major savings and loan, yet her nights and weekends reflected her commitment to us children. On dozens of Friday nights, she would stuff us all in her car, hook on our little "teardrop" trailer, and off we would go to the mountains in northern Arizona or to the beach in Mexico to camp out with other families.

Camping was an acquired interest for my mother. Coming from an affluent home in Indiana, her only camping had been at Holiday Inns next to a campsite. Yet she knew that three growing boys needed the rigors of outdoor life and the male companionship of several married friends who treated each child in the "camping club" as their own.

I can say without question that my brothers and I learned about the blessing long before we could read about it in the

Scriptures. From meaningful touching to attaching high value to us, to picturing a special future for each son—we learned the elements of the blessing by experiencing them. My mother is a very loving person; but she is also very wise. Wise enough not to question how adequate her love was, when after several years, my father sought to re-establish contact with us.

Today, my brothers and I enjoy a growing relationship with our father and still are very close to our mother. We have these good relations in large part because the natural desire to make contact with our father was not held against us. The blessing of both of my parents has never been used as a bargaining chip to play one against the other. Even in a home situation that is less than God's ideal, we have found help to make up for missing a part of the blessing.

We realize that not all divorces and parental relationships end up like the story described above. In part, that is why we will spend an entire chapter talking about how we deal with the lack of a blessing. However, we would like to share two other avenues for helping single-parent families in particular.

Two programs at our church have proved particularly helpful for single-parent families. The first is a "Big Brother/Little Brother, Big Sister/Little Sister" program designed to provide for the needs of boys and girls who are missing the elements of the blessing from a mother or father. By matching an adult male with a young boy and an adult female with a young girl, gaping holes caused by a missing parental blessing can begin to be filled.

The second program is an "Adopt a Grandparent" program that matches a single-parent child (or even children whose grandparents live out of state), with a member of the seniors' department. Often, these godly, older saints can provide a little boy or girl a precious commodity. As one little six-year-old commented, "Grandparents are the only adults who have time to listen." Match these children with a senior who needs to be needed, and each can become a source of blessing to the other.

Any parents who are considering divorce need to face facts squarely. Splitting apart a marriage can severely affect each child in a negative way. While these children can learn to live without the blessing of both parents, a growing marriage is the best place for it to be given and developed.

## When One Parent Deserts the Family

Desertion by a parent can be harder on a child than losing him or her to death. When a parent dies, a child knows that in this life the opportunity to regain a missing part of the blessing from that parent is gone. When a parent deserts his or her children, they know that "out there somewhere" is a living person who still has the power to bless. Some children can catch a glimpse of that missing person's face in an airport or on a crowded street. But when they run to get a closer look, the likeness disappears, and they are left face to face with a stranger.

When a father or mother suddenly, unexpectedly, deserts the family, it can have serious effects on a child. In a seminar we attended on the effects on "displaced" children, one of the speakers used this quotation:

> *The father who deserts his family suddenly and never sees them again can leave a daughter forever afraid to allow herself to be vulnerable to a man, sure that he too will leave her. . . . His daughter's resulting anger may give her trouble with men all her life. She may totally avoid men, or keep seeking the father she never had.*[2]

With the Lord's help, such a prediction does not have to become a reality. However, nagging questions can remain in the mind of a child whose parents just walk out, questions Laurie asked herself for years.

Laurie's mother had walked out on her family. Surprisingly, wives leaving their families is not an uncommon occurrence any more. One popular secular book that noted this fact was even titled *The Runaway Wives*.

Laurie's mother was having an affair with her supervisor at work. When he was transferred across the country, she packed her bags one day when the rest of the family was gone and went with him. She did not leave a note written to Laurie, or even call to talk to her. Her mother just sent a certified letter that arrived addressed to Laurie's father, delivering notice of a pending divorce.

Laurie and her father did very well together through the grade school and high school years. She even went to secretarial school and landed a nice job as an executive assistant. Yet lurking in the shadows every time Laurie became serious in a dating relationship was a nagging fear deep inside.

Every time Laurie would think seriously about marriage or having a family, a little voice would say, "Don't do it. You'll be just like your mother and leave them too." The counsel of a helpful pastor and learning about how God could meet the missing part of her blessing finally helped her be able to marry and set up a happy family.

Desertion leaves so many important questions unanswered. It is a cruel dealer who passes out only half the cards a child needs to gain the blessing.

## Dealing with the Questions Raised by Adoption

We see yet another group of children in counseling who commonly struggle with gaining only part of the blessing. These are adopted children who struggle with the question, "Why did my natural parents leave me?"

We know many parents of adopted children who do a tremendous job of giving them the blessing. These parents more than make up for any loss a child might feel by being separated from his or her natural parents, especially if the child was adopted quite young. However, in even the best of homes where a child is totally secure in his adoptive parents' love, the question can still arise: "Why did my natural parents leave me?"

Sometimes this questioning comes in the form of misbehaving to see if his or her adoptive parents will "leave me like my natural parents did." These children will test the limits of their adoptive parents' commitment in an attempt to reassure themselves that they really are loved. Other children will join clubs or pay organizations to find their natural parents, all in an attempt to regain that part of the blessing they lost in years past or to hear it one last time.

Adoptive parents should expect some behavior of this sort, especially when the child gets old enough to ask such questions for himself or herself. However, by providing the five elements of the blessing, backed by God's unchanging love, adopted children can have the security and self-confidence to face these questions in a healthy way. They may still ask the questions, but they are not dependent on their natural parents' blessing to lay the foundation for their lives. God's love, demonstrated through providing them the blessing, can bring them the certainty they need about themselves and the certainty that they belong to a family that truly loves them.

## WHEN BLENDED FAMILIES FAIL TO "BLEND"

As we travel across the country, we are constantly asked how remarriage affects the blessing. While many, many blended families do a wonderful job of giving the blessing to "yours," "mine," and "ours," children in these homes can still bear significant hurts. For younger children especially, three reactions to this new family can lead a son or daughter to actually work to see that a blended family doesn't blend, thus blocking the giving or receiving of the blessing.

First, almost all children will generate tremendous *expectations* concerning the possibility of remarriage, either negative or positive. Some children will look at a "new father or mother" as an idealized person, particularly if there have been fights between the husband and wife prior to the divorce. Someone who won't argue, someone who won't disappoint them or their custodial parent *ever*, or someone who will make up for hurts in the past. When the child learns that like anyone else, the new parent isn't perfect, anger and resentment can follow, sometimes blocking a parent's blessing.

Second, they often *fear* that accepting a new person into their lives is a form of betrayal of their natural, non-custodial father or mother. Family loyalties that go unaddressed can act like invisible stumbling blocks, making it difficult for a child to receive a new parent's blessing.

And finally, there can even be *panic* in the heart of a child who fears that this new person will crowd out his or her place in Mom or Dad's heart. If several years pass before a remarriage, a child can feel terribly threatened by a new person who is now competing for Mom or Dad's time.

It's important to realize that you will never be able to outlogic the emotions of these children. Lecturing a child that he has no reason to be fearful, shouldn't panic, or feel disappointed doesn't erase his feelings. Patience and understanding are needed to draw these deep-felt issues out of a child's heart.

Helping a child receive and accept the blessing from a blended family takes a concerted effort from both parents. We'd like to recommend a book to you! It's by our friend, Dr. Robert Barnes, and is called, *"You're not my Daddy! Winning the heart of your stepchild."*[3]

## WITHOUT THE BLESSING, CHILDREN CAN BECOME . . .

### The Seekers

We have looked at several examples where children have re-acted to missing the blessing by beginning a life-long search. Seekers are people who are always searching for intimacy, but are seldom able to tolerate it. These are the people who feel tremendous fulfillment in the thrill of courtship. But after marriage, their lack of acceptance from their parents leaves them uncomfortable in receiving it from a spouse. Never sure of how acceptance "feels," they are never satisfied with wearing it too long in a relationship. They may even struggle with believing in God's unchanging love for them because of the lack of permanence in the blessing in their early lives.

### The Shattered

These are the people whose lives are deeply troubled over the loss of their parents' love and acceptance. Fear, anxiety, depression, and emotional withdrawal many times can be traced to a person's missing out on his or her family's blessing. Their unhappy road can even lead them to the terrifying cliffs of suicide, convinced they are destined to be a "Cipher in the Snow."

### The Smotherers

Like a two-thousand-pound sponge, these people react to missing their parents' blessing by sucking every bit of life and energy from a spouse, child, friend, or entire congregation. They are left so emotionally empty from their past that they smother other persons with their unmet needs and, like a para-site, drain these others of their desire to listen or help.

Unfortunately, when the other persons trying to make up for years of unmet needs finally tire of carrying these smothering persons' entire emotional weight, the message the smothering persons receive is that they are being rejected. Deeply hurt once again, they never realize that they have brought this pain upon themselves. They end up pushing away the blessing other people offer when actually they desperately need it.

## The Angry

As long as people are angry at each other, they are chained to each other. Many adults are still emotionally chained to their parents because they are angry over missing the blessing. They have never forgiven or forgotten. As a result, the rattle and chaf-ing of emotional chains distract them from intimacy in other re-lationships. Many children thus go into life with a chip on their shoulders put there early in life when they believed they could never experience love and acceptance in their homes.

## The Detached

An old proverb says, "Once burned, twice shy." This motto is used by some children who have missed out on the blessing. Af-ter losing the blessing from an important person in their lives *once,* they spend a lifetime protecting themselves from its ever happening again. Keeping a spouse, children, or a close friend at arm's length, they protect themselves all right—at the price of inviting loneliness to take up residence in their lives.

## The Driven

In this category line up extreme perfectionists, workaholics, notoriously picky housecleaners, and generally demanding peo-ple who go after getting their blessing the old-fashioned way: they try to "Earrrrrrrrn it." The only problem is that the bless-ing is a *gift;* you cannot buy the blessing. You can find some counterfeit blessings that are for sale—at an incredible price—but they last only as long as the "showroom shine" on a new car. In real life travels, such counterfeit blessings rust and corrode once they leave the showroom floor. Missing their parents' blessing challenges these driven people to attack a windmill named "accomplishment" in an illusory attempt to gain love and acceptance.

## The Seduced

Many people who have missed out on their parents' blessing look for that lost love in all the wrong places. As we mentioned in an earlier chapter, unmet needs for love and acceptance can tempt a person toward sexual immorality—all in an attempt to try to meet legitimate needs in an illegitimate way. Also in this category fall substance abusers. All too often, a drink or a pill is taken initially to try to cover up the hurt from empty relationships in the past or present. Alcoholism or drug abuse can become a counterfeit way to try to gain the deep emotional warmth that is a part of experiencing the elements of the blessing.[4]

In a recent study of compulsive gamblers (especially those struck with "lottery fever"), over 90 percent of the men studied were found to have "dismal childhoods, characterized by loneliness and rejection."[5] In other words, missing out on the elements of the blessing in a home can seduce a child into choosing immoral relationships, alcoholism, or even compulsive gambling as an attempt to fill missing relationship needs.

There is help to leave the ranks of those above and join the ranks of "the blessed." That help begins by discovering the reality of a spiritual family blessing that our Lord holds out to everyone and being willing to courageously face the past.

As we look past these homes that withhold the blessing, we will discover that every one of the elements of the blessing we might have missed out on can be ours. Rather than being locked into repeating the past, we can be free to grow into the people God wants us to be.

We shouldn't look down and lose hope if we grew up without the blessing. We should look up instead to the incredible provision of a blessing for our lives that can leave our lives overflowing, the kind of blessing that can even replace a curse with contentment.

# Chapter Ten

## Learning to Live Apart
## from the Blessing

Several years ago, I (John) counseled with the parents of a very disturbed twenty-one-year-old named Dean. Even though the problems these parents faced had existed for some time, they had put off coming in for help.

Dean had serious mental problems that had placed a tremendous burden on his family. Often he was angry and belligerent, occasionally becoming violent. Yet life had not always been so damaging for this family.

Dean's problems first began to develop after a car accident when he was eleven years old. The accident occurred soon after the family moved to Texas. Before the accident, when they were living in Michigan, Dean and his family had gotten along beautifully. In fact, they were a model family at the church they attended and in their community.

When Dean's behavior began to change following the accident, his concerned parents took him to specialist after specialist. They always received the same diagnosis: their son's problem had no medical solution. Perhaps time and understanding would work things out.

Dean's mother loved him dearly. Even when he was mad and sullen, she would spend hours trying to reason with him and read him verses of Scripture to make an impression on his life. Always she hoped that his "thorn in the flesh" would be removed and that their lives would be restored to what they were before the accident.

With Dean's brothers and sisters, and even with her husband, Dean's mother would constantly downplay the severity of her son's problems. In an attempt to alleviate the mounting pressure because of Dean's behavior, she would often set up family socials and special holiday events. She wanted to re-create a time when the whole family could be "all together again, just like in Michigan." However, as soon as Dean arrived on the scene, he would ruin the party with his angry words.

This loving mother refused to acknowledge that Dean's problems were as bad as they were. Her husband and the rest of the family could think what they wanted to; she knew that things would get better. Life would once again be just like it was "in Michigan." She even dreamed about this—until one day her dreams turned into a nightmare.

Dean's father was nearing retirement age, and he and his wife were looking forward to his retirement. This couple had been good stewards of the money God had entrusted to them, and they had saved a sizable nest egg to buy that dream retirement property up in the mountains.

Six months before Dad officially retired, Dean's parents called their realtor and said it was time to put their house on the market. They had talked this over with their children, and each of them was excited for their parents—all except Dean. Even though he had been living on his own for several years, he still made his parents' home his headquarters. This was almost a necessity because his violent temper had driven off every roommate and all but the staunchest friends.

When Dean came to his parents' home one night and saw the "For Sale" sign in their yard, he went berserk. He banged on the door repeatedly, but his parents were not at home. Finally, he pulled up the sign from the front yard and used it to bash in the glass in the front door window. Then he proceeded to tear up the house.

Dean's parents returned home several hours later. Chairs were overturned and lamps had been smashed. Dean had even ripped an inside tree out of the planter box and had stuck the "For Sale" sign in its place. Upstairs and down, the house was in a shambles. Yet of all the things that Dean had done, one thing literally broke his mother's heart. In fact, nothing he could have done to her home could have shattered her as much.

In his anger over their plan to move to a retirement home, Dean had gone into the hall where all the family pictures hung and cut every one of them into pieces. From baby pictures on up to their last family portrait with all the grandchildren, each one was torn beyond repair.

Dean's mother, like every parent, had treasured her children's pictures. They were irreplaceable and beyond price to her, especially the pictures of the family before Dean's accident. They had always given her hope that one day things would be just like before, just like "in Michigan."

Dean's mother learned a very painful lesson that night. A lesson that many people have to come to grips with who have missed out on the blessing from their parents, their spouse, a loved one, or a friend.

Dean's mother finally had to recognize and acknowledge that she now lived in Texas and life would never be like it was "in Michigan." Even if Dean made a dramatic recovery, things were not and could not be exactly the way they were. Instead of living with the dreams that Dean's problems would go away, or trying to convince herself that the last ten years of Dean's outbursts "really weren't that bad," she was forced to come to grips with the past and take responsibility for dealing with her problem in the present.

We see this same twofold tendency in person after person who has missed out on his or her parents' blessing. Many will try to explain away and put off admitting the obvious in their lives. Drawing imaginary pictures of their past or denying the real problems that exist can often keep them from honestly facing their past and their parents. By protecting themselves or their parents, they effectively prevent a cure.

If we never face the fact that we missed out on the blessing, we can postpone dealing with the pain of the past, but we can never avoid it. The legitimate pain of honestly dealing with this situation is what leads to healing and life. When we try to avoid this legitimate pain, we are actually laying on top of it layers of illegitimate pain.

Dean's mother refused to make the painful acknowledgment that her son had a serious problem, and she ended up suffering an even worse pain of guilt, anguish, and remorse. People who put off coming to grips with their past often reap the same kind of harvest, a harvest where pain is multiplied and sorrows doubled, all because they did not face the legitimate pain that comes with facing the truth.

In the pages that follow, we want to recommend several things that can help people who are suffering from missing out on the blessing (or help those who work with them). These recommendations are not a simple formula, nor do they guarantee an instant cure. However, in counseling men and women all across the country, we find that many who have applied these principles have received hope and healing.

The road to blessing that we would like to point people toward begins with the very difficult first step we tried to illustrate with Dean's mother. We need to be honest with ourselves.

## BEGIN BY BEING HONEST WITH YOURSELF

John 8:32 is a verse in the Scriptures that we require our counselees to memorize. Jesus is talking in this verse, and He says, "And you shall know the truth, and the truth shall make you free." The truth Jesus is talking about in this verse refers to knowing Him in all His purity. Christ offers no cover-ups, no denying there is a problem when there really is one. When we know the truth, we are walking in the light that exposes darkness; and it alone can begin to set us free.

Many of us need to turn on truth's searchlight and shine it on our past. Only then can we be free to walk confidently into the future. Greg was able to do this, and it paid rich dividends in his life.

Greg was four years old when his parents told him that a new little brother or sister was on the way. As with most four-year-olds, nine months seemed like nine years as he waited for his new playmate.

The day finally came when Greg's mother left for the hospital, and he knew he wouldn't have to wait much longer. That next day, Greg went with his father to the hospital to see his new baby sister. However, when Greg came into his mother's hospital room, he had a surprise. He had two baby sisters, two beautiful twin girls who were already becoming the apples of their mother's eye.

Greg was certainly not loved any less when the twins came home, but things had definitely changed. Big brother was now having to share his parents' time and attention with not only one sister, but two. When the twins got older, things became even worse from Greg's perspective. The same people who stopped his mother to comment on how cute the little girls were in their double stroller rarely lifted their eyes to notice an older brother longing for the same affirmation.

Greg's parents loved him deeply. In no way did they intentionally try to overlook Greg or cater to the twins. Also, Greg loved his sisters. He was the perfect big brother, looking out for his charges and showing them the ropes when they got into school. Yet as the years went by, even the special bond between the twin girls became a minor source of jealousy for Greg. He just could not compete with the special closeness between his two look-alike sisters, and it bothered him.

Long after he and his sisters were grown and out of the house, Greg attended one of our seminars where he heard for the first time about the family blessing. In many ways, Greg knew that he was loved and accepted and that his parents had tried hard to provide him the blessing. Yet in his heart of hearts, he questioned whether he had really received it after the twins were born. For years he had had a nagging insecurity in his life that he could trace directly back to this fact.

Greg knew that all his family would soon be gathering at his parents' house to celebrate the holidays. After the conference ended, he also knew that he needed to deal honestly with his feelings of missing out on at least a part of the blessing. With every bit of courage he had, Greg decided he would bring up the subject with his parents.

The first morning he was at their home, the opportunity came up for him to discuss his feelings with his parents. The three of them were alone at the breakfast table; everyone else had gone out shopping for Christmas ornaments or a last-minute present.

Greg began talking with his parents by sharing with them much of what he had learned about the blessing at the seminar. The concept was new to them as well, and they perked up and got right into the discussion.

He then took several minutes to praise his parents and thank them for the way they had put into practice several elements of the blessing.

Finally, he brought up his feelings of missing out on part of the blessing when the twins had come along. In a loving, nonaccusatory fashion, he shared one of the deepest secrets of his heart with his parents.

As soon as Greg began sharing his concern, his mother began to cry. Greg immediately tried to comfort her and told her he wished he had never brought it up. "No!" said his mother. "Please don't be sorry. I've wanted to talk about this for so long. I've always thought it might have bothered you, but I didn't know how to bring it up."

Almost instantly, Greg and his parents were drawn into unity. They cried and laughed and hugged each other as if they had just been introduced after years of being apart, and in fact they had.

That night the now grown children and their parents sat down for a family council, something they hadn't done in years. The topic of conversation at the breakfast table that morning was shared with the twins, and they had their chance to cry, to share, and to reaffirm their love for their brother and their parents. Any nagging guilt they had over the situation was now resolved and turned into gratitude for a courageous older brother.

By Greg's willingness to share his feelings honestly with his parents and his twin sisters, if ever a part of the blessing had been missing in his life, it had certainly been filled up. Greg was even more confident at work in the weeks that followed, something that his employer noticed almost immediately.

We can't stress how important it is to be honest with your feelings regarding missing the blessing. It is the important first step toward healing and restoration.

## SEEK TO UNDERSTAND
## YOUR PARENTS' BACKGROUND

The next recommendation we make to anyone who has missed out on his or her family's blessing is to understand as much as they can about their parents' background. Following this one bit of advice can free many people from wondering why they never received the blessing, something I (John) discovered firsthand.

For years I felt pain about the relationship I had with my father. It would often be years between our visits, and he never made contact on his own initiative. His silence trapped a layer of hurt in my life that seemed untouchable . . . until I met "Uncle Max."

I transferred from a junior college in Arizona to Texas Christian University in Ft. Worth. I studied hard, and spent a good deal of time in the library. One day a research librarian, who was helping me with a project, asked, "Are you any relation to Max Trent?" In talking with her, and later with my mother, I discovered that I did have a great-uncle named Max Trent. He was living in Dallas, and was the head librarian at a rival college, Southern Methodist University. It took a good deal of courage, but I called Uncle Max, and informed him that he had a nephew in Ft. Worth. Could I come and meet him? We did meet, and for the first time, I took a step towards really understanding my father's background.

I discovered what it was like when my father was born, and what life was like in his home. I learned much about his war years, and the personal and alcohol-related problems he'd suffered as a result of those years.

It was like slowly turning on a light in a darkened room. I often wondered why my father resisted communication; now I saw numerous things that shaped his behavior. I never could understand certain patterns he developed—and then I discovered that they actually ran *generations* deep.

What I learned from Uncle Max was something that my father wouldn't talk about, but I hope all children will take into consideration. In the vast majority of cases, parents who do not give the blessing to a son or daughter never received it themselves.

Andrea, like me, took this advice to heart, and it totally changed her perspective on her father. Andrea heard about the concept of the blessing at a singles retreat I spoke at. For years she had struggled with how distant her father seemed to her. He was always cordial to her, and he never raised his voice with any of the children. But what was missing left Andrea with nagging questions about whether she had received the blessing. Besides an occasional hug, her father had not demonstrated, to her way of thinking, any of the five elements of the blessing she had learned about.

Andrea was still living at home, and she took the first opportunity she could after the retreat to talk to her father about what she had learned. (What Andrea found out in that conversation was a key to understanding her father, the key she had never known before.)

After her father had listened to his daughter talk about the blessing (he was always a good listener, just not a good talker), he cleared his throat and shared with Andrea something of his past. Andrea had never met her grandparents on her father's side. They had both died a few years before she was born. And as he had been an only child, her father had no brothers or sisters to become aunts and uncles to pass down family stories.

Andrea's father had grown up in England and his parents were very British. Apparently, they even held claim to a small title of nobility.

When their son, Andrea's father, was born, he was raised with all the dignity and care afforded any English citizen of high birth. During his early years, he had a nanny who helped raise him, while his parents kept the respectable distance proper for teaching children discipline and manners. His relationship with his parents was so formal, anytime he addressed his father it was to be prefaced by "Sir." No using "Dad," "Daddy," "Papa," or anything of the kind in this household. "Sir" was the proper form of address.

In addition to the requirement to formally address his parents, meaningful touching was strictly taboo, and words of praise were as rare as hen's teeth (which, in case you weren't raised on a farm, are quite rare).

In the course of one hour, Andrea learned more about her father's background than she had in the nineteen previous years. As a result of seeing how her father was raised, she gained a new compassion and understanding for his actions toward her and her brothers and sisters. She even found out that compared to his parents, her father felt he was a fanatic in trying to make sure each of his children received the blessing. And all the time she thought he was withholding it!

If we will stop and take the time to look beyond our parents' actions in the present and back at their past, it will be time well spent. As we will see in a later chapter, often we will find out that our parents need the elements of the blessing from us just as much as (or more than) we need these elements from them!

## UNDERSTAND THAT EVEN A CURSE CAN BE CHANGED INTO A BLESSING

Some children have a difficult time relating to the concept of a family blessing. From their perspective, they have received a curse from a mother or father in place of a blessing. Can such people ever move past this hurt and pain and feel genuinely loved and accepted?

If you had asked Helen this question four years ago, her answer would have been an emphatic no. In her mind, the pain she had endured from an abusive father had forever trapped her in a cycle of insecurity, fear, and unrest. Many times she thought about a permanent way out of her pain. But she never had the courage to go through with it.

After years of anger, anxiety, and resentment, three years ago Helen discovered a way of escape. She began to understand and apply God's spiritual family blessing, something we will discover more about in this chapter.

No one had to pay Helen's father to curse her. He seemed to enjoy making her life miserable. In fact, Helen would stay at school in the library or at a friend's house as long as she could before she had to go home. At least then maybe her father would have passed out from drinking too much. However, all too often he was awake and propped up in front of the television set when she came home. Then his "fun" would begin.

"Come over and give your father a hug," he would say when Helen tried to sneak past the living room door. She had no place to hide in her home. Her mother worked nights (and often didn't come home during the day), and Helen was left alone much of the time with her father. Without going into the tragic details, Helen was repeatedly subjected to the physical abuse of a sick father. Always careful that he didn't leave "marks that show on the outside," he was daily leaving heart-wrenching scars on Helen's inner life.

Spending so many evenings in the library to avoid her father paid an unexpected dividend to Helen. She graduated near the top of her class in high school and gladly accepted a scholarship to an out-of-state school.

However, physical distance does not equal emotional distance. Even though she was miles away in another state, Helen was still sitting next to her father emotionally.

Only after a number of years was Helen finally able to come to grips with her tragic past. She learned from a caring friend for the first time that God could take a curse from the past and turn it into a blessing.

What Helen learned about God's family blessing is what we would like to share with you now.

## THE POWER OF A CURSE

In Biblical times, there was no mistaking the terrible power of a curse. It could freeze people in fear, or drive them from a place of safety.

When David first met Goliath, the army of Israel was paralyzed by this giant's size and cursing. Every day, Goliath stormed out and cursed Israel and the Lord God.

"Am I a dog, that thou comest to me with sticks?" he shouted at the youth. And then for good measure, he "cursed David by his gods." Years later, when the Moabites realized that Israel had come up and camped against them, their King summoned Balaam, a powerful warlock, and hired him to "Curse this people . . . that we may smite them and . . . *drive them out of the land.*"

In Old Testament times, people took the power of a curse seriously, and in homes today, people should too. People like Alan.

Alan grew up with a giant in his home. While his father's 6'3" frame might not qualify him as a Goliath, it certainly made him a giant to one small child who faced this man's terrifying anger. Alan would shudder in fear as his father towered over him and cursed him with angry explosions that inevitably left him in tears, often with toys shattered, and always feeling helpless.

Today, Alan is taller than his father, but he still feels mouse-size. The fear, anger, and hurt that were trapped in Alan's life cause him to struggle with truly feeling loved and accepted by God and all others in his life.

In Hebrew, the word *curse* means to consider something of little value or worth. Like mist, or steam, it's something of so little weight that, like a worthless irritation, it's to be brushed aside. In Old Testament times, nothing was as powerful as a curse—with one exception. A more powerful blessing.

Maybe you feel like you received a curse, perhaps you come from one of the homes that withhold the blessing we talked about earlier. In the next few pages, we'll look at what a curse can do to you, how to break its hold on your life, and who holds the only power to truly set you free from the curse.

## How a Curse Cuts Us Off from a Special Future

Living under a curse from a parent often leaves three tragic consequences that directly affect a person's future. A brief understanding of these three consequences, and how to move beyond them, is crucial if we're to receive the blessing from others, and give it ourselves.

### When We Learn to Be Hopeless

The first common effect of living under a curse is illustrated in a research study done nearly twenty years ago at the University of Pennsylvania. Researchers made a surprising observation concerning animals.

For several months, researchers conducted two independent studies with laboratory dogs. One group was put in a maze, with various hurdles to climb over to reach their food. The average hungry dog would quickly navigate the set up barriers, and, in under a minute, would be chomping on dog biscuits.

At the same time, another group of dogs were subjected to a pain tolerance test. These dogs were put in immovable, unescapable full-body harnesses, and then given strong electrical shocks. In fact, they would receive sixty-four random shocks in a sixty-minute period. Unable to move, unable to predict when the shocks would come, they were held prisoner in a painful situation, powerless to escape.

With the pain study concluded, researchers decided to use these same animals the next day to run the maze test. The scientists predicted that the dogs would quickly jump the barriers and get their food like the dogs before them, but they were wrong.

When the dogs who had been in a painful, inescapable situation started through the maze and ran into the first barrier they laid down. Even when the dogs were later shocked to "motivate" them to jump over the barrier and move towards the food, they'd simply hunker down, sit still, and endure the pain.

Physically, these dogs had not been harmed by the shocks they'd received. They had both the strength and ability to get over the obstacles. But what had been shocked out of them was the confidence or the willingness to even try.

What were the conclusions drawn from these and a number of other related studies? Namely, that uncontrollable, prolonged, negative experiences can freeze an animal, making him passive, pessimistic, and withdrawn in the face of obstacles.[1]

We know that there is danger in drawing conclusions from animal research and applying them to the more complex reasoning of humans. But the comparisons are striking, especially with those we see in counseling who have received a curse from their parents.

Experiencing a major trauma, like losing a job or losing our parents' blessing, can deeply affect us. And for some of us, it not only marks our past, but immobilizes us as we face the future. Instead of actively trying to solve our problems, we can become passive, dependent, and depressed. And unfortunately, we can also live out two other negative responses to a curse.

## Someone Has Stolen the Key

If we've labored under a curse from our parents, in addition to feeling a deep inner hopelessness when we face later trials, we can also begin to feel that there is absolutely nothing we *can* do to improve our situation!

Take Brian for example. He was the older brother. In his thinking, if Dad had to make a choice, he should have bonded with *him*, not his younger brother! He wore his heart out trying to please his father. But no matter how far he stretched towards him, he could never reach the arms of acceptance he wanted.

In a climate of unfair comparison and favoritism, Brian made a subtle, but terribly damaging, decision. Deep inside, he equated his missing blessing with something he could never become—*younger*. And because he focused on something that could never happen as his key to happiness in the future, he became a committed pessimist in the present—and eventually pushed himself right into clinical depression!

Pessimists persistently look backwards.[2] For example, pessimists look back, wanting to be younger, optimists look forward and wish they were older! By never being able to "forget what lies behind" they stay stuck in their pain, rather than "looking forward" to a positive future.

Listen to a more humorous example of someone who illustrates this point. One man wrote us with the following complaint.

> "I'm thirty-four years old, and I've been married three times. (Not my fault; always seem to pick losers.) My problem is my hair . . . or lack of it.
>
> "I know that many men feel there's nothing wrong with being bald, but I do. I started losing my hair when I was in high school, and have since tried everything I know to stop what's happening to me. I know that my first wife left me because of my hair. My latest wife even told me straight out that I was obsessed with my hair, and that was why she was leaving. My lack of hair is ruining my life! I went to a plastic surgeon recently and offered to pay him, in advance, to transplant whatever skin I needed to fix my head. All he did was to insult me by saying that I shouldn't waste my money on scalp surgery, but should spend the money on a psychiatrist!
>
> I'm sure that doctor wasn't a Christian. That's why I'm writing you to ask your advice . . ."

When it comes to facing the future, this man has a major problem. In his mind (or actually on top of his mind), is something that forever keeps him from finishing first in life—or even coming in a strong second. He can't picture a successful future for himself without thick, curly locks of hair. And by picking out something that he is powerless to change and making it the source of all his problems, he directly affects his future.

If we've labored under a curse that makes us feel powerless, and if we feel that the only key to change is forever out of our reach, there's a final consequence.

## I'm All Alone in My Pain

During the experiment we described above, the dogs who had been shocked were verbally, and then physically encouraged to jump the barrier when they ran the maze. But it didn't help. They drew so far into an inner, protective shell that the fear of more pain made them oblivious to outside encouragement.

How many times have we seen this same type of behavior in people we've counseled!

Take just one example. Jim remembers a time when he was nine years old. One Sunday he was sitting next to one of his friends at the back of church. His father was the preacher, and in the midst of his sermon, he saw the two boys whispering to each other. Suddenly his father's voice rang out. He ordered his son to come up front. Before the entire congregation, he laid into him about what a disrespectful and dishonoring son he was. And then he stopped the service, took Jim outside (but in full view of the congregation from the windows), and gave him a whipping he's never forgotten.

Many years later, when his marriage began crumbling, Jim still carried the effects of many episodes like this where he received a curse, not a blessing from his father. As an extension of the pain and powerlessness he felt as a child, whenever his wife would begin to complain or criticize him, he would become almost comatose. When he saw her angry words coming, he beat a hasty, inner retreat. And instead of being open to counsel, or translating what she said as cries for help, he just pulled further inside—which made her even *more* vocal and frustrated.

If all our efforts don't count, if the key to change seems out of reach, and if we feel a deep sense of loneliness and isolation, chances are we're still laboring under a curse from the past. But there is a power stronger than any curse.

## THE ONE FORCE MORE POWERFUL THAN A CURSE

There was a power that young David drew on that kept his heart from freezing in fear when cursed by Goliath. When the mighty warlock, Balaam, was hired to curse God's people they were terrified at the time. But someone acted for them to not only frustrate Balaam's words . . . but to turn them completely around. At the dedication of the wall in re-built Jerusalem, Nehemiah told the great story of someone even more powerful than Balaam who could not only stop, but also reverse, the curse: *Almighty God*. We're told that not only did God frustrate Balaam's effort, but, also ". . . our God turned the curse into a blessing."

Turning wrongs around is something God specializes in, particularly for those who have received a curse from their homes. But how? Briefly, here are three crucial elements to see a curse lifted off your life.

### A Life of Learned Hopefulness Begins with Commitment

If some of us have learned to be hopeless through shouldering a curse in the past, then the first step towards reversing the curse and learning to be hopeful comes from making a whole-hearted commitment.

Several years ago, I (John) worked with a man who has carried the curse of hurtful words for years. While it's driven him to succeed, it's never left him with a moment's inner rest or peace. As part of our conversations, I asked him clearly if he had ever truly committed his life to Jesus Christ. "Absolutely," he said. And while he had only recently trusted Christ, he bore a strong, convincing testimony.

"Do you want to be the husband and father God would have you be? And are you willing to do whatever it takes to be the man God wants you to be?" Again, the answers were a resounding "yes." *"Would you put that commitment in writing?"* I asked. And he did.

That day, and now for over two years, that single sheet of paper has hung in his office, becoming for him an important milestone in overcoming the curse he's been under.

Recently, we completed a workbook for this book you're reading, *The Blessing Workbook* (Nashville: Thomas Nelson Publishers, 1993). And guess what is in the first section of the book? A page for you to put in writing your commitment to Christ, to your family, and to personal growth—a milestone to remind you that in Christ, you are "a new creation; old things have passed away; behold, all things have become new" (2 Cor. 5:17).

A key to sorting out the inner confusion that comes with receiving a curse is making clear, definite commitments. Then once we've made those commitments, we begin to gain:

## Increased Energy to Pursue Self-Control

One glaring problem that surfaces for many of those we counsel who have grown up with a curse, is a lack of self-control. And not surprisingly, *the degree of self-control in an individual is directly proportional to their self-worth.*

The *lower* value we have of ourselves (remember, the word for curse literally means, "of little value"), the *less* energy we'll have to discipline our attitudes, appetites, and actions. We'll reward ourselves with junk food instead of consistently exercising; let five hours a night go by before we finally turn off the television and stumble into bed and a fitful sleep; or procrastinate on those things we must do at work.

Out of strong commitments come renewed energy to view ourselves differently, more positively, and to gain more self-discipline and self-worth as a result. And that positive gain is increased as we gain something else.

## Moving Towards a Clear Challenge

For those of us who have labored under a curse, our God can break its impact on our lives, renew our commitments, and re-store the energy to be self-disciplined. One way He does that is to give us a clear challenge.

Many studies have shown how crucial it is to maintain a clear purpose and challenge in life. In fact, many of these studies cen-ter around the fact that the only challenge most men have is their work. That's why the average man in the United States dies within three years of retirement! (Or in Coach Bear Bryant's case, three weeks after spending a quarter century of coaching football.) The Scripture is true, "Without a vision, the people perish." Yet the future painted for many people who have grown up with a curse is anything but clear. How clear is your purpose in life? Do you have a challenge that is big enough to last you a lifetime? To move you forward each day? You do if you are seek-ing to give the blessing to others. *For one of the most powerful ways of reversing a curse you've received, is to give the blessing to others.*

For the Lord, the opposite of the curse was giving His chil-dren the blessing. As His servants, we're called to be a blessing to all the earth. The five elements of the blessing that we've de-tailed in this book can give you a simple, biblical plan to bless your children, spouse, friends, and others.

Commitment, self-control, and a significant, therapeutic chal-lenge to be a blessing: these are the three things that can help break the negative cycle of the curse. And they're the very thing God desires for your life.

Look at God's Word to see just what kind of future He calls you to. For as He looks at you, He sees a future totally free of a curse.

> *"For I know the thoughts that I think toward you, says the* Lord, *thoughts of peace and not of evil, to give you a future and a hope."*
>
> *(Jer. 29:11).*

## AT HOME WITH GOD'S FAMILY BLESSING

Some children will never, in this life, hear words of love or acceptance from their parents. People like Helen. Some will try to break down the door to their parents' hearts to receive this missing blessing, but all too often their attempt fails. For whatever reason, they have to face the fact that their blessing will have to come from another source.

When Helen finally realized this and turned to listen to the voice of her heavenly Father calling her, she discovered an open door of blessing. She found a spiritual family blessing that provided her with every element she had missed in her home.

"God's spiritual family blessing" begins with the fact that when we have a personal relationship with Jesus Christ, our spiritual parentage is secure.

### As Believers, Our Spiritual Parentage Is Secure

Helen was never secure in her relationship with her father. His anger had frozen within her heart a sense of insecurity. Yet when Helen trusted Jesus Christ as her Lord and Savior, she found out that she had a source of blessing that would be with her each day of her life and beyond! Helen discovered verses like these that speak of how stable her heavenly Father is and how permanent her relationship is with Him:

> *"My sheep hear My voice, and I know them, and they follow Me. And I give them eternal life, and they shall never perish; neither shall anyone snatch them out of My hand."*
> *(John 10:27–28)*
>
> *And Jesus came and spoke to them, saying, . . . "lo, I am with you always, even to the end of the age."*
> *(Matt. 28:18, 20)*
>
> *For He Himself has said, "I will never desert you, nor will I ever forsake you," so that we confidently say, "The Lord is my helper, I will not be afraid. What shall man do to me?"*
> *(Heb. 13:5–6 NASB)*
>
> *The Spirit of the Lord GOD is upon me,/Because the LORD has anointed me/To bring good news to the afflicted;/He has*

> *sent me to bind up the brokenhearted,/To proclaim liberty to captives,/And freedom to prisoners; . . . To comfort all who mourn, . . . Giving them a garland instead of ashes,/The oil of gladness instead of mourning,/The mantle of praise instead of a spirit of fainting./So they will be called oaks of righteousness,/The planting of the LORD, that He may be glorified.*
>
> *(Isa. 61:1–3 NASB)*

The first thing Helen had to consider when she came home at night was what kind of mood her father would be in. One night it would be anger, the next indifference; and occasionally he could even be very nice. His vacillations kept her so off balance, it left her insecure and questioning herself. Now she had a relationship with a heavenly Father characterized by the words, "Jesus Christ is the same yesterday and today, yes and forever" (Heb. 13:8 NASB).

Those who have personally believed in Jesus and trusted their lives to Him have a secure relationship with their heavenly Father. Yet there is even more to God's spiritual family blessing that they receive when they trust their lives to Him.

## As Believers, We Gain a Spiritual Family to Bless Us

In Chapter Three we told the story about a little girl who was very scared and needed "someone with skin on" to hug her. As we saw in that chapter, our Lord knows all about our need for meaningful touch. He also knows our need for the physical companionship of others to build up our lives and encourage us.

That is why when we accept Christ, we gain not only a secure relationship with our heavenly Father, but we join an entire family of brothers and sisters in Christ! Men and women "with skin on" who can hug us and hold us and communicate God's love, wisdom, and blessing to us!

In many ways the early church provided a very good model for us to follow. They were often in each other's homes (the earliest churches started in homes) and shared meals together. They were literally a family of the faith, and that is just how Paul expected Timothy to treat the believers he met. Listen to the counsel this noted apostle gave his young charge:

> *Do not rebuke an older man, but exhort him as a father,*
> *younger men as brothers, older women as mothers,*
> *younger women as sisters, with all purity.*
>
> *(1 Tim. 5:1–2, italics added).*

Timothy was not related to these people by physical birth, but Paul points out clearly that he was related to them through spiritual birth. They all shared the same heavenly Father, and they were all necessary members of one another.

For both of the authors, this principle of having a spiritual family has been a tremendous personal help, particularly the way God used an older man in each of our lives to become a spiritual father to us in times of need.

Gary was in college when his father died, leaving a huge vacuum in his life. At this crossroads period in his life, a godly man named Rod Toews stepped in and became a spiritual father. Rod is a nationally prominent speaker and Christian educator. He could have easily let his busy schedule crowd out time for a hurting collegian. However, Rod attached high value to Gary and took him under his wing to shepherd and support. Both verbally and by his presence at a critical time, Rod gave Gary the blessing that was missing in his life now that his natural father had died.

John was a freshman in high school when he met a man who would become his spiritual father. Doug Barram, at the time a Young Life area director, had come to watch a freshman football game. Besides a few parents who were dyed-in-the-wool fans, *nobody* goes to freshman football games. Yet Doug was there, standing along the sidelines every game, offering words of encouragement to a young man who had not yet heard about Christ.

In the years that followed, this man took a fatherly interest in John and his two brothers. In a single-parent home, Doug added spiritual support to three boys who very much needed it. Each brother and even John's mother would come to know Jesus Christ and His heavenly Father personally! All because of this man's deep love for his Savior, a love that was reflected in his fatherly love for us.

To return to Helen's story, she had a similar experience in learning how God's family can become that missing source of blessing she sought. Only hers came with a spiritual sister who blessed her at work.

Helen worked for a major oil company in the accounting department. One day, with the retirement of a woman at the office, Karen came to work. Karen was a committed Christian, who had prayed that God would provide the opportunity for her to share His love with someone who worked in her new office. That someone turned out to be Helen.

Karen was a mystery to Helen at first. She always seemed to have such a positive attitude and such a calm spirit even when there was great pressure at work. Perhaps more than anything Karen's lack of anxiety and inner peace drew Helen to want to be around her.

Soon, Karen and Helen had struck up a friendship and were sharing stories about the "rigors of dating" and their frustrations at work. But Karen also began sharing with Helen the good news about a heavenly Father Helen could come to know. At first, Helen didn't want anything to do with such talk. She had had enough of fathers to last a lifetime. Yet gradually, in spite of herself, the Holy Spirit working through Karen's life drew Helen to a saving knowledge of Christ.

Karen took Helen to church with her for the first time in Helen's adult life. Helen couldn't believe what happened. She was asked to stand up as a visitor, and she was greeted by the pastor. After church a number of people stopped her to say they were glad she had come. One elderly lady even hugged her! Helen went with Karen to the singles Sunday school class. People shared prayer requests before a short message, and they actually held hands and prayed for each other.

Helen found people who had never laid eyes on her treating her like a sister and encouraging her to come back. For the first time, Helen had seen the source of blessing a church family could be, and God used that experience literally to change her life.

Any person who has missed out on all or a part of their parents' blessing can acquire a spiritual family of fathers, mothers, brothers, and sisters who can fill that void. With a personal relationship with a heavenly Father that is secure, and through a spiritual family that can offer warmth, love, and acceptance, every element of the blessing can be ours and overflowing.

## For Believers, Each Element of the Blessing Is Available Today

Just in case you have forgotten (or are one of those readers who begin a book in the middle!), let's review the five elements we saw that are a part of the blessing to see how we can give it to each other:

- Meaningful touching
- A spoken message
- Attaching high value
- Picturing a special future
- Active commitment to see the blessing come to pass

Karen provided each element of the blessing to Helen, and it brought Helen to the Savior and to His church. By introducing Helen to a loving group of friends at church, Karen was able to see her blessing multiplied as many people took an interest in Helen's life.

As we will see in more detail in a later chapter, God has equipped the church, the local body of believers, to provide each aspect of the blessing to people in need. Where churches are growing and thriving anywhere in the country, you will find a body of believers who are practicing these five elements of the blessed. These are also the churches that are drawing in the unsaved, not simply luring other believers away from the church down the street.

The past three years had brought tremendous changes for Helen. She had come from feeling isolated and alone to feeling truly blessed for the first time in her life. Helen could retire now in the shelter of her caring friends at church and forget all about the past, right? Not quite. Her life still needed to go full circle.

Helen had received God's blessing from others. Now she would need to become a source of blessing to others around her. People in the office and at her apartment building for the first time could be thought of in terms of what she could give, not just what she needed from them. Because her life was filled with God's blessing through His Spirit and His people, she could love and serve them without needing it to be returned in response.

Helen had eaten fully and had drunk deeply from the feast of life God had provided her in His blessing. However, one final thing was left for Helen to do if she truly wanted to be free from her past. She would need to be a source of blessing not only to her friends at church and work, but to her enemies as well and to one enemy in particular.

## Giving the Blessing to Others—Even Our Enemies

As incredible as it may seem, Helen needed to become a source of blessing to her father, the very one who had caused her so much pain and had caused her to begin her search for acceptance in the first place.

"Couldn't I just skip over this part?" Helen asked her pastor when she found out her need to bless her father. Yet in her heart of hearts she knew she would never be truly free of his grip over her life until she could do this.

In a later chapter we will discover the way Helen went about re-establishing contact with her father and how she approached their first meeting in years. Suffice it to say that in spite of her change in attitude about blessing her father (which went from adamant refusal, to quiet acquiescence, to firm resolve, to wanting to chicken out at the last minute and not get on the plane to go see him), it was the second most meaningful day in her life.

Her most meaningful day was when she met the Lord Jesus, the One who changed her life by meeting her missing need for the blessing. He gave her a spiritual family to bless her in the present and provided her the power to be truly free from the yoke of the past.

Jesus is the Person who can change our life, or the life of loved ones who are struggling without the blessing, by providing us and them with God's spiritual family blessing. A blessing that not only parents need to give to their children, and vice versa, but also one that can enrich your relationship with your spouse, intimate friends, and church family.

# Chapter Eleven

## When You Know You Will Never Receive a Parent's Blessing

**O**ver the years, we have received literally hundreds of letters telling us about dramatic turnarounds with a parent. At seminars, we have heard countless stories of men and women who went back to a father or mother who hadn't blessed them. They gave that parent the blessing, and saw their life radically transformed. Many were "deathbed" conversions, where in the last days, weeks, or months of their life, parents not only turned around and gave their children the blessing, but also asked forgiveness from them, and sought salvation from Christ.

That was the kind of happy ending I always pictured for my own father. For years, I prayed for him, and tried to give him each element of this blessing you've read about. I felt sure that one day, he would return it to my brothers and me. We would talk about the hurt and loneliness, and close the loop on any painful memories with caring words. Even more important, I just knew that with all my prayers and sharing, with all the prayers *others* around the country had made for him, he would come to know Christ as well.

This chapter is for those of us who live with less than happy endings.

## WHEN HEARTACHE DIALS YOUR NUMBER . . .

"He's in bad shape, John . . . Really bad. You'd better come down right now."

It was August 9, 1992. The call came from my older brother, Joe, and it was one I'd been dreading.

It was a crystal clear Sunday morning, with the promise of yet another scorching day in Phoenix. Cindy and I had just gotten the kids ready for church. Even two minutes later, and I'd have missed the call. But with everyone heading towards the car, I stopped and picked up the phone.

On a day that would hit 111 degrees, Joe's words shook me like a blast of cold air. There had been several times over the past two years when I'd received similar calls, on those occasions I'd always known Dad would pull through. Somehow on this day, I knew deep inside: This was my father's last day on earth.

Cindy, Kari, and Laura all gathered around me, and we knelt in a little circle and prayed for Grandpa. Then I urged them to go on to church, and I drove the short distance to the hospice where my father was dying.

I can't describe to you the feelings I had as I sat in the car before I went in. Sadness, hopefulness, anger, and compassion, all jumbled together. I just knew that something positive was going to happen . . . *that it had to happen.*

I arrived at 8:10 in the morning and found my father sitting on the edge of the hospital bed. Even then he was fighting for breath, his chest heaving as he sought to bring in enough air to fill his collapsing lungs. He was losing his life to lung cancer, complicated by congestive heart failure. A terrible reward for chain-smoking over the years, and a horrible way to die.

For the next eight hours, my brother and I would take turns sitting beside him, holding his hand, praying for him when he'd let us, shifting his pillows, trying to help him be more comfortable. And time after time, when I'd look at him, pictures would pop into my mind . . .

## PRESS THE BAR . . . FEEL THE PAIN

One picture was of meeting my father for the first time since my childhood. My parents divorced when I was three months old, and while my father always lived within a few miles of us, it wasn't until my teenage years that he called and finally made contact with us. When he did, it was to come and see my twin brother, Jeff, and me play in one of our high-school football games.

You can imagine how hard we played that game. For the first time, our *father* was coming to watch us! He hadn't come down on the field before the game like we'd hoped, but we were sure he was somewhere up in the stands, cheering like crazy, proud of his sons. But we were wrong. He had gotten sidetracked at his work, and didn't show up at the game.

What happened to me emotionally that day reminded me of a study I would read about years later by animal researchers who trained mice to press a bar in a cage—and out would drop a pellet of food. Mice are extremely motivated by food: they quickly learn to press the bar to get it.

But then, while the mice slept, the experimenters would link up an automobile battery to the back of the metal bar. The next time the little mouse got hungry—he'd walk over, press the bar, and *zzzzaaaap!* He received his food pellet all right, along with a tremendous shock!

Reeling and disoriented, the mouse would move far away . . . but eventually his hunger pangs would overcome his confusion. Finally, he'd come close and gingerly reach out and press the bar a second time to get his second pellet—*and* a second shock.

The researchers kept plenty of water in the cage for these mice, but the only way to get a pellet of food was to press that bar. Something a mouse would do a third time . . . and a fourth . . . and occasionally a fifth. . . . But there it ended. They wouldn't take the shock a sixth time. In fact, they would die in the cage, rather than go back and press that bar.

As I watched my father dying before me, I kept reliving picture after picture of times I had pressed the "bar" with him. Only I wasn't looking for physical food.

I was looking for his blessing.

Going to Father and Son banquets with a neighbor's dad was like pressing the bar—and getting a shock. Having him not show up at a major holiday, never getting a birthday card, or later, his forgetting the names of my children were like pressing the bar—and getting a shock. And over the years, there were times, when my feelings toward him died. I'd rather walk away, than be shocked again.

And there were other times when I thought the shock had been turned off . . . I remember an afternoon, a year before his death, when I sat in a different hospital room, waiting for him to wake up from yet another heart surgery. We talked for a short while after he was awake. Having been there for several hours, I needed to go home, and I told him, as I always did in leaving, "I love you, Dad."

As I turned, I heard him say, "I love you, too, John."

I stopped and turned around, in shock at what I'd heard. I had never heard those words from my father.

"What did you say?"

"I love you, too, John," he repeated.

As you can imagine, I walked out of that hospital on cloud nine. That night, I did a national radio program with Gary. On "Life Perspectives," an outstanding radio program we're on with our good friend, Don Hawkins, I told the entire nation that for the first time in forty years, I heard my father say he loved me!

The next morning, I went back to the hospital to see my father, and to ask him if he would call my brothers (one in California and one in Michigan at the time) and tell them what he had told me the previous night. Perhaps his words would turn off the shock for them as well.

"Tell them what?" he said suspiciously.

"Tell them what you told me. You know . . . before I left . . . that you loved me."

My father not only refused to make the call, he denied that he'd ever said those words at all. "It must have been the drugs they have me on!" he joked. But I wasn't laughing. In retrospect, I'm sure his words of love were buried beneath the surface, like most parents. But at the time, it was another example of pressing of the bar—and feeling the shock.

## THE END OF THE BATTLE . . .
## THE BEGINNING OF THE WAR

And now, I was pressing the bar for the last time.

As the day unfolded, it became clear that years of praying and hoping weren't leading to an ending I would have chosen. My father was the first person, besides Cindy, I gave a copy of *The Blessing* to—and it remained unopened to that day. So too had the Bible I had given him years before. He had resisted talking with me about the blessing and about his personal faith, and now as his breathing became more labored, I realized that even any last words he might have spoken were being stolen along with his breath.

It was a hard battle for an old warrior that day. The hospice nurse occasionally came in to administer pain medication, and she told us his struggle could go on for hours, even days. For weeks thereafter, I would wake with the horrible sounds and sights of his struggle in my mind. After staying by his side faithfully all day, my older brother had to leave for a short time to run an important errand.

Before he came back, I sat holding my father's hand and praying for him. It had been eight hours since I had arrived. Eight hours of being next to the man who helped give me life, and whom I didn't even know. Eight hours of wishing there were some way I could help him, some way I could reach him even now.

At 4:40 P.M., his condition finally changed. God mercifully allowed him to fall into a fitful sleep. As I watched him, his breathing gradually began to slow. His worn out body began to relax. At last his battle was ending. In the quiet space of only a few minutes, I could tell that his life was slipping away.

It was like reaching out and trying to catch the wind. I didn't want him to go. Not with words of love left unsaid. Not without his coming to know Christ. Not without his laying his hands on my children's heads and blessing them, *even once.* His breathing stopped, and I buried my head on his shoulder, and cried my heart out in an empty, sun-splashed room.

## WHEN THE BLESSING IS
## FOREVER OUT OF REACH

Some of you have felt that same pain of reaching out for the blessing, and receiving a shock instead. Others, like me, have lost a parent without words of love or forgiveness ever being spoken. Yet, as I've sought to pick up the pieces of a shattered dream these past few months, God has encouraged me in four specific ways. It's my prayer that if you've lost that chance to receive the blessing these will be helpful principles for you as well.

### Having Done All . . .

As I have reflected on my father's death, there have been times when I've felt tremendous guilt. Often, I've caught myself thinking, *Maybe you could have been clearer in presenting the Gospel . . .* or *John, How can you talk about giving the blessing to so many people, and yet* you never received it yourself? *Maybe if you'd spent more time with him,* or at rock bottom, there've been the cutting words, *Maybe if you'd have been a better son . . .*

Guilt, piled upon guilt. Reinforced by so many stories of people whose parents *did* turn around. What was wrong with my prayers? With my love? Why couldn't I have broken through his hard, outer shell, and drawn out the love and softness that I knew were there? Like a broken gumball machine, I felt like my father's blessing was always just beneath the surface. I could see it! But I never could get to it, no matter how many emotional coins I put in the slot.

Perhaps you've felt an aching failure at not turning your parents around as well. Perhaps you've felt that all your efforts ended up slipping out of your hands. If so, the apostle Paul's words in the book of Ephesians can be an encouragement to you as well: *"Having done all . . .* stand" firm in the faith (Eph. 6:13, italics added).

For many of us, it isn't that we haven't done enough . . . in fact, we may have done *more* than enough. We may have paid for their hospital bills, kept up their medications, helped move them into our home, or from there to care center after care center. We may have listened to endless complaints. We did our best. We prayed hard. We sought their forgiveness for things we did wrong. We tried to give them an example, to give them the blessing in practical, tangible ways.

Yet effort doesn't always equal a desired response. There are times when we've done it all, and our all isn't enough. But that's another tremendous advantage of being a Christian. The apostle Paul who had labored long and well didn't have to measure his efforts in human terms. He could rest on the fact that he had "done all." He could stand on the fact that his faith and acceptance rested in a God who would rather have us give Him our hearts than our sacrifice.

Recently, I sat down with a large company that was looking for some consulting work. Several of their top managers had been promoted to significant positions, only to be served divorce papers by their wives, and their performance at work had come crashing down.

"We're thinking of adding a new employee benefit," they shared. "Perhaps marriage and family counseling would help head off what's happened to our executives." But as I listened to them, I was struck by the words of their corporate head. "You understand, Dr. Trent, we measure everything here by one standard—*results*. If we're going to put money into counseling, we want to see results—and fast."

In pure, unvarnished language, that's the way the world measures success. Not in how a life is lived, or by the sincerity of our efforts. But in the bottom line, in measurable success or failure according to worldly standards.

Isn't it great to know that when it comes to our acceptance from Christ, we're not on the performance track? Certainly, He calls us to do our best. To lay down our lives if need be. But Christ's bottom line is love, not results.

No matter how many voices tell me I failed, I don't have to feel shame that my father didn't receive Christ; and neither do you. I can stand firm in the faith, knowing I faithfully laid the Gospel before him. While the world may measure our efforts in terms of a balance sheet, God looks at our hearts, and His love covers us no matter what.

And yet, even armed with this fact, there is something else I had to learn.

## You Can't Guard Against the Unguarded Moment

Four weeks had passed since my family assembled at the National Veterans Cemetery to pay last respects to my father. Because of his combat experience and decorations during World War II, he received a full honor guard, a 12-gun salute, and a clear-as-a-bell salvation message from a retired Army chaplain (that I wish he could have heard).

I was up early one morning, coming in from jogging, when I ran right into our seven-year-old daughter, Kari, just walking out of her room. She was sobbing.

I dropped to my knees, and she fell into my arms, her little shoulders shaking.

"What's the matter, Honey?" I asked in confusion. My mind was racing, trying to think what could have upset her so much from the happy night before.

"It's Grandpa," she said. "He's gone now . . . *and I never got to hug him.*"

I can't tell you how much that "unguarded moment" cut my heart. I had Scriptures memorized to remind me of my wholeness in Christ (Col. 2:10). I had God's word that I was His child, and a much loved son (Hebrews 12:7; John 3:16). I knew that He would never leave me or forsake me (Hebrews 13:5). Yet I also discovered that I wasn't quick enough to out-logic an emotion.

Let me repeat that. We'll never be fast enough to out-logic an emotion.

To illustrate this, think about being at church or at work last week. A dear friend you haven't seen in ages rushes up to hug you, and they accidentally step right on the top of your foot with the tip of their high heels! And to top it off, you're wearing sandals!

What is your instantaneous, *emotional* reaction?

Pain!

And then what?

Anger at being stepped on by a clumsy friend!

But when you stop hopping around, hear their profuse apology, and slowly begin to be able to put weight back on your aching foot, your emotions die down. After possibly wanting to chant a Lithuanian curse over the person, you can even begin to laugh at the situation and assure them, "Oh, . . . It's all right!"

God made us with emotions. Jesus felt them. We're told in Scripture, "Be angry, and do not sin" (Eph. 4:26). And no matter how many verses we memorize, we may still run into an unguarded moment that stomps on an emotional weak spot like a size 14 boot.

That's what happened to me that day in the hallway. All the hurt, all the pain, all the memories of empty arms, and even more painfully empty arms for my children, spilled out. Both Kari and I cried in the hallway. We grieved his loss all over again.

It's important to realize that while we may be grounded in God's truth, we often aren't, nor should we be, cut off from our emotions. David grieved and cried at the loss of his sons. The nation of Israel mourned the loss of Moses. Jesus wept at the death of a friend.

It's been almost a year now since my father died, and still I run into those unguarded moments. Perhaps it's at a movie that pictures a father/son relationship I never had. Or it comes when hearing someone else's story in counseling or at a conference. It was C. S. Lewis who observed that the only place we are truly safe from the pain love can bring is in hell. Here on earth, we shouldn't feel defeated, or fail to honestly grieve the loss of our parents.

Yet we should commit ourselves to a third, important principle.

## After a Season of Grieving . . .

When David's child by Bathsheba fell ill, we're told that David "fasted and went in and lay all night on the ground" (2 Sam. 12:16). Yet once news reached him of his son's death, he "arose from the ground, washed and anointed himself, and changed his clothes; and he went into the house of the LORD and worshiped. Then he went to his own house; and when he requested, they set food before him, and he ate" (2 Sam. 12:20).

A calloused response to a painful time? Not at all. David honestly grieved, and prayed before the Lord for days. But he also worshiped the God whose ways were higher than his own. After a season of pain, he began the difficult process of moving on in daily life. He didn't allow "sackcloth and ashes" to become a permanent garment.

We live in a society where victims abound. While the recovery movement has done many tremendous things in many people's lives, it can also leave others stuck in recovery. Let's face it, under an intense enough spotlight of parental faultfinding, we can all find someone who will classify us as co-dependent, addicted, or somehow "victims."

I am no way discounting the genuine pain that many parents have caused, nor am I negating the very real time (sometimes years) where healthy grieving can and should take place. However, like David, there must also be a time when we worship a mighty God, wash and eat, and get back into life.

The fact that we are forever victims is something that is not true for the Christian. Because we're related to a mighty God who's worthy of our worship, we can even sing again. There may be sadness in the night, but "joy comes in the morning" (Ps. 30:5).

These three things God has taught me after losing my father, and also a fourth.

## A Lifelong Commitment . . .

There is nothing more precious than watching your children sleep. Returning from a trip, I often get home after Cindy and the kids are in bed. Without fail, I'll walk down the hallway and stop first in Laura's room. Her beautiful brown hair all a tumble, she melts my heart even when she's asleep. Then there's Kari, our precious first-born, the one who always kicks off her covers—and who always knows that Dad or Mom will put them back on.

Even watching Cindy sleep, I'm reminded of how much I love her, and how much I want each of them to know they're loved. And believe it or not, that has been a powerful, positive legacy from my father's death.

I know the heartache of missing out on loving words—and of having them denied if they were once spoken. And that's one pain I'm determined that my own family won't have to face. I can't protect them from every problem. I can't ensure that they won't experience sorrow. But I can ensure that they'll hear my blessing on a daily basis. Something that Kari taught us is extremely important, even for a young child.

Since Kari and Laura were born, Cindy and I have made the decision that every morning, we'd wake them up with a blessing song. While it sounds much better when Cindy sings it than me, it's the words, not the talent behind them, that we want to communicate. The little rhyme put to music goes like this:

> *Good morning, good morning, how are you today?*
> *The Lord bless you and keep you throughout the day.*
> *We love you. We love you. We love you, (Kari, or Laura).*
> *The Lord bless you and keep you throughout the day.*

As Kari has gotten older, she even comes in and sings it to Laura as well.

Nearly four years ago, when Kari was not yet three, we were putting her to bed. We had brought in water, her favorite stuffed animals, and even a puzzle she loved, and arranged them all "just so" on her bed. Then we prayed with her, and left the room. But before we'd gotten very far down the hall, she yelled out, "Night, Mom. Night, Dad. And don't forget to *bless* me in the morning!"

Not even three, and still she knew her blessing was waiting for her in the morning!

Is it time you washed your face and hands of the long road of hardship, worshiped the King of kings, and got on with life? Is it time you made a commitment to blessing your own family each day? I can't think of anything that has helped me more in these last several months than that powerful combination of worship and reaching out to give others the blessing, beginning with my own family.

May God indeed heal all your hurts, as He is healing mine. As I pray for you who read this book, I would ask for your prayers for our family as well. And may each of us never leave a doubt in a loved one's mind, that each time they wake up, our blessing will be there in the morning.

# Chapter Twelve

## Giving the Blessing to Your Spouse and Friends

*E*arly in our research on this book, I (John) went through this material with several couples in a Bible study group. I asked for the participants' honest evaluation of the material during the sessions, and then had them fill out an evaluation at the end.

One of my favorite comments was written by a wife in the group. Commenting on what her husband had learned during the class, she wrote:

> Dennis has learned so much about how to "bless" the children. It has made a real difference in his relationship with them. How about teaching him how to bless me!!!

This woman's request was right on target. The elements of the blessing are not just limited to the parent/child relationship. We feel strongly that they can be found at the heart of *any* healthy relationship.

Let's continue to discover just how valuable applying the five elements of the blessing can be to three important relationships besides those with our children. First we will look at how the blessing can and should be given to a spouse and the relationship gains that can happen as a result. Then we will look at how friendships can be strengthened and developed through applying these same elements. Finally, in the next chapter, we will look at what can happen when a church family begins to apply these blessing principles to reach out to those beyond the church and especially to those within.

## BEING A SOURCE OF BLESSING TO YOUR SPOUSE

Laura was fed up with her husband and with all the upheaval in their lives. He often traveled out of town, and when he was home, he drank and made life miserable for her.

In her frustration, Laura came within an eyelash of throwing in the towel and filing for divorce, but her good friend Gayle talked her into going to see her pastor who she felt might be able to help. Even though Laura was reluctant at first, she was at the end of her rope. Against her better judgment, she made an appointment and went to see him.

For nearly forty minutes this wise pastor simply listened to her story. After Laura had shared her nonstop description of every one of her husband's faults, she finally sat back with a loud "Humph." Smugly she waited to hear an "Amen" from the pastor or at least a hearty confirmation that hers was the worst husband he had ever heard about.

At first the pastor didn't say a word. Deeply engrossed in thought, he literally waited several minutes before he spoke. Finally he sat up, looked her in the eye, and said gently, "Laura, have you ever forgiven your husband for all his many faults?"

You could have heard a pin drop. Laura had not expected to receive this kind of advice. ("No wonder his counseling is free," she thought.) Of course she had not forgiven her husband! He had never asked her to, and she wasn't about to bring it up. He had caused her to suffer, and she wasn't going to let him off the hook that easily.

"Laura, would you think about what I've said today, and would you promise to come back and see me next week?" As she grabbed her purse and headed for the door, she heard herself mutter something like "That would be fine, Pastor"; but she never thought she would be seeing him again. Yet something happened that week that began to change Laura's perspective on her marriage. Something drew her back to this man's office the next week.

In spite of telling herself repeatedly that she should simply forget what he had said, Laura did a great deal of thinking during the week. While it didn't all make sense, it began to dawn on her that it wasn't her husband who was on the hook—she was! He didn't lose any sleep about his behavior; she was the one getting ulcers.

Laura was still confused and had a great many questions for the pastor the next time they met. However, God had already begun to do some miraculous things in Laura's life. That afternoon, in the quietness of the pastor's study, she surrendered her life to Christ. She also decided to give up her need for revenge, to forgive her husband for all he had done, and to learn to love him unconditionally.

Laura's husband was a truck driver, and almost a week went by before he returned home. When he came into the house, he could have sworn he was at the wrong address. He couldn't believe how peaceful things were. Just a week ago everything he did made his wife mad; now she was going out of her way to do things for him.

When this rowdy truck driver found out Laura's change of heart had something to do with religion, he tossed her behavior aside as though it were another diet his wife had discovered. While it made things a lot nicer in the short run, soon her willpower would fade and they would be back at each other's throats.

After five months, Laura's *husband* made an appointment to see the same pastor she had seen. "You've got to tell me about what happened to Laura," the truck driver said. "She's changed so much. It's made me realize what a rotten husband I've been these past years. Pastor, I have a drinking problem, and I need help with it."

What made all the difference for this couple was that Laura, in spite of the fact her husband didn't "deserve" it, decided to give him the blessing. For years she had made just the opposite decision. She had devalued him and even cursed him to his face. She hated his occupation that took him out of town and filled his clothes with the smell of diesel fuel.

When Laura's life was changed by the Source of blessing Himself, she was able out of the overflow of her life to attach high value to her husband and bless him. Instead of riding him about getting another job, she found ways to build him up and encourage him. Where once she had gone days without speaking to him when she was angry, now she told him her feeling, but without anger and hate. Meaningful touching even began to come back into their relationship, something that Laura had withheld from her husband when her spirit was unforgiving and bitter. As a result, her husband became so convicted about his behavior at home that he also made an appointment to see the pastor.

Granted, this is a dramatic example of what can happen when one spouse decides to be a source of blessing to the other. Their problems were of the major league variety and they needed to make a great deal of changes. However, in everyday households all across the country, with everyday problems and tensions, providing the elements of the blessing to a spouse can revive, encourage, and rejuvenate a marriage.

Let's look briefly at each element of the blessing and see just how important they can be to a healthy marriage. In fact, show us a couple that is growing together, and we'll show you two people practicing these principles of blessing.

## Meaningful Touch in Marriage

The same need for meaningful touching we saw with our children is equally important in a marriage. One wise husband realized the importance of this need during a difficult time for his wife, and it did more to minister to her than anything else he could have done.

When Marilyn was getting dressed one morning, she noticed something that didn't seem quite right. She noticed a small lump on her breast that she had not been aware of before.

Marilyn wasn't overly concerned, but she knew enough from reading magazines and watching television to know that she needed to get it checked. She told her husband, Art, what she intended to do, and then called the doctor for an appointment.

Two weeks later, Marilyn went to the doctor to have a biopsy done on the lump. Three days after her appointment, she was lying in a hospital bed facing a radical mastectomy. Besides coming to the hospital twice to deliver their two boys, this was the first time in her forty-seven years Marilyn had had to undergo an operation.

For Marilyn, the hardest thing she faced after the surgery wasn't her recovery, but what Art would think of her now. Would she still be attractive to him? How would he feel about touching her? Questions like these ran over and over in her mind.

The morning she was to be released from the hospital, Marilyn and Art were alone in her room. Her husband sat on her bed and took her hands in his. "Sugar," he said. "I want you to know something. You're as beautiful to me now as you were on our wedding night. Don't you ever forget that." Then Art looked over to make sure the door was shut, winked at her, and said, "After you get home and get rested up, we're going to have to get the lock fixed on the door."

Marilyn hugged her husband, and tears came to her eyes. She knew exactly what he meant by that last statement. Early in their marriage, when someone had forgotten to lock the door, one of the boys had walked into their room at a most inappropriate time. The result was that a new lock was installed on the door the next day, and a new saying began for them. "We're going to have to get the lock fixed on the door" became their private password to an intimate evening.

What had concerned Marilyn was not only how her operation would affect their sexual relationship, but also whether it would keep Art from touching her outside the bedroom. His words and actions that morning assured her that this important element of the blessing would still be a part of their relationship.

Sexual touching is important in any growing relationship; however, it should not be the only time a couple touches. Our friend, Dr. Kevin Leman, notes this in his book, *Sex Begins in the Kitchen*. He points out that genuine intimacy is developed in the small acts of touching in the kitchen, or walking through a mall together hand in hand, or sitting close together on the sofa watching television.

Speaking of "sex beginning in the kitchen," we heard a true story from a recent participant in a seminar who tried to apply the concept of meaningful touching with his wife, and it left him in an embarrassing situation!

After hearing the concept of meaningful touching talked about over and over, it really stuck with this man. One afternoon after cutting the grass, he came in to take a shower and clean up. He had left the bedroom door open and when he finished his shower he walked over to the rack to get a towel. From where he stood, he could see his wife standing in the kitchen preparing their dinner.

*What a time for meaningful touching,* he thought to himself. Without a moment's thought, he ran down the hall in his birthday suit and burst into the kitchen to give his wife a big hug. What he couldn't see from the bedroom or as he raced down the hall was his neighbor's wife who had come over to visit. That shocked neighbor saw a great deal more of this husband than she had ever expected! His timing was terrible, but no one could fault his commitment to meaningfully touch his wife!

Meaningful touch can enrich your relationships in many ways. Studies show that regardless of gender, people who were comfortable with touching were also more talkative, cheerful, socially dominant, and nonconforming; those uncomfortable with touch tended to be more emotionally unstable and socially withdrawn. Those more comfortable with touch were less afraid and suspicious of other people's motives and intentions, and had less anxiety and tension in their everyday lives.[1]

Yet as powerful as touch is, it is not enough to sustain, alone, a growing marriage. Researchers at the University of Illinois used three measures of intimacy to assess marital satisfaction and happiness. They found that each form of intimacy made its own important contribution. However conflict and divorce potential were most closely linked with a lack of the next two elements of the blessing—emotional and *verbal* intimacy.[2]

## A Spoken Message Attaching High Value to a Spouse

Let's combine the next two elements of the blessing into one way of making sure your spouse receives the blessing. When we decide to place high value on our spouse, and then back that up with spoken words to that effect, it can do wonders for a relationship.

Using a word picture to praise a character trait of our children or our spouse is something we spent several pages discussing in Chapter Five. Like that royal couple we looked at in the Song of Solomon, husbands and wives can take on that look of royalty when they hear how highly we value them with our words.

A popular bumper sticker slogan reads, "Have you hugged your kids today?" Another, equally important phrase that you can copy and paste to your refrigerator, bathroom mirror, or forehead is:

> ## Have You Praised Your Mate Today?

An everyday dose of praise, whether in the form of a word picture or just a statement like "Great dinner, Honey" or a "You are so kind to other people" or even a "You make me so proud the way you handle the children" can do wonders in a relationship.

Spoken words that attach high value to our spouse are so powerful that they can enrich almost any marriage. Why not try a project in your home to discover just how true this statement can be.

For one month, thirty days, praise at least one thing you appreciate about your spouse each day. Be sure you point out things about his or her character (being kind, generous, thoughtful, punctual, organized, and so on), as well as what they accomplish. Don't tell your husband or wife you're doing this. We give this assignment to many couples in counseling, and it in itself has caused positive changes in relationships.

While we have talked exclusively about using word pictures to praise a husband or wife, they can also be used to help discuss an important issue or avoid a heated argument. By using a word picture to convey a concern we have, instead of lashing out with damaging words, we can often motivate our mate to change and get across a message we can't seem to get across with only words.

One woman at a conference Gary was leading had a concern she had unsuccessfully tried to communicate to her husband for years. Yet by using a single word picture, she so affected him that he was willing to write her a $150,000 check right on the spot to build her dream house!

When we were talking through this story for the book, we kiddingly talked about asking people to mail in a dollar with a stamped self-addressed envelope to find out the word picture she used. We'd be rich in no time! We're sure every wife in America would like to know what she did to motivate her husband to respond the way he did.

You'll be glad to know that at absolutely no extra charge, we have decided to go ahead and tell you the word picture she used. Actually this story is not just about how one woman got her dream house. It is a beautiful example of how attaching high value to a spouse (in this case, not wanting to devalue a spouse in any way) can be powerfully communicated through a word picture.

Don and Bee are dear friends who have attended several relationship seminars that our ministry, Today's Family, has put on. As part of these seminars, Gary teaches couples and singles how to use word pictures with their spouse, their children, or in any meaningful relationship.

Bee had been struggling with something in her marriage for quite a long time. Something that ate away at her self-confidence and caused her constant embarrassment over the years. She was bothered about the condition of their house.

The Lord had greatly prospered Don's business, and much of their resources went into supporting their church and various ministries. They were both generous with their time as well. Don especially was always inviting a new couple at church home to dinner or offering to put up this missionary or that speaker.

Bee was every bit as hospitable, but she was the one having to struggle in an undersized kitchen to feed all the guests, or skip taking a shower because the hot-water heater allowed only three hot showers, or somehow finding a place for six or even ten people to sleep when there were only two beds in the house.

It was not a question of finances that held Don back from moving into a larger home; rather it was his desire not to be ostentatious and flaunt what God had given them. Bee understood her husband's motives and made do with the situation as best she could.

When Gary came back to their city for a second time, they signed up immediately for the seminar as a "refresher" course. After listening again to Gary share about using word pictures to communicate a concern with her spouse, Bee decided she would share one with her husband to describe her feelings toward the home she was living in. That night, she did share with her husband, and here is the word picture she used.

"Don, I feel like you're the game warden who takes such good care of the trout in the waterways around our house. You help keep the streams and ponds clean, and even make sure that when the trout are spawning, they have help getting upstream.

"When we were first married, I felt like I was one of those trout in the stream. I could see you standing on the bank, and I longed for you to scoop me up in a net and take me to the stream by your house. Then one day you did come for me with a net and gently picked me out of the water. It was the happiest time of my life; but instead of ending up in the little stream, you put me in an old, rusty barrel filled with fresh water.

"For twenty-two years you've made sure I had plenty of food and you've kept the water clean, but I long for the day when you will pick me up in your net and put me in that little stream by your house. Don, that's the way I feel about living in this house. I feel like we're living in a rusty barrel, and it makes it hard on me and the people we have over to the house."

Bee's years of longing came to an end that night. She had talked to her husband numerous times about this subject and had even tried to share her feelings with him about their living situation. Yet Don had never seemed to understand how important it was to her, until she shared this word picture with him.

Don loved his wife deeply and had attached high value to her throughout their marriage. He did not want to devalue her in any way, so when he finally understood through this story how she really felt about their house, he responded immediately. Don wrote her a check that night to hire an architect to draw up the plans for a new home, a home where she could enjoy having people over, serve them better, and have a comfortable place for them to stay.

We were so convinced of the benefits of using word pictures that we wrote an entire book on the subject, *Language of Love* (Focus on the Family, 1989). And we hope by this story you can see their usefulness in a marriage. Whether you use a word picture in praising your spouse or in sharing a concern, it can be a helpful tool to communicate words of high value to your mate.

## Providing a Special Future for Your Spouse

The other night my (John's) wife and I were watching part of a comedy show on television that we thought was funny. The scene was a forest meadow where an outdoor wedding was taking place.

There in the clearing were the bride and her attendant, and the best man alongside the bridegroom, who looked worried and out of place. The minister asked the bride to say her vows, which she had made up especially for this occasion. Unhesitatingly, she launched into goal after goal, commitment after commitment, and dream after dream she had for herself, her husband, and their marriage. In fact, she went on so long night fell in the forest.

When she finally finished, the exhausted minister turned to the groom and asked him to repeat the vows *he* made up. Looking around nervously, his only words to the minister were, "Well, I hope this works out!"

His vows were not the kind of words that a new bride could build a secure future on. They were funny all right, but they did not provide the kind of security a wife needs to know that she has a special future ahead of her.

In a marriage, our mate needs to know that he or she is a special part of our future. What's more, our spouse needs to know that the way we look at him or her today leaves room for positive change and growth in the future. Tod learned this lesson the hard way with his wife, Betty.

Betty was not the world's best house cleaner. Her home was not what you would call neat and clean before they had children, and with three little ones running around, she had nearly given up on their home ever being clean. Like what happens in many marriages, her husband, Tod, had a different temperament. He was incredibly neat and clean. Tod even kept his work-shop, where he spent time on his hobbies, so clean a person could safely eat off the floor.

Tod was so frustrated with his wife's sloppy ways, he spent much of his time berating her for being a poor house cleaner. She would *always* be messy and could *never* change. Tod told her stories about how, in the future, their house would become so dirty that their grandchildren would catch incurable diseases and the County Health Department would come out and shut them down.

Not only was Tod not placing high value on his wife, he was helping to see that the very thing he sought to change became a lasting part of their future! By painting a picture of his wife with no window of hope or door for change, he literally boxed her in to viewing herself as the "world's messiest housekeeper" that he thought she was.

In a Sunday school class, Tod saw for the first time how his words of a negative future had hurt his wife, not helped her. He learned that he was effectively killing any motivation his wife did have to change. His words of a negative future were telling his wife that it was impossible for her ever to please him. So why should she bother trying?

Tod thought back on what he had said to his wife. The times she had tried to make a dent in the house cleaning chores, he had met her with a "Finally!" or a "Why can't you keep things like that all the time?" But then he began to change.

Tod started to praise small things Betty did and to put aside the criticism of her poor performance. He even began to change his picture of her future and their house to a positive one. Change is always slow to take root, but it can grow ten times faster in the soil of encouragement than in the hard, rocky soil of criticism.

By picturing a special future for his wife in this area and en-couraging her for small accomplishments, a miracle began to happen. Even though the house is not up to Tod's workshop standards, no longer does he have to fight his way through the laundry in the washroom or fear going into a shower that has things growing in it.

Whether it is the fear of entertaining, the need to go on a diet, failing to discipline the children promptly, or keeping a messy house, we do not motivate our mate to change by picturing a negative future. Our mate needs to hear words that picture a special future in the same way our children do, positive words that provide our spouse the room to become all that God can help him or her to become.

## Active Commitment to Your Mate

As we have discovered in earlier chapters, providing the individual elements of the blessing without the glue to hold them all together is not enough. That glue is our active commitment. In fact, this final element of the blessing is at the heart of "cleaving" in a marriage.

When the Scriptures tell us we are to "cleave" to our spouse (Gen. 2:24), the root word in Hebrew means "to cling, to be firmly attached."³ It takes a firm decision to be committed to blessing your spouse, a decision that will not remain intact if you don't make room for your mate's fallibility.

In the 1929 Rose Bowl game, Georgia Tech came to California to meet the mighty football team from the University of California. In that game, something happened that demonstrated how fallible even a star could be.

Roy Riegels was a starter and star athlete for California. He had performed admirably during the regular season and was expected to make a great contribution to the team that day. What actually happened was that Roy made a winning contribution to the *other* team!

In a brilliant defensive play late in the first half, Roy intercepted a pass, fought off several would-be tacklers, and headed for the end zone and a touchdown. What he didn't know was that in fighting off the tacklers, he had gotten turned around and he actually scored a safety for the other team! When the half ended, Georgia Tech had gone ahead of California because of Roy's safety, and they hung on to win by that margin.

At halftime, everyone was wondering the same thing. Would Roy's coach, Nibbs Price, yank him out of the game? When it came time to announce the starting lineup for the second half, Price called out Roy's name! This coach had watched Roy work hard all season, and he remained committed to him even when he made a major mistake.

Another football coach, at the University of Texas, made famous an old country saying. Darryl Royal was like Coach Price; he remained committed to his starters in the game, even if they were fumbling the ball or missing a tackle. The press constantly asked him about this, and his reply was always the same, "You dance with the one who brung ya"—not good English, but an excellent example of active commitment.

What these two coaches had, and what every man or woman owes his or her spouse, is the willingness to stay committed, even if the other person fumbles the ball. Amy did this, and it was the very thing her husband credits with saving his life.

Grant owned a manufacturing business that had done quite well. His business was small, but it found its niche in the marketplace and was growing by leaps and bounds. Borrowing against the property and expecting his profits to continue, Grant took out a large loan to expand the facilities. No sooner had construction begun on his new plant than a multinational manufacturing concern decided to go into competition with Grant's product.

With cash flow tight because of the huge interest payments on the loan, Grant did not have the resources to put more salesmen on the street. Neither could Grant lower the price on his product because of the profit margin needed to keep the business afloat.

In less than a year, Grant had literally gone from riches to rags. His competitor had undercut his prices drastically to get into the marketplace, and it literally drove Grant out of business. Saddled with unpaid employees, lawsuits from suppliers, and with the bank breathing down his neck, Grant had to shut down his plant and liquidate his equipment at a fraction of its actual worth. He even lost his home that had been collateral for the note and had to move into a small apartment. Perhaps the crowning blow came when he had to explain to his children at midyear that they would have to change from the private school they loved to public school.

Grant was not a believer at the time of his business's collapse, and he was devastated as he had never been before. He even contemplated suicide, but one thing held him back:

*"I didn't know the Lord at the time my business went under, and my whole world seemed to end. I would like to say it was the thought of my children that kept me from ending it all, but that wouldn't be true.*

*"The one thing that kept me from it was Amy and the way she constantly believed in me and blessed me with her love. Listening to her pray for me at night and having her hold me and let me cry were what pulled me through. I tell everybody she saved my life "twice." The first time was when the business failed; the second was when she led me to Jesus Christ!"*

Grant could no longer provide for his wife and family "in the manner to which they had become accustomed." Yet because of this loving wife, who based her blessing for her husband on active commitment instead of material possessions, their relationship remained strong and secure.

Every husband and wife will drop the ball and prove themselves fallible time and again. If we are to be people of blessing, our commitment will rest on our decision to love our spouse "in spite of." Our love must be the kind of love that motivated our heavenly Father to bless us with His Son, in spite of the fact we didn't deserve it and because He knew we needed that blessing so much in our lives.

The blessing can make a tremendous difference in marriage, but it takes work to pull these principles off the page and apply them with our spouse. Even so, we know you won't regret a minute of time you spend cultivating each of the elements in your home, especially when you see the harvest of love and happiness that can result.

## BEING A SOURCE OF BLESSING TO YOUR FRIENDS

We constantly meet people who "wish they had a close friend." Many of those same people would not have to make that comment if they knew how to be a "close friend." We discovered in studying the blessing in the Scriptures that an important part of becoming a close friend is to apply each element of the blessing in a friendship.

In all the Scriptures, perhaps the most universally acknowl-edged model of a close friend is Jonathan. His relationship with David is a graduate course in what makes a lasting relationship. These two young men were not a likely pair to strike up a friend-ship.

Jonathan was the heir apparent to his father's throne. He was also a mighty warrior in his own right. He led Israel's armies in battle and even attacked twenty Philistines with only his armor carrier to back him up and defeated them all (1 Sam. 14:6–14).

David and Jonathan first met just after David had slain Go-liath. With all the attention David was getting, Jonathan could have looked at David as an arch rival and enemy. Yet we are told in the Scriptures that "the soul of Jonathan was knit to the soul of David, and Jonathan loved him as his own soul" (1 Sam. 18:1).

One reason that their friendship was unique is that it was a friend-to-friend relationship that included, and models for us, every aspect of the blessing.

Without the fear that exists today among men of appearing like homosexuals, David and Jonathan demonstrated meaning-ful touching in their friendship. In their last meeting, Jonathan had to tell David it was no longer safe for him to be around his father, Saul. We read that they "kissed one another; and they wept together, but David more so" (1 Sam. 20:41).

While men giving each other a kiss and crying in each other's arms is almost taboo in our culture, it was not considered strange in ancient Israel nor is it unusual in many foreign coun-tries today. Friends in these cultures demonstrate their love for each other with a kiss or a hug.

A friend today will include meaningful touching in blessing his or her friend. Withholding a hug or even a handshake from a friend can freeze that relationship at a surface level.

In giving us another picture of what it means to be a close friend, Jonathan spoke of his appreciation for David and placed high value on him. Let's look back on Jonathan's actions toward David when they first met.

David certainly stole the spotlight on that day. Yet we are told that "Jonathan took off the robe that was on him and gave it to David, with his armor" (1 Sam. 18:4). A warrior only lays down his weapons in front of someone he considers his better.

Jonathan placed such high value on David that he was willing to sacrifice his symbols of authority (his armor and his robes) in order to honor his friend.

Jonathan also made a verbal covenant with David that he would be his close companion for life (1 Sam. 20:13). He said to David, "The LORD be with you as He has been with my father." No words of blessing were spared in what Jonathan said to David.

The last words Jonathan spoke to David illustrate his active commitment to David and his desire that God bless David in the future. "May the LORD be between you and me, and between your descendants and my descendants, forever" (1 Sam. 20:42).

Who are your true friends? Just think a moment about someone in your life who has been an intimate friend. Almost without exception, a close friend will be someone like Jonathan, a man or woman who has demonstrated each aspect of the blessing in his or her relationship with you. A close friend will be someone like Larry, who decided to provide each element of the blessing to his boss, Glenn.

Glenn was not an easy person to befriend. For one thing, Glenn didn't seem to *need* any friends. He was a tremendously successful businessman who always seemed on top of everything. Also, Glenn had been trained in the old tradition of maintaining professional distance from his employees and competitors. "Don't let anyone get close" was the unspoken motto Glenn lived by, that is, until the day his teenage son was picked up for selling illegal drugs to his classmates.

In order not to be taken advantage of by others, Glenn had built a wall around himself at work and at his church. He was constantly around people, yet he had no close friends. Glenn didn't even know how to be a friend to his wife or children, and the rebelliousness of his son and Glenn's total ignorance of his son's drug problem graphically pointed that out to him.

Now, in a time of dire need, Glenn needed the emotional support of a man he could pour his heart out to; and no one was there. No one was there until Larry noticed that something seemed wrong with his boss and decided that Glenn needed a friend, in spite of his nonverbal language that said just the opposite.

Larry was already an accomplished "Jonathan." He knew the importance of supplying another person with the elements of the blessing, and he had a number of close friends. But befriending Glenn was a different matter. He was his boss, and besides, Glenn certainly did not look as if he wanted any company.

Day by day, watching Glenn suffer in silence, Larry became convinced that he needed to befriend him. Their friendship began one Tuesday morning when Larry gathered up his courage, walked into Glenn's office, and laid his hand on Glenn's shoulder.

"Hey, old buddy," Larry said, "you just don't seem to have been yourself for a while. I may be way out of line, and you can tell me so if you want, but you seem to be really hurting. I just want you to know that if you ever need somebody to talk to, I'm around." Larry expected to be dismissed with a curt rebuff, but instead Glenn didn't say a word. Finally, after a long pause, he looked up at Larry, close to tears, and said, "I'll remember that, Larry. Thanks a lot."

Larry thought that was the end of things when a few days went by without hearing from Glenn. However on Friday, his secretary gave him the message that Glenn wanted to have breakfast with him one day that next week.

During that meeting, Larry listened, and listened, and *listened* to Glenn pour out a heart full of hurt. Larry didn't try to lecture Glenn, nor did Larry try to lessen the emotions that were present by saying, "Well, it's not all that bad" or "You're a Christian, Glenn, just pray about it." When Larry heard Glenn share the heartbreak that only comes when dealing with a rebellious child, he cried with him. The only time Larry remembered saying more than a sentence or two was when he prayed a short prayer with Glenn in his car after their breakfast.

Over the next several months, Larry met every week with Glenn to listen, talk, and pray about Glenn's relationship with his son. Larry couldn't directly relate to Glenn's hurt (Larry's children were just entering grade school), but he could still shake Glenn's hand and let him know that day or night, he had a friend he could turn to.

An interesting thing began to happen around the office as a result of Larry and Glenn's meeting. Glenn actually began to soften a little in his strict rule of professional distance. For the first time in years, Glenn had a friend who cared about him, and the result was that he was rediscovering how to be friends with others again.

Through Larry's providing each element of the blessing to his boss—by shaking his hand or patting Glenn on the back (meaningful touch); in speaking encouraging words to Glenn (spoken message); through pointing out the positive character traits that Glenn did have and the way he was trying to make a fresh start with his wife and the other children at home (attaching high value); by providing him with the hope of a special future that God could bring to pass regardless of how his son responded (special future); and by committing himself to be available to his friend when he needed someone to talk to (active commitment)—these two men's hearts began to be knitted together.

Things finally did get better with Glenn's son and as a result Glenn had *two* things to thank the Lord for. One was the new way his son responded to him as he began to become a better friend to him, and the other was an employee named Larry who had taught Glenn about genuine friendship by modeling for him the elements of the blessing.

Understanding the relationship elements of the blessing can communicate parental acceptance to a child, enrich a marriage, and deepen a friendship. But that is not all. The blessing can also provide helpful guidelines for a church family to use in remaining or becoming a place of blessing. Both to those outside the church and especially to those within.

# Chapter Thirteen
## Giving the Blessing to Your Parents

**O**ur portrait of the blessing is almost complete. In past chapters we have used broad strokes to illustrate how the blessing was viewed down through the centuries. We have also used the fine strokes of the literal meaning of the word *blessing* to bring out the subtle nuances of this concept. Five predominant patterns run throughout the painting, each an important element of the blessing, and together they provide the viewer with a sense of structure and balance. Stories of people, past and present, have been used to bring color and depth to the picture. Some of these colors are dark and subdued and stir our compassion. These are the stories of Esau and others like him who never received their family's blessing. Yet we have also tried to paint the brilliant colors of joy, happiness, and security from the lives of those who have received the blessing.

However, before we lay down our brush and move away from this portrait of the blessing, we need to paint one final corner. In fact, this corner is a key to completing our picture and truly capturing its total scope.

In our final strokes to complete this portrait of the blessing, we need to illustrate the importance of seeing the blessing go full circle. We began painting in a corner of the canvas that showed how parents need to give their children the blessing; we will end by seeing how these same children need to return the blessing to their parents. Helen returned the blessing, even though it was the most difficult thing she had ever done in her life.

## A STORY OF BLESSING

Let's look back at the story of Helen. Helen had been physically abused by her father the entire time she was growing up. He was an alcoholic whose changing moods left her insecure, fearful, and distressed. The first chance Helen had to leave home, she was out the door. From her perspective, she didn't care if she ever saw her father again, an attitude that was confirmed when he and her mother were divorced while she was in college. Helen had absolutely no reason to go home now and refused even to consider the thought.

Then Helen met a coworker named Karen, and her whole life began to change. For the first time, she heard about and received God's blessing of salvation and His provision of a spiritual family at church to help meet her needs. With spiritual fathers galore at her church, Helen felt even less of a need to make peace with her natural father.

Gradually, Helen began to notice that some areas of her spiritual life were lagging behind. She had grown by leaps and bounds, but still had a tendency to criticize others. She had come a long way, but her temper still needed control. For a long time, Helen thought these nagging tendencies did not disappear because of a lack of faith or knowledge of God's Word. Countless times she had committed herself afresh to study God's Word. Yet her struggles continued.

Then one day Helen discovered what was at the heart of her problem. She did not lack faith; she was not willing to honor her father. The deep bitterness and resentment she felt still had an iron grip on part of her life, an area she had not opened up to God's leadership, healing, and love.

When Helen looked closely at her life, she found she was becoming more and more like the person she hated most in life— her father. Until and unless she dealt with the stranglehold he still held on her life, she would find a continuing struggle in her spiritual life and possible destruction in her personal relationships.

At first, Helen tried to push away the growing conviction that she needed to deal with her relationship with her father. Even thinking about him again hurt her. This is always the case when we remember something painful from the past. Memories bring back with them feelings, and sometimes those feelings are the things we don't want to face. However Helen knew what was right. While her emotions didn't agree, she knew that God honored those who honored their parents. By remaining at enmity with her father, she was doing what was wrong and was draining herself of life.

Helen went to see her pastor and explained what God had been showing her over the past several months. After several sessions of prayer and counsel, Helen decided to visit her father. Whether he would respond or not, she was determined to bless and honor him.

On June 14, sitting in the pastor's study, Helen made the most difficult call of her life. She had found out her father's phone number from an old family friend and, after praying with her pastor, picked up the phone and dialed the out-of-state number.

She made the call at 3:00 P.M., and secretly Helen hoped her father would be at work and not be there to answer the phone. But on the fifth ring, her father answered the phone. God gave Helen the strength to choke out, "Hello, Dad?" After a long silence on the other end, he replied, "Helen?"

In a short conversation, Helen told her father she was going to be flying to his city and asked if she could see him. "Please do, Helen," her father said. She got directions to his apartment and hung up the phone.

The first skirmish had been won, but the battle still lay before her. A hundred times in the four days before her flight Helen talked herself in and out of going to see her father. Yet each time she decided to back out, that still, small voice within her convicted her of what was right. If she received nothing from her father except the pain she had gotten in the past, she knew she still needed to go for *her* sake and do what was right.

Helen did board the plane, and her pastor and several friends came with her to the airport to encourage her and see her off.

The flight was both the shortest and longest airplane flight of her life. Helen rented a car when she arrived at the airport and drove the thirty minutes to her father's home. With a deep sigh and a short prayer, Helen walked to his apartment and knocked on the door.

An old, tired-looking man opened the door. (Why had she remembered him as being such a giant?) Sitting on the couch with her father, Helen poured out her heart to him. She told about becoming a Christian and the difference it had made in her life. Then, hardest of all, she admitted the anger and hatred she had carried toward him for years and asked his forgiveness.

By the time Helen finished talking, they were both in tears. For fifteen years Helen's father had denied the burning conviction of his wrongs against his daughter. He asked her to forgive him for being such a terrible father and lamented over all the pain he had caused in her life.

After four hours that seemed like only four minutes, Helen left. At the door she put her arms around her father and heard herself say the words that she never thought she could say: "I love you, Daddy." All the hurt he had caused in her life had not stopped her from loving him. Even during the times when she hated him the most, she still felt an attachment to him and a love for the man who had brought her into the world. Where once she could not express that love or even feel it, now she felt compassion, pity, and warmth for a man who had shattered his own life when he shattered hers.

Helen went back to her home, her office, and her church a new person. Not looking different on the outside, but knowing that on the inside she was more free than she had ever been in her life.

When she had come to know Christ, He had freed her from the guilt of every sin and unlocked the shackles that kept her chained to the past. By having the courage to face her father, to honor and bless him, Helen finally took off the shackles Christ had unlocked. She walked away from her father's house that day free to truly live in the present, because she was at last unchained from the past.

## THE FIRST COMMANDMENT WITH A PROMISE

What Helen was willing to do in facing her father took a tremendous amount of courage. However, Helen had a God who understood her tears and gave her the strength to face them.

Is it only those like Helen, who have such a hurtful past, who need to bless their parents? Certainly not. In fact, the Scriptures direct every child to give the blessing to his or her parents.

In the book of Ephesians, Paul goes into detail about what it means to have healthy family relationships. In the fifth chapter of this book he gives a beautiful picture of God's design for the husband/wife relationship. With the man as a loving leader and the woman as a highly valued partner and responder, the stage is set for children to come into a loving home.

Paul's next instructions are for those children. While under the roof and protection of one's parents, children are to "obey your parents in the Lord" (Eph. 6:1). Then Paul gives a general admonition for children of all ages: " 'Honor your father and mother', which is the first commandment with promise: 'that it may be well with you and you may live long on the earth' " (Eph. 6:2–3).

What does it mean to honor your parents? We can see that if we will look at the word *honor* in the Scriptures. In Hebrew, the word for "honor" is *kabed*. This word literally means, "to be heavy, weighty, to honor."[1] Even today, we still link the idea of being heavy with honoring a person.

When the President of the United States or some other important person speaks, people often say that his words "carry a lot of weight." Someone whose words are weighty is someone worthy of honor and respect. However, we can learn even more about what it means to honor someone by looking at its opposite in the Scriptures.

In Chapter Ten, we discovered that the literal meaning of the word *curse (qalal)* was "to make light, of little weight, to dishonor."[2] If we go back to our example above, if we dishonor a person we would say, "Their words carry little weight." The contrast is striking!

When Paul tells us to honor our parents, he is telling us that they are worthy of high value and respect. In modern-day terms, we could call them a heavyweight in our lives! Just the opposite is true if we choose to dishonor our parents.

Some people treat their parents as if they are a layer of dust on a table. Dust weighs almost nothing and can be swept away with a brush of the hand. Dust is a nuisance and an eyesore that clouds any real beauty the table might have. Paul tells us that such an attitude should not be a part of how any child views his or her parents, and for good reason. If we fail to honor our parents, we not only do what is wrong and dishonor God, but we also literally drain ourselves of life!

## WHAT HAPPENS WHEN YOU HONOR (OR DISHONOR) YOUR PARENTS?

Paul goes on to remind us in this passage in Ephesians that a promise is available to all those who will keep the commandment to honor their parents. However, we need to understand something about the promises of God before we look any further. The first thing to remember is that God's promises are always fulfilled. What God promises, He will see come to pass.

The second striking reality we need to see about this promise is that it is conditional. If you fulfill the conditions of the promise, God will honor that in your life. God's promise to you cuts both ways. If you will honor your parents, this promise will apply. But if you dishonor them, you will have to live life apart from God's promise.

Paul tells us that two aspects to this promise relate to those who would honor their parents. The first reflects on our relationship with God.

### "That It May Go Well with You"

In New Testament Greek, this entire phrase is captured in the tiny word, *eu*. In ancient Greece, this word was used to salute someone with the words, "Well done! Excellent."[3] When you honor your parents, the first thing you can know for sure is that God is saying to you, "Well done! Excellent!"

For God's people, doing what was right before God has always included doing what was right by their parents. In Leviticus 19:3, Moses commands the people, "Every one of you shall revere his mother and his father, and keep My Sabbaths: I am the LORD your God." Linked with the importance of setting aside a special Sabbath day each week to honor God is the command to be consistent in revering and honoring your parents.

Jesus felt just as strongly that the actions you take toward your parents reflect your heart toward God. If you are dishonoring your parents, you are following the tradition of your times, not the Word of God. Listen to the strong rebuke Jesus gave the Pharisees and scribes who willfully chose to dishonor their parents:

"Why do you also transgress the commandment of God because of your tradition? For God commanded, saying, 'Honor your father and your mother.' . . . But you say, 'Whoever says to his father or mother, "Whatever profit you might have received from me is a gift to God" then he need not honor his father or mother.' . . . Hypocrites! Well did Isaiah prophesy about you, saying:

> *'These people draw near to Me*
> *with their mouth,*
> *And honor Me with their lips,*
> *But their heart is far from Me'."*
> *(Matt. 15:3-8).*

For Jesus, doing what was wrong in dishonoring your parents could never be linked with what was right in God's eyes. Anyone who urges you to dishonor your parents speaks words of hypocrisy and falsehood. You will only hear a "well done" from your heavenly Father when you honor your parents, not if you dishonor them by treating them as a speck of dust.

Not only does it affect your relationship with the Lord when you follow what is right in honoring your parents, God promises that it will affect your own life in a positive way as well!

## "That You May Live Long on the Earth"

God promises that those who will honor their parents actually receive life! How can this be? Just ask many physicians, counselors, or pastors. They have seen in their offices the shattered lives of those who dishonor their parents, with their strength drained away as a result.

Each of you has only so much emotional and physical energy, and you choose how you will spend it. What physicians and researchers are finding out more and more clearly today is that a close link exists between what we think and how we physically react.

Positive attitudes have been linked with positive physiological changes while negative attitudes can open the door for illness or disease.[4] When persons choose to hate or dishonor their parents because of anger, bitterness, or resentment, they pay a spiritual, emotional, and physical price.

The Scriptures have shown the strong connection between the words we speak and how they affect us physically. In Proverbs 16:24 we read, "Pleasant words are like a honeycomb,/Sweetness to the soul and health to the bones," and in a later passage, "A merry heart does good, like medicine,/But a broken spirit dries the bones" (Prov. 17:22).

When you decide to honor your parents, you are placing high value on them. God says such actions will increase your life on the earth. However, if you decide to see your life dried up by holding on to bitterness or resentment toward your parents (attitudes of dishonor), you eat up your strength and shorten your very life.

Some people have been dishonoring their parents for years. If that is something you have been doing through your actions or attitudes, you need to deal with it as soon as possible and begin the process of making things right. Otherwise the words of King David can ring true in your life, "When I kept silent about my sin, my body wasted away/Through my groaning all day long./For day and night Thy hand was heavy upon me;/My vitality was drained away as with the fever-heat of summer" (Ps. 32:3–4 NASB).

Paul's words have clearly demonstrated to us that we need to honor our parents. Yet, practically, how do we do this? Once again, we find ourselves at the doorstep of the blessing.

## HOW DO YOU HONOR YOUR PARENTS?

The book of Proverbs was written to teach us the skill of right living. We have already seen that honoring your parents is the right thing to do, but how is it done? You honor your parents by acting as wise people, not as fools.

Many of the Proverbs talk about and illustrate different kinds of fools. All are people who are not applying God's principles for right living. One vivid description of a destructive fool is found near the end of the book. Look at this description of a worthless, treacherous man. Then go back and see what heads the list of things that characterize him:

> *There is a kind of man who curses his father,*
> *And does not bless his mother.*
> *There is a kind who is pure in his own eyes,*
> *Yet is not washed from his filthiness.*
> *There is a kind—oh how lofty are his eyes!*
> *And his eyelids are raised in arrogance.*
> *There is a kind of man whose teeth are like swords,*
> *And his jaw teeth like knives.*
>
> (Prov. 30:11–14 NASB)

The man pictured above brings pain to those at home and those outside the home. As we have already seen, he also robs himself of life by cursing his parents. However, he is not only being rebuked in this passage for cursing them, he is also being scolded because he did not bless them.

If you want to be a person who honors your parents, you will be a person who blesses them. In providing the blessing to your parents, you truly honor them, do what is right in God's eyes, and even prolong your life.

We have talked at length in earlier chapters about the five elements of the blessing. We have seen these elements applied to our children, our spouse, our friends, and our church family. Yet where these elements can be of tremendous importance is in providing a blessing for our parents. Each one can be a useful tool in honoring them.

To begin with, your parents need you to *meaningfully touch* them. Even if they have struggled with hugging and touching you when you were young, as they grow older they need the re-assurance that comes from being touched.

They also need *spoken words* from their children. Isn't it interesting that Mother's Day is the busiest day of the year for interstate phone calls! For many mothers, these will be the only encouraging words they hear from their children until the next year. Unfortunately, many fathers will hear fewer words of praise. You need to be consistent in your contact with your parents. They need to hear your voice and the spoken words of blessing they carry.

It is common for a parent to think back in guilt on the past. The things that often seem to stand out to a parent are not the many positive things they did, but the times they spoke out in anger or did something that accidentally hurt their child. When you bless your parents with words that *attach high value* to them, you can be a tremendous encouragement in their lives. You do not have to pretend a wrong was never committed, but you can forgive them and keep them from self-pity. You can decide to value them highly, to honor them because of the great worth they have to you and to God.

Parents need words that picture a *special future* for them. In fact, for many parents the reason they can only look back to times past is because they do not feel a sense of a future in their lives. You can point out useful and beneficial aspects to your parents' lives, even if those useful qualities are different from when they were younger. You can also point them to the Scriptures and the encouragement that their future with their heavenly Father and spiritual family does not end when this life does.

Something that can help is assuring your parents of their important place in the family as the years go by. In some homes with older parents, the grown children will take over the finances and all major decisions and toss aside an older parent's advice or input. Nothing is wrong with providing a helpful service to your parents, but you should be sure you still honor them in the process. By continuing to ask for their wisdom and advice, you can provide them with a picture of a special future.

One last thing that can encourage a special future for your parents is letting them be a part of your future, the future wrapped up in your children. Providing the time for grandparents and grandchildren to meet and interact can be a tremendous tool for providing your parents with a special future. If you will let them know how they can be and have been a blessing to your children, you honor them in a very valuable way.

Of all the ways you can bless your parents, the genuine commitment to walk with your parents through each step in life is particularly important at the end of their lives. Particularly when one parent dies, the other will need an extra measure of your love and commitment to lean on in his or her journey through life.

## BLESSING OUR PARENTS WHILE MAINTAINING HEALTHY BOUNDARIES

Thus far, we've talked about giving the blessing to our parents in a positive, honoring way. But it's important to state that honoring a parent does not mean that we have to drop all healthy boundaries.

For example, my (John's) father had an explosive temper that came out many times when I was with him. In fact, the very first time I ate dinner with him at a nice restaurant nearly turned into a brawl!

My father had re-established a relationship with us, and after closing a large business deal, took us out to a nice restaurant to celebrate. While World War II had ended twenty years before, in many ways my father had never left the battlefield. And one evidence of that was his thinly veiled hatred for anyone of oriental descent.

It didn't matter that our waiter was of Chinese, not Japanese origin. With each round of drinks he ordered, he became more upset with his "slanty eyes," his "poor" service, and "smart #@$#[$>" attitude.

Finally, when the waiter was slow getting us our check, my father blew up in anger. He stood up, challenged the man to fight and started towards him. I feel sure that if my older brother Joe hadn't grabbed him and forced him outside (even then Joe was

6' and 220 lbs.), we'd have witnessed the battle of the Pacific all over again.

Keeping his explosive nature in mind, I put strict boundaries around his behavior when he was in my home. He could say or do anything he liked when I was at his home. But like everyone else who came over to my house, if he chose to smoke it would have to be outside. If he chose to drink before he came over, he should hold off on coming that night. And at all times, his words should be civil and without profanity in front of the children.

As you might imagine, the first time I sat down with my father at a Denny's restaurant and explained these family "rules" was an invitation to an explosion. However, we had just moved back from Texas to Arizona, and I knew the time to set loving boundaries was then.

Without judgment, and without a doubt, I wanted to make sure he knew that I loved him. I didn't preach, or condemn him in any way. But I also had a wife and little ones to consider, and a home where I didn't want anyone, even my father, to cross the line into dishonor.

Healthy boundaries with a difficult parent aren't incompatible with giving them the blessing. I'll have to admit there were times when our family boundaries acted like a wall to him. But every stone was built from his side of the fence.

If you have a parent who consistently "crosses the line" into dishonor, you too may have to establish clear boundaries with them, and have the strength to enforce them despite their reactions.

## COMING FULL CIRCLE WITH THE BLESSING

In honoring our parents as very valuable, we have come full circle in our look at how the blessing in the Scriptures can enrich and encourage healthy relationships. Many of us have never thought in terms of providing our parents with the blessing. But if we will, we can leave them a tangible gift of love that they can carry throughout their lives, just as Don and his brother and sisters did for their parents.

Cindy and I (John) have been to some very creative parties over the years. From "re"gressive dinners to "Roaring Twenties" nights, we thought we had seen them all. Then an invitation came that really caught our attention. We were being asked to attend a surprise, "This Is Your Life" party for an older couple in our church.

The party had been planned by the children in this family specifically to honor their parents for years of loving care and sacrifice. It wasn't anybody's birthday, nor was it tied in with an anniversary. It was simply an evening to remember and say thank you for years of commitment to friends and family.

There was not a dry eye in the place by the time the evening was finished. Thanks to the oldest son's, Don's, initiative, their parents had received an evening of blessing from their children. As we left this older couple's house, you could see in their eyes that their hearts were bursting with pride, appreciation, and love. These children had provided their parents with an evening that was worth far more to them than any department store gift from their children ever could be.

Please don't assume that "my parents would never let us do something like that for them." If Don's parents had known what was coming, they would have probably tried to talk their children out of the evening. Yet regardless of how difficult it can be for some parents to let their children give back to them, we need to make an effort to bless them. In Appendix A at the end of this book, we have included suggestions on how to plan a special evening of blessing for those you love. Has it been too long since you honored your parents with words of blessing? All you need is an active commitment to give back to them what God has already richly given you.

# Chapter Fourteen

## Giving the Blessing to Your Older Children

**W**hen our children were young, Norma and I (Gary) made a commitment to give our children the blessing. We knew that simple acts of unconditional love could make a major difference in their lives. We have seen the fruits of the blessing by watching them mature, leave home, and increase their desire to enrich the lives of others. *But what I never realized, or ever dreamed, was how powerful—and how necessary—the blessing would become to my older children.*

Kari, Greg, and Michael have now grown up and left the house, Kari and Greg to spouses and homes of their own, and Michael to college at an out-of-state school. Our home is much quieter, but not empty. Their laughter, voices, pictures, and love still echo from each wall in our house. And what's more, instead of their growing out of their need for our blessing, they've grown to appreciate it even more. So if you have older children who have moved away from home, they're never out-of-reach of the blessing you can continue to give them. Here are eight important ways you can bless your children to show them your love and appreciation for who they have become as adults.

## Older Children Fall Back on Our Praise

While we've spoken at length about the need to verbally praise our younger children, I've seen with my own grown children how important affirmation continues to be. In fact, as the decisions they make become more serious, and the trials they face become more real, praise is a tremendous source of security and strength for them.

Children of all ages have an "affirmation bank," that requires constant deposits. When we do verbalize our love, we continue to give them a foundation that operates apart from any trying circumstances they might face.

Recently, I saw two examples of how important words of praise are for older children. First, I met a bright, energetic young woman in her early twenties who, already, is building an outstanding career. She is poised, confident, and always wears a smile. And that's someone who only gets paid commission sales in a highly competitive field, and who faces rejection every work day of the week! What keeps her going as she faces so many closed doors? What is the main thing she credits for her top honors as a sales rep?

"Without a doubt, it's my parents," she told me.

"I deal with rejection from people every day, but I've never gotten anything but acceptance from my parents. For example, I can't think of a single time when I've been alone with my father—and I mean since I was a child—that he didn't verbally affirm me about something. Let me tell you, there are a lot of days that I draw on his praise, and it keeps me going." Now as an adult, facing criticism and stiff competition, her parents' words of praise for who she is, and what she does, are like a lighthouse on a stormy night.

The second example of the power of praise came from my son, Greg. In fact, he taught me a lesson I'll never forget about this important aspect of the blessing.

Last May, Greg married a wonderful young woman named Erin. After their honeymoon, Norma and I had the privilege of traveling a good part of the summer with them before they headed to graduate school and their new home in Colorado.

In my own life, I'm always looking for ways to strengthen my marriage and parenting skills. Perhaps that's why, without realizing it, I began pointing out things that I noticed in Greg's interaction with his new bride.

If he did something I felt was somewhat insensitive, or not completely loving, I found myself taking up Erin's defense. Without meaning to, I made him feel uncomfortable around me, even defensive.

I had no idea how deeply this affected Greg until one night after we'd been traveling for almost four weeks. My son pulled me aside when Norma and Erin were out of the room and we had a "son-to-father" talk.

"Dad," he said, in a serious tone. "I need to have a talk with you."

He outlined his feelings and concerns in a very loving way. But sandwiched in between his words of appreciation for me, was the clear message that my "helpful" pointers were being taken as criticism of him as a brand new husband.

As we talked, Greg reminded me of a crucial lesson. "Dad," he told me. "I'm not perfect, but I'm *trying*. This is all new to me. Do you think that for the first year or so, instead of concentrating on the negative things I'm doing, you could praise me for what you see me doing correctly? I think that would help me a lot more than what you're doing now."

Greg's words made an immediate impact on me. He gave me a reminder that praise is one of the most positive reinforcing tools God has given us as parents!

Since that conversation, Greg hasn't had to come to me one time about my "help." But what he has heard from me is consistent encouragement and praise for the many things he is doing right.

Look for anything your children are doing, saying, acting, or experiencing that you believe is valuable and healthy for them, and that honors God and others. Like the fourth chapter of Philippians says, "Whatever is honorable," these are the things we should think on, and praise in our children.

Remember that even the smallest act of praise can be an encouragement to our children. Michael, our youngest, has even expressed how he appreciates seeing bumper stickers on our cars that read, "Our son and our money go to Baylor University!" I have two other smaller Baylor logos stuck on my car windows as well. Small thing, but to him they say, "I'm proud of you, I'm proud of your college and of the way you're working so hard at school."

Without question, praise inhabits the best of homes. And as our children grow older, their need for our affirmation becomes even greater, not less.

## Older Children Need a Written Record of Our Words

Written words become a lifelong legacy for a child to keep. In a letter, you can express your pride in them, or share what you're learning from the Scriptures, or what you're doing that fills them in on your life. Whether they're waiting in the mail-line in the military, reaching into their mailbox at school, or thumbing through their letters in their own home or apartment, written words of blessing from a parent are incredibly powerful.

How powerful? John was involved in a wedding several years ago where a young woman graphically demonstrated the power of written words.

At some reception dinners, words of love and blessing are easily spoken from both sets of parents. But in Angie's case, her father was a very quiet, extremely shy person. He did manage to stand up and share briefly—and nervously—how much he approved of the marriage. But then his daughter did something that expressed his love better than any speech he could have given.

Without his realizing it, since she was a young child, she had kept *every* card and note he had ever written her. Somewhat awkward with his spoken words, he eloquently expressed his love for her through written words. And she treasured and kept every one. Even recent letters that expressed how proud he was of her, and how much he looked forward to her marriage.

In front of the entire crowd (whose eyes were all filled with tears), she had her dad come up and stand beside her as she talked about how much he loved her; how meaningful his support had been over the years. And his love for her was all recorded in written blessings, captured in the several thick scrapbooks she had brought to the dinner.

With the kids out of the house, do you find yourself with a little more time? Then why not take some of that extra time and put your blessing for your children into written words. Even if they don't keep every card or letter you write in an album, they'll keep your words of love in their hearts forever. Often, our written words of love become priceless treasures when we're gone—a paper trail of love! a written memorial to our blessing to them.

If you're reading this chapter as a son or daughter, let me tell you how this same principle can be a tremendous encouragement to your parents. For years, I've greatly appreciated my daughter, Kari's, thoughtfulness in leaving Norma and me little notes around the house. Sometimes on a door, sometimes on the sink or refrigerator we'll find the words, "Mom and Dad, I was just thinking about you and wanted you to know how much I love you and look forward to the fun times we'll have in the future!" In many ways, Kari has taught the rest of us the power of written words of encouragement.

## We Bless Older Children by Helping Drain Anger Out of Their Lives

I began my book *The Key to Your Child's Heart* by stating that the single most important factor in maintaining harmony in any home is to resolve anger as soon as possible. Even today, the single greatest problem I observe in homes across the world is the epidemic of broken relationships, most destroyed by unchecked, unresolved anger.

Too many people are simply not aware of how much damage anger heaps on any family or friendship. I label this unresolved anger as "closing a person's spirit." The more a family member "closes the spirit" of another, the greater the disharmony and distance in the relationship, and the less interest in spiritual things you'll see. Prolonged anger can lead to depression, ulcers, or high blood pressure. These are just a *few* of the emotional and physical problems that can accompany anger!

Most of us can recognize a closed spirit in another family member. They usually won't talk with us openly or cheerfully, and they dislike our reaching out to hug or touch them. They tend to argue more, and we can sense their subtle (or obvious) avoidance of us. With older children who have a great deal of anger, they may move away at the earliest opportunity, or even deliberately choose any path to take, except the one we've pointed them towards.

For anyone serious about reducing family friction, blessing older children, and dealing with anger in a healthy way, here are five brief, practical suggestions on opening another person's closed spirit. For greater detail, see *The Key to Your Child's Heart*.

## Five Steps to Reopen a Child's Spirit

Years ago, I disciplined my son Greg in anger after he was screaming while I was on the telephone. Without finding out the reason why he was yelling, I spanked him and watched his little spirit "close" towards me.

When I realized what I'd done, I applied the five principles (not steps) I'll share with you, and in a matter of minutes I witnessed his spirit reopen.

Today, almost twenty years later, I *still* use these same principles if I see I've done something to put anger in Greg's heart. What's more, I've even used these guidelines to help him deal with the anger others may have placed there over the years.

## 1. Become Tenderhearted

The first step that I needed to take to open Greg's spirit was to reflect tenderness and softness in my words. "A soft word turns away anger," the proverb says, and gentleness has a way of always melting anger.

We communicate several things to the person whom we have offended when we soften our tone. First it says, "You're valuable and important." Second, it shows that we are willing to slow down long enough to correct what has happened. Finally, by adopting gentleness we communicate that we are open to listen, that it is safe for him or her to share what has happened, and that we don't want anyone to maintain a "closed spirit" in our home.

## 2. Increase Understanding

The second step to open a person's spirit is to increase our understanding of the pain he or she feels.

As Greg has grown older, when I have stopped to listen and softly ask Greg why he was hurting, I've found his resistance to talking begin to drain away. As my spirit became even softer, I had deeper understanding and could feel his pain. Many times just these two factors—being soft and then understanding a person's pain—will open a person's spirit.

This is particularly important as children get older. The gift of listening with understanding to an older child is often all they need to make the connection between what they're hurt or frustrated about, and dealing with that hurt in a positive way. Avoiding lectures, and increasing careful, honoring listening can be very helpful for a child of any age.

## 3. Recognize the Offense

The third step to opening a person's spirit is admitting that we were wrong. One of the hardest things for many parents to do is to admit when they are wrong. I find it is especially hard for fathers. I do not necessarily like to find out when I am wrong, and it's not always easy to admit when I am. But I must remember that a hardened, resistant attitude is extremely detrimental to children.

One of my favorite Christian camps is Kamp Kanakuk, in beautiful Branson, Missouri. Jim Brawner was for years one of the directors of the camp (now our National Homes of Honor Director!), and one summer, he made an incredible discovery.

He asked each of the several thousand teenagers who came to camp during the summer, "What is the one thing you wish your parents would do more often?" The answer wasn't, "Say, 'I love you,'" more often, or even, "Spend more time with me." They didn't even say, "Send more money!" The overwhelming number of teenagers said the very same thing: *"I wish my mother and father would admit when they're wrong."*

There is tremendous bonding power when we become strong enough to admit our mistakes to our children. While some children may use our apology as ammunition to shoot back at us, most will be moved to a level of closeness—and a freedom from anger—that would shock you.

Softness, listening, and admitting we're wrong. These three factors are crucial, but there are two more actions that are equally important to making sure the spirit has reopened.

## 4. Attempt to Touch

The fourth factor is attempting to touch the offended person. Why? First of all, he needs to be touched. If he reaches out and responds to our touching, then we know his spirit is opening or the anger is draining out. This is an extremely important time to take his hand, put an arm around him, or otherwise touch him in a meaningful way. Even with an older child, that touch lets him know that we care, that we love him, and that he is very important.

Second, touching often allows us to find out if the child's spirit is *not* opening. If my child pulls back or moves away when I try to touch her, it is commonly an indication that she isn't ready to open her spirit. She may need more time or greater understanding from the one who offended her.

For all the reasons we listed in the chapter on meaningful touch, we encourage you to practice appropriate hugs, handshakes, and kisses with your older children.

## 5. And Finally, Seek Forgiveness When Warranted

The final step we need to take is to seek forgiveness from the one we offended. When we have offended someone, we must not only be willing to admit we're wrong, but also to give that child a chance to respond. For me, the best way is to say something like, "Could you find it in your heart to forgive me?" When Greg was young, this is when I knew I had reopened Greg's spirit, for when I asked for his forgiveness, he would rush into my arms.

Once they're talking to us again, allowing us to hug them, and speaking to us in honoring tones, we can say at this point that true restoration and forgiveness has been gained. And usually, most of the anger is gone.

Praising our older children; leaving them a written legacy of our love for them; and helping to drain anger out of their life.

All three are powerful ways of giving the blessing. And a fourth way is equally powerful.

## Give Them the Inheritance of a Good Name

Not everyone can leave a $100,000 inheritance to their children, even if they want to. I remember when Norma and I were first married, her father took us out to dinner and told us we were going to receive a $100,000+ inheritance very soon. In our minds, that very night we began to spend that inheritance in one hundred different ways! Thank the Lord, we never actually went out and bought things based on his words, because the economy went into a deep slump. Her father lost all the money he had verbally promised (and far more) nearly overnight.

So, while not everyone can leave a monetary inheritance to their child, and we shouldn't always count on that kind of inheritance anyway, every one of us can leave our children the inheritance of a good name.

In Proverbs, we're told that a "good name" is better than jewels. It's a priceless gift that we can pass down to our children, and they can pass down to their children in turn. Our name is something that, no matter what, we will pass down to our kids, and it can either be a blessing to them, or a curse.

Take Darwin Smith, and his son, Darwin, Jr. While this is an extreme example, it illustrates the importance of looking ahead two, and even three generations, on the impact we have on future family members. Darwin, Sr. came from an abusive home, and the home he made for his son was incredibly unstable. He was fired from over a dozen jobs all because every boss he had was terrible. But what his instability led him to do one winter day was even more terrible still.

After being dismissed from yet another job, Darwin, Sr., took a rifle, a handgun, and pockets full of ammunition and killed four people at his former plant, and then killed himself as the police moved in. His father left a name to remember all right, only Darwin, Jr. had to carry it as well. Every day at school, and every time his name was spoken in their small community, the name his father left him became a curse, not a blessing.

How different when we see a person whose parents have loved God and spent a lifetime helping others. The name these people have leaves a sweet fragrance for those who hear it and a powerful blessing to the children and grandchildren who carry it. How is your character today? From truthfulness, to consistency, to Christ-likeness, we need to leave our older children a name they can be proud of, not ashamed of.

## We Bless Our Older Children By Taking Care of Our Own Health

While it may sound unimportant, one of the most important ways we can bless our older children is to maintain our own physical, mental, and spiritual health! When we pay attention to what we eat, the vitamins and prescription medications we take, and even exercise regularly, it's bound to help us live longer. And in my case, hopefully, it's extending my ability to be around to bless my children and their children even longer.

In my family, my father died of a massive heart attack at the age of fifty-eight. My oldest brother had a similar heart attack at age fifty-one and has had by-pass surgery since then. My next oldest brother died of a heart attack at age fifty-one.

I have the same genetic tendencies that the other Smalley men do and have had for generations—high cholesterol.

Yet instead of my health's becoming a cloud that my children have to worry about, I've done all I can to maintain a healthy life-style. Through the help of my doctors, diet, and regular exercise, I've seen my cholesterol move to a level below even the average risk factor.

For almost twenty years, I've vigorously exercised one half-hour each day—walking, tread-milling, stair climbing, bicycling, and occasionally jogging. And there's a reason. Whether we realize it or not, our children do worry about our health as we get older, even at times, more than we do. That's why actively taking care of ourselves not only blesses us physically—it's a way of giving our children the blessing as well.

Recently, I just went through a procedure, angioplasty, where a camera was literally inserted into my heart arteries, allowing a doctor to see if the Smalley "curse" of high cholesterol had caused any heart damage. The result? To my amazement, and the doctors', all the efforts and prayers I've made over the years seemed to pay off one hundredfold. I was told by the doctor when I finally awoke from the procedure,

"Smalley, get out of here and go home! You've got a 'baby' heart, it looks so good. Yours is the best looking heart I'll see in here all year."

Many supportive friends celebrated with me about how positive my health has become, but none celebrated as much as my own spouse and children. Our daughter, Kari, called me in the hospital and said, "Dad, call me the minute you get out of the operating room and tell me everything's OK. Because if it isn't, I'm jumping on a plane and coming out right now!" It's natural for our children to worry about us. However, they've seen me take an active role in doing all I can, not to become a burden on them through ill-health, and to avoid being any kind of burden to them for years to come.

While the previous five blessings for our children involve who they are in their relationships, this sixth blessing can become a tremendous, personal help to them.

## Teach Them Financial Responsibility

When our children were young, we were responsible for them financially. But in the years that follow, we need to teach them financial independence and responsibility.

There is a tremendous temptation to try and rush in and provide financial help, resources, or even luxuries that a grown child needs. However, at times, this can lead to over-controlling, and even short-circuiting the learning process when it comes to being financially responsible. Rather, like Sam Walton, the founder of Wal-Mart stores, we need to help our children see the value of hard work, savings, and thrift.

Norma and I see each of our children learning to work hard and plan financially for themselves and their own families. We've tried to instill within them an understanding of three important financial guidelines:

1. What do they believe God wants them to do in serving other people? The highest calling for each of us is serving people in love.

2. Once they decided on what area of serving others is best for them, anything from medicine to selling a helpful service,

they then need to commit to gain the best knowledge and practical skills possible to become an expert in that field.

3. They must continually practice and increase their skills in their chosen area of service.

I've watched God honor and reward people all over our world who have held to these three guidelines. You'll notice that the focus isn't on money. It's on serving others with an expertise that leads to their efforts being recognized and rewarded.

My children know that they can't depend on others to take care of them forever. They have to find their own plan for satisfying service, knowing that "the greatest among you is the servant of all."

## Avoid Over-Controlling

As we've visited Michael, our youngest son, at college, he's mentioned many times a major problem of parenting—and blessing—older children. Namely, well-meaning children can find themselves with a parent who is far too controlling for their good.

Mike has actually told us that instead of these parents' being appreciated by their children, they look at them as actually withholding the blessing from them. One example he gave was of a junior in college who still has to call her mother every time she plans to do anything significant, either in-town or out-of-town. Instead of communicating concern, this checking-in has become a control device that her mother uses to live her own life through her daughter.

When our children are young, it's important that we remain in control as their parents. But as they grow older, there's a balance that must come into play. Namely, that we lead them by example and love, encourage them always, and support them with a listening ear or personal counsel—but not control. Rather, we should bless our children out of a desire that they take *positive control* of their own lives as they grow older.

## Give Your Children the Chance to Return the Blessing to You

For me, it's easier to give a gift than to receive it. But as I've learned over the years, it's important that the blessing become a two-way street. While we need to travel the road first and give our children the blessing in every way, they also need to be able to express their blessing back to you.

Without question, one of the greatest rewards of giving your children the blessing is having them grow up one day and return it to you. That's what happened to me a few years ago, when I received something incredibly meaningful from my son.

While it might not catch your eye, if you were to walk into my (Gary's) office, you'd see something hanging on my wall that's priceless. It's not an oil painting, or a bronze sculpture. It's a small plaque that my son Greg created and gave me that carries a picture of the two of us, a father's day card, and his words of blessing returned to me.

All of us have tough, discouraging days at times. But not everyone has the words of love and appreciation I have hanging behind me. Words of blessing returned to me from my oldest son, Greg, that brighten the darkest day.

The Father's Day card that I can't read without mist gathering in my eyes says,

### This Is For You
*This is for you, Dad, for the father I love,*
*For the one who has cared all these years,*
*but has never heard enough about how much I care.*
*So this is for you,*
*For the one who has helped me through,*
*all my childhood fears and failures,*
*And turned all that he could,*
*into successes and dreams.*
*For the man who is a wonderful example,*
*of what more men should be.*
*For the person whose devotion to his family,*
*is marked by gentle strength and guidance*
*And whose love of life, sense of direction,*
*and down to earth wisdom,*
*make more sense to me now,*
*than nearly any other thing I learned.*
*If you never knew how much I respected you,*
*I want you to know it now, Dad,*
*and if you never knew how much I admire you,*
*let me just say that I think you're the best father*

> *that any child ever had.*
> *This is a card filled with love,*
> *and it's all for you . . . Dad.*

And then added to Adrian Rodgers' beautiful poem are my own son's words of blessing.

> *"Father, my wish and prayer on this special day, is that we can share another fifty years of friendship together. To the molder of my dreams, yet still, to my best friend. I love you."*
>
> *Gregory T*

Greg's words are precious to me because they come out of a commitment Norma and I made years ago to provide our children with the blessing. We've looked at it as our gift to give our children to help them have a wonderful, meaningful life. But it is so humbling and encouraging when they return the blessing to us, it can make our hearts want to burst.

While I've spoken and given Greg numerous examples of my love and commitment (and Kari and Michael as well), I need to be able to receive the blessing from them, too. Not look for it. Demand it. Or pout if we don't get it. But be open to receiving it should they complete the loop by blessing us as well.

### Eight Ways to Bless Your Older Child

1. *Praise*
2. *Written words of blessing*
3. *Drain anger from their lives*
4. *Leave a positive inheritance*
5. *Teach financial responsibility*
6. *Take care of your own health*
7. *Avoid being over-controlling*
8. *Let your children return the blessing to you*

While the applications of the blessing may change when they're older, their hearts don't change. Even grown children are waiting for words of love to be spoken and heard.

# Chapter Fifteen

## A Church That Gives the Blessing

$J$im had struggled in his marriage, in his job as a mechanic, and in his life in general for many years. The only time he went to church was when he and his wife attended a wedding or when he was forced to attend an occasional Christmas or Easter service.

From Jim's perspective, the most encouraging place of fellowship he knew was at the bowling alley with his Wednesday night bowling league. Jim lived for Wednesday nights when he and some of the guys from work would arrive early, have a few beers, and then bowl in league play.

From the slaps on the back for making a strike, to the closeness and camaraderie of being on a team, Jim looked at bowling as a shelter to get away from the storm clouds at work and the problems with his family. Unfortunately, after an evening at the lanes, Jim still had to go back home that night and to work the next day and face the reality that his life was falling apart all around him.

During the next year, through the example and loving commitment of a new mechanic at work, Jim heard the gospel for the first time. The new mechanic's name was Ed, and he was a deeply committed Christian. Jim quickly grew to respect Ed's skill in repairing engines, but it was his personal life that Jim envied even more. Ed was not perfect, but he had an inner peace and a growing marriage that Jim longed to have. Ed did not force his belief on Jim; rather he did something much more powerful. Ed lived a positive Christian life in front of his coworker, which was like giving salt to a thirsty man.

With Jim's marriage on the rocks and with his bordering on having a drinking problem, one afternoon Jim asked Ed why his life was so different from his (Jim's). Over the next several months, Ed met regularly with Jim and taught him about his need for the Savior and the new life he could have in Christ. On a cold day just before Christmas, Jim prayed with his friend Ed to receive Christ. After thirty-seven years of failing at life on his own, Jim finally turned to the Source of life Himself to lead him and guide him.

Like Jonathan in the Old Testament, Ed was a source of blessing to his friend. His personal caring helped Jim feel secure. Jim's personal life and his marriage began to change for the better as a result of God's working in his life. Ed also encouraged Jim to attend a church where he could learn more about God's Word.

Jim and his wife did begin to attend a fairly large church near their house. This church had an outstanding reputation as a Bible-believing church. However, they never seemed to feel comfortable and accepted there. The preaching didn't bother Jim; in fact, he loved to learn from the pastor who was an excellent communicator. What hurt and confused him was the lack of personal relationships or warmth once the preaching was over.

Everyone was polite to Jim and his wife, but no one with bright eyes gave them a warm greeting, and dinner invitations after church were nonexistent. To try and develop some deeper friendships with other people at the church, they began attending a Sunday school class. However, after several months of attending the class, they were little closer to the people in the class than they were on the first Sunday they attended.

When Jim's friend Ed took a job at another auto shop out of state, Jim was crushed. He particularly ached over the lack of personal relationships with other men at the church. Since Jim had become a Christian, he had given up his Wednesday night bowling league to attend midweek services. Yet without any committed Christian friends, he was getting lonelier and lonelier. Even when he tried to initiate a conversation with someone else at church, after an initial "Hi, how are you doing?" the strain to find topics to talk about would become uncomfortable. Finally Jim gave up trying at all. There were pockets of friendly people, but Jim noticed that they were friendly to the same people week after week.

This was Jim's first experience at a church and he began to feel that somehow Christians didn't need friends. He tried to immerse himself in studying the Bible and hoped that would take away his need for meaningful relationships. However, as time went by, Jim felt more alone when he was surrounded by the people at his church than he ever had at the bowling alley. The thought of switching churches never really occurred to Jim. This was the only church he had ever gone to and he felt certain this must be what they were all like.

With his only Christian friend gone and with no one at church who took a personal interest in his life, Jim began to spend more and more time with his old friends at work. As a result, he began to slip back into the old patterns he had before he became a Christian. Unfortunately, that included beginning to drink again.

Jim stopped attending Sunday school and attended only the church service. As the weeks went by, no one in his Sunday school class called to ask why he was no longer attending or even stopped him after church to say more than "Hello." While their lack of concern may have been from a feeling of "I didn't want to pry" or "We don't want to put pressure on him," in Jim's mind their indifference confirmed to him that they didn't care. Soon his attendance at the church service was sporadic.

With all the people at this growing church, no one seemed to miss one man who began drifting away from the fellowship; that is, until the pastor unexpectedly ran into Jim's wife one Saturday at the market.

"Hi," said the pastor. "How are you and Jim doing?" It was only an innocent question, but it was met with tears and sobs right in the middle of a supermarket aisle. "Pastor, Jim won't come back to church with me. He said that he has better friends at the bowling alley than he ever did at church."

Jim had been searching for closeness in relationships and a blessing from his church family, but he never found it. In less than ten months, Jim had gone from sitting at the midweek service at church to drinking beer again with his buddies back at the bowling alley. Perhaps Jim should have been mature enough to stay in the church and to concentrate on giving to others, never receiving love back himself, but he wasn't. And neither are many new believers just like Jim.

Is this simply the story of one man who had too little faith? We wish it were. Unfortunately this story can be told of many churches today that talk about the blessings of genuine fellowship *(koinonia)* in a sermon or in a Sunday school class, but do not practice it with people within the church. While we may not like to admit it in the evangelical community, many people who come to our churches find more of the elements of the blessing in a bowling alley than they do inside the church walls.

Instead of letting this discourage those of us inside the church, it should encourage us to learn how to be a people of blessing. We need to learn how to make significant relationships within the church, not superficial ones. From the first time God called a special people to be His own until today, we as believers have always been called to be a blessing to others.

## OUR CALLING IS TO BE A PEOPLE OF BLESSING

From earliest times, God's people have been called to be a blessing. When God first came to Abraham, He gave him a very specific promise. We read: "I will bless you/And make your name great;/And you shall be a blessing. . . . In you all the families of the earth shall be blessed" (Gen. 12:2–3).

Centuries later, in the book of Acts, Peter tells us what form this blessing took for all nations. The blessing came in the body of the suffering servant, Jesus, a descendant of Abraham's who has the power to bless our lives by freeing us from sin. Peter said:

> *"God . . . says to Abraham, 'Through your offspring all peoples on earth will be blessed.' When God raised up his*

> *servant, he sent him first to you to bless you by turning*
> *each of you from your wicked ways."*
>
> *(3:25–26 NIV)*

Introducing people to Jesus Christ is the first and foremost way a church can bless others. When men and women are introduced to the Source of blessing, they come face to face with Someone who can be their best friend and their very source of life.

If we have been called to provide people with the blessing of knowing Christ, what is the best way to see that happen? Let's let our Lord answer that question. "A new commandment I give to you, that you love one another; . . . All [people] will know that you are My disciples, if you have love for one another" (John 13:34–35). What does that mean to us?

People outside the church will never care how much we know about Christ until they know how much we care for each other. When a body of believers becomes committed to loving each other, then they can truly be called a church that is serious about winning others to Christ.

## THE BLESSING:
## A CHURCHWIDE GUIDELINE
## FOR LOVING OTHERS

If Jesus commanded us to be people who deeply love each other, why do so many churches struggle with being warm and sensitive to the needs of others? Is it a lack of loving people in the church?

We fully believe that it is not the lack of caring believers in the church that results in people like Jim going away unblessed. Rather, these people lack the knowledge about how they can practically meet the relational needs other people have once they come to know Christ.

The church needs to be first and foremost a place where the gospel is preached and where Christ is honored as our Lord and Savior. But God designed the church to be a caring community as well. We can't escape the fact that when we fail to bless and love our brothers and sisters in Christ, we are failing in our duties as a family of God. When one member of the body rejoices, we should all rejoice. When one member weeps, we should all weep (1 Cor. 12:26).

The exciting thing about the concept of the blessing is that it can be a guideline for all kinds of loving relationships. Obviously it can provide a tangible way for parents to bless their children. We have also seen how a marriage and even an intimate friendship can be built up by the elements of the blessing. However, it doesn't stop there. Some churches today train and encourage their people to provide each aspect of the blessing to others. And thankfully more and more churches are learning to do this training.

In fact, show us a church anywhere in the world that is meeting the genuine needs of its members and drawing others to Christ, and we'll show you a church where God's Word is being taught and where the relationship elements of the blessing are being applied.

What happens when a church, or even a department within a church, gets hold of the concept of the blessing? Let's look at how the principles of the blessing, applied in one church's singles department, literally turned their ministry around.

## A CASE STUDY OF APPLYING THE BLESSING WITH GOD'S PEOPLE

Mark was the leader of a large singles Sunday school class. In fact, on any given Sunday, they could have more than 150 young men and women in attendance. Like many church groups, Mark's class struggled with the problems of turnover and building deep relationships. They had the heart for ministry to others, but that caring desire never seemed to move out of their class leaders' meetings and into their class.

Almost two years ago, we shared the principles in this book at a conference Mark attended. He jumped on every bit of information we could give him about the blessing and asked us to speak at a class retreat he had coming up. God used that conference Mark attended and the ensuing class retreat to plant the biblical principles of the blessing within the hearts of the people in the class.

We found out only a few months ago that after the retreat, Mark formed a group of people within the class called the Blessing Bunch. Their goal was to identify people in the class who particularly needed one or more elements of the blessing and then actively to commit themselves to be the person who provided that need.

With one young lady in the class who had broken an engagement, providing the blessing meant simply taking her hands and crying with her. For a man, it involved a brother in Christ picturing a special future for him that gave him the confidence to tackle a difficult new assignment. Still another woman needed to know she was of high value to her friend and to the Lord after a week of listening to her employer say she was worthless.

Having a strategy for meeting needs within the group by teaching and applying the elements of the blessing became a real help to this leader. In fact, Mark talked about the principles of blessing so much, many of the class members would say to each other in fun, "Have you had your blessing this week?"

"Have you had your blessing this week?" These people meant this as a joke, yet making the people in that class aware of the elements of the blessing opened many doors of ministry, doors to a number of men's and women's lives that had once been tightly closed. But what happened in this singles group did not stay confined to their classroom. Giving the blessing began to spread throughout the entire church.

Several of the members of the class became convicted about their relationships with their parents as they learned about the concept of the blessing. One young man in particular walked out of the classroom one Sunday morning and right to a pay phone where he called his father for the first time in more than four years. Other people began to share the principles of the blessing with their family members at the church and it, too, led to a time of healing.

The singles class even talked about the concept of the blessing at a Sunday evening service a few weeks following their retreat. One thing Mark shared was that the married people in the church could bless the singles by not expecting them to get married tomorrow and by inviting them into their homes. This began an "adopt a single" program that helped bring a once nearly isolated group into the mainstream of church life.

This story is of just one department that decided to get serious about blessing other people in their lives. The results spread throughout the entire church and helped bring a new sense of warmth and caring to many people.

Imagine what would happen if an entire church decided to bless those in their fellowship and were trained how to do it! We would have a church where relationship needs were actively being met by a welcoming handshake or hug (meaningful touch); where appreciation for a fine sermon, working in the children's department, or simply listening to a hurting brother or sister was verbally acknowledged (spoken message). We would have groups of believers who acknowledged every member's true worth (attaching high value) and who gave them words of hope and encouragement to reach their God-given potential (a special future). All these elements would be wrapped in the willingness to let people fail and not let them walk away unnoticed, because a decision had been made already that they were valuable (an active commitment).

This church sounds like the kind of church most of us would like to belong to, and it can be. All it takes is one person to start a Blessing Bunch to begin to meet the needs of those around them. Even more than that, this kind of church can become the kind of place that those outside the church long to be a part of, a true place of blessing.

A church that is committed to applying the principles of the blessing can make a tremendous impact on the unsaved. Once church members learn about this concept and experience it within the church, they can begin to transport it outside the church walls. Monday through Saturday they can provide the elements of God's blessing to a non-Christian society desperately in search of genuine security and acceptance.

An employer can evaluate how well he or she is doing in being a blessing to his or her employees. A school teacher can learn about the blessing and recognize the telltale signs of a child's growing up without parental acceptance. A student can befriend a fellow classmate and point him or her toward a secure source of blessing through Christ.

## HITTING THE TARGET WHEN IT COMES TO
## LOVING EACH OTHER

Aristotle once observed, "You stand a far greater chance of hitting the target if you can see it." At first glance, this statement might not sound too profound, but it really is. Churches, parents, spouses, and friends stand a far better chance of hitting the target of loving each other if they can see how to do it.

Following the guidelines provided in the blessing can help our words and actions score a bull's-eye when we want to communicate God's love and acceptance to our loved ones. Coupled with sound teaching from the Word of God, the elements of the blessing can also provide a tremendous tool for evangelism. The blessing can even help us fulfill the Great Commission to "Go therefore and make disciples of all the nations" (Matt. 28:19). If the mark of disciples is that they "love one another" (John 13:34), applying the principles of the blessing can help God's love radiate to a needy world.

As we end our look at how the blessing applies to our church family, we are nearing the end of our journey in this book. However, we have one more important stop to make. There are two people in our lives who can especially profit from a blessing we can give them—our parents.

Before we look at how we as children can give back a blessing to our parents, let's listen to the words of a song that capture the kind of place the church needs to be: a shelter for those who have faced the storms of life, and a place where God's love radiates to a needy world; a place where the blessing is given to others and where authenticity is a password to fellowship. A place Ken Medema pictures in these haunting words:[1]

### If This Is Not a Place . . .

*If this is not a place, where tears are understood,*
  *then where shall I go to cry?*
*And if this is not a place, where my spirit can take*
  *wings, then where shall I go to fly?*
*I don't need another place, for trying to impress you,*
  *with just how good and virtuous I am,*

*No, no, no, I don't need another place, for always*
*being on top of things. Everybody knows that it's a*
*sham, it's a sham.*
*I don't need another place for always wearing smiles,*
*even when it's not the way I feel,*
*I don't need another place, to mouth the same old*
*platitudes; everybody knows that it's not real.*
*So if this is not a place, where my questions can be*
*asked, then where shall I go to seek?*
*And if this is not a place, where my heart cry can be*
*heard, where, tell me where, shall I go to speak?*
*So if this is not a place, where tears are understood,*
*where shall I go, where shall I go to fly?\**

# *Chapter Sixteen*

## A Final Blessing

**O**ne hope that discovering more about the blessing in the Scriptures has challenged each of you to have a new reason and a new way to honor your parents, your children, your spouse, your friends, and your church family. Our prayer for each reader is that your life will be one where each element of the blessing is given and received.

Remember, we build the blessing into a person's life on a daily basis. You never know what small act of love and encouragement will be the one that your children, spouse, or friends remember as a key way in which you blessed them. How do we know this? In seminars throughout the country and in numerous counseling sessions with couples and individuals, we asked people this question: "What is one specific way you knew that you had received your parents' blessing?" Let's look at how one hundred people responded to this question. Through their responses we can discover how powerful a parent's everyday actions and attitudes are in communicating the blessing to their children.

### One Hundred Homes That Gave the Blessing to Children
1. *My parents would take the time to really listen to me when I talked to them by looking directly into my eyes.*

2. *We were often spontaneously getting hugged even apart from completing a task or chore.*
3. *They would let me explain my side of the story.*
4. *We went camping as a family. (This response was repeated often.)*
5. *They would take each of us out individually for a special breakfast with Mom and Dad.*
6. *My father would put his arm around me at church and let me lay my head on his shoulder.*
7. *I got to spend one day at Dad's office, seeing where he worked and meeting the people he worked with.*
8. *My mother always carried pictures of each of us in her purse.*
9. *They would watch their tone of voice when they argued.*
10. *My parents made sure that each one of us kids appeared in the family photos.*
11. *My parents would make a special Christmas ornament for each child that represented a character trait we had worked on that year.*
12. *They were willing to admit when they were wrong and say "I'm sorry."*
13. *They had a "king or queen for a day meal" for us that would focus individual attention on each child.*
14. *As a family we often read and discussed the book* The Velveteen Rabbit, *which talks about how valuable we are.*
15. *I saw my parents praying for me even when I didn't feel I deserved it.*
16. *My folks wrote up a special "story of my birth" that they read to me every year.*
17. *We read Psalm 139 as a family and discussed how God had uniquely and specially designed each of us children.*
18. *They attended all of my open houses at school.*
19. *My father loved me by loving my mother.*
20. *They would tell us character traits we possessed that would help us be good marriage partners when we grew up and got married.*
21. *My mother would tell us "make believe" bedtime stories that illustrated positive character traits she felt we had.*
22. *They tried to be consistent in disciplining me.*

23. My mom was always willing to help me with my math homework.
24. My folks really tried to help me think through where I should go to college.
25. My dad would constantly tell me that whoever I married, he'd be committed to him and our children for life.
26. My parents openly discussed and helped me set limits in the sexual area.
27. My mother and father would ask us children our opinions on important family decisions.
28. When my father was facing being transferred at work, he purposely took another job so that I could finish my senior year in high school at the same school.
29. My mom had a great sense of humor, but she never made us kids the brunt of her jokes.
30. My parents wouldn't change things in my bedroom without asking me if it was OK with me.
31. My folks pursued resolving conflict with me instead of letting issues build up.
32. When I wrecked my parents' car, my father's first reaction was to hug me and let me cry instead of yelling at me.
33. My dad could correct me without getting all emotional or lecturing me.
34. My parents were patient with me when I went through my long hair stage in high school.
35. My mother tried really hard to keep her promises to me.
36. My dad would ask me all the time, "What would it take for this to be a 'great year' for you?" and then try to see that it was.
37. Even though my dad had played football in college, he never forced me to go out for sports when I didn't want to.
38. At least once a year around my birthday, my dad would take me out of school for a special lunch where he would let me know I was special to him.
39. My parents would tell me over and over that I was a good friend to my friends.
40. Even when I was in high school, my father sometimes would tuck me into bed like when I was little.
41. My mother would pray with me about important decisions I was facing, or even that I would have a good day at school.

42. When I was thirteen, my dad trusted me to use his favorite hunting rifle when I was invited to go hunting with a friend and his father.
43. We would have "family meetings" every two weeks where everyone would share their goals and problems.
44. If it was really cold, my mom would get up early and drive me on my paper route.
45. When I had my appendix out, my parents were right there with me before and after the operation.
46. Sometimes when I would get home from school, my mother would have left a plate of cookies on the counter with a special note saying she loved me.
47. My parents used to take me and friend out for a special dinner sometimes.
48. When I had a teacher that didn't like me, my parents defended me and stood up for me.
49. My mother got interested in computers just because I was interested in them.
50. They could have just shipped my stuff, but my parents drove a U-Haul trailer over 1,800 miles when I went off to college.
51. My dad gave up smoking because he knew how much it bothered Mom and us kids.
52. My father taught me how to budget my money.
53. Even though I didn't like it at the time, the chores my parents made me do helped me learn responsibility.
54. My parents would always make sure I knew why I was being disciplined.
55. My father let me go with him on some of his business trips.
56. I realize now how hard my mother worked to take care of us all.
57. My parents were good examples to me of how a Christian marriage should function.
58. When I was down about my boyfriend breaking up with me, my father took extra time just to listen to me and cry with me.
59. My parents never acted like they were perfect, and they never expected us to be perfect either.
60. Now that I'm an adult, I really appreciate how my father taught me to communicate with him. That has helped me know how to talk to my husband now that I'm married.

61. My mother would let me explain my point of view on issues—even when she disagreed with me. She always made me feel that my opinion was important.

62. My parents didn't compare my abilities with those of my older brother or the other kids at school, but helped me see my own unique value.

63. My parents allowed me to give back to them when I got older, like picking up the tab at dinner.

64. I appreciated my father working to keep a good relationship with me when I was a teenager. I can see now that helped keep me from some really bad dating relationships.

65. When I asked for it, my mother would give me advice on dating and other areas of my life.

66. I always had the best sack lunch at school of anybody in my class.

67. My folks were always willing to hang in there with me and help me work through conflicts with my friends.

68. My father went with me when I had to take back an ugly dress a saleswoman had talked me into buying.

69. My mother was always interested in what I was doing at school, but she wasn't interfering.

70. My father acted more excited about getting to spend time with us kids than he did about working at the office.

71. My father helped me buy an old Mustang that had been wrecked and worked with me to rebuild it into a beautiful car.

72. I never felt like I had to perform to gain my father's approval.

73. My father worked with me for hours on my soap-box derby racer.

74. Some people's parents criticize them behind their backs, but I was always hearing something positive from my parents' friends that my parents had said about me.

75. My mother had a Bible study with me every Monday morning before I went to school.

76. Even though I didn't appreciate it at the time, I know that my parents were protecting me by putting a curfew on when I had to be in on a date.

77. When I first started wearing make-up, my mother never made fun of how much time I spent in front of the mirror.

78. *Even when I was very overweight in high school, my parents still made me feel I was attractive.*
79. *My mom took on a part-time job to help me earn enough money to go to a Christian summer camp.*
80. *My parents paid for me to take several vocational tests when I was struggling to find out what I wanted to do for a living.*
81. *My father would reward me for a job well done on the yard by taking me to Dairy Queen where we would both get a sundae.*
82. *My father let me share in his failures as well as his successes.*
83. *My father went with me to six different used car dealers to help me find my first car.*
84. *My parents would always make sure that each of us children was introduced to their friends when they came over to our house.*
85. *My parents quit using a "nickname" that really hurt me.*
86. *My mom used to rub my legs after cheerleader practice.*
87. *My father would always point out my good table manners to others.*
88. *My mother would see to it that I had the necessary tools to complete a project (crayons, ruler, and so on).*
89. *My father would put a special note on our pillows when he had to go out of town on business.*
90. *My parents would involve the whole family in planning family vacations.*
91. *My father took me and my sisters out on a very special date on our sixteenth birthdays.*
92. *They would always go to my piano recitals and act interested.*
93. *My father would let me practice pitching to him for a long time when he got home from work.*
94. *We used a special red plate at dinner to designate birthdays or outstanding achievements.*
95. *Every Saturday morning, my father would get up before anybody else and cook us all pancakes and bacon.*
96. *We always went out to eat as a family after church and discussed what we had learned at Sunday school.*

97. *My father would ask to talk to each of us kids personally when he called in from a trip.*

98. *We would all hold hands together when we said grace; then when we finished, we would squeeze the person's hand next to us three times, which stood for the three words, "I love you."*

99. *My mother would slow down when I helped her cook to let us accomplish the task together.*

100. *Even though I had never seen him cry before, my father cried during my wedding because he was going to miss me no longer being at home.*

Sounds like a lot of small things, doesn't it? Yet these small acts of love and acceptance left a lasting impression on these people's hearts. Each act was actually a decision a parent made to provide an element of the blessing to a child. A blessing that even now, years later, is remembered and cherished.

We could have included a list of "one hundred ways to bless your spouse, friends, or church family," but we're sure you get the idea. Providing the blessing to those we love can encourage and enrich their lives. It also does wonders for the one giving the blessing as well. We have looked at the children of one hundred families who provided the elements of the blessing to their children. Our prayer is that your family will become number one hundred and one.

## A PERSONAL MESSAGE

As we close this book and our look at the blessing, we hope you've been encouraged and challenged to be a person of blessing. But we don't want to leave you with just our thoughts on these pages. We would also like to leave you with our blessing for your life.

If we could reach out to each of you reading this book right now, and place our hands on your shoulder, our final blessing to you would be the words of Aaron, in the Old Testament (Num. 6:24–26).

May God enable you to become a mighty source of blessing, and may these words always ring true in your life:

*"The* LORD *bless you and keep you;*
*The* LORD *make His face to shine upon you,*
*And be gracious to you;*
*The* LORD *lift up His countenance upon you,*
*And give you peace."*

Gary Smalley                    John Trent

# Appendix A

## Evenings of Blessing to Apply with Your Loved Ones

*I*t's good to talk or read about the blessing, but putting its elements into practice is even better. That's why we want to give you four sample "Evenings of Blessing" that you can adapt and use with your loved ones.

What follows are suggestions we have either tried ourselves or know have been successful with other people or groups. The best way to use them is to take ideas from the sample evenings that follow and add your own special touches. (Then write us at Today's Family, 1482 Lakeshore Drive, Branson, MO 65616, and tell us the ways of blessing you've come up with and how your evening went. We're always looking for new ways to bless people and would love to hear yours.)

None of these ideas is sacred. One husband actually had a "Morning of Blessing" instead of an "Evening of Blessing" for his wife that included breakfast in bed. Be creative and have fun. Most of all, know that you can waste precious time on a thousand different things, but you will never waste one minute in blessing your loved ones.

## AN EVENING OF BLESSING FOR YOUR CHILDREN

*Goal:* That your children will know and experience your love for them in a special setting and in a unique way.

*Basic Idea:* Whether this evening happens once or several times a year, each child in the family would have a time when he or she experiences the elements of the blessing from his or her parents (or parent in a single-parent home).

*Possible Program:* We know several people who have tied their time of blessing in with a birthday celebration. Again, feel free to vary these suggestions so that they bless your uniquely special child.

1. Give your child(ren) several days' notice that this evening is coming. Half the fun for children is anticipating an event, particularly when it involves a special time for them!

2. Ask your child ahead of time what his or her favorite meal would be and use that as your guide for a festive dinner to begin the evening. Be prepared for peanut butter and hot dogs as a main course, topped off with chocolate cake for dessert (and then Rolaids on the side). Remember, this is your opportunity to honor them. That doesn't mean that you can't sneak in a vegetable or something nutritious, but it should be a meal your child feels is fit for that "king" or "queen" in your household.

3. Beginning with holding hands when you say grace at the meal, meaningful touching or hugging should be part of this time of blessing.

4. You can bless your children with a spoken message in several ways, attaching high value to them and providing them with the picture of a special future. Here are a few things you could try after dinner.

- Put together a slide show or picture album showing each year of the child's life that you have on film.
- Each parent can list five to ten things about that child that the parent has appreciated over the past year. (Try to pick character traits as well as accomplishments.)
- Each parent could also say a word about how these charac-

ter traits will help the son or daughter be a godly, helpful, or loving person in the years to come.

- Pick out an everyday object and use it as a word picture to share praise with your child, or to point out a talent God could use in the future. One dad we know used a sponge to picture his son! "Henry," he said, "this past year you've reminded me of a sponge. You've soaked up your Sunday school lessons like a sponge and then squeezed out big drops of love all over your little brothers and sister and your mom and me."

- Present your child with a homemade gift. This isn't the time for an early Christmas present. Make sure if you do give a gift it's something that your fingerprints are all over. One mother we know gave her daughter a beautiful afghan she had spent months working on that became the beginning of her daughter's hope chest.

- Some parents like to write out a "story of their child's birth" and read it to their child. This story talks about the special events of the nine months before birth, their mad dash to the hospital, and the indescribable joy of seeing their little one for the first time. It blesses children to know that they were planned and looked forward to (regardless of whether they came in our timing or not).

5. While it can be short, take the time to formally bless and pray for your child. (Be sure to look at Appendix B to see several sample blessings based on scriptural passages you may want to use.)

- Sing a hymn or a familiar chorus as a way of transition from slides or a fun story.

- Candles fascinate children (and many adults). The lighting of candles is an important part of blessing children in orthodox Jewish homes, and it's something you might want to try. This act can also be a good way to get the other children in the family involved.

- If your denomination permits, sharing Communion with older children is especially meaningful. This can also be a time to ask forgiveness if we have offended anyone in the

family and a chance to focus together on the cup of the blessing that represents Christ's love for us.
- Write out a few short sentences for you to read that express your love and appreciation for your child. This would be a special time to lay your hand on the child's shoulder or head while you bless him or her. Whether as a prayer, or with eyes open, your words can be something like the simple blessing below. Here's an example of a blessing for a boy named Joseph. (Again, look in Appendix B for other examples based on scriptural passages.)

"Thank You, Lord, for our son, Joseph. We ask that You be the source of his joy and the Source of his life. Help us as parents to love Joseph as You would have us love him. Thank You for the way he is already growing into the unique person You designed him to be. Lord, we know how special Joseph is to You, and tonight may he realize how valuable he is to us now and forever. May he become all You intend him to be, and we are honored that we are his parents. Bless us all now, for it's in Jesus' name we pray."

*Closing comments:* Again, these are just a few suggestions on how you could design an evening of blessing for your children. For some children, ending the evening with a special family activity or even a VCR movie they have picked out would be a "10" to them. Others may just want to talk to you or have a hug. However you design this evening, it can be a special and meaningful time for you and your children.

## AN EVENING OF BLESSING FOR YOUR SPOUSE

*Goal:* To set aside a meaningful time to provide your husband or wife with each of the elements of the blessing.

*Basic Idea:* Plan an evening for your spouse that will be a memorable time as he or she experiences your love and high value for him or her. While this evening can adopt some of the same elements that were a part of blessing a child, you can personalize this time for a husband or wife in several ways.

*Possible Program:* An anniversary is always a good time to provide a spouse with an evening of blessing. However, any evening apart from the children and away from the phone will do.

1. If there is money available, you might want to consider going to a hotel room for the night. Many nice hotels and resorts have special weekend rates when their weekday business guests are gone. If money is tight, why not try swapping houses with a close friend for one night. This means that you trade houses with another couple for one night (leaving your kids for them to babysit) and agree to swap with them at some future date. Swapping houses cuts the cost way down and still lets you have the privacy to really focus on each other.

2. As with the times of blessing in the Scriptures, a special meal is always a great way to start things off. Remember to include your spouse's favorite dish. Even if you have a coupon for a steak dinner, if he or she would rather have fish, honor that request.

3. You can communicate your love to your spouse by expressing your commitment to your marriage and by pointing out several of your spouse's endearing qualities. Here are some practical ways to do that:

- Write a "story of our marriage" where you recapture some of the drama and excitement of your courtship and of each season of your marriage. If you're not a writer, try making a tape recording of your fond memories. While talking into a microphone may seem a little awkward at first, this can leave a lasting record for your spouse of some of the things you appreciate about him or her.

- Photographs of special times together can be very endearing. Pictures bring back memories and memories bring back feelings. Just looking again at a few happy times you have shared together (without going overboard and showing ten trays of slides of your one fishing trip together) can do wonders to set a positive tone for the evening.

- Select one or several everyday objects to use as a word picture to communicate things you appreciate about your spouse. One husband used a bottle of "White Out" correcting fluid as a word picture to praise his wife. "Sweetheart," he said, "you remind me of this little bottle of 'White Out.'

Every time I make a mistake or do something to hurt you, you cover over my faults with your love like covering mistakes on a page. Every day with you, I get to start with a clean sheet of paper." Don't underestimate the power of such pictures! As we have stressed before, word pictures can leave a lasting positive impression on your spouse.

- One way to picture a special future for your spouse is to dig out your original wedding vows and repeat them. Something else that is special is to write a new set of vows that expresses your love and commitment. If you did not memorize and repeat your own set of vows during your wedding, here's your chance to do it!

Appendix B can give you some good ideas that you can apply to blessing your spouse.

- If your denomination permits, partaking in Communion as you re-commit your life to your spouse can be a beautiful and meaningful part of an evening of blessing.
- List ten reasons why, of all the guys or girls in the world, you would choose your spouse again to be your life-partner.
- Take an extended time to pray together, thanking God for each other and asking God to keep your love as fresh and refreshing as spring.

4. Since you've gone to all the trouble to get away for the weekend, meaningful touching as a married couple can take on a whole new meaning after a special evening of sharing words of love and commitment.

## AN EVENING FOR CHILDREN
## TO BLESS THEIR PARENTS

*Goal:* For children who have now grown up to take a special time to provide the elements of the blessing to their parents.

*Basic Idea:* Many parents are used to giving the elements of the blessing to their children, but they may not be as used to receiving them in return. In this evening, children have a chance to give back words of love and acceptance that they have received as a way of honoring their parents.

(If one parent has died or if your parents are divorced, do not avoid such an evening simply because it might remind the parent too much of the departed loved one. While we need to be sensitive, we can still honor the memory of a parent who has died and provide needed words of love and encouragement to the parent who remains behind. If your parents are divorced, at another private time you could share a time of blessing with your other parent.)

*Possible Program:* You might want to turn to the end of Chapter Thirteen to see some of the ways Don and his brother and sisters designed a special evening of blessing for their parents. Each set of parents is different, and it can be difficult for some parents to receive these words of love from their children. However, time and time again we have heard that embarrassed or uncomfortable parents have warmed up to their children's words of blessing and then treasured them for the rest of their lives.

PLEASE NOTE: While grandchildren are special in and of themselves to their grandparents, for this one evening they should be left at home with a babysitter. Children are wonderful and delightful, but they can also be distracting. The children should have their special time of blessing. This should be a time to focus all our attention on our parents.

1. If possible, try to gather each brother and sister together for this time of blessing. If someone absolutely can't make it for some reason, get them to send a tape recording of some words of blessing they can share with their parents. Why a tape? Listening to a person's voice has a way of putting them right in the room with you. Also, like taping the entire evening, it can give a parent a record of this missing child's thoughts.

2. What would an evening of blessing be without a special dinner! Parents like to eat, too—especially if you cook some of their favorite items, and then forbid them to help clean up the dishes.

3. Slides or old family photo albums can be a tremendous tool for remembering fun times in the past as a family. Again, don't overdo it. Remember the words Jack Benny once said to a reporter who asked him, "What do you want to be remembered for?" Benny replied, "I would like to have carved on my tombstone, 'Here lies a man who never bored his friends with home

movies!' " Pictures won't be boring to your parents, but be sensitive about how many you show.

4. Each child can then share five positive character traits that their parents built into their life. In other words, how are you a different person today because of the parents God has given you? Don and his brother and sisters shared in this way and it had an incredible impact. As you can tell, this activity will take some advance planning and careful thought on the part of each child. But the results will be well worth it.

5. Homemade gifts or a special portrait of the children might make a special gift for your parents at an evening of blessing.

6. Let's not forget how an everyday object used as a word picture can bring encouragement to your parents' hearts. One person we know told her mother, "Mom, when we were growing up, you reminded me of a fork. Your eyes were always sharp enough to catch us when we were doing something wrong, and you had more than one good point!" While you may not want to use a fork, we're sure at least twenty objects in the very room you're sitting in could be used to point out the high value of your parents.

7. A special time of prayer for our parents, with everyone gathered around them arm in arm, can be a memorable way to close such an evening. Don't expect this to be an emotionless time. While we can share love with each other by laughing together, it is also healing to cry together. This is not to say we should try to force any emotions, but rather allow both tears and laughter to be a part of the evening.

*Closing Comments:* Many people wait too long to share words of blessing with their parents, or they simply don't know how to do it. Armed with all the suggestions above, what's stopping you from honoring your parents with an evening of blessing? Forget about giving them an all-expense-paid trip to the Bahamas as a way of showing you love them. Expressing your love and appreciation for them is the best present you could ever give them. (But don't let them know you substituted their trip to the Bahamas for this time of blessing!)

## AN EVENING OF BLESSING
## WITH YOUR CHURCH FAMILY

You say it has been too long since you had a church potluck dinner? Here's a special evening with your church family that can help you get to know new people, honor those who have served the Lord in a special way, and learn more about blessing God all in one!

*Goal:* To provide an evening when our church family can come together to bless each other and bless the Lord.

*Basic Idea:* Invite church families to a potluck dinner that centers around the theme of "blessing."

*Possible Program:* Talk about having fun while you're doing something meaningful. Watching a popular television program can't hold a candle to the excitement and light of God's love that can flow through a time when the church family is gathered to bless each other.

1. Ask each family to bring a main course to feed their own family, and then a dish to share that says something about their roots. For example, one family's origins might be Swedish and they could bring Swedish meatballs. Another family might be French and they could bring pastries or even French onion soup. If they are all-American they can bring hot dogs or even apple pie. If they're not up on their ethnic roots, they could bring a dish that represents their geographical roots. For example, if one family is from Washington State, they could bring baked apples. Each family should label their dish as to its origins. Sharing a meal like this is a great way to get to know a little bit about the background of people in the church.

2. As an admission ticket to get into the dinner, each adult should be required to bring a verse from the Bible that has been a blessing in his or her life. Just before grace is said, or later in the program, the pastor or program leader can randomly call on a table and have someone there share his or her favorite verse. Or each person could share his or her verse with the others at the table as a way to encourage each other and get to know each other better.

3. You will bless the children and parents who attend by providing child care for the little ones before the more serious part of the evening begins. After the meal would be a good time to have the little ones march out to a movie or to special games.

4. We are told in the Scriptures to bless the Lord. What better way to do so than with our church family and friends. Here are some ways this can happen during the evening program:

- Sing several songs in your hymnal that focus on the theme of God's blessing us or our blessing Him. Hymns or choruses like "Make Me a Blessing" and "Bless the Lord, O My Soul" can be a meaningful way to bless our Lord with song.
- We are told to bless God's holy name. Ask the pastor or a church leader to talk briefly about the names of God in the Scriptures and how each name gives us a new reason to praise Him.
- Communion is a tremendous way for us to come face to face with God's priceless blessing in sacrificing His Son for our sins. Even the Scriptures tell us that Communion is a "blessing." In 1 Corinthians 10:16 we read, "The cup of blessing which we bless, is it not the communion of the blood of Christ?" In keeping with preparation for Communion, perhaps if someone in the congregation has dishonored someone else in some way, he or she can be encouraged to go to that person and ask his or her forgiveness to set things right.
- In some churches, a foot-washing service could be another way to bow the knee to our brother or sister in Christ by humbling ourselves to wash another's feet.
- One church had a large, blank poster at the front of the room. Each table had pencils, paper, and straight pins. After a short message on how faithful God had been in blessing the congregation over the years, the pastor asked people to write down one way in which God had blessed them over the past year. Then anyone who wanted could come up to the front, read or share how God had blessed them, and pin their paper on the blank poster. By the end of the evening, dozens of testimonies to God's gracious blessings were pinned to that poster.
- This time can even be used to bless other people in the

church for a job well done or simply for being a good friend or godly example. You might even want to ask people to come prepared to share word pictures that illustrate traits they appreciate about another member of the congregation.
- Close the ceremony of blessing by holding hands and singing a closing chorus or benediction. If the early church could greet each other with a holy hug and kiss, we should at least be able to take each other's hands as we close this time of blessing.

Can you imagine what would happen if parents, spouses, adult children, and even entire churches put these evenings of blessing into practice? So many people's lives would change for the better that it would drive us out of a job when it comes to marriage and family counseling. And we'd love it! We hope you'll adopt even one evening of blessing described above as a model for designing one of your own and that it will prove to be one of the most encouraging times in your loved one's and your own life.

# Appendix B

## Sample Blessings
## Based on the Scriptures

*These are some ways that you can bless your children or even your mate by inserting his or her name where the blank is on each passage.*

*H*ow blessed _____ will be because you do not walk in the counsel of the wicked, nor stand in the path of sinners, nor do you sit in the seat of scoffers. But as your parents we have seen you delight in the law of the Lord. You have been thinking about His law day and night. May God make you, _____, like a tree firmly planted by streams of water. May God allow you to grow and bear His fruit in His season and your life will not wither and whatever you shall do, it will prosper!" (Psalm 1)

"O Lord may _____ always abide in Thy love. May [he] dwell in Your holy presence. May [he] walk with integrity and do works of righteousness. May [he] speak truth in [his] heart and not slander with [his] tongue nor do evil to [his] friends, nor get revenge on [his] friends.

"May _____ despise being a reprobate and value those who honor You. May [he] always keep [his] word for the good of others and not cheat [his] friends or use their misfortune for "[his] benefit, nor take bribes against the innocent. Consequently You Lord, have promised that _____ will never be shaken." (Psalm 15)

"O Lord, may _____ come to know Your wisdom and instruction. May [he] discern the sayings of understanding, may [he] receive the instruction in wise behavior, righteousness, justice, and equity. May You Lord give [him] prudence, knowledge, and discretion. May [he] truly listen and increase in learning, always seeking wise counsel. May [he] come to understand the greatest of all Your instructions, to love and value You with all [his] heart. Then will [he] begin to know knowledge." (Proverbs 1)

"Lord, may _____ trust in You with all [his] heart and may [he] not lean on [his] own understanding. But may [he] seek to know what You would want [him] to do in all [he] does. Then You have promised to make [his] paths straight." (Proverbs 3:5–6)

"May _____ never try to be wise in [his] own eyes, but may [he] learn to value You above all else and keep turning away from evil ways and thinking.
"Then You have promised to heal [his] body and refresh [his] bones." (Proverbs 3:7–8)

"Lord, may _____ never lose the willingness to turn from reproof. Behold then You have promised to pour out Your spirit on [him] and to make Your words known to [him]! If [he] does not turn to Your ways You have also promised to refuse to listen to [his] cry or grab [his] hand in distress.

"May _____ never neglect Your counsel nor turn from Your counsel nor turn from Your reproof." (Proverbs 1:23–25)

"My [son or daughter] _____:
If you will:

- Receive and believe what God says
- Treasure with high value His commandments

- Listen attentively to His wisdom
- Draw your heart to understanding Him
- Cry out for discernment
- Raise your voice for understanding
- Seek Him more than silver or hidden treasures

"Then you, _____, will understand how to honor God.

"God will give you knowledge and wisdom. From Him you will receive understanding for God has been storing up wisdom for you because you have sought Him above all else.

"He will be your shield, your bodyguard, and He will preserve your way." (Proverbs 2:1–8)

"Oh Lord, may _____ never forget Your teaching. Let [his] heart keep Your commandments. Then, Lord, You will give _____ many more days and years to [his] life and You will add peace to [his] life.

"May kindness and truth never leave [him]. Lord, may [he] bind them around [his] neck and write them on [his] heart.

"Then, Lord, You will give [him] favor and a good reputation both with You and man." (Proverbs 3:1–4)

# *Notes*

## Chapter 2

1. Gerhard Kittel & Geoffrey W. Bromiley, *Theological Dictionary of the New Testament, Vol. II* (Grand Rapids, MI: W. B. Eerdmans Publishing Co., 1964), p. 755.
2. Francis Brown, S. R. Driver, and Charles A. Briggs, *A Hebrew and English Lexicon of the Old Testament* (Oxford: Clarendon Press, reprinted edition, 1974), p. 139.
3. David Hunt & T. A. McMahon, *The Seduction of Christianity* (Eugene, Ore.: Harvest House, 1985), pp. 28-29.
4. Nathan Ausbubel, *The Book of Jewish Knowledge* (New York: Crown Publishers, 1964), p. 98.
5. J. A. Thompson, *The Bible and Archaeology* (Grand Rapids: Wm. B. Eerdmans Publishing, 1972 edition), p. 26.
6. K. A. Kitchen, *Ancient Orient and Old Testament* (Chicago: Inter-Varsity Press, 1966), p. 154.
7. C. H. Gordon, "Illustrations from Pre-Nuzi Data on Biblical Archaeology," *The Biblical Archaeologist*, vol. 3, 1940, p. 5.
8. Changing the blessing between children was indeed quite common in the Ancient Near East during Biblical times. For example, a father named Tupkitilla of Nuzi sold one son's blessing to another

for three sheep! C. H. Gordon, *Tyndale House Bulletin*, vol. 17, (1966), p. 71.

9. Ausbubel, *Book of Jewish Knowledge*, p. 355.
10. A. Cohen, *Everyman's Talmud* (New York: Schocken Books, 1975), p. 171.
11. Ibid.
12. How do we know that this group of children was both boys and girls? The Greek word used for *young children* in Mark 10:13 is *paidion*. (See William F. Arndt and R. Wilbur Gingrich, eds., *A Greek-English Lexicon of the New Testament and other Early Christian Literature* [Chicago: University of Chicago Press, 1957, p. 609].) This was a general word used for little children of both sexes. There are specific Greek words that could have been used if the group was of all boys or all girls.

## *Chapter 3*
1. Robert Salt, "Affectionate Touch between Fathers and Preadolescent Sons," *Journal of Marriage and the Family*, vol. 53, August 1991, p. 545.
2. Job 41:15–17; also see Brown, Driver, and Briggs, p. 621.
3. Robert Salt, "Affectionate Touch Between Fathers and Preadolescent Sons," p. 545.
4. Ibid.
5. Ibid.
6. As we mentioned in Chapter Two, the blessing of Ephraim and Manasseh also had a unique spiritual message. When Jacob "crossed" his hands and blessed the younger with the older son's blessing, it was a picture of God's election.
7. Charles F. Pfeiffer, Howard F. Vos, and John Rea, editors, *Wycliffe Bible Encyclopedia* (Chicago: Moody Press, 1975), p. 750.
8. Harvey Richard Schiffman, *Sensation and Perception: An Integrated Approach* (New York: John Wiley & Sons, 1982), p. 107.
9. Frank A. Geldard, "Body English," *Psychology Today*, December 1968, p. 44.
10. Dolores Krieger, "Therapeutic Touch: The Imprimatur of Nursing," *American Journal of Nursing*, May 1975, p. 784.
11. *UCLA Monthly*, Alumni Association News, March-April 1981, p. 1.
12. *Reader's Digest*, vol. 140, January 1992, p. 21.
13. *Current Health*, vol. 13, no. 2, 1986, p. 13.

14. *Parents,* vol. 64, no. 2, 1989.
15. L. W. Linkous & R. M. Stutts, "Passive Tactile Stimulation Effects on the Muscle Tone of Hypotonic Developmentally Delayed Young Children," *Perceptual and Motor Skills,* vol. 1, no. 3, December 1990, pp. 951–954.
16. F. B. Dresslar, "The Psychology of Touch," *American Journal of Psychology,* vol. 6, 1984, p. 316.
17. Marcia Mark & Perla Werner, "Agitation and Touch in the Nursing Home," *Psychological Reports,* vol. 64, no. 3, part 2, 1989, p. 1020.
18. Ibid., p. 1023.
19. *Health,* vol. 21, no. 10, October 1989, p. 73.
20. James Hardison, *Let's Touch* (New Jersey: Prentice-Hall, 1980).
21. Helen Colton, *The Gift of Touch* (New York: Seaview/Putnam, 1983), p. 102.
22. *Reader's Digest,* p. 21.
23. Edgar Wycoff & Jill Holley, "Effects of Flight Attendant's Touch upon Airline Passenger's Perceptions of the Attendant and the Airline," *Perceptual and Motor Skills,* vol. 1, no. 3, part 1, December 1990, pp. 932–934.
24. Colton, *The Gift of Touch,* p. 49.
25. Arthur Janov, "For Control, Cults Must East the Most Profound Pains," *Los Angeles Times,* Dec. 10, 1978, part 6, p. 3.
26. Marc H. Hollender, "The Wish to Be Held," *Archives of General Psychiatry,* vol. 22, 1970, p. 445.
27. Ibid., p. 446.
28. Ross Campbell, *How to Really Love Your Child* (Wheaton, Ill.: Victor Books, 1977), p. 73.
29. Alfred Edersheim, *The Life and Times of Jesus the Messiah, Part Two* (Grand Rapids: Wm. B. Eerdmans Publishing Co., 1972), p. 329.
30. Sidney Jourand, *Psychology Today,* vol. 22, no. 3, March 1988, p. 31.

## *Chapter 4*

1. Gary Smalley, *The Key to Your Child's Heart* (Waco, TX: Word Books, Inc., 1984). See the chapter on "Balancing Loving Support Through Contracts," pp. 77–107.
2. Jack Burton, "Goodbye . . . Be good to each other." Article in *USA Today,* August 19, 1985, p. 1.

## Chapter 5

1. To "value" something in the Scriptures is captured in the word *honor* that we looked at in Chapter Two. See also, Arndt and Gingrich, editors, *A Greek-English Lexicon of the New Testament and other Early Christian Literature* (Chicago: The University of Chicago Press, 1957), p. 825.
2. Brown, Driver, and Briggs, *Hebrew Lexicon*, p. 139.
3. Ibid.
4. That is why Psalm 95:6 translates the word *bless* as "to bow the knee" when it says, "Come let us worship the Lord and *bow before Him*" (literally *bless* Him).
5. J. D. Douglas, "Lion of Judah," *New Bible Dictionary* (Grand Rapids: Wm. B. Eerdmans Publishing, 1971 edition), p. 742.
6. Some circles dispute how Solomon, with all his many wives, could be a model for a godly marriage. One can see a commentary on the Song of Solomon for a fuller explanation, but in brief here are two reasons why we feel Solomon's story can still help any married couple today. First, Solomon did not begin to take foreign wives and concubines until later in life, after his visit by the Queen of Sheba. This book is dated by most scholars as being written early in his reign as king. Most importantly, *any person* including Solomon could leave their first love when they stop walking with God. During Solomon's later years when he took many wives, his fellowship with God was certainly not where it was when he asked for the gift of wisdom.
7. S. Craig Glickman, *A Song for Lovers* (Downers Grove, IL: Inter-Varsity Press, 1974), p. 48.

## Chapter 6

1. M. J. Cohen, *The Jewish Celebration Book* (Philadelphia: The Jewish Publication Society of America, 1946), p. 108.
2. Jay Stifler, *The Epistle to the Romans* (Chicago: Moody Press, 1983), p. 119.
3. While we do not recommend the book because of its secular bent and conclusions, William S. Appleton's *Fathers and Daughters* (New York: Berkley Books, 1984) has a number of chilling studies that have been done on the destruction that happens when a father has a poor relationship with his daughter.

4. We would like to extend our special thanks to Dr. Jeffry M. Trent, Associate Professor of Medicine, University of Arizona, for putting this example into "everyday English" for us.

## Chapter 7

1. For a helpful discussion on this point, see Charles Swindoll, *You and Your Child* (Nashville: Thomas Nelson Publishers, 1977), pp. 27-32.
2. Gary Smalley, *The Key to Your Child's Heart* (Word, 1984), Chapter Two, "Expressing Loving Support—The Most Important Aspect of Raising Children."
3. Smalley, *The Key to Your Child's Heart*, Chapter Seven, "The Secret of a Close Knit Family."
4. Dewey Roussel, "Message of the White Dove," published in *Reader's Digest*, September 1984, p. 29.

## Chapter 8

1. For an excellent discussion of our need today for a time of "Sabbath rest," see Gordon MacDonald's *Ordering Your Private World* (Nashville: Thomas Nelson, 1984), the chapter titled "Rest Beyond Leisure."
2. Quoted by Roger Hawley, "The Family Blessing: Implications for Counseling." Unpublished paper presented at the Texas Council of Family Relations Conference, 1983.

## Chapter 9

1. H. Norman Schwarzkopf with Peter Petre, *It Doesn't Take a Hero* (New York: Bantam Books, 1992), p. 19.
2. Quotation by Rev. Steven Lyon in "Loving Your Children God's Way," unpublished message given in Dallas, Texas, 1983.
3. Robert Barnes, *You're Not My Daddy! Winning the Heart of Your Stepchild* (Dallas: Word Books, 1992).
4. An excellent book we would recommend that deals with the impact family influences can have on both the creation and cure of substance abuse is entitled *Good News for the Chemically Dependent* by Jeffery VanVonderen (Nashville: Thomas Nelson, 1985).
5. Richard A. McCormick, "Affective Disorders Among Pathological Gamblers Seeking Treatment," *American Journal of Psychiatry*, vol. 141, no. 2, p. 215.

## Chapter 10
1. See the book by Martin Seligman, *Learned Optimism* (New York: Pocket Books, 1990).
2. Christopher Peterson & Lisa M. Bossio, *Health and Optimism* (New York: The Free Press, 1991), p. 81.

## Chapter 12
1. Stephen Thayer, "Close Encounters," *Psychology Today,* vol. 22, no. 3, March 1988, p. 33.
2. Ibid., p. 34.
3. *Hebrew Lexicon,* p. 174.

## Chapter 13
1. *Hebrew Lexicon,* p. 457.
2. Ibid., p. 866.
3. Arndt & Gingrich, *Greek-English Lexicon,* p. 317.
4. Gerald C. Davison & John M. Neale, *Abnormal Psychology* (New York: John Wiley & Sons, 1978), pp. 135ff.

## Chapter 15
1. Ken Medema, sound recording, *Through the Eyes of Love,* Word Records.

# The GIFT of HONOR

# Contents

*Chapter 1*  Joining the Battle . . . . . . . . . . . . . . . . . . . . . . . . . . 273

*Chapter 2*  The Gift of Honor . . . . . . . . . . . . . . . . . . . . . . . . . 284

### We Give Our Children the Gift of Honor By . . .

*Chapter 3*  Extending the Gift First to Our Own Parents . . . . . . . 295

*Chapter 4*  Helping Our Children Find Value in
              Troubled Times: Part 1 . . . . . . . . . . . . . . . . . . . . . . 313

*Chapter 5*  Helping Our Children Find Value in
              Troubled Times: Part 2 . . . . . . . . . . . . . . . . . . . . . . 326

*Chapter 6*  Recognizing Our Own Parenting Strengths
              and Style . . . . . . . . . . . . . . . . . . . . . . . . . . . . . . . 339

*Chapter 7*  Providing a Healthy Balance in Our Homes: Part 1 . . 352

*Chapter 8*  Providing a Healthy Balance in Our Homes: Part 2 . . 362

*Chapter 9*  Establishing Loving Boundaries: Part 1 . . . . . . . . . . 379

*Chapter 10*  Establishing Loving Boundaries: Part 2 . . . . . . . . . . 389

*Chapter 11*  Establishing Loving Boundaries: Part 3 . . . . . . . . . . 401

*Chapter 12*  Establishing Loving Boundaries: Part 4 . . . . . . . . . . 411

*Chapter 13*  Building Positive Loyalties: Part 1 . . . . . . . . . . . . . . 419

*Chapter 14*  Building Positive Loyalties: Part 2 . . . . . . . . . . . . . . 430

*Chapter 15*  Understanding the Dark Side of Family
              Loyalties: Part 1 . . . . . . . . . . . . . . . . . . . . . . . . . . 438

*Chapter 16*  Understanding the Dark Side of Family
              Loyalties: Part 2 . . . . . . . . . . . . . . . . . . . . . . . . . . 448

*Chapter 17*  Offering Honor to God . . . . . . . . . . . . . . . . . . . . . . 463

*Chapter 18*  Honoring Others in Action . . . . . . . . . . . . . . . . . . . 473

*Notes* . . . . . . . . . . . . . . . . . . . . . . . . . . . . . . . . . . . . . . . . . . . . . 480

# *Dedication*

*This book is dedicated to Zoa Trent, John's mother. A tremendous model of a parent who honors her children, she was a great help on this book.*

# Acknowledgments

We would like to express our deepest thanks to the following people:

To Darryl DelHousaye, Bill Yarger, and Tom Rietveld, three of our supportive pastors in our home church who took the time to review and critique this book and offer their suggestions.

To Doug Childress for again being a loving "critic" and a great source of encouragement.

To Diana Trent, for her hard work in proofreading the manuscript.

To Larry Weeden, Susan Salmon, and the rest of the editorial staff at Thomas Nelson for working so diligently with us in meeting deadlines.

To Terry Brown, our teammate in ministry, for covering even more bases than usual while we were away writing this book.

To Ken Gire at Insight for Living and Steve Laube at our local Christian bookstore for taking time out of very busy schedules to give us their wisdom and insights into the concept of honor.

And to Wendy Ragan, our dear friend at Thomas Nelson, who has been such an encouragement to us and to many other authors at Thomas Nelson over the years.

# *Preface*

Whether we realize it or not, the value we attach to God, our children, and ourselves can greatly determine the success or failure of all our relationships. Indeed, nothing will do more to build healthy families than learning to give and receive the gift of honor.

No matter how old our children are, it's never too late to start honoring them. As we learn more about the biblical concept of honor and as we apply this principle, we do all we can to save our children the heartbreak of damaged relationships. We give them the foundation they will need to develop a deeper maturity when leaving home and cleaving to their mates.

*If you would like more information about the authors' national speaking schedule or other books and cassette tapes, please write to:*
*Today's Family, P.O. Box 22111, Phoenix, AZ 85028.*

# Chapter One

## Joining the Battle

Something took place in the fall of 1944 that can explain a major reason many children are facing a losing battle in today's families. It was late October when an officer commanding a platoon of American soldiers received a call from headquarters. Over the radio, this captain learned his unit was being ordered to recapture a small French city from the Nazis—and he learned something else from headquarters as well. For weeks, French Resistance fighters had risked their lives to gather information about the German fortifications in that city, and they had smuggled this information out to the Allies.

The French Underground's efforts had provided the Americans with something worth its weight in gold: a detailed map of the city. It wasn't just a map with the names of major streets and landmarks; it showed specific details of the enemy's defensive positions.

Indeed, the map even identified shops and buildings where German soldiers bunked or where a machine-gun nest or a sniper had been stationed. Block by block, the Frenchmen gave an accounting of the German units and the gun emplacements they manned.

For a captain who was already concerned about mounting casualty lists, receiving such information was an answer to prayer. Although the outcome of the war wouldn't depend on this one skirmish, to him it meant that he wouldn't have to write as many letters to his men's parents or wives telling them their loved one had been cut down in battle.

Before the soldiers moved out to take their objective, the captain gave each man a chance to study the map. And wanting to make sure his men read it carefully, he hurriedly gave them a test covering the major landmarks and enemy strongholds. Just before his platoon moved out, the officer graded the tests, and with minor exceptions every man earned a perfect score. As a direct result of having that map to follow, the men captured the city with little loss of American lives.

Nearly thirty years after this military operation took place, an army researcher heard the story and decided to base a study on it.[1] The project began in France, where instead of a platoon of soldiers, he arranged for a group of American tourists to help him with his research.

For several hours, the men and women were allowed to study the same map the soldiers had, and then they were given the same test. You can guess the results. Most of the tourists failed miserably.

The reason for the difference between these two groups was obvious—motivation. Knowing their lives were on the line, the soldiers were highly motivated to learn every detail of the map. For the tourists, being in a research study provided some motivation. But most of them had nothing to lose but a little pride if they failed the test.

What does this story have to do with honoring our children? Actually, a great deal. What took place in that village years ago is applicable to the war taking place in many homes and affecting many children today.

In our secular society, when it comes to the battle our children face with feeling insignificant and of low value, many of us act like tourists. With all the intensity of people on a month-long vacation, many of us look at the Scriptures or a Christian book as we do passing scenery through a car window. Not realizing what's at stake, we expend little energy on discovering and putting into practice specific ways to value our children. Little do we know that many sons and daughters, perhaps a child living right under our own roof, may be under tremendous attack in a losing battle to honor God, themselves, or others.

Thankfully, not all parents are so naive. Just the fact that you're reading a book like this marks you as concerned and special! Like the soldiers who knew what was at stake in studying that map, some parents have the motivation and desire to learn how to raise their children's sense of value.

What we hope to do in this book is to alert parents to the battle going on in many children's lives and to the terrible results that can come from experiencing the emotional wounds of a dishonoring home. Even more, our desire is to provide parents with a detailed map that points out not only enemy strongholds to avoid but also seven different safety zones that moms and dads can use to build high value in their children.

In calling parents to arms, we're certainly not saying that this is the "final" book on building self-worth in a child or loved one. Of first importance we have the Scriptures, and there are many other good, biblically based books that can help us encourage our children.[2] Yet regardless of what books we take down from the shelf, we need to have an intensity and a willingness to learn and apply biblical principles. Only then can we attack a problem that can emotionally cripple our children.

## BLESSING CHILDREN AND BEYOND

How serious a problem is growing up without love and acceptance? Is it really a "battle" our children face or simply an insignificant skirmish?

Several months ago, we looked at these very questions in a book we wrote called *The Blessing*. In that book, we looked at the Old Testament concept of "blessing" children and what it was like for children today to grow up with or without their parents' love and acceptance. In particular, we discussed five specific things parents did in biblical times, and could do today, to attach high value to their children. We also looked at several homes that commonly withhold this blessing and the emotional damage that often faces children who grow up in them.

Since that book was published, we have been flooded with letters and calls from men and women who have told us their tragic stories, and even more tragic results, of missing out on their families' blessing. And while we knew from our counseling and conferences that this was a problem, we had no idea how deeply it ran and how many people it affected.

While *The Blessing* seemed to unearth this problem and gave parents several practical ways they could encourage and build up their children, we began looking in the Scriptures for additional tools they could use. Our search led us to study in depth the concept of "honor" and, as a result, to seven additional steps parents can take to build a lasting sense of love and acceptance into their children. Unfortunately, it also taught us more than we wanted to know about the devastating results of growing up in a "dishonoring" home.

How deeply can it hurt a child to grow up being dishonored and feeling of little worth to parents and other loved ones? Just ask Denny. Years of living in just such an environment not only significantly damaged him in all his relationships, but also brought him to the breaking point one winter night.

## THE DAMAGING RESULTS OF A DISHONORING HOME

Football practice was over, and Denny was sore from head to toe. He walked slowly down the rows of aging apartment buildings, each drab gray in the fading winter sun. Coming to his own building, he pushed open the heavy aluminum door and began to walk slowly up the two flights of stairs to his family's apartment. The stairway walls were covered with years of graffiti and holes where the plaster had been torn loose, yet nothing caught Denny's attention—until he reached the second floor landing.

Suddenly, his head shot up and his schoolbooks dropped from his hands. Shivers ran up and down his body as he heard through the apartment door the all too familiar sounds of his mother's screaming.

For years Denny had tried to calm his father during his many angry rampages. His dad's drunken fits of rage usually left one of Denny's brothers or sisters (or more often his mother) black and blue. Yet this time would be different. This was the last straw!

An award-winning football player in a city famous for hard-nosed athletes, Denny ripped open the door and charged at his dad. Not caring about the consequences of his actions, he could only think of the times he had been brutalized by his father.

As a boy growing up, Denny could never find a place safe from his father's anger. He had tried hiding under the house, and his father found and beat him. Another time, he had crawled into the narrow space between the refrigerator and the kitchen cabinet to hide, but his father discovered him and kicked him into the corner until he finally tired of the sport. Too many nights, his mother would meet him at the door, and the family would drive around town, waiting for his father to get so drunk he finally passed out.

This had to stop. Although Denny was several inches shorter than his father, working with weights had made him stronger than his dad, who had been a steel worker for years. Now, his eyes red with fury and his adrenaline pumping, Denny tore his father off his mother. He hit him twice in quick succession, and as his father reeled back, he screamed and rammed into his father like a raging bull, knocking him to the floor. Then, with years of burning memories giving him lion-like strength, he lifted his father and threw him through the second-story window.

The deafening sounds of shattering glass, his mother's screaming, and his father's crashing from an aluminum canopy down to the yard below echoed inside the room. Denny ran down the stairs and over to his father, who was already sitting up in the yard. They were amazed to see that although his father was shaken and had a number of superficial cuts, nothing was broken. Grabbing his father by the front of his shirt, Denny pulled him up and with cold fury spat the words into his face, "If you ever touch any of us again, I'll kill you!"

Shortly after this incident, Denny left home for good, but no matter how far he traveled, he never escaped its memories. Because he had come from a dishonoring home, he knew how to live with anger and mistrust, but not with warmth and love. Every relationship Denny entered—including two marriages and a string of friendships shattered by his fiery temper—turned into a repeat performance of the tragedy he had left behind. Unfortunately, at the root of many of his problems was alcoholism—something Denny had sworn would never destroy his life as it had his father's.

Just another story of someone with a tragic background? Hardly. In the last chapter of this book, we'll reveal what Denny learned during the lowest point in his life that totally turned him around. What he learned and decided to apply in his life is what this book is all about.

Through a caring friend at work, Denny learned for the first time what it meant to give honor to God and how, for most of his life, he had done nothing but dishonor Him. All his life he had longed to be valued and accepted, and now he discovered the very source of significance and life itself.

Not only did Denny learn to honor God, but he also learned to apply honor to each of his important relationships. Denny discovered that instead of being an abstract concept, honor was something he could and should give to his wife, his children, his friends—and miraculously—even to his father. As Denny learned about the positive benefits of honoring God and others, his life changed so dramatically that years after throwing his father through a window, he was able to call him on the phone and tell him he loved him—an event that opened the door to dramatic changes in his dad's life.

## A NEEDED INGREDIENT IN EVERYDAY HOMES

We realize that Denny's story represents an extreme. Thankfully, most parents do their best to genuinely love their children, and most children never have to face the degree of dishonor and hurt that Denny did. However, all parents need to know what actions honor their children and which ones lower their sense of self-worth.

You might be thinking, *But my little Jimmy and Suzy are doing great! Why do I need to invest time in learning to combat a problem they're not even facing today?*

What we have discovered in talking with people across the country is that the results of dishonoring parental actions accumulate over time. On numerous occasions, we have counseled with well-meaning mothers and fathers who sat in our office in bewilderment and shock over their son or daughter's self-destructive behavior. Others have been just as shocked when they discovered drug abuse, promiscuity, or other damaging patterns in their children's lives.

As youngsters, many of these children showed little or no evidence of the problems they face as adolescents today. And very often as we began to look back into the history of these children, we found that their parents had no idea of honoring actions they were leaving out of their children's lives and dishonoring actions they were allowing to accumulate.

During World War II, Winston Churchill said, "All that has to happen for evil to prevail in the world is for good men to do nothing." In our twisted society today, parents need more than simply good intentions when it comes to raising secure, confident children—they need a plan. And while things may be going well today, we need to take the offensive to understand what it means to honor our children and raise their sense of self-worth and what actions to avoid that can lower it.

"It could never happen to my child!" some might say. Let's look, however, at some of the problems children from "average" homes often face, children whose parents never understood the tragic results of their dishonoring actions.

## COMMON EFFECTS OF DISHONORING HOMES

- Drug and alcohol abuse[3]
- Chronic lying[4]
- Procrastination[5]
- Extreme pride and self-centeredness (narcissism)[6]
- Workaholism and the need to achieve more and more[7]
- Vicious emotional cycles[8]
- Repeated absences from church and school[9]
- Extreme submission[10]
- Unhealthy legalism[11]
- Severe withdrawal from society[12]
- Sexual difficulties in marriage[13]
- Lower academic achievement[14]
- Feelings of loss of control[15]
- Stress-related heart problems[16]
- Homosexuality[17]
- Deep feelings of loneliness[18]
- Suicidal thinking and attempts[19]
- Problems with delinquency[20]
- Poor mate selection in marriage[21]
- Clinical depression[22]
- Poor decision making[23]
- Lowered career achievement[24]
- A pattern of outbursts of anger[25]
- Low energy in accomplishing school or work tasks[26]
- Extreme self-criticism[27]
- Gravitation toward cults and fringe religious groups[28]
- Having unrealistic expectations of self and others[29]

Emotionally healthy parents wouldn't want to see their children experience the terrible heartache represented in these problems. Yet without realizing it, some parents lead their children down these very paths.

How can we work to avoid these things in our children's lives? How can we do battle against such problems and build value into their lives? At the heart of making our children or anyone else feel valuable, loved, and accepted is a decision to *honor* them.

## THE GIFT OF HONOR

When you think of what it means to honor someone, what may come to mind is attending a retirement party, meeting the president, or standing with a crowd of fans cheering for a favorite team after they've won "the" game. It's also normal to think of it as something that goes only in one direction—usually toward a superior or someone who has "earned" or "deserves" it. However, as you will see throughout this book, when the Scriptures talk about giving honor to God or to loved ones, they don't leave such a fuzzy definition. Instead, they give a crystal clear picture that honoring someone involves viewing him as a priceless treasure and treating him with loving respect. They also show that while honoring God is based on His worthiness, honoring others is something that can be passed on to loved ones regardless of whether they "deserve" it or not. We believe the next statement summarizes this entire book:

> **Honor is a decision we make to place high value, worth, and importance on another person by viewing him or her as a priceless gift and granting him or her a position in our lives worthy of great respect; and Love involves putting that decision into action.**

When Jesus was asked to name the great commandments in the Scriptures, He didn't hesitate in the least. He told a young lawyer, "Love the LORD your God with all your heart, with all your soul, and with all your mind. . . . You shall love your neighbor as yourself."[30] Loving God, loving others, and finding value in ourselves. Without a doubt, these three aspects of love are the most effective weapons against the destructive power of low self-worth, and communicating loving actions is what this book is all about.

Genuine love is a gift we give others. It isn't purchased by their actions or contingent upon our emotions at the moment. It may carry with it strong emotional feelings, but it isn't supported by them. Rather, it is a decision we make on a daily basis that someone is special and valuable to us.

Like genuine love, honor is a gift we give to someone. It involves the decision we make *before* we put love into action that a person is of high value. In fact, love for someone often begins to flow once we have made the decision to honor him.

Our goal in this book is to combat low self-worth by explaining how to treasure our loved ones and how to communicate to them that they have a special place in our lives. As we've seen in Denny's case and in each of the effects of a dishonoring home, this is especially important for children. When we give our children the gift of honor—that is, when we learn how to communicate to them in tangible ways that they are deeply loved and highly valued—it goes a long way toward combating future problems in their lives.

That's why we're excited about sharing with you a practical definition of what it means to honor others and seven ways you can apply it in their lives. These are seven aspects of honor that you can apply and act out on a daily basis and raise your children's value as a result. These are honoring attitudes that can

---

**We give our children the gift of honor by . . .**
- extending it first to our own parents.
- helping them find value in troubled times.
- recognizing our own parenting strengths and style.
- providing a healthy balance in our homes.
- establishing loving boundaries.
- building positive loyalties.
- offering honor to God.

---

shape parenting actions and encourage children. These *aren't* a seven-part formula or seven simple, foolproof steps. Each of the seven aspects of honor will be expanded in a later section of the book.

While we'll be directing these seven aspects of honor primarily toward our children, they can help us enrich each of our relationships. They can help us increase our value of God and enable us to learn what it means to honor a spouse. Friends can give honor to one another, and churches to those they seek to minister to. Employees can find a new reason to value their employers, and employers to respect their employees.

## GETTING BACK TO THE BATTLE

We began this chapter by sounding the call for parents to join the battle against a major destroyer of children—their feeling valueless and insignificant. We can't stress enough how important each day is in waging this war. If we sit back, fold our hands, and neglect building self-worth in our children, one day King Solomon's words may come true in their lives or our own. When this wise king wrote about the sluggard, he made this comment:

> *A little sleep, a little slumber,*
> *A little folding of the hands to rest;*
> *So your poverty will come like a prowler,*
> *And your want like an armed man.*[31]

If we act like tourists or sluggards when it comes to building value into our children, heartache may enter our homes as stealthily as a prowler, or discouragement may burst upon us as forcefully as an armed man.

No matter how old your children are, it's never too late to unfold your hands and start honoring them. When you consistently apply this concept, you save them the heartache of damaged relationships, and you also give them the foundation they will need to truly value God, themselves, and others.

Parents, do your children (and yourself) a great favor. Give them a gift that can strengthen them their entire lives—a gift that can continue to build up and bless your children and even your grandchildren—*the gift of honor.*

Where do we begin? By getting a clear picture of a key marked "honor," and understanding how dishonoring our own parents can lock the door to building value into our children.

# Chapter Two

## The Gift of Honor

*H*ave you ever been handed the wrong key to a hotel room? Regardless of how much effort you may put into opening the door to your room, or how sincere you are about its working, if the desk clerk hands you a poorly cut key or one that fits a different door, you're sincerely wrong when you try to use it.

The same thing is true of building value into your children. It's not enough that you are handed a set of keys or principles to unlock the door to self-worth. If they aren't cut correctly or are missing a few of the teeth that match the lock, they may open another door, but they won't fit the one marked "self-worth."

That's why we want to take a close look at the biblical concept of honor as we begin this book. If a key isn't cut accurately, it doesn't matter how practical it is. We want to make sure that you're making proper use of the key marked "honor" and that you can spot a counterfeit key named "dishonor."

We know that definitions can bore some people, but we feel strongly that getting a clear idea of what it means to honor God or loved ones is at the heart of all healthy relationships. With that in mind, let's look more closely at the concept itself and at how it can be applied in the home.

We'll look first at the opposite of honor, namely, dishonor. By contrasting the two, we can gain insight into what honor avoids, as well as what it builds, in a person's life.

## AS LITTLE VALUE AS A VAPOR

A few months ago, we flew over to southern California to be on our good friend, Al Sander's, radio program, "VoxPop." After we had finished the program (and our favorite chicken dinner at Knott's Berry Farm), we hustled to the airport to catch our plane.

When we arrived, we discovered that all air traffic was being delayed by a light mist that had drifted in from the ocean. As we sat in the terminal and waited to board our plane, we watched that light mist turn into a gripping fog, closing down the airport and forcing us to spend another night in California.

Who would have thought that something as insignificant as a little mist could have turned into a major problem that disrupted our schedules, inconvenienced hundreds of other people, and proved costly to the airlines? Just a vapor! Yet it had the power to disrupt so many schedules and lives.

We see a similar occurrence in family relationships. People who grow up feeling worthless and unlovable—those who were dishonored in their home—have usually grown up in an environment where unloving acts have surrounded them like a vapor.

Like the mist that drifts in from the ocean at night, dishonoring actions by a parent may start with a critical word or an angry glance—not cause for major problems at first. But if left unchecked, one day that mist can build up and turn into a gripping fog. That disabling fog of hurtful words and actions can become self-destructive to children, creating boys and girls who grow up with damaged emotions and problems in future intimate relationships.

In the Scriptures, the word *dishonor* is used of "something or someone who has little worth, weight, or value."[1] One word picture used to describe it is the same one we faced at the airport and some children face at home—a "mist or vapor."[2] In one instance, it was used to describe the steam that rises from a boiling pot of water.[3]

When the Greeks thought of a word picture to describe something of the least value imaginable, they thought of mist or steam. It referred to something of such little weight and significance that it was good only to be waved or wiped away as a nuisance.

In relationships, when we dishonor people, we consciously or unconsciously treat them as if they have as little weight or value as a vapor. When do we treat someone like that? How about when a preschooler has just asked the same question for the thousandth time; a youngster leaves his toys out at night again so that others trip over them in the dark; a teen-ager seems to selectively forget what he's been told; a spouse has the nerve to try and ask a question or to do a chore when the best part of the game or TV program is on; an elderly parent has become critical, even though extra effort is required to provide his room and board in a nursing home; or God's Word clearly states that a decision is wrong, yet the decision is "right" for the business.

Anger, sarcasm, unjust criticism, unhealthy comparisons, favoritism, inconsistency, jealousy, selfishness, envy, racism, and a host of other ills are "justified" as legal weapons to use against people we consider of little value. Even with our family and loved ones, our anger toward them often comes as a result of something they've done to us that's lowered their value in our eyes.[4] Here's something everyone ought to write on a card and read every day:

> **The lower the value we attach to a person, the easier we can "justify" dishonoring them by yelling or treating them with disrespect.**

God's Word makes it clear that we're to give honor to Him: "Sing out the honor of His name; Make His praise glorious" (Psalm 66:2).[5] The apostle Paul told us that with other people, including our children, we should "in honor [give] preference to one another" (Romans 12:10). If we're serious about honoring God, our children, and others, we'll begin to combat our natural bent to dishonor them by taking them lightly. How can we do that? We can begin by understanding two specific aspects of the definition of honor. Each acts as part of the foundation on which the remainder of the book will rest. Each applies first to how we can honor God and then to how we can honor our family and other loved ones. The first aspect of this definition calls us to look on each loved one as a priceless treasure; the other to grant each individual a high place of honor and the loving respect that accompanies it.

## A PRICELESS TREASURE

In ancient writings, something of honor was something of substance (literally heavy), valuable, costly, even priceless.[6] For Homer, the Greek scholar, "The greater the cost of the gift, the more the honor."[7] The same is often true for biblical authors.[8] David used the word *honor* this way in the psalms, saying, "How precious [literally, honorable] also are Your thoughts to me, O God!" (Psalm 139:17). In essence David was saying, "What a treasure, or how priceless it is, to get to look in on God's thoughts—something believers can do every day in His Word."

In the New Testament, when Paul wrote to Timothy to encourage believers who were straying into sin, he asked them to be honorable vessels for the Lord—not inexpensive pots of clay that were used for dishonoring purposes, but costly vessels of "gold and silver" (2 Timothy 2:20).

For Christians, the greatest example of a priceless treasure is Christ's death on the cross. The apostle Paul certainly recognized this in his writings. When he sternly corrected the Corinthian believers for their immoral lives, he referred to Christ, the priceless sacrifice, to convict them: "You were bought at a price [literally, with *honor*]; therefore glorify God in your body" (1 Corinthians 6:20). Every angel and the hosts in heaven recognize the price the Father paid to redeem His people when they sing, "Worthy is the Lamb who was slain / To receive . . . honor!" (Revelation 5:12).

In several places in the Scriptures, the word *honor* actually means "glory."[9] In our relationship with God, honor comes naturally whenever we draw near to Him whose "glory fills the earth" (Psalm 145:5). We can see a picture of how something that is glorious and of great value commands honor in the instructions set forth for His priests and for His tabernacle.

In order to convey the great dignity and importance of the priesthood, the priests' garments, or "royal robes," were designed to be of unusual beauty (Exodus 28:2, 40). From the intricate wood carvings to the priceless ornaments of gold and silver, everything that would stand near God's presence was made with a glorious form (Exodus 35:30—36:1; 40:34).

God isn't impressed by costly robes and priceless vessels, but He knows that we are. Few people can stand next to the Hope diamond, one of the largest diamonds in the world, and not spontaneously be moved by its magnitude, its weight, and the price it commands. When we catch sight of something precious and valuable in creation, our reaction to that treasure gives us an object lesson in how we should respond to God's surpassing glory and beauty.[10]

What does all this have to say to those of us who want to honor our children? One way we honor God is by recognizing that His worth is beyond any price. Similarly, we honor our children by considering them to be special treasures God has entrusted to us.

The Scriptures declare that children are a "gift" from the Lord (Psalm 127:3). They, too, are priceless treasures that we should treat with special care. Why is it so important to look at children as costly gifts or special treasures?

## Children Are Gifts of Great Price

Let's be honest. There can be days when that precious little bundle you brought home from the hospital can become a pain in the neck (or someplace farther south). However, as a parent, you can make a decision to treat your child like a valuable treasure. When you do, you raise your positive feelings for that child—even on days when circumstances make all your feelings start out to be negative ones.

At the time we're writing this chapter, it's been six months since my (John's) wife Cindy had a beautiful baby girl. I can't think of a mother who loves her child (or her husband) more, but I also know it isn't always easy. Particularly this past week when combined with Kari's colic, her baby shots, and a stuffy nose cold, she's started teething!

It's times like these when even the most loving parent could be tempted to drop the value of her child. But there's a certain attitude Cindy adopts that steadies her through sleepless nights and equally trying days. Because Cindy makes a daily decision to treasure our daughter, her feelings for Kari rarely drop. How does that work?

Our Lord answers this question in one of our favorite statements: "Where your treasure is, there your heart will be also" (Matthew 6:21). The more you treasure God and His Word, the greater your desire to pray and read His Word. When you learn to treasure your children, your positive feelings for them go up as well.[11]

To get a better handle on what we mean by treasuring some-one, try to picture a tangible thing you value. Perhaps it's a new car, an expensive painting, a family heirloom, your father's watch, or a mountain hideaway. For sake of example, let's say you have an expensive, almost priceless painting that's the center of attention in your living room. You would take steps to protect it by making sure it was hung securely and away from direct sun-light; you would highlight it with indirect lighting and a subtle yet elegant frame; you would certainly brag on it to your friends and family because it means so much to you. Because it's of such value, just coming home from work and looking at it could raise your spirits and give you a special feeling inside.

Parents who treasure their children develop many of the same responses. When you treasure a person, you want to protect her; you'll go out of your way to see that she succeeds, and you'll high-light her best points; a valuable loved one would be mentioned frequently in conversations in a positive way. When you place honor on a child, the thought of coming home to her after a long day at work can give you energy, not drain it all away from you.

Isn't it interesting how inanimate objects, such as paintings, tend to keep their value over the years while living objects, such as children, often see their value drop? For parents of toddlers and teen-agers in particular, the decision to treat the children as priceless treasures sometimes has to be made on an hourly ba-sis! But it pays rich dividends.

Children are incredibly perceptive. When it looks as if you value the house, job, car, or pet poodle more than them, your actions speak far louder than your words. In the chapters that follow, we'll look at a number of ways you can actively communi-cate to your children that they are treasures to you.

## A HIGHLY RESPECTED POSITION

There's a second meaning of the word *honor* that can help us understand how it builds value into our loved ones. Not only does it signify something or someone who is a priceless treasure, but it is also used for someone who occupies a highly respected posi-tion in our lives, someone high on our priority list.[12]

In ancient Greece, the word *honor* was reserved for "men who are in a high position."[13] It was used to designate a king or those of his inner circle. Later it came to apply to anyone who deserved special mention for the place he held in someone's life.[14]

In the Scriptures, the classic example is Christ. Because of His sacrifice and because of His calling, He takes the place of honor as our High Priest before the Father.[15] The more we understand about the place He holds with the Father, the greater our respect for who He is and what He continues to accomplish in and through us.

For the Greeks, giving people honor because of the positions they held or what they had accomplished was inseparable from treating them with respect. The very word *respect* means "to look behind."[16] In other words, it involves looking back and seeing a person's accomplishments, then treating him as very valuable.

One way we honor God today is to look back on all He has done for us. That's why the writers of the psalms call on us so often to "remember."[17] One way we honor our loved ones, parents, and family members is to give them a high position on our priority list and look back in thanks on how they've enriched our lives.

But what if you look back at your parents or other loved ones and find that they *don't* deserve your thanks? For example, what if through ignorance or through a lack of caring, your parents failed to provide you with the actions or memories that deserve your respect? What if they used their position in your life for harm rather than good?

Like counting someone as a valuable treasure, granting a person respect is a decision you have to make. Emotionally, you may or may not "feel" like giving honor to your parents, but you can still make a decision to do so.

> **One way we honor our loved ones, parents, and family members is to give them a high position on our priority list and look back in thanks on how they've enriched our lives.**

We know that some mothers and fathers haven't earned the right to be honored. But we also know that the highest form of love bestows honor on someone who doesn't deserve it. And as we'll show, *the only way to achieve real freedom from the effects of a dishonoring parent is to honor that person.*

What place do your children feel they have in your life? Some parents really don't want their children to answer this question. Hearing a child say he feels as though he's fifth place in your life can be a crushing blow, as it was for Walter.

Walter was a pastor who heard us describe what it meant to honor a person, and he went home and asked his son what kind of position he felt he occupied in his father's life.

"Do you really want to know?" asked his teen-aged son.

"Certainly," his dad replied.

"All my life, I've felt like it's been ministry, ministry, ministry, ministry, family, and then ministry."

When children grow up feeling low on their parents' list of priorities, major problems can result. Many children will spend a lifetime languishing in an emotional cubbyhole from being "low-listed"—afraid and unwilling to break out of it.

Thankfully, many parents take steps to make sure that children occupy a place of significance in the home. The knowledge that they rate high on their mother and father's list can be, in and of itself, a tremendous boost to their feeling valuable and significant.

## APPLYING HONOR IN OUR HOMES

Thus far we've looked at the biblical concept of honor from three different angles and seen three clear reflections from the literal meaning of this word (and its opposite) that can guide us throughout the book. But how do we apply this to our loved ones, especially our children? How does this knowledge help us raise their self-worth and battle any feeling of inferiority they may have?

The pages that follow focus on seven ways parents can practically apply honor in their most important relationships and see their children's feeling of value raised as a result.

We're excited to help you discover (or be reminded of) what we've seen make a tremendous difference in families across the country, including our own. We want you to walk with us through the next few pages as we give you a thumbnail sketch of the various ways you'll be able to help your own children to honor God and others and feel of great value themselves. Throughout this book as you understand and apply each principle, you'll be **giving the gift of honor when your children see you. . .**

## Extending It First to Your Own Parents

Many of us do not realize that when we dishonor our parents, we not only hurt them but also rob ourselves of a sense of value and fail to pass down value and acceptance to our own children. Not only that, we give our children a model and an excuse for dishonoring us and repeating a negative cycle generation after generation.

Punching holes in our parents drains away our physical, spiritual, and emotional energy. And the less worth and energy we have ourselves, the less we have to pass along to our children.

## Helping Them Find Value in Troubled Times

In looking at this aspect of honoring our children, we'll be tackling one of the most frequently asked questions in counseling and at conferences: "How do I help my child work through some of the most discouraging and damaging experiences he or she faces?"

Many moms and dads are afraid of what their children might experience in life, but few of them are equipped to help their children through major difficulties should they actually occur. While it is our hope that neither our readers nor their children will ever go through tragedies, the Scriptures tell us various trials will come (James 1). What then?

We can learn a method of walking our children (or ourselves) through discouraging, even devastating experiences that would ordinarily lower their sense of self-respect or value. These same negative experiences can then be used to increase their feelings of worth. Parents can even begin to see their own sense of anxiety lowered as they learn how to face the very experience most people only know how to avoid.

## Recognizing Your Parenting Strengths and Style

Why are some parents stricter than others? Why do some children leave home seemingly secure and confident and others do not? Why does one parent seem assured while the parent next door suffers great insecurities?

At least in part, the answers to these questions lie in the different parenting strengths and styles men and women possess. In these sections, we want to help you discover your primary parenting strengths and how God can use these natural gifts to build value into your children. We also want to help you see how each parenting style can build up a child's sense of value or, if pushed to an extreme, break it down.

## Providing a Healthy Balance in Your Home

Another important question that often surfaces when we talk with parents is some variation of this theme: "How do we know how to balance staying close to our children yet releasing them to develop healthy independence?"

We deal with this question by illustrating a healthy balance, a biblical balance, between "belonging" and "separateness" necessary in each family's home. Specifically, we'll share ways parents can help their children feel the warmth of belonging, as well as ease them into independence. We'll also highlight what happens to children who grow up in out-of-balance homes, where they are forced to live at either extreme.

## Establishing Loving Boundaries for Them

Throughout the Scriptures and in numerous current studies, we are told that providing loving limits for our children helps raise their value and sense of self-worth. Each time we make the effort to provide a loving boundary for our children, we not only protect them but help to produce security and confidence in their lives.

Providing protective fences for our children and learning how to maintain them is one of the most important ways we can encourage our sons and daughters. Loving boundaries can also help a child answer four crucial questions every person needs to answer to combat temptation and truly feel valuable.

## Building Positive Loyalties into Them

In every home, invisible lines of loyalty stretch across thousands of miles and through decades of time. Even adults who have long since moved away from home can still stumble daily over these cords from the past.

Because of the nature of children, every home and every parent builds lines of loyalty into a child. There is little debate over the fact that children repeat patterns they see in their parents. What remains a toss-up is whether the patterns they adopt will be positive or negative when they become adults.

Every day we are laying down lines of loyalty for our children. To make sure these patterns are positive, we'll focus on the way God establishes positive loyalties with His children through His "loyal-love," including several specific patterns we can adopt in building value into our children.

## Offering Honor to God

Finally, in this section, we see that the same elements that help us build value into our children can also help them raise their value of God! As we discover ways we can teach our children to honor God, we will also learn a major reason why many of us have such a difficult time reading God's Word or spending time in prayer. These are lessons which we can pass along to our children to help them have a more consistent spiritual life.

Seven aspects of honor, each with the power to make a major positive difference in our child's life if applied. However, before we as parents are truly free to build a sense of value into our children, we must first understand why honoring our own parents or their memory is so important. The decision we make in this area can either leave us stuck on a muddy road or well on the highway toward giving honor to our loved ones.

# Chapter Three

## Extending the Gift First to Our Own Parents

*T*ami was thirty-two years old when she realized that most of her shattered relationships could be tied directly to her lifelong struggle with her father. Emotionally, she had been fighting him and her painful past for years, and her energy and joy in the present had been drained away.

He hadn't been the best of fathers, and for years she took every opportunity she could to remind him of that fact. Twice she married men just like him; twice she ended those marriages in frustration and bitterness.

What made Tami feel a need for counseling was the way her children were beginning to act toward her. She never wanted to see her family go through the same kind of struggles she had, but when she took an honest look at what her children were experiencing, she saw a mirror reflection of her own life as a child.

One of the first things Tami learned in counseling was also one of the most difficult things she had to do. Even though she understood how much it would help her, she was only willing to accept it when she understood how much it would benefit her children.

What did Tami have to face? As a parent who wanted to honor her children by building value into their lives, she had to begin by becoming aware of the need to honor her own mom and dad. By attaching significance and worth to her parents, she would benefit personally, and she would model for her children how they should act toward her.

As much as some people would like to ignore this fact, the Scriptures make it clear that one of the first steps on the road to honoring others begins with honoring "your father and your mother, . . . that your days may be long, and that it may be well with you" (Deuteronomy 5:16). Why is this so important? Some individuals may live thousands of miles from their parents. Others may not have thought of them for years. Still others, whose parents are deceased, may be able to deal with them only through memories (which can be just as vivid, or more so, than life).

In the pages that follow, we'll look at four reasons why it's crucial for us not to short-circuit God's command to honor our parents. But before we address this issue, there's something we need to highlight, particularly for those who grew up in a less-than-ideal home situation.

## WHAT? HONOR *MY* PARENTS?

We're sure that there will be individuals who read this book (perhaps even you) and bristle with anger at the mere suggestion of giving honor to parents. "Honor *my* parents? After what my father did to me? After all I had to go through with my mother? Are you kidding? Give me a break!"

Without a doubt, there are some parents whose insensitivity and unloving actions have hurt their children deeply. We know well that some mothers and fathers don't appear to deserve honor. We're not saying their actions weren't hurtful, nor are we explaining away the negative effects they may have had over the years. However, we are saying that the only way to be free from the hurt they have caused you is to honor them. In short, *continuing to nail your parents to a cross years after the fact* **hurts** *you more than it does them.*

Most of us grew up with loving parents who tried their best to build value into our lives. For those of you who did not, the next chapter is directed toward you. There we'll show how the trials you suffered at the hands of a dishonoring parent (or anyone else for that matter) can be used to bring positive gain into your life.

But for now, let's look at four reasons each of us has for honoring our parents, whether or not they're alive today.

## REJECTING OUR PARENTS IS ROBBING
## FROM OURSELVES

Brad didn't hate his father, but he didn't like him either. His father had always been very demanding of him as a child, and for years Brad continued to resent it. Perhaps that's why he said so often to his wife and children (and anyone else who would listen) that he had little respect for his dad.

Invariably, as Brad would be watching a television show and a villainous character would come on, he would make some wise-crack about his father. Whenever he did something special for his children, he would always preface it with the remark, "You wouldn't find *my* dad doing something like this with *his* kids."

Long before they ever met him, the children had a vivid image of their grandfather. On a good day, they knew he must be a cross between Attila the Hun and Archie Bunker. The very first time David, Brad's five-year-old son, met his grandfather, he walked up to him, doubled up his fist, and took a swing at him!

In some ways, it made Brad feel better to put down his dad. When he was growing up, he never had anyone to talk over his frustrations with, and as an adult, he felt justified in getting them all off his chest. What Brad didn't realize (and what other "Brads" and "Bettys" often aren't aware of) was that *every time he dishonored his father, he was lowering his own self-worth.* How does this happen?

All of us are very much like our parents and very much a part of them. We pick up many of their emotional characteristics and bents, and our physical bodies are forever marked by them, too. Chromosomes are God's building blocks for our physical development, and at conception, half of them came from each parent. From that one fact alone, it should be obvious that we can never escape our parents. Each of our cells bears the vestiges of their stamp on our lives.

When God tells us to honor our parents, it's with good reason. When we lower their value and cut them down, we're dishonoring a part of ourselves. Brad was doing even more.

When Brad's children met their grandfather, they were surprised by two things. First, he didn't seem as big as they thought he would be. Second, he acted so much like their father!

It causes incredible confusion in a child's mind when he's been taught to dislike characteristics in his grandparents that he sees every day in his own mom or dad. Like a marksman firing off a scatter-gun at close range, a child who blasts out at his grandfather knows he will hit his father as well.

For years, Brad didn't realize the harm he was doing to himself. The more he dishonored his father, the lower his own sense of self-worth sank. The lower his worth, the more difficult he became to live with and the harder he was on his children and wife.

It bears repeating that people with low self-worth tend to act out their feelings of anger and inadequacy. If their feeling of dislike for themselves is deep enough, they often strain every relationship and get other people to treat them in the negative way they feel about themselves. People with low self-worth aren't easy to live with, and that was certainly true of Brad.

Brad tried all his life to get away from the hurtful memory of his father, but by dishonoring him, he ended up staring at him every morning in the mirror. His children knew it, too. Brad hated the way he had been treated by his father, and his children knew exactly how he felt because it was exactly the way Brad treated them.

As we have seen, making the decision not to honor our parents gives our sons and daughters their first lesson in how to dishonor us. And just as in Brad's case, the lack of joy and the shortened life we get out of dishonoring them[1] keep us from being able to love our children as we should.

Besides draining away our capacity to love others, dishonoring our parents does something else. It builds a wall around relationships that can block us from truly developing our masculinity or femininity.

## IN SEARCH OF MASCULINITY AND FEMININITY

For any child, his first look at masculinity comes from observing his father, and his first look at femininity from observing his mother. What happens when a child cuts himself off from his parents? Pushed to an extreme, it can edge a person toward homosexuality.

Although many factors are involved, much current research on homosexual behavior is centered on boys who were cut off, emotionally or physically, from their fathers.[2] When a male child grows up disliking and avoiding his father, he also runs the risk of being blocked from identifying with his maleness. All too often, an overly involved mother comes into the picture with a son who is being shunned or not accepted by his father, and she is all too willing to pick up the slack. Because of an uninvolved or uncaring father, the mother-son attachment can grow incredibly strong.

In extreme cases, young boys identify almost totally with their mother and her actions, yet they remain in search of an idealized "someone" to replace their absent father. Such boys and young men are easy prey for a homosexual encounter.

While homosexuality may represent the extreme of being unable to identify with a father, dishonoring our parents can affect each of us in more subtle ways.

Recently, we met a middle-aged woman named Dayna who grew up in a dishonoring home. For years, even after she became a Christian, she hated her father with a passion. His continual drinking and lack of support for the household required her mother to work full-time and kept Dayna from having any of her friends visit her at home. By the time she was old enough to marry and move out of the house, her anger toward her father—and toward men in general—had been honed to a razor's edge.

Dayna's first marriage lasted two years—two years of constant criticism and fighting after she discovered on their honeymoon that her husband's social drinking was much more than that. Her second marriage had lasted years longer, but she was unable to be satisfactorily intimate with her husband.

When we saw this couple in counseling and suggested that the way she continually dishonored her father had a role in her marriage problems, she became so upset that she got up and walked out of the room. Only after several weeks of her husband's pleading was she willing to come back for another session.

In no way were her father's actions justified. They caused hurt for her mother and incredible pain for her. His sin was wrong, and he stands accountable for it to the Lord. But twenty years later, it wasn't her father who was continuing to suffer, it was Dayna.

By refusing to forgive him, she chained herself to the very person she wanted so desperately to avoid. By doggedly holding on to hurts in the past, she moved further and further away from enjoying life in the present.

Dayna's inability to identify with the most powerful masculine figure in her life, her father, also contributed to the continual struggle she had with every other man who tried to get close to her, including the men she married.[3] Listen to what she told us near the end of our time of counseling:

> *Deep down inside, all my life I have thought that men were nothing but sleazeballs. I couldn't even enjoy my husband holding me because he reminded me so much of my father. I even resented the fact that God gave me two boys and no girls.*
>
> *I want to be close to my husband and my children, and I want to be close to God. But I know because I view them as men I don't really trust them.*

And therein lies one of the worst effects of dishonoring her dad. It's bad enough that it can cut her off from forming a close attachment to her spouse or her children, but it's even worse that it can block her from a fulfilling relationship with the heavenly Father, especially His masculine side.[4]

Similar problems can result if someone cuts herself off from the most powerful feminine figure in her life, her mother. If she dishonors her, watch how few nurturing qualities, how few relationship skills, and how little sensitivity develop in her life.

Not being able to identify with a difficult, uncaring mother was the very thing that led a young woman named Marian to become every inch a "man" by her dress and actions. Deep inside, Marian became so angry with her mother, who presented a very feminine side to people, that she wanted nothing to do with dresses or make-up or anything that made her look more like her mother. She managed to look very different from her mother on the outside, yet she acted just as controlling, angry, and manipulative on the inside.

Besides lowering our value and threatening to cut us off from significant relationships with other men or women, and even with God, there's a third negative result of dishonoring our parents. According to the Scriptures, we pay a terrible *physical* price for lowering our parents' worth.

## THE PHYSICAL EFFECTS OF DISHONORING MOM AND DAD

Some people refused to quit smoking until the surgeon general came out with his warning labels and long list of physical ailments linked to cigarettes. Although we don't pretend to be surgeons, we've come across some interesting studies that we hope might help people stop treating their parents with as little value as a light mist.

In God's first commandment with a promise, "Honor your father and your mother,"[5] you can't get away from the physical side effects that come from agreeing with or tossing aside God's Word. Either your life will be lengthened and your days brightened, or you run the risk of shortening your life and darkening your days.

In a simplified way, we'd like to share with you one reason why dishonoring mom and dad does such physical damage.[6] It all begins inside the brain, where the decision you make to harbor negative feelings toward your parents can set off a series of physical events you would do well to avoid.

To better understand this concept, try to think in terms of an outer brain and an inner brain. The outer brain, basically located in the outer cortex, acts like the programmer, the person who punches the raw data into a computer. He gathers all the incoming information from each of the five senses, makes a decision on it, and sends the equation that matches the decision down to the inner brain.

The inner brain acts like the computer itself. Once it receives the equation, it follows the instructions to the letter. The inner brain doesn't worry about making the right decision. It simply responds to what it has been commanded to do.[7]

Let's see how this applies to honoring or dishonoring parents by going back to the story of Brad. He had real problems with his father, and dishonoring him had become almost second nature. What Brad didn't realize was that every time he made a decision (outer brain) to dishonor his father, chemicals were being released into his body (by the inner brain) that could shorten his life. To understand how this happens, we need to know more about how the brain functions.

Let's say a man is out jogging one afternoon when a neighbor's large dog starts to run toward him. Instantly, the jogger's outer brain kicks into action to make a decision about what to do.

For example, his outer brain might be saying, "Okay, my eyes tell me there's a dog running at me. It's a big dog. In fact, it's one of the *biggest* dogs I've ever seen! He doesn't look all that friendly either. In fact, his hair is standing straight up! If I try to outrun him, he'll jump on me and eat me alive! This isn't a good situation. I mean, I'm really in trouble! I know I can't outrun him, so I think I'd better stop, stand still, and hope for the best."[8]

Once a decision has been made in the outer brain, it's transferred down to the inner brain. The inner brain reads the instructions it's handed and relays its instructions verbatim to the many important glands it controls. If we could listen in, we might hear something like this:

"Okay down there! Listen up quick! Let's release a bunch of adrenalin to get our heart moving quicker. Double the blood pressure! Lungs, you'll have to move oxygen in and out faster to keep pace! Pituitary gland! Work on increasing the sugar content in our system, and while you're at it, make it easier for our blood to clot just in case the dog decides to bite. To be safe, it says here in the instructions we need to dilate those pupils so we can see the dog better. And for right now all digestion and elimination is to come to a halt. Got it? Good, you've only got about two seconds to get everything ready before the dog gets here."

Our jogger has made a decision (outer brain) about a stressful event, and his body responds (inner brain) dramatically to that decision. Let's say that in this case the dog happens to be a big, lovable animal who is lonely for some company. He runs over to the man, stands up and puts his paws on the jogger's shoulders, and licks him in the face.

Petting the dog for a few moments and slowly moving along his way, the jogger suddenly feels faint and starts to shake. That's the natural result of his body's trying to get back to normal after all those chemicals were dumped into his blood stream. Even once the threat has been reduced to a nonthreatening, playful dog (even a big one), it takes the body quite a while to get everything back to normal!

## Staying on the Alert Too Long

How does all this concern Brad and his decision to dishonor his father? Just suppose that last night Brad was watching a rerun of "Little House on the Prairie," and he got steaming mad at the controlling, manipulative Mrs. Olsen. Then he started thinking about how manipulative and controlling his own father was while he was growing up, and he got even angrier. As though that wasn't enough, just before bedtime he remembered that his father was coming the next day for one of his obligatory visits, and oooh, he didn't want to see him.

Understanding what's happening inside Brad's brain at this point gives us at least one illustration of how our lives can be shortened. If Brad realized this, perhaps he would understand why he's been having such a hard time falling asleep at night and why, when he awakens, his stomach is churning and his jaws are sore from grinding his teeth. With all the stress Brad puts on his body each year, it's no wonder he gets the flu or a cold so often that everyone at the doctor's office calls him by his first name.

When Brad makes a decision that his father is worthless, a pain in the neck, or nothing but trouble, his body goes on the alert. When the inner brain gets the message that there's a stressful situation out there (in this case a "bad dad"), it doesn't ask questions—it just reacts. Brad's body can easily release as many chemicals and disrupt as many bodily functions when he is angry with his father as it would if he were being chased by his neighbor's dog.

What happens when our bodies stay on the alert too long? Undesirable things such as clinical depression, colitis, bleeding ulcers, anxiety attacks, lowered resistance to colds and flu, heart and respiratory failure.[9] Some researchers believe that cancer can and does take place.[10] Such stress on our bodies can shorten our lives on this earth; thus the negative promise in God's Word may be fulfilled.

If you haven't been challenged to answer the question yet, let's ask it pointblank: To what degree are you dishonoring your parents today? For any of us who are majoring in lowering our parents' value, at the same time we're **minoring in lowering** our own self-worth and that of our children, risking cutting ourselves off from intimate relationships with other men, women, and God Himself, and physically damaging our bodies. As if this isn't enough, there's more!

## THE DARKNESS FROM DISHONORING
## OUR PARENTS

There's a fourth reason why we need to honor our parents. Actually, it should be reason enough, in and of itself. God commands us to do so: "Honor your father and mother ... that it may be well with you and you may live long on the earth" (Ephesians 6:2–3).

In the psalms, we're told that God's Word is a light to our paths and a lamp to our feet.[11] When we decide to ignore His Word, we walk away from the light and into the darkness. Our loving heavenly Father knew the pain we would have if we stumbled around in the dark so He provided His Word as a clear light for our paths.

None of us can afford to forget the truth that persistent anger directed toward anyone leads us right into darkness (1 John 2:9ff.). Darkness keeps up from knowing or walking in the light of God's path. Making a decision to honor our parents, even if we have to call on God for the strength to do so, keeps us out of darkness and our children from learning a negative pattern.

There may be times when the path God's Word illuminates is not the same one we want to take—like the road that leads to honoring our parents—but a loving God knows it will be far worse for us in many ways to experience the illegitimate pain of falling in darkness than to face the legitimate pain of dealing with our past in the light.

## HOW DO WE GIVE HONOR TO OUR PARENTS?

Honoring our parents follows the pattern we have described earlier in the book: making a decision to treat them (or their memory) as a valuable treasure, and granting them a position of high respect in our lives. However, before we look at specific ways in which we can do this, we need to evaluate how highly we're valuing them today.

### Evaluate Current Attitudes and Actions

Assessing our current attitudes and actions toward our parents is particularly important for those people who may have kept their parents at arms' length as a way of dealing with past hurts. If you recall from chapter 2, the picture the Scripture gives of dishonoring someone is treating him like an insignificant mist. Each of us needs to ask, "Do I brush my mother and father aside, or do I count them as weighty and valuable?"

Jim would never have thought or admitted that he was dishonoring his father, but he was. Jim's mother and father had divorced when he was very young, and it wasn't until his early teens that he and his father re-established contact. For Jim, however, now that the years had passed and he had a family of his own, spending time with his father or checking in with him occasionally was something he continually put off.

Anger didn't bubble over on the surface when he did see his father, but it was always lying just beneath the surface. Their conversation was usually shallow when they got together, filled with talk of sports or the weather. Instead of bringing up the tension that had dominated their relationship for years, they walked around issues that desperately needed confronting as carefully as if they were walking through a minefield.

Jim was not openly dishonoring his father, but his ignoring him for months on end was a subtle way to accomplish the same thing. Instead of facing the hard issues and working through them himself or with his father, he let silence and procrastination shut out his unhappiness.

Jim's case isn't unusual. Even when there hasn't been a major family fracture, many people who live within an hour of their parents only contact them on a yearly basis.

When you ignore your parents, even when you're busy with your own lives and family, you dishonor them. You don't have to call them four times a day or invite them on every vacation, but putting off making contact with them as a subtle form of punishment or insensitivity dishonors them.

How can you combat the tendency to slip parents beyond the back burner? Let's look at some practical ways of applying the twofold instructions of our definition of honor.

## Take Time to "Look Back"

Attitudes influence actions, and that is particularly true when it comes to your parents. If you place your present view of your parents on a value line, perhaps you can determine how much you treasure them. On a line marked off from 1 to 10, if 10 means high value and 1 means low, where would you put your present value of your parents?

My Present View of My Parents

1    2    3    4    5    6    7    8    9    10
Little value                                    High value

The reason many of us fail to call or write our parents is that their present value in our busy lives is probably at a 4 or below. Remember the principle we gave earlier: What you treasure is what you'll have good feelings for.[12] If your parents are near the bottom of your value line, you may not feel like contacting them or expressing any thanks for what they've done in your life. But if

---

### Biblical Instructions on Honoring Our Parents

1. It honors our parents to listen carefully to their counsel. (Proverbs 1:8, 2:1, 3:1, 4:1, 5:1, 9:8, 10:1, 13:1, and 15:5)
2. It honors our parents when they see their children acting wisely. (Proverb 27:11)
3. Sharing "good news" with our parents can bring "health to their bones." (Proverb 15:30)
4. Praising our parents brings light to our lives; cursing them will snuff out our lamp. (Proverb 20:20)
5. It dishonors ourselves and our parents when we act foolishly. (Proverb 17:25)
6. Involvement in immoral relationships not only affects us, but also causes our parents to grieve and lose their energy. (Proverbs 5:1ff, 31:3)
7. Pride and a "haughty spirit," saying we're "pure" when we're not, expressing critical and judgmental words like a "mouth full of knives," and mocking our mother and father bring dishonor to a parent. (Proverbs 30:12–17)

---

you make a decision to move up their value, your feelings for them may move up as well.

The Scriptures say that the wise man honors his mother and father, and the fool ignores and hates them (Proverb 30:17). Making a decision to treat them as special treasures can be one of the wisest things you ever do.

The second aspect of the definition of honor can help to accomplish the first. The way to treasure your parents is by "looking back" at them with respect. In the previous chapter, you saw that to respect a person literally means to "look back." But very few people develop the honoring habit of "looking back." In Jesus' day, in one instance it was only one out of ten. Do you remember the story in the New Testament about Christ's healing ten lepers? (Luke 17:11–19). That was no small feat or act of love. These lepers were tremendously needy, and Jesus met their deepest physical needs. But how many turned back? One! Only one man out of ten who could have stopped to express thanks and appreciation, bothered to do so.

As we look around, we still see as few as one in ten taking the time to look back and say thanks to their parents. But practically, how can we do that? First, let's look at a list from the Scriptures that can give us insight into what honors and what dishonors our parents.

Below are responses from parents of various ages who were asked the question "What could your children do or have they done to make you feel honored?"

## What Could My Children Do to Honor Me?

1. *On a day other than Mother or Father's Day, it would mean so much to get a card or letter from our children letting us know they're thinking of us.*
2. *The greatest present I ever received from my son was a cassette tape that looked back on several specific things I had done for him in the past.*
3. *Even though it's difficult for me to do, my daughter always makes a point of hugging me when we get together.*
4. *As a single mom, when my (school-age) children do chores without being asked, or additional chores, I feel honored.*
5. *It honors me to see my children reaching out to help others who have been less fortunate than they.*

6. *I feel flattered and humbled when my daughter asks my advice on struggles and needs in her life.*
7. *We appreciate the way our children tell us the truth, even when it means disagreeing with us or expressing an opinion different from ours.*
8. *We know our children are praying for us every day and that honors us.*
9. *When I see my daughter seeking after God, I can't think of anything that brings me more honor.*
10. *When my children were in their teen-age years, they came to us to talk about "taboo" areas like drinking, sex, and drugs.*
11. *My son and I have often disagreed over the years, but it means so much that we've cleared up past hurts.*
12. *Receiving a special thank you after we've babysat the grandchildren is a real encouragement.*
13. *I think the greatest way my daughter honored me was to name her daughter after me.*
14. *When I see my (school-age) children do their best in school or on different projects, it honors me.*
15. *A while ago, I learned from a neighbor that my son had praised me and actually defended me in front of several people when I wasn't present.*
16. *My son's admitting he was wrong in the way he was treating his wife and agreeing to get marriage counseling was something for which I'll always be thankful.*
17. *When my children let me spend time with the grandchildren, I feel honored.*
18. *Although he knew he didn't have to, my nineteen-year-old son helped out by paying some of the grocery and rent costs when we were having a tough time making ends meet.*
19. *At my husband's funeral, I cried when my two sons and one daughter came up to me and told me they would love and take care of me as I grew older.*
20. *Watching the way my son treats his wife and children, and then hearing him say he learned it from us, is something that is more valuable than any present he could give me.*

(In *The Blessing*, look at the chapter "Giving the Blessing to Your Parents" for other suggestions.)[13]

We know there will be people who read these comments and respond by saying, "If my parents had done some of those things for me, maybe I would take the time to honor them!" Out of anger over the message of this chapter, you are certainly free to skip this section, read ahead, and put into practice the other aspects of honor we offer in this book. But you will never see the short- or long-term effects on your life or your children's lives if you do.

How can you learn to honor a dishonoring parent? How can you stop chasing past hurts and be at peace in the present? At the beginning of the chapter, we promised we would speak to the special needs of those of you who came from deeply dishonoring homes—people who may still be saying, "There's no way I could ever respect my parents, you've never met them!"

In the next chapter, we'll look at how negative events can bring some of the most positive effects to our lives. But for now, let's meet a man named Jerry, who never believed anything positive could come from his relationship with his parents, especially his devastating relationship with his father. Although he would never have considered it at one point in his life, Jerry was free from the hurts in his past only when he learned to honor his father and find value in trials.

## COULD ANYTHING GOOD COME
## FROM JERRY'S HOME?

Jerry was plagued with feelings of worthlessness and discouragement most of his life. These feelings also made it difficult for him to receive love from his wife or to give love to her and their children. Where did such negative feelings begin? Just like many other "Jerrys" we've met—in a dishonoring home.

Jerry's father was a deacon in the church, and the family spent a lot of time at church. But if someone had peeled away the thin veneer of happiness and spirituality that greeted outsiders, he would have seen a terrible problem eating away at this family from within. Because Jerry's father had begun to question God's Word on right and wrong and on what makes healthy relationships, this "model" family was beginning to deteriorate.

Children, even very young children, are incredibly perceptive about picking up signs of strain in their parents' marriage, and Jerry knew his parents were struggling in theirs. Increasingly, his mother and father would ride separately to church and sit with other people when they got there. Also, at least in front of the children, they had quit touching or hugging each other. As a twelve-year-old boy, Jerry was concerned about his parents' marriage. Yet what hurt him the most was the knowledge that, for whatever reason, he no longer lived up to his dad's expectations.

Jerry could see this firsthand every Sunday after church as he sat at the dinner table with another boy his age whom he could tell his father idolized. Jerry's mother had a close friend who would come over after church and bring her teen-age son, Don. For Jerry, it was the hardest time of the week. He had to listen to his father say things to another boy that he longed for his father to say to him. Jerry's father never seemed to run out of questions about Don's week at school or praise for the way he had played in his latest football or baseball game. And every time Jerry's father put Don up on a pedestal, he lowered his own son's value.

Occasionally, when his father's rapt attention would become too obvious, Jerry's mother would shift the conversation and ask something about Jerry's week. But from the look his father gave him and the way the conversation would invariably swing back to Don, it was all too clear that his father wasn't interested in or impressed with anything he was involved in.

The way his father *looked* at the other boy tore holes in his heart. While Jerry would hardly receive a glance, his father's eyes would brighten and his face would soften at the very sight of Don.

By now, you've guessed that Jerry's father had his value system out of whack, but he couldn't (or wouldn't) see it. As a result, what should have been of utmost worth to him, his relationship with the Lord and his family, became of little value.

One mark of mental health is that people can differentiate between what is truly valuable and what is of little worth. The roots of mental illness can be reflected by people such as addicts who view drugs as being more valuable than the person's possessions he steals or the workaholic who trades in his relationship with his family for a minor promotion. *When people begin a habitual pattern of dishonoring others, they are only a few steps away from trading in the permanent for the immediate.*[14]

For months, Jerry endured this torturous Sunday lunch-time ritual. Then one day it happened. On a school night, Jerry's mother came up the stairs and gently knocked at his door. She sat down on his bed, and at first all she could do was put her head in her hands and weep. Finally, through broken words, she told

Jerry that she and his father were divorcing. And then she told him the rest of the story. *Jerry's father was going to marry Don's mother!*

The ultimate way to dishonor another person in marriage— divorce—will happen hundreds of thousands of times this year alone.[15] The tearing apart of what God has meant to last a lifetime invariably results in a husband and wife deeply devaluing each other, and it greatly affects the children as well. Anger, lowered self-worth, guilt, fear, and even a high suicide rate are found among those experiencing the trauma of divorce.[16]

In the more than twenty years since Jerry's parents divorced, he has seen his father only one time. That was when he found out from his uncle that his father would be flying through his home- town and would have a two-hour layover between flights. He called his dad and asked if he could see him at the airport.

## The Death of a Dream

Jerry was filled with expectation. He took along pictures of his children his father had never met and even a copy of an article he had written for a Christian magazine. He thought about all the things he wanted to share with his dad, but he never got the chance. From the time they met at the gate until only a few min- utes were left before he had to leave, Jerry's father talked on and on about what Don and his family were doing.

When he could stand it no longer, Jerry broke in and asked his father, "Don't you want to know what's been happening in *my* life?"

His father stopped and looked down at his shoes. "Jerry," his father said slowly as he looked up, "I'm sure whatever you're doing is going very well."

Those were the last words the two men spoke to each other. A heavy silence hung over them until the call came from the reser- vation desk announcing his father's flight. After his dad left, Jerry walked out to his car, buried his head in his arms, and cried—heart-rending sobs that come only when you know you've seen a loved one for the last time.

Jerry's father has never visited Jerry's home, but his ghost haunts every room. Two times in the past five years, Jerry has sent a letter to his father. Neither time has he received an answer.

Jerry's father made a decision years ago. He started walking away from God's Word, and as a result, he began dishonoring it and other people. The same thing is true of anyone who puts aside God's Word and begins walking in darkness.

Jerry and his mother were treated as people with little value or worth. As a result, it has left a legacy of hurt feelings and emotional pain that they continue to wear like a heavy pinecone wreath. It's uncomfortable and constantly pricks at them (especially on anniversaries, birthdays, and holidays), and it keeps them from letting others get close enough to wound them again. In Jerry's case, that has included keeping his own wife and children at arm's length.

As we pause here, perhaps you're wondering how anything good could come out of a story like this. With all the rejection this man has felt over the years, and still experiences today, what possible benefit could come from all his trials? How could such treatment lead to anything but low worth and the problems associated with it?

The next chapter provides some answers. Jerry looked back, faced his past, and made a decision to give his father honor. He developed the ability to treasure his father as a valuable person in spite of the way he had been treated. You'll see how he turned the terrible experience with his dad into higher self-worth and how even his own family benefitted from what he learned.

The same things Jerry learned can help us all deal with difficulties and heartache in our lives and teach us how our children can learn to respond to suffering in a way that honors God and themselves. Teaching our children to find value in trials is the next vital step in honoring them and building value into their lives.

# Chapter Four

## Helping Our Children Find Value in Troubled Times: Part 1

*I*t was early evening when Mary's mother walked by her daughter's room on the way to the kitchen. An active junior in high school, Mary rarely stayed home on a Friday night. Perhaps that was why her mother stopped outside her door for a moment and listened.

She couldn't be sure, but she thought she heard muffled crying. As she gently knocked on her daughter's door, it opened a few inches, and she could see her daughter lying on the bed with her head buried in a pillow.

"Mary? What's wrong, honey?"

"Nothing," Mary replied as she sat up quickly, trying to stifle the emotion in her voice and pull herself together. "Nothing's wrong."

Her mother opened the door, walked over to the bed, and sat down beside her. "Mary, you know you can tell me if something is wrong. Your dad and I love you very much, and we're here for you if you need us."

Unable to control her emotions, Mary laid her head in her mother's lap and sobbed uncontrollably. "I'm so sorry, Mom. I'm so sorry . . . I just can't believe it . . . I just can't believe it happened to me."

After letting her daughter cry for some time, Mary's mother

finally urged her to sit up. "Honey, don't you think you'd better tell me what's bothering you?"

Looking down at her hands, in a voice that sounded foreign even to herself, Mary choked out the words, "Mom . . . I'm pregnant. I went to a doctor and had the test done, and it was positive."

Looking up at her mother, Mary began to cry again. "How am I going to tell Dad? What do I do about school and my friends? Oh, Mom, what am I going to do?"

## WHEN TRIALS CRASH INTO OUR CHILDREN'S LIVES

For most parents, these words would represent one of the greatest tragedies their child could face. About to begin college or a career, the child sees lifelong dreams and hopes suddenly go up in smoke. In their place stand the cold, harsh realities of an unplanned pregnancy and the emotional scars that often result.

As parents, we may never have to experience the pain that comes from children caught up in immorality, but our children will experience many types of trials. The Scriptures assure us of that.[1] Trials and difficult times are unavoidable. Although we may work overtime trying to protect our children from pain, we'll never be able to isolate them totally from being hurt by their own or by others' actions.

As loving parents, one way we can honor our children and build value into their lives is to help them see the positive gain in troubled times. Whether we like it or not, before they leave our homes, our sons or daughters may experience moments or even days of doubt, discouragement, loneliness, disappointment, or depression.

They may be betrayed by a friend, fail to get into the college or the profession of their choice, be dumped later in life by a spouse, or perhaps experience the disabling results of experimenting with drugs or alcohol. And with each painful experience their child suffers, Mom and Dad feel the aftershocks in their hearts.

If a child doesn't know how to deal with trials in a positive way, he stands a great chance of being emotionally and spiritually handicapped, and his relationships later in life can suffer. Whether he's stuck with fears and anxiety or saddled with deepening bitterness and resentment, he can have a difficult time trying to cope with his negative experiences, and his lowered self-worth can adversely affect his emotional development.

This is exactly what happened to Jerry, whose story we told at the close of the last chapter. His last meeting with his father was so traumatic and painful that he was almost frozen in a perpetual state of emotional anguish. He was afraid of being hurt again if he tried to re-establish contact with his father, but the pain deep inside from being separated hurt just as badly. Thankfully, Jerry discovered how to find value in troubled times, and he was able to begin the process of "unthawing" emotionally and moving away from his pain.

It is certainly not wrong to avoid pain when we can. But it is wrong to deny problems, ignore them, or try to explain them away.[2] One of the all-time-great truths is that life is difficult and often unfair. The better we are at seeing through trials to what they can produce in our lives and our children's lives, the better able we'll be to provide calmness, assurance, and genuine love to our children, even in the midst of trying times. In fact, trials have the capacity to bring strength, maturity, courage, genuine love, righteousness, and perseverance to those who are willing to be trained by them.[3] The very things we fear might happen to our children can make them stronger people, depending on their response and our response to their difficulties.

Before we proceed any further on this point, we want to set the record straight. We're not saying that parents should stand by and let children suffer trials if it's within their power to help them, nor that parents should create or actively seek out difficulties children can experience.

The apostle Paul was asked whether we should create evil that "grace may abound" (Romans 6:1). Put another way, should we cause troubled times for our children so that God can build good things into their lives? In Greek, his answer was *Me Genota*.[4] That's the strongest way possible in his language to say, "Absolutely not! No way! Don't even think about it!"

Children who are mistreated may one day gain positive things from the trials they experience, but that is because of God's grace, not their parents' sin. It would be better for a millstone to be hung around our necks than to deliberately hurt any little one.[5]

In this chapter, we'll take a closer look at what we mean by trials coming wrapped as opportunities for growth. We'll also suggest three actions you can take that set the stage for finding value in troubled times. Then in the next chapter, we'll describe five specific benefits that can be a part of any trial you or your children experience. While our emphasis will be on teaching children to uncover these benefits, those who grew up in difficult home situations can apply this as the basis of being free to give honor to their parents. These are the same steps that helped Jerry begin to honor his father.

## WHEN HURT COMES WRAPPED UP AS OPPORTUNITY

Several years ago, we heard a story about a man who was walking along the sidewalk outside his high-rise apartment. It was early on a bitterly cold winter morning, and he was headed for the local twenty-four-hour convenience store. Suddenly, from out of nowhere it seemed, he was hit on the shoulder by a heavy object and knocked to the ground.

For several moments he lay on the sidewalk, trying to clear his head and feeling to see if his shoulder was broken. Finally, he sat up and looked around. The street was deserted, so he ruled out having been hit by a car. He looked up at the apartments above him, but he could see no open windows.

Struggling to his feet, he looked around one more time and saw a shoe box lying near him. It was heavily taped from end to end. As he bent down to pick it up, he found it was so heavy he had to use both hands.

Later that morning, as he sat in his apartment nursing his bruised, hurting shoulder, he took his scissors and cut through the tape wrapped around the box. Lifting the lid, he saw three fairly large cloth sacks in the box. As he lifted out one of the sacks and opened it in the light, he gasped and sat back in his chair. There were dozens of small gold bars and coins!

Talking to the police, he was told that more than likely, the gold had been stolen jewelry that had been melted down. Whether it had fallen from an apartment or from a plane overhead, they could never determine. However, after he waited six months to see if anyone claimed the gold, the shoe box legally became his property.

Most of us would suffer through a sore shoulder to end up with a box filled with gold! However, we have a similar opportunity to find value when we are hit by trials. Every trial is a box containing valuable treasures. It may knock us to the ground and bruise us, but once we learn how to open the box, we can find great gain inside.

For you who want God's very best,[6] He places in every trial you experience rare coins that are worth a great deal. This is true even if those trials include being hated by your brothers, nearly losing your life, being sold for pennies into a foreign slave market, being framed for adultery, being thrown into jail without a trial, and then being forgotten by the very person who could have won your release. At least that was Joseph's perspective after he experienced all the above![7] Looking back on all the trials he went through at the hands of his brothers, he was able to say to the very ones who caused him such problems, "But as for you, you meant evil against me; but God meant it for *good*, in order to bring it about as it is this day, to save many people alive."[8]

You have the privilege of explaining to your children that each trial contains value. Some have more value built into them than others; some of the less painful trials you experience may not be as valuable as the more painful ones you struggle through. Trials are painful, but unwrapping them to see what they can produce in your lives can be a tremendous source of help for you and your children.

How do you honor a child helping him find value through trials? To answer this, let's start by looking at an example close to home. Over the years, I (Gary) have had to repeatedly unwrap trials with my younger son, Michael.

## A CASE STUDY IN CATASTROPHES

For some reason, Michael is the accident-prone one in the family. When he was two weeks old, he almost died from severe stomach problems that required major surgery. For the next several years, he suffered through a series of childhood illnesses, but when he was three years old, he went through two terrible trials.

First, I was digging in the back yard and unearthed a yellow jacket nest. Sadly, Mike happened to be standing right where the nest came out, and he was stung repeatedly before I could get him inside. Then in the same year, Mike nearly drowned in a motel swimming pool. It was only by means of mouth-to-mouth resuscitation that we were able to revive him.

Since then, Mike has fallen off everything and onto anything possible in our house. And his accidents aren't limited to our home. We were at a business associate's home one evening when Mike was young, and they were roughhousing in the living room. Our friend was swinging Mike around by his feet just for fun when he suddenly lost his grip and Mike smashed into the coffee table, splitting his head open.

For as long as I can remember, Mike has had something in his mouth. At first it was a retainer to enlarge his mouth and then braces to pull his teeth in tighter. From accidents to inconveniences, you name it and Mike has experienced it. And it doesn't seem as though he's slowing down a bit as the years go by!

This past summer, at age thirteen, he was in a major car accident, and he broke his nose and his arm. He was showered with so much broken glass, it took the doctors two hours to take out all the glass slivers from the side of his face and from his eyelid (thankfully, it never penetrated to his eye).

What do you say to a child who has gone through so many trials? Let us tell you now the three actions we promised to describe earlier, the approach we take during and after each trial. These principles aren't in the form of a simple formula that you can wave over a hurting child and use to take away his pain. Rather, they are attitudes and actions you can develop toward suffering, actions that begin with your very first response.


## BUILDING VALUE THROUGH TROUBLED TIMES

### 1. Helping Your Child Grow through Trials Begins with Your First Response.

Have you ever seen a toddler fall down and then turn around and look up before he decided whether or not to cry? Very often, a child's first response is to look to his parents when a trial comes to get some kind of reading on how worried he should be.

Often, the first response by parents can set the tone for how traumatically an event will be taken. When an accident occurs, a breakup with a boyfriend or girlfriend takes place, or there's a problem with someone at school, we've found that being soft and calmly accepting when our children first come to us does several positive things. For one thing, it gives them energy they need at the moment—energy to deal constructively with the problem. With my (Gary's) children, I've seen this time and again.

When Kari was eighteen years old, she slammed into the back of a car during a terrible rainstorm. The accident occurred when another woman tried to turn left from the wrong lane. That also turned out to be the day that Kari received a vivid lesson in differing responses to trials.

Norma and I were away when she got home, but one of our friends had dropped by the house to see us. When he saw the damaged car, he burst into angry words and lectured her about what a careless driver she was and how she could have killed herself or someone else. Just about that time, we pulled into the driveway. Kari was already crying over what this friend had said, and when we got out of the car, she cried even harder.

At that first moment, all we did was hold her and let her tell us the story. In a little while, she was able to wipe her eyes and smile for the first time. Our friend was so surprised by the contrast, he apologized to Kari for being so upset with her. He may have learned in his home that hurts were first met with angry words or emotions, not softness and a gentle touch.

When one of my children is hurting, compounding it by reacting with angry words doesn't add to the solution. If anything, such a reaction often freezes things in a problem state.

Responding with initial softness helps the child see that if Dad and Mom aren't panicking, maybe there is a light at the end of the tunnel. If the child sees his parents panicking or moving into anger, he is often barred from responding in any other way.

> **When parents know ahead of time that the very things that have potential to devalue their children can be used by God to build character into their lives, they are strengthening their grip on their emotions.**

One young boy we counseled with told us how difficult it was to share minor hurts or problems with his mother because every negative thing was blown way out of proportion. Once he came home from school and told her that he thought he may have flunked a test. Dropping the mixing bowl, she threw up her hands and began crying. "What are we going to do with you?" she said between sobs. "What are we going to do?"

How did such a response affect her son, who was the one experiencing the trial? "When my mom would panic like that, I can remember thinking, *How do I know what we're going to do with me? I'm only in the tenth grade! That's why I came to you!*"

Where does the ability to initiate softness and keep from panicking come from? *From a decision forged in quiet times apart from trials to believe that God works all things unto good* (Romans 8:28).[9]

In the middle of a fire, there isn't time to think about ways to prevent a fire. Parents who react emotionally in anger or panic to problems instead of having a plan for responding to them can increase the tension in the air. When parents know ahead of time that the very things that have the potential to devalue their children can be used by God to build character into their lives, they are strengthening their grip on their emotions.

When Michael was in his serious automobile accident this past summer, my first words to him could have been a lecture, something like these: "Were you wearing your seat belt, young man? What was the driver doing? Did you distract him?" or "Mike, did you know that this makes the ten thousandth time you've been banged up? *Did you?* Do you have any idea how embarrassing it is to send in another claim form on you? *Do you?* Do you realize that it's senseless accidents like yours that are causing health care costs in the country to rise dramatically?"

Even if I hadn't been angry and lectured him, I could have used my most pious voice at the hospital and said, "Michael, do you realize how exciting this is? You're going to grow so much spiritually from this! Don't you want to thank God right now that you're hurting so much?" When Mike lay in the hospital room, all Norma and I did was lovingly and calmly stand by him and encourage him through the initial pain.

The book of Proverbs says that having enthusiasm in the face of sorrow is like walking outside on a bitterly cold day without a coat (Proverb 25:20). Meeting someone else's trial with enthusiastic words about how much he can learn through the pain he's suffering can do much the same thing. When a difficulty first happens, don't lecture your children, panic, or become sickeningly pious. Calmly comforting them at the beginning of a trial lays the foundation for them to find value in their experience. Calmness comes from within us when we are confident in God's Word. Painful trials produce maturity, which leads to love! (See James 1:2 and Hebrews 12:10, 11.)

## 2. Keep Tabs on Your Child's Thinking Process During and Following the Trial.

People in California who have lived through several earthquakes know the truth of the old baseball slogan, It ain't over 'til it's over. The first quake may have ended, but they know better than to let their guard down or move back into their houses too soon. It's likely there will be aftershocks that can be nearly as deadly as the first quake.

A similar thing is true when you help your children deal with trials. You need to learn to listen and watch for their reactions following trials to make sure that the aftershocks of emotion won't chip away at their self-worth.

Are they disappointed? Are they angry? Those emotions are common and normal. But are they *staying* angry? Are they repeatedly discouraged? Do they get depressed easily after the event? Does everything have a way of directing their attention back to that trying time, or do they try just as hard to avoid mentioning the subject?

After your children have experienced a trial, you should stand back and watch what's happening with them. If they continue to struggle, you can move in to help them. If they are handling the problem well, you can be just as quick to encourage their response to the trial.

We've observed that when people go through a painful experience, it often enables them to go through a similar experience in the future with less effect. Michael had already been through so many things that the automobile accident wasn't that traumatic for him. Even during the two hours they worked to take all the glass from his face, he was calm and joked with his brother who was "helping" in surgery. A week after the accident, Mike's attitude was still positive when he learned that he'd have to go through the Arizona summer with a cast on his arm and wouldn't be able to swim.

Watching Mike's attitude gave us an opportunity to praise him for the way he was handling the situation. However, several months after the accident, we make a mental note to keep tabs on what's happening with his response to that trial. By doing so, we can spot early warning signs like depression or anxiety that could grow into major problems later on.

### 3. A Few Days After a Trial, Look for an Opportunity to Discuss How God Could Use It in Your Child's Life.

When is the best time to say that there is value in troubled times? How can you do it in a way that sounds genuine, not saccharine sweet? Perhaps several days or weeks may go by before a child is ready to hear the message that God can bring forth value in troubled times.

One way I bring up the subject is to say, "Are you satisfied with what you're experiencing out of the trial you've been through?"

If he hasn't talked about the trial yet, almost always he'll say, "No, I'm not. I'm miserable and unhappy."

At this point I may ask, "Would you like to spend some time this week 'unwrapping' the trial you've received?" I may also give him a hug and a reassuring smile or look.

If his answer is yes (and nine times out of ten it is), that's when I can discuss with him what God's Word has to say about troubled times—the very things we'll be saying in the next chapter. If his answer is no, I don't panic. I just come back another day and softly but persistently give him the opportunity to open up the box his trial came in to see the precious coins inside.

When you teach your children what God's Word has to say about troubled times, you're providing a lamp unto their feet.[10] Biblical principles are like powerful flashlights that can light up even the darkest trial your children may experience.

Because you know this, you can verbally and nonverbally convey this message to your children as they watch your response to their trials. And you can also ask them if they are willing to look for what God has to teach them in the difficulty they've experienced.

One man's life provides a dramatic answer to the question, Can God indeed bring positives out of troubled times?

This young man's name is David, and he is an awesome picture of God's using difficulties for good.[11] For years he viewed trials as something that affected only his external world, and any blow to what he owned or how he looked would discourage him and leave him feeling cheated.

Today, David travels around the world, talking with people about how he discovered that no matter what happens to the outside, it's the internal life that trials really touch. Just like what happened in Jerry's life (whose story we shared in the last chapter), the bigger the trial, the more potential to see God's power and peace at work in the inner person.

## FINDING VALUE IN THE WORST OF TRIALS

During the Vietnam War, David went through rigorous training to become part of the ultraelite special forces team the navy used on dangerous search-and-destroy missions. During a nighttime raid on an enemy stronghold, David experienced the greatest trial of his life. When he and his men were pinned down by enemy machine-gun fire, he pulled a phosphorus grenade from his belt and stood up to throw it. But as he pulled back his arm, a bullet hit the grenade, and it exploded next to his ear.

Lying on his side on the bank of a muddy river, he watched part of his face float by. His entire face and shoulder alternately smoldered and caught on fire as the phosphorus that had embedded itself in his body came into contact with the air.

David knew that he was going to die, yet miraculously he didn't. He was pulled from the water by his fellow soldiers, flown directly to Saigon, and then taken to a waiting plane bound for Hawaii. But David's problems were just beginning.

When he first went into surgery—the first of what would become dozens of operations—the surgical team had a major problem during the operation. As they cut away tissue that had been burned or torn by the grenade, the phosphorus would hit the oxygen in the operating room and begin to ignite again! Several times the doctors and nurses ran out of the room, leaving him alone because they were afraid the oxygen used in surgery would explode! Incredibly, David survived the operation and was taken to a ward that held the most severe burn and injury cases from the war.

# The Gift of Honor

Lying on his bed, his head the size of a basketball, David knew he presented a grotesque picture. Although he had once been a handsome man, he knew he had nothing to offer his wife or anyone else because of his appearance. He felt more alone and more worthless than he had ever felt in his life.

But David wasn't alone in his room. There was another man who had been wounded in Vietnam and was also a nightmarish sight. He had lost an arm and a leg, and his face was badly torn and scarred.

As David was recovering from surgery, this man's wife arrived from the States. When she walked into the room and took one look at her husband, she became nauseated. She took off her wedding ring, put it on the nightstand next to him, and said, "I'm so sorry, but there's no way I could live with you looking like that." And with that, she walked out the door.

He could barely make any sounds through his torn throat and mouth, but the soldier wept and shook for hours. Two days later, he died.

That woman's attitude represents in many respects the way the world views a victim of accident or injury. If a trial emotionally or physically scars someone or causes him to lose his attractiveness, the world says "Ugly is bad," and consequently, any value that person feels he has to others is drained away.

For this poor wounded soldier, knowing that his wife saw no value in him was more terrible than the wounds he suffered. It blew away his last hope that someone, somewhere, could find worth in him because he knew how the world would perceive him.

Three days later, David's wife arrived. After watching what had happened with the other soldier, he had no idea what kind of reaction she would have toward him, and he dreaded her coming. His wife, a strong Christian, took one look at him, came over, and kissed him on the only place on his face that wasn't bandaged. In a gentle voice she said, "Honey, I love you. I'll always love you. And I want you to know that whatever it takes, whatever the odds, we can make it together." She hugged him where she could to avoid disturbing his injuries and stayed with him for the next several days.

Watching what had happened with the other man's wife and seeing his own wife's love for him gave David tremendous strength. More than that, her understanding and accepting him greatly reinforced his own relationship with the Lord.

In the weeks and months that followed, David's wounds slowly but steadily healed. It took dozens of operations and months of agonizing recovery, but today, miraculously, David can see and hear.

On national television, we heard David make an incredible statement.

> *I am twice the person I was before I went to Vietnam. For one thing, God has used my suffering to help me feel other people's pain and to have an incredible burden to reach people for Him. The Lord has let me have a worldwide, positive effect on people's lives because of what I went through.*
>
> *I wouldn't trade anything I've gone through for the benefits my trials have had in my life, on my family's life and on countless teenagers and adults I've had the opportunity to influence over the years.*[12]

David experienced a trial that no parents would wish on their children. Yet in spite of all the tragedy that surrounded him, God turned his troubled times into fruitful ones.

Knowing that the almighty Creator of the universe can take the greatest trials and use them to His glory should be an encouragement to us as parents. The same God who can trade tears of agony for the oak of righteousness (Isaiah 61:3) can take our children's trials and build value into their lives.

In the next chapter, we'll look specifically at five assets that lay wrapped up in each trial our children or we ourselves can open and experience. These are positive elements that can build self-worth and high value into our lives.

# Chapter Five

## Helping Our Children Find Value in Troubled Times: Part 2

Seeing my (Gary's) son lying on a blood-stained stretcher, not moving, with a plastic brace taped to his head, I thought that he wouldn't live through this one. The paramedics calmed me down by assuring me he had only minor injuries and would recover rapidly.

Some of my earliest thoughts were, *What possible benefit did that have? What benefit is there in any trial a child may go through?* I was already assured by the Scriptures and my own experiences that God could and would use this trial in our lives for great benefit to us and glory to Himself. Today, I'm aware of at least five positive benefits that came out of that trial and that we've seen to be wrapped up in any trial. These are benefits that parents can point out to their children and thus raise their value through troubled times.

That's not to say that people can't become bitter or deeply angry when they experience a traumatic experience or loss. Nor does it explain away healthy tears that should be cried nor condone negative actions of others that may have caused the pain. But when we learn to teach our children that God can bring good out of trials, we take the first step in opening up their lives to these positive effects.

## WHEN OUR CHILDREN EXPERIENCE
## TROUBLED TIMES . . .

### 1. They Can Gain an Increased Awareness of Others' Needs and Pain.

In Shakespeare's *Romeo and Juliet*, Romeo says, "He jests at scars, that never felt a wound."[1] For many people who have never been through any kind of deep emotional pain, empathy can remain only a dictionary definition.

Dr. Gary Collins, a Christian psychologist, says that the mark of a person who truly knows how to **love** others and be an effective "people helper" is being able to empathize with their pain.[2] Children or adults who go through difficult times almost always gain a deeper understanding and compassion toward others' needs and pain. For example, we know of a pastor in the Midwest whose counseling ministry was transformed by a major trial he faced.

Bob is a tremendous teacher, but by his own admission he has always struggled in the area of counseling. He wasn't a good listener to people who were hurting, and he tended to cover even the most difficult problem with a hastily found verse and a quick closing prayer.

Although he wouldn't say it to anyone who came into his office, deep inside he often felt that people who came in "crying" were just weak and weren't trusting God with their problems. They simply needed to tighten their belts and "gut it up." But that all changed one afternoon when news arrived of his father's sudden death.

Bob and his father had the natural ties of a father and son, but they were best friends, too. And while he knew his mother had health problems, his father's sudden death due to an aneurysm took him totally by surprise.

Bob had preached at dozens of funerals, but suddenly *he* was the one sitting in the front row with the family. For the first time in his life, his heart went through the anguish of losing a loved one, and it changed him forever—by softening and sensitizing his heart.

Today, Bob is still a tremendous pastor and teacher, but he has more depth to his messages. And since his father's death, he has listened more and cried more with the people in his congregation than in all the other years of his ministry combined.

Bob became aware of what we feel made King David able to write such moving, emotional psalms. In many ways, they both knew the heartbreaking pain of suffering.

The psalmist who wrote the uplifting words, "O Lord, our Lord, / How excellent is Your name in all the earth" (Psalm 8:1), was the same who wrote, "All night I make my bed swim; / I drench my couch with my tears. / My eye wastes away because of grief" (Psalm 6:6–7).

In spite of all his glorious victories, cheering crowds, and magnificent prayers, there were many times when David cried himself to sleep. He was hunted down in the desert by a man who had once loved him.[3] He grieved over the death of his best friend, Jonathan.[4] His wife grew to despise him and his devotion to God and mocked him to his face.[5] He had a rebellious son whose attempt to overthrow David's throne ended in the young man's brutal death.[6] David's own sin left one man dead and a woman in shame and eventually led to the death of a little baby he helped conceive out of wedlock.[7]

David was able to write about a Shepherd who walked with him through the valley of the shadow of death because he had been there. Hunted down by those who had once said they loved him, he slipped into the inky blackness of trials, yet he came out into God's light. The same thing can remain true for any of us today.

Like David, Nancy went through a terrible ordeal of physical and emotional pain, but her suffering was caused by her father's sexual abuse. For three years, she experienced perhaps the greatest blow imaginable to a person's sense of value and self-worth from a man who should have been her greatest encourager and help.

When parents violate a child's boundaries in this way, they cut as deeply as the greatest hurt and can leave lasting scars that can affect a young boy or girl for life.[8] But in Nancy's case, those scars have also brought an incredible sensitivity. Although we can't explain exactly how, Nancy can spend only a few moments with other women, and she can sense with uncanny accuracy those who have been abused sexually.

There was nothing good in what Nancy suffered in her dishonoring home. Yet good has come out of it. Without any formal training, she has a trememdously effective "coffee cup counseling" ministry with other women suffering the effects of abuse.

In my (Gary's) home, there is no question about who is the most sensitive person. No one feels the hurt of others or even of animals as deeply as Mike does, and he is the one who has suffered the most. By pointing this out to Mike and by sharing with him how much God will be able to use that sensitivity in his own family and ministry in the years to come, I've seen his eyes brighten as he sees positive gain in his trials.

How often in our own lives has someone ministered to us during a difficult time with caring eyes and loving concern, and later we learned that person had been through a similar trial? The writer of the book of Hebrews tells us that Jesus is able to aid those who suffer because of what He Himself suffered (Hebrews 2:18).

As you begin to look for and teach your children about positive gains through trials, one clear benefit is that God can make them more aware of others' hurts. This increased sensitivity can help them become individuals who help others, and it is a **major factor** in their ability to genuinely love others.

## 2. They Can Learn Humility.

One common denominator in facing difficult times is that they are almost always humbling. Whether it's the boy who fell while walking up the steps at school or the girl who had such a hard time explaining her divorce at the ten-year reunion, trying experiences often bring people back to rock bottom.

After Mike's automobile accident, several scars remain on his cheek, his eyelid, and his lip. Since he is in junior high, walking around with scars on his face can be humbling. Of course, at first it was something to brag about with the guys; but as time has passed, even though the doctor has assured us the scars will eventually become less noticeable, it's been a very humbling experience for Mike.

What possible benefit is there in being humbled? Do these verses sound familiar? "Blessed are the meek, / For they shall inherit the earth" (Matthew 5:5). "God resists the proud, / But gives grace to the humble" (James 4:6). One lifelong benefit you receive from going through painful situations is the increase of

God's grace. You get more of His undeserved, unearned favor[9] and more of His power to live successfully.

Recently, we were on a friend's radio call-in program. During the breaks when we were off the air, we learned about this man's childhood. As a boy, he had been assaulted sexually by a relative. The experience was so traumatic for him that he was never able to tell his parents, who loved him dearly and treated him accordingly. In a sense, he has felt that the relative robbed him of the blessing his parents gave him.

Because he was so ashamed of what had happened to him, the tragedy of that event would rush to his mind every time he accomplished something significant and keep him from enjoying it. Even though he had reached the top of his profession, he had terrible insecurities and doubts about himself. But in the last year, he had learned an important truth.

In studying the Scriptures, he ran across a statement the Lord directed to Paul: "My grace is sufficient for you" (2 Corinthians 12:9). Paul was experiencing a trial that was humbling to him, and he wished God would take it from his life. Yet he lived out his life with his thorn in the flesh and the words, "My grace is sufficient for you."

As our friend thought about his own trial that had humbled him so much, he suddenly remembered another verse, "God gives grace to the humble." He had certainly been humbled, and he knew God's grace was sufficient. But at last he put the two together, and the words moved from his head to his heart.

Our friend is one of the best counselors we know, with a tremendous sensitivity to hurting people who call in. Every time we're with him, we listen in wonder at how accurately he can pinpoint what a caller is struggling with, even though he has learned only a few details of the situation. Yet he admits that he would never have been as effective in feeling compassion and helping others in pain had he not gone through what he did.

While the experience itself was and continues to be a heinous sin and a humbling incident, God's grace has proved more than sufficient. That relative left our friend's self-worth in "ashes," but God has turned the negative effects of the experience into beauty in his life.

### Being Humbled Can Teach Us Lessons in Helping Others

Being humbled by a trial showers us with God's grace and also helps us become better servants. That may not sound too appealing to some people who have no desire to be servants. After all, servants have a low social status, don't they? When God counts valuable people, however, they're the first He points to, and He says they're the greatest (Matthew 20:26). Do you know what Jesus said was the highest calling in life? Not preaching. Not teaching. Not even evangelism. But *serving* (John 13:1ff.).

I (John) found that being humbled made me a better servant. When I was entering high school, my mother had to go through a series of operations due to her rheumatoid arthritis. We used to call her the "Bionic Woman" because she had so many artificially replaced joints that she had to carry a card to get through the metal detector at airports.

During much of her recuperative time, my mother had to walk very slowly using a cane or use a wheelchair that one of us boys would push. Pushing a woman around in a wheelchair might have gotten me a merit badge if I had been a Boy Scout, but in the crowd I hung around with before I became a Christian, it only brought mocking and abuse.

To be very honest, it was humbling at times. But do you know what I quickly learned? The humiliation I felt at the hands of a few callous friends made me a better servant. Even though I was in high school, responding to my mother's needs taught me incredible lessons in servanthood. Those lessons I learned in my teens are still helping me today in my ministry with others and with my own family.

Being humbled helps us gain more of God's grace, and the power of His grace in us provides the ability to enrich the lives of others. That ability, in turn, increases our sense of self-worth. In Lori's case, it did more than that. It held the key to how God would use her in the future.

For years, Lori hated herself and even God for making her the way she was. Many little girls were taller than the boys in grade school, but as time passed, Lori kept her height advantage. Feeling self-conscious and alone, she adopted eating habits that soon left her with a weight problem, too.

She just knew that being born big boned and heavyset had reduced her chances of getting dates, and she hated the way she stood out in a crowd. Even after she became a Christian during high school, she couldn't find a single thing to thank God for when it came to her appearance.

Then one day Lori's high-school business education class visited a nearby hospital on a career field trip. That afternoon Lori's life changed on the spot, and it happened when they were visiting the physical therapy room.

As the class stood listening to a nurse tell about the different equipment being used in the room, a minor emergency occurred. A young woman with a spinal cord injury slid from her exercise machine onto the floor. As the girl began to cry, almost without thinking Lori hurried to lift her up and put her gently in her wheelchair. It would have been a task for at least two nurses, but Lori's size enabled her to lift the girl with ease.

It has been seven years since that field trip, and when we talked to Lori last year, here's what she said about it: "For years I looked at the way God made me as a curse, not a blessing. But that day at the hospital, I learned that He could use me just the way He made me! That young woman needed my strong arms. That afternoon, for the first time in my life I was able to thank God for who I was and even for making me big."

Lori has completed occupational therapy training, and today she is on the staff of a major southwestern hospital, feeling valued and needed as she serves hurting children and adults—just the way God made her.

Trials can be humbling. It may not be pleasant if your child drops a pass in the end zone, is the only one to forget a piece at the piano recital, wets the bed at a friend's slumber party, or has to repeat the second grade; but your child can receive God's grace when it happens. Trials can make his heart more sensitive to others, and God may use them to make him a better servant in years to come. For some children, trials can hold the key to discovering lifetime goals.

## 3. The Trials Can Deepen Their Maturity and Give Them Endurance.

Have you ever noticed that many people who suffer tend to develop a maturity and strength far beyond their years? Carol benefited from her trials in that very way. She lived in a single-parent home with her mother who was an alcoholic. In high school, she was definitely part of the "in" crowd, but in some ways she stood apart from them. Because of the things she suffered at home,

Carol made some decisions early in life that many of her more immature friends had to learn the hard way.

When the group began to take bottles to parties, Carol had already seen where social drinking could lead. Her girlfriends had never seen someone passed out on the floor, lying in her own vomit. Carol had. And the pictures of her mother made it easier for her to say no to the offers to "share a drink." Seeing the part alcohol played in her parents' divorce also made her set her dating standards higher than those of many of her friends.

People who come from alcoholic homes are more likely to become alcoholics than those who come from nonalcoholic homes. Often a person coming from an alcoholic home has such a low self-value that she acts out her low worth by repeating her parents' problems. However, instead of being controlled by the trials she experienced, Carol learned how to look for positive things in her background that could build her worth.

For Carol, coming from an alcoholic home acted as a deterrent to drinking. In addition, she was working and maintaining an after-school job and a household long before many of her friends. She learned lessons in responsibility then that helped her in her career and with her own husband and children.

Growing up too soon can be a hurtful trial. Yet today, years after she has left home, Carol is able to thank God for the responsibility and maturity her trials built into her life. In her endurance and capacity to deal with difficulties, she's head and shoulders above many her age. And there are others like her— Alan, for instance.

Alan's sister died of leukemia when she was a senior in high school and he was a freshman. As devastating as that trial was, he changed greatly after her death. Suddenly, little things he had once taken for granted took on a more precious nature. Alan ceased to look at life and death and spiritual things in a childish way. The growth and maturity that event wrought in his life helped carve out a capacity to care and a burden to share Christ with others that have made him one of the finest pastors in the country today.

As in Carol's and Alan's lives, nature has its own way of picturing this spiritual truth. Every fall, those of us with yards have to go through the ritual of "scalping" our grass. Cutting it down so short makes it seem it will be forever kept from sprouting. Yet every spring, it grows up even more lush and green because of the cutting. The Scriptures tell us that every branch that bears fruit, the Lord prunes back at times to help it grow and bear more fruit (John 15:1–8). As difficult as the pruning process is, the results are the fruit of the Spirit that can change our lives and those around us (Galatians 5:22).

No one who is familiar with Joni Earricksen Tada's story will deny the beautiful life God made from her terrible accident. When she is on a television program or a radio talk show, her maturity radiates how much God has taught her through her suffering. Maturity is a third wonderful benefit you can look for and point out as you honor your children by helping them find value in troubled times.

In a healthy body, when one member of the body suffers, all the other parts suffer along with it (1 Corinthians 12:26). The same thing is true in a healthy family. When one person suffers, the rest of the family can be drawn closer through the sharing of that sorrow. That's the fourth benefit of going through trials.

## 4. The Difficult Times Can Draw Us Together as a Family.

One of the most emotional experiences we've witnessed was the closing moments of a reunion of World War II veterans. A few summers ago we were staying at a hotel in The Loop in Chicago where a reunion of former tank artillerymen and commanders for General Patton was being held. The officers and men had fought from Italy to France and made a heroic rescue of surrounded Allied troops at the Battle of the Bulge. Most of them had lost a number of close friends in the war. All of them had experienced major trials together.

We were in the lobby when the reunion was breaking up and many of the men were saying their good-byes. In one way, it was almost comical. Because of the incredible noise inside the tanks when their cannon were fired (tankmen in World War II didn't have the protective equipment artillerymen do today), many of the men suffered severe hearing loss.

As a result parting conversations were much louder than they would be for people with normal hearing, and requests to get the other person to repeat something he had just said were commonplace. Yet in spite of all that, we will never forget the tears, the embraces, and the love the men showed for one another over forty years after they had fought together. They may have lost their ability to hear as they once could, but their ability to love one another more than made up for it.

Experiencing troubled times welded these men together into a family. When children experience a trial, it can have a similar effect on each member of the family.

For years, when I (Gary) asked my son Michael, "Why does Dad love you so much?" he would smile and say, "Because I brought you back to the family."

Michael came along at a time when I was at the "height" of my career. The other children were getting older, and I was able to travel more to minister to others. At the time, the last thing I wanted was more responsibility around the house.

To be honest, in some ways I resented Michael in those first days when we brought him home from the hospital. But all that changed one day when we were swimming in a motel pool and I looked over to see three-year-old Michael's small body at the bottom.

I'll never forget thinking, *Oh, Lord, we've lost him,* as I dived into the deep end and brought him up to the surface. Laying him on the side of the pool, I gave him mouth-to-mouth resuscitation, and very shortly he coughed and began to cry. From that moment on, it was as if that trial bonded me to Michael in a special way and brought me back to the family. That experience was a major reason for my asking my boss for a different job that would keep me off the road and closer to home.

Throughout the years, trials that the other children have experienced have drawn the rest of us closer together as well. But because of all that has happened to Michael, it seems God has used him time and again to pull us together as a family. Take last Christmas, for instance.

A favorite tradition around the Smalley household is having a marinated steak fondue on Christmas Day. We were all busy sticking pieces of bread and steak with the long fondue forks and dipping them into the fondue when Michael suddenly let out a blood-curdling scream!

As he tried to stick his fork through a piece of steak, it slipped and rammed all the way through the palm of his hand! For several minutes while Greg and I ran for pliers to cut the fork loose and Norma and Kari ministered to Michael, pandemonium broke loose in our house.

Finally, after we had bandaged his hand and he was feeling much better, Michael began to laugh. Soon we were all rolling on the floor laughing at the hectic things that had happened with all of us running around and shouting.

When everyone quieted down, Michael looked at me with a smile and said, *"Hey, why is it that I'm always the one who brings the family back together?"*

Have you been able to identify a common thread that runs through the benefits we've discussed so far? They can all help children become more loving.

## 5. They Can Become More Loving.

The greatest coin we can discover as we unwrap any trial is love. Troubled times have a way of cutting deep channels into our lives that can carry God's love to us and our love to others.

In the weeks after my son's car accident, I had the opportunity to sit down with him several times and list some of the benefits that were a part of his trial. Because we've done this with so many of his trials, he was quick to point out ways in which he had become more sensitive, had gained maturity, and had seen the positive side of his humbling scars. Yet the greatest gift trials can bring him is their ability to make him more loving.

Perhaps the thing I appreciate the most about people like Joni and my son, Michael, is the deep love for the Lord and for others that has developed through trials. As C. S. Lewis said, "God speaks to us in our joys; He shouts to us in our sorrows." [10] People who look for and thank God in advance for the benefits He can bring through a trial not only help themselves, but they can also look for and share these principles with their children.

Children don't have to be shut up in their pain forever. Our God is as good as His Word, and His Word tells us that all things work together for good for those who love Him (Romans 8:28). He is so trustworthy, we can thank Him before seeing immediate benefits from our trials (1 Thessalonians 5:18). In the process of time and with loving parents to help them cut the tape and remove the lid from difficult times, sons and daughters can gain love through the trials that once threatened to take it from them.

## FURTHER HELP ON FINDING BENEFITS
## IN TRIALS

Before we close this chapter, we have a few other comments to make about how to respond to trials. With problems such as unwanted pregnancy, major accidents, cancer, death of a parent, and other traumatic events, don't expect your child to see benefits from his trial overnight. In some cases, it may take a year or longer.

For Nancy, whose story of abuse we shared earlier, it took almost a year of continually looking for positive benefits from her abusive background before she was able to see anything positive from that terrible experience. However, once she began to see how God had made her more sensitive, a better servant, and more loving to her own family and others, she was able to make a decision to forgive her father and for the first time move away from the pain of the past. Every day for almost eight months Jerry, who struggled with his father, had to make a decision to unwrap his trials and look for benefits God had supplied him before he too loosened the painful grip of the past.

Experts say that it takes at least thirty days of repeating something consistently before it becomes ingrained as a habit. You need to be lovingly persistent in looking for positive benefits God has worked or will provide in your life if you're to find value in troubled times.

We're not explaining away the possibility that some people can go through difficulties and become anything but more loving in the process. It's natural for someone to go through a stage where he's angry over what has happened to him, but making a decision to *remain* angry can desensitize him to spiritual truth. That decision can lead to bitterness and resentment. It can harden his heart and weaken his relationship with God and others.

The mark of a person who does or does not grow through trials is not the amount of tears he has cried. It is the degree to which he is willing to take God at His word. If he only listens to the wisdom of the world, trials that touch him on the outside will almost always lower his sense of value. If he listens to God's unchanging Word, however, even when it is only a still, small voice amidst the storm or a troubled time, his inner life can be opened to maturity and gain.

Why sit down with your children and teach them that there can be value in trying times? Because of something Solomon, the wisest man who ever lived, once said:

> *Remember now your Creator*
> *in the days of your youth,*
> *Before the difficult days come,*
> *And the years draw near when you say,*
> *"I have no pleasure in them"*
> *(Ecclesiastes 12:1).*

If you consistently ignore the benefits that can come from trials, you can watch the joy go out of your life. As Solomon said, if you live long enough, you will see enough sorrow and storm clouds to make your joy of living disappear.

If you're wise, you'll turn your children toward what God can build in their lives, even during trials, *before* the harsh realities of life rob them of their joy. This process begins by reminding them and yourself that where there is defeat, that's where God's strength is available. Where there is loneliness, that's where God's presence is. Wherever there are bad things happening to you, there is God giving you the power to gain value in Him and to serve and love others in need.

Let's now turn our gaze on another aspect of honor, recognizing our own parenting strengths and style.

# Chapter Six

## Recognizing Our Own Parenting Strengths and Style

*T*wice, in quick succession, her father slaps her across the mouth as he firmly takes hold of her arm. "You little smart mouth!" he shouts at his ten-year-old daughter. "Keep it up! I've got all day to see to it that you clean up your room!"

Mother is now in the battle trying to defend Geri, her youngest daughter, but it's much too late. Dad has already lost control of his temper and stands screaming at her, "I want this room to look perfect! Look at these socks behind the door. Does this room look clean to you? You can forget about going over to your friend's house this afternoon. Starting now, you're grounded for a month. Do you hear me, young lady?" he yells into her ear as if she were deaf.

Why are some children raised with so much severity while others live in a healthier, more relaxed home? Why do some parents have incredible expectations of their children, but others encourage and motivate them to reach their own potential? Why do some homes seem to produce confident children, but others send sons or daughters away feeling insecure and unstable?

What we continue to see in our work with families is that parents who understand and develop their own particular positive parenting style raise confident children who feel of high worth. In other words, parents who have a better understanding of *who they are* and *what their strengths are* honor their children and build value into their lives.

In this chapter, we'll be discussing the four most common types of parents we see and the strengths they bring to the parenting task. Although there are numerous excellent individual personality books and tests on the market, we want to look at how these different individual "bents" can build value into children.

Also, we've found that while a person may act one way at work or with friends, he often has a different bent when it comes to his parenting style and how he relates to his children. Why is it so important for parents to understand their strengths in the parenting setting? I (John) discovered one vital reason on my first day of seminary.

## UNDERSTANDING OUR PARENTING STRENGTHS

At the seminary I attended, all incoming students took the class "Bible Study Methods" that was taught by Dr. Howard Hendricks, a nationally known Christian educator and family expert. He was the finest equipper and discipler I've ever met, and his motivating courses on the Christian family were the very reasons why I decided to minister in the areas of counseling and family enrichment. To all of us at seminary, he was known affectionately as "Prof."

As I took my seat in the crowded classroom the first day, my anxiety was already sky high. Looking around the room, I knew that many of the men and women there had graduated from Christian colleges. Some had probably been to Christian grade schools and high schools as well.

Having graduated from a secular university and become a Christian just recently, I knew that I didn't have the background in Bible courses these students did. Would I pass the course? Could I make it through the rigors of the next four years? Was I smart enough to do the work?

After opening the class in prayer, the next thing Dr. Hendricks did raised my anxiety level another ten notches. In his brisk, energetic way, Prof pointed his finger at us and said, "Men and women, I'm about to give you a test. If you pass this test, I can almost guarantee you'll be successful in the ministry. If you fail this test, there's a great chance you'll wash out and won't make it. Now, get out a three-by-five card, and let me give you the test."

*Oh no!* I thought to myself as I fumbled for an index card. *He's going to ask us to name all the books in the Old Testament or list all the names in Christ's genealogy or at least give the "hidden" Greek meaning to some theological word that everybody who has been to Bible college already knows.*

With my head down, I was already thinking about what I would say to my family and friends when I flunked out of seminary. It was my first day in graduate school, and I already felt I was going to let down the Lord and my family.

Prof's words cut short my thoughts when he said, "On one side of the card, I'd like you to write down your three greatest weaknesses."

*Three greatest weaknesses?* That wasn't hard! The only difficult thing about that was limiting it to three. As I glanced around the room, I noticed that no one else seemed to have any trouble writing down weaknesses either. Pens moved furiously the next few minutes.

After a short time, Prof said, "Okay, that was the warm-up. Here's the real test."

*I knew it!* I said to myself. *Here comes the question about all the books in the Old Testament.*

Very deliberately, Prof said to us, "I want you to turn your index card over, and I want you to list your three greatest strengths."

It was so easy to write about weaknesses, but take time to write down strengths? After all, this was a Christian school, wasn't it? Shouldn't we talk only about our weaknesses? Even coming from a secular school, I knew that "pride cometh before a fall." Instead of the fast and furious writing of just a few moments ago, pens and pencils dangled in our hands as most of us struggled with our answers.

In the years that have passed since that "exam," I've often thought back to Prof's words when our time of writing was up. I can still picture him confidently stating, "In all my years of teaching, I've rarely met someone who can't quickly tell me his weaknesses. But if you don't know the strengths God has given you that you can develop, you'll never be a success in the ministry."

When we think about Christ's ministry, that statement makes

very good sense. Our Lord knew who He was and where He had come from (John 16:5). He knew His relationship with His Father and what He could or would not do (John 5:19ff.). His confidence in the Scriptures made Him unafraid to meet even the most learned Pharisee in a face off of words.[1] In short, He knew His strengths and used them to serve God and us.

But how does this relate to you as a parent who wants to raise the value of your children? A parent who is aware of personal strengths is better able to serve children. If you can't write down three strengths you have right now, very likely your own value is so low you'll struggle in raising your children's worth above your own. Until you're aware of the strengths, characteristics, and traits God has built into your life, you can never understand your greatest weaknesses as a parent.

## WHEN STRENGTHS BECOME PUSHED TO AN EXTREME

For most of us, our weaknesses are usually our strengths pushed to an extreme. That's worth repeating. Weaknesses are often strengths pushed to an extreme. Take the apostle Peter, for example.

When we think of Peter, the Rock, one strength he certainly had was his willingness to jump in wherever he sensed a need. On the day of Pentecost, this strength led him to preach such a powerful sermon that over three thousand people were saved. But what happened when that strength of "jumping in" was pushed to an extreme?

How about questioning whether Christ should go to the cross? Or nearly causing a massacre in the Garden of Gethsemane when Jesus was being arrested, or quickly turning away from the Lord when several women questioned him before the Crucifixion?[2] Peter certainly had a strength in being quick to make up his mind. However, he often jumped regardless of the wisdom of doing so.

Maybe one of your strengths is making quick decisions. Being decisive can be a strength, but pushed to an extreme, it can lead you to become bossy or demanding.

Perhaps one of your strengths is listening. Taking the time to actively listen to a child can be a tremendous tool to build value into her life. But what happens when a person pushes the strength of listening to an extreme? Then you have a situation like Faye's.

Faye tried repeatedly to go to her mother for help with her problems. Every time Faye went to her mother with a major issue to discuss, however, she would listen, listen, listen. But because she felt insecure inside, she never felt confident enough to offer any suggestions to her daughter. Faye would often become so frustrated that she would say, "Mom, just tell me *something* I could do, would you?" Listening is a strength all of us need to develop, but for Faye's mother, it caused frustration instead of building value into her daughter.

Once a person understands what his strengths are, he becomes better able to recognize his weaknesses. An extremely conscientious mom can thank God for her natural bent toward orderliness, but she needs to guard against becoming obsessive with her house cleaning or excessively picky with the children. A dominant dad can thank God for his determination and efficiency, but he needs to guard against going too far with his dominance in the home and becoming harsh, pushy, and domineering.

There's one other reason why knowing your parenting style and strengths can help you. It helps you know which child you'll probably struggle with the most (the one with most of your same strengths), and how you can best encourage and equip each of your children by using their natural personality tendencies.

We know that there are parents reading this book who think they might not be able to come up with a single strength to put down on an index card. As you read about the four basic parenting styles, however, we hope you won't just look for areas you need to change. We hope that perhaps for the first time, you'll be able to see and thank God for your natural strengths, strengths you can use to build value in your children.

## Are You a Take-Charge Charlene (or Charlie)?

*Take-Charge (TC) parents* like to get immediate results when they ask their children to do something. If they're really strong in this respect, their favorite line might be something like this, "When I tell you to jump, don't ask me why. Ask me how high."

They like challenges in life and may stir up a little excitement if things get too steady and relaxed. TC parents want to see results from the things to which they give their time (and money). They expect to see quick results like positive grades from their son who is being tutored or a minirecital from their daughter who is taking piano lessons.

TC parents speak directly and boldly. One great thing about TC parents is that you know just where you stand with them. Children don't need to guess whether Mom or Dad is angry, happy, or sad. It's right out in the open instead of being hidden behind a mask. However, as good as TC parents are in being forthright, they sometimes can say something very blunt to their children and walk away without realizing the possibly damaging impact of their words.

If TC parents have a teen-ager in the house, sparks can fly. TC parents don't like it when their children question the status quo, and they can get angry when they're questioned.

When talking to TC parents, children might find some resistance if they don't "get to the point" in sharing a request or story. TC parents aren't great chitchatters; they like to get on with conversations and get back to the challenges of life.

Finally, if TC parents see something they feel they need to respond to, they'll move right out. If they feel Bobby's room needs redecorating, they can spend hours that same afternoon shopping for new things. If Jayne wants to be the only child in her school who takes bagpipe lessons, within hours a TC parent can track down the only bagpipe tutor in town and get her child enrolled.

Like the apostle Peter, a TC person has the natural strength of decisive action, but she also needs to be sure she has talked to Bobby first about the decorating plan instead of changing his room when he's at school and figuring he'll appreciate all her efforts.

How can TC parents use their natural bent to build value into their children?

• By using their tendency to respond quickly to meet their children's or their spouse's needs.

• By speaking directly and without manipulation.

• By taking the lead to serve the family and setting a positive direction for family members to follow.

How can TC parents work to keep their strengths from being pushed into weaknesses?

• They can work on developing their sensitivity to other family members' feelings.

• They can slow down enough to let others ask questions and verbalize "why" they've made a decision. (We know of one TC father who never told his wife or children they were moving until he had already bought a house in a new city and put the For Sale sign up at their house!)

• They can pace themselves and make sure there are family fun times when everybody (including the TC parent) can relax.

## Are You a Fun-Loving Freda (or Fred)?

If *Fun-Loving (FL) parents* were animals, without a doubt they'd be otters! Have you ever seen an otter in the wild or on film when he *didn't* look like he was having the time of his life? Even the act of opening an oyster or sliding down a hill can become nonstop fun for an otter.

FL parents treat life in much the same way. They love to gather their friends and their children together and talk, talk, talk. In many ways, they're a party waiting to happen! With their children, they're quick to ask about their day, and they love to get into long discussions with them. They're optimistic and good motivators, and even if they do tend to forget the food and leave two hours late for a family camping trip, they'll have fun when they get there.

Remember how each pattern has strengths and weaknesses? While an FL parent is very encouraging and motivating to children, he can also do things that can lower his children's worth. One common problem is saying yes to so many other people and opportunities for work or play that there isn't any time left for the kids. Saying no is a skill FL parents need to learn. Even if it's only to a second piece of pie, they should make it a habit to say no to at least one thing a day.

FL parents can stray into another trap. In the book of Proverbs, we are told, "In the multitude of words sin is not lacking."[3] In their excitement to tell a story or relate some fact, sometimes FL parents can bend a story or slip in a "fact" here or there. In their need to be liked by others, instead of telling someone "I'm too busy," they'll stay up all night to get a project done and then be too tired to spend time with their families. Children (or spouses) who live with this can become frustrated at times, feeling they are number three or four (or seven or eight) on the list of priorities.

How can FL parents use their natural bent to build value into their children?

• By using their extensive network of friends and contacts to meet their children's (or mate's) needs.

• By showing enthusiasm over things their children (or spouse) accomplish.

• By structuring and initiating fun times and experiences that build family unity.

How can their strengths be pushed into weaknesses?

• By allowing their poor control of time to cost them time with the one group who "has to love them"—their family.

• By saying yes to things they know they need to say no to.

• By wanting too much to be liked by their children and failing to be firm with them as a result (particularly if they tend to have little of the Take-Charge parents' traits).

## Are You a Loyal-Friend Lisa (or Larry)?

*Parents like Loyal-Friend (LF)* Lisas and Larrys usually don't have as many friends as Fun-Loving parents, but the friendships they do have are much deeper. While Fun-Loving parents tend to know hundreds of people one-inch deep, Loyal-Friend parents have a deep desire to know a handful of people in depth. Not only that, but LF parents are incredibly loyal to their children, spouses, or friends. Of all the different kinds of parents, LF's can absorb or listen to tremendous amounts of pain or hurt when it involves the family or a close friend.

LF parents would rather stay home with their children than spend every night at the movies. They are excellent listeners and are empathetic when their children share hurts. They're good at calming things down when little Sammy is screaming that he's bleeding to death because of the scratch on his knee. And wherever they live—in a one-room apartment or a twelve-room mansion—their home reflects a warmth and a "This is home" feeling.

Just as we've seen in other parenting patterns, LF parents can do things by stressing their natural strengths to an extreme that can lower their children's worth. For example, their love for a stable, steady environment can make changes hard to take. Particularly if a child (or a spouse) is a Take-Charge or Fun-Loving person, things are going to change every day! And that leads to the next strength of an LF parent that can be pushed into a weakness.

Loyalty is unquestionably a tremendous quality. Yet sometimes LF parents will listen to another person's hurt so long and so intently that they never leave time to share their own hurts and needs. They tend to be very sensitive to their children's pain, but they also need to allow them room to grow up and not stay in the nest long after their wings need to be exercised. And as we note in the chapters on the dark side of family loyalties, sometimes being lovingly loyal means not only listening and hoping problems will work out, but (gasp!) confronting them as well.

How can LF parents use their natural bent to build value into their children?

• By using their excellent listening skills to demonstrate interest in what their child (or spouse) is saying.

• By modeling depth of communication instead of just flippant talk.

• By showing a commitment to each family member that in and of itself builds value in their loved ones.

How can they keep their strengths from being pushed into weaknesses?

• By learning that change represents an opportunity for growth instead of just a reason for concern.

• By taking risks to express their own hurts and needs instead of letting them pile up.

• By doing one thing a week (going to Bible study, having lunch with a friend, taking time alone to shop, reading a book of interest) that fills their emotional tank, which they so readily empty for others.

## Are You a Let's-Be-Right Rita (or Randy)?

Fun-Loving parents ask, "Are we having fun yet?" *Let's-Be-Right (LBR) parents* ask, "Are we following the directions correctly yet?" If you lean toward being "right" and doing things by the book in everything you do, from the minute you find out you're pregnant (or your wife is), you've qualified as a genuine LBR person. Now that you're going to be a parent, you'll need to schedule the *right* number of doctor visits; take the *right* prenatal vitamins (are generic brands really as good as the others?); eat only the *right* things and avoid all the junk food the Fun-Loving parent sneaks on the side; and make sure you read the latest research about the *right* color to paint the nursery for a newborn.

Accuracy is an LBR parent's trademark, and her house, office, and children's rooms reflect that fact. She does a tremendous job of setting and keep boundaries for herself and her children, but those boundaries can sometimes shift over to the rigid side.

A tremendous strength of LBR parents is their consistency and their "quality control" tendencies. Like Loyal-Friend parents, they'll be at the party when the invitation says, or when they think it is the "correct" time to be there. If a child has a big paper coming up in school or transportation has to be worked out between soccer practice and music lessons, you can be sure it'll be done right and on time.

LBR moms and dads give children orderliness and predictability that build their security and worth. However, like each of the parenting styles we've looked at, this one also can use natural strengths to drop a child's worth.

Pushed to an extreme, LBR parents' critical thinking and attention to detail can move into legalism and unhealthy perfectionism. Expecting their children or themselves to be perfect can add burdens instead of building worth. Fear of doing something wrong (like not reading this chapter correctly) and damaging their children for life can paralyze them and keep them from doing anything at all. Finally, when problems come or they get mad at their children (or spouse), they can step back several paces to avoid the pain instead of facing the anger or hurt and dealing with it.

How can LBR parents use their natural bent to build worth into their children?

• By providing a careful, predictable environment that encourages stability.

• By being diplomatic when an argument breaks out between the children and using logical thinking to straighten things out.

• By teaching their children that doing things correctly and working heartily unto the Lord can give them a sense of quality and accomplishment (and keeps them from having to do it again!).

How can these parents' strengths be kept from being pushed to an extreme?

• By seeing to it that "deep" cleaning, keeping the house in order, and spending the day "according to plan" don't get put ahead of taking time to play and talk with a child (or spouse).

• By keeping in mind that they can become very stern critics of the same people they once felt had so many positive qualities (and nine times out of ten still do).

• By facing up to conflict when it's necessary instead of avoiding it.

So far, we've looked at four different parenting types, each of which can build value into a child (or lower it if strengths get pushed to an extreme). As you looked over this list, perhaps you could easily pick yourself out, or you may have seen more than one pattern that describes you.

Some personality experts say that people are one "type" only or that certain types are totally incompatible with each other. We don't agree. We feel this puts too tight a label on people who are each tremendously complex. For example, we've seen a mother who was primarily a Fun-Loving Freda also have strong Let's-Be-Right Rita tendencies. We've seen a father who 90 percent of the time was a Loyal-Friend Larry become a Take-Charge Charlie at home the 10 percent of the time when his boss put him under extra pressure at work.

*We feel that every parent has within himself or herself the capacity to develop and demonstrate each parenting style.* Perhaps you've already seen this in yourself. Have you seen your parenting style change with the arrival of a new child or when your child reached a certain age?

To be able to build value in children throughout their lives, parents need to develop positive aspects of each parenting type. With toddlers who don't have the judgment yet to stay away from certain things, quick responses and take-charge characteristics are important. What grade-schooler doesn't need the nonstop entertainment a fun-loving parent can provide? Could a parent ever have enough loyal-friend patience and listening skills when dealing with an adolescent? And for children of any age, lets-be-right training can help them follow God's Word and stay on a positive path.

Wouldn't it be great if we could take the best of every personality bent and mold it into our lives? We have a model for that, you know. The better we know our heavenly Father, the more we'll see the incredible balance and maturity in the way He treats His children.

## COMBINING THE BEST

With His disciples, Jesus put each parenting style into practice. Can you think of ways in which He treated them with take-charge tendencies? How about telling Peter to get behind Him, standing up for the disciples when they were challenged by the religious leaders, directing their ministry and mission, and setting His face "like a flint"[4] to go to the cross for them?

The Savior of the world modeled fun-loving characteristics to His disciples. Where was the first place He took them? To a wedding. What was He constantly accused of by the Pharisees? Being "a glutton and a winebibber."[5] He talked with the "sinners" at length, and He often mingled with crowds of needy people.

While Jesus felt compassion for the crowds He went amongst, He also modeled depth in relationships with His disciples. Could there ever be a better, more loyal friend to sinners than our Lord? Within the disciples, there was an inner circle of three. Within that circle, He had an even deeper relationship with the "beloved disciple." Most intimate of all was His relationship with the Father, as seen in the times—even hours before dawn—when He drew away to enjoy that intimacy. Loyalty marked our Savior's life, a loyalty that led all the way to the cross and beyond.

Can anyone convict Jesus of doing wrong? As long as He was with His disciples, He demonstrated to them and called on them to follow God's Word, which could guide and free them. His carefully worded answers to the disciples and every life He touched reflected a quality moment.

Each style of person, each style of parent can be seen in our Lord. It should be seen in our lives as well. Most incredible of all, He can give us the inner desire and strength to build the best aspects of each style into our own parenting patterns.

## TAKING THE NEXT STEP

Why not make a study of positive traits from each parenting style that you can build into your life? Choose one trait from each of the four you especially want to work on in the next six weeks, and ask your spouse or a close friend to hold you accountable at the end of that time.

We would also encourage you to take the time to explain to your children which parenting type you are most like today and admit to them your strengths and weaknesses. With just a little effort, you can help them identify their personal bent and see how their strengths make them special and valuable parts of your family.

If you find that in a family of four, each of you has a different pattern that predominates, don't lose heart. Each of you can make a decision to build balance into your life and develop the best from each bent.

Finally, don't crush or bend a child into a different pattern simply because you're most comfortable with your own pattern. You'll probably lean in one direction, but you can learn to shift, bend, and still keep your and your children's worth and identity intact.

Wise men and women seek wisdom and understanding.[6] Deepening your understanding about your own parenting strengths can help you live wisely with your children. In this third aspect of honor, you can find a key to opening each child's heart, filling it with love and self-worth. You can also find new value in yourself and the way God created you and wants you to develop.

Now that you're better aware of your parenting strengths and style, you can use this information and your individual bent to help you personally apply the principles in this book. And in particular, understanding yourself better can help you keep your home in a healthy balance, which is the next aspect of honor.

# Chapter Seven

## Providing a Healthy Balance in Our Homes: Part 1

*I*t was two days before my (Gary's) fourteenth birthday when I paid a steep price for losing my balance. All my friends had been urging me to try to walk across a thin pine tree that had fallen across a deep, narrow ravine—a feat we called the suicide walk.

It really didn't look that difficult. All I had to do was keep my eyes glued to the end of the tree, walk a straight line, and not look down at the trees and razor-sharp rocks below. My first few steps across the fallen tree were confident, but my friends stopped cheering when they saw me lose my confidence, then my balance, and fall nearly twenty feet onto an old oak tree down below. Thankfully, that tree broke my fall and perhaps saved my life. But because of the impact when I hit, I was badly shaken and had a number of deep cuts and bruises.

It's not always easy to keep things in balance, even in a home, but in some cases it's extremely important. We're not trying to panic you by making you think your home is precariously perched. However, it's important for you to understand two crucial elements in building a high sense of value in your children that flow out of your decision to honor them—elements you need to work at keeping in balance. If a home is shifted too far in either direction, major problems can result.

These two important elements are (1) meeting their need to belong while (2) easing them into separateness and independence.

Let's look at each element and how it can provide lifelong help to children.

## BUILDING ON BALANCE

There's an old story about two young children who were standing on the corner, bragging about who had moved from state to state the most. One little boy said, "My family has moved three times in the last three years."

"Hey!" said the other little boy. "That's nothing. My parents have moved five times this year—and I found them every time!" It's safe to say that this second boy came from a home without a strong sense of belonging.

### Meeting a Child's Need to Belong

*Belonging is the need each person has to feel a special, needed, and important part of the family.* It's a feeling that we fit in with our parents and our brothers and sisters and that our contribution to the family is valued. It's knowing that we were planned (even if our timing was a surprise) instead of being an accident that somehow showed up to disrupt the family. Even more, it's knowing that God Himself designed our button nose or curly hair. (See Job 31:15; Psalm 119:73.)

Children who grow up with a strong sense of belonging gain ground on those who don't. The seeds of acceptance that are sown in children who feel they belong will bear fruit in giving them the ability to give and receive love and acceptance later in life.

Take Judy, for example. Although she missed out on belonging in her own home, it was served at every meal with her grandparents.

Judy grew up in a home where her parents showed little love and acceptance. Not only that, but as the youngest child of six, she also had to constantly put up with being teased by her brothers and sisters. If it wasn't her scraggly hair or her turned-up nose they made fun of, they loved to lie to the neighborhood children and tell them their parents found Judy when she was a baby abandoned in a vacant lot—and they were ready to send her back!

Yet in spite of this, Judy grew up feeling very special and valuable. Why? As she thought back, she realized it was the hours she spent in her *grandparents' home* that had molded her sense of belonging. Her grandparents lived just a few houses down from her family as she was growing up. Her grandfather was a retired carpenter, and her grandmother had the best lap to sit on for miles around. Every day after school, she would run into her grandparents' home for a cookie or snack before heading home. And every day she would gain a gift—a sense of belonging—even sweeter than the chocolate-chip cookies she would devour.

When her parents were too busy to listen, Grandma and Grandpa had nothing but time. When there was a problem with another girl at school, she received counsel, not an impatient lecture. When Judy was feeling hurt or discouraged, Grandma would cradle Judy's head in her lap and gently stroke her hair as she spoke loving, comforting words and sounds like "Mmm-mmm" and "My, my" and "Bless your poor little heart." Judy even received reassurance from her grandparents that her parents and brothers and sisters really did love and value her. They just didn't know how to show it.

Today, Judy has one of the best marriages we know, and it didn't come from a vacuum. It came from loving grandparents who blessed her with a sense of belonging. And she, in turn, is blessing her children in the same way.

## Meeting a Child's Need for Separateness

On the other side of the coin is separateness, the need each person has to feel he can accomplish things on his own, that he has unique skills and talents within the family. This is a concept that Kevin, as an identical twin, had to come to grips with. Being an identical twin brought Kevin a good deal of attention. With a carbon copy walking beside him, he felt little need to develop a uniquely individual identity in dealing with others—that is, until his brother decided to leave home to attend a military academy.

When we first saw Kevin in counseling, he was going through an intense time of depression. Alone for the first time, he felt abandoned and unprepared to face others. As long as his brother was present, he knew exactly how to act. But now that he had to make friends, set his own schedule, and make decisions without consulting his brother, he felt at a loss about where to begin.

> **On the other side of the coin is separateness, the need each person has to feel he can accomplish things on his own, that he has unique skills and talents within the family.**

Children who grow up without a healthy independence from their parents or siblings are in trouble. Procrastination, mood swings, difficulty in maintaining intimate relationships, problems with getting and staying motivated, and a deep-seated fear of being alone often hold them back from becoming all that God intends them to be.

In each household, there's a need for individual expression as well as for a strong sense of belonging. Both concepts need to be present in children if they are to take off and grow. Although these factors may look like irreconcilable extremes, each provides a sense of balance to the other.

It would be wonderful if every home perfectly balanced these two elements. However, that's not always the case. Some homes take a perfectly good family trait and push it to an unhealthy extreme.

## PUSHING FAMILY STRENGTHS TO EXTREMES

The Taylors have a real strength in their family. They love to kid and joke with one another. Humor is often an important part of a close-knit home, but pushed to an extreme, it can become anything but funny.

Mary is the oldest daughter in the family, and in spite of her sensitivity to her weight problem, she knows that the next fat-girl joke is right around the corner. Like the day she wore a new red-white-and-blue dress for the first time and her sister announced at the dinner table, "Hey, everybody, did you notice Mary's new dress? Mary and I were standing on the corner today, and somebody came up and tried to mail a letter in her." Ha, ha, ha.

Even the parents get into the act of making fun of each other. Take the last time they went to the airport. As they pulled up to the terminal, a sky cap asked, "Take your bag, mister?"

"No thanks," Mr. Taylor said. "She can walk!" Ha, ha, ha.

When humor is pushed to an extreme, soon the only safe conversations are shallow ones. If we cover all of life with humor, we are also covering over wells of important feelings and emotions that need to be expressed. Family members need to be able to share tears of sorrow as well as tears of joy.

A similar thing happens in homes that push separateness and belonging too far. Without a doubt, each is a family strength. However, a family can become so strong in one area that it throws the family off balance in another. That's exactly what happened to Joan.

## When Belonging Is Shifted to an Extreme

Joan's family stressed belonging . . . and stressed it . . . and stressed it! To outsiders, this emphasis may have passed for an unusually strong sense of togetherness, but to Joan, it meant being trapped in a web of manipulation that she felt powerless to cut through.

Joan participated in home schooling long before it was fashionable to do so. Her parents' decision was made not from a fear of what was being taught in public schools but from a fear of the influence outsiders might have on her. Joan's only friends were her brothers and sisters, and they were all strictly forbidden from playing with the "inferior" neighborhood children.

Even in high school, when she was allowed to attend the public school, she was expected to come home immediately after class. "After all, there are so many things we have to do as a family, there just isn't time for all those 'other' people." That was the typical response to any request she would make to take part in outside activities.

Her parents' constant discouragement of participation with her peers did much to deepen Joan's shyness, and she found herself withdrawn and fearful of other teen-agers at school. Hearing the other girls talk about a slumber party might bring pains of loneliness, but an even greater fear of being away from her family for the night pushed loneliness aside.

Together with her parents, Joan shouted out the message, "We only have time for each other!" Alone at night she whispered, "Why don't I fit in with others outside my family?"

Today, as an insecure twenty-nine-year-old, Joan lacks any real confidence that she can exist outside her family context. She has held several jobs and has spent a short stint at a community college. Yet every time she encounters trials or interpersonal struggles, she either quits her job or ends a relationship—and draws further back into a faltering coexistence with her parents.

Angry with them for her lack of healthy independence, she pouts and broods when she's at their house. But afraid of alienating her only source of acceptance, she's unwilling to give up the stifling relationship she has with her parents. While she often dreams of a Prince Charming who will ride up and take her away, she always awakens to a king and queen who hold her heart in a dishonoring home.

In this home, the family strength of belonging has been taken so far to the extreme that it has thrown Joan's life out of balance. A very similar result came about in George's home, where separateness was pushed to an extreme.

## When Separateness Is Pushed to an Extreme

George came from a strong ethnic background. His parents walked off the boat and right into work at a shoe repair business. In the almost thirty-five years since then, they have worked day and night. The same thing was expected of each of the children who came along. "Get yourself up, and get to work!" the kids heard often.

At forty-three years of age, George can never remember his parents' telling him they loved him or were proud of him. What he remembers clearly are the times he was told he could make it on his own or he would never make it at all.

He vividly recalls one incident. When he was a boy, his family lived in a neighborhood where they were the only ones from their ethnic background. One day, three older boys followed him home from school, taunting him about his accent. When George said something cutting back to them, they gave him a terrible beating and left him lying in the street.

George's head and face throbbed with pain as he lay there sobbing and fighting for breath. When he was finally able to roll onto his side, he looked up and saw his father standing on their front porch only yards away. He had been standing there the whole time.

"Why," George cried, "why didn't you help me?"

Before walking back into the house, his father told him, "Let it be a lesson to you. No one can fight your battles for you."

In some ways, having to stand up for himself did make George stronger. He got much better at fighting and developed an independent spirit that he took on to college and the business world. The only problem was that he took that same "stand alone" attitude into his marriage.

Growing up with separateness and an exaggerated emphasis on being self-sufficient, he longed for the love and warmth he saw in his wife during their courtship. However, feeling comfortable only with separateness, he didn't know how to give or receive that love, and soon his callousness had strained their marriage to the breaking point. George could stand on his own two feet, all right. What he couldn't do was put his arms around anyone else, including his wife and children.

Take separateness to an extreme and you have the potential to produce the loneliest people in the world. Nothing is more pitiful than watching a thirsty man who lies with fresh water just out of reach. Watching someone who is supremely *independent* but who can never be *interdependent* inspires just as much compassion.

Always longing to hear words of love and acceptance, he will stiff-arm those very words if they finally come his way. Even though he knows intellectually that he needs to verbalize his love for his family, he's never able to relinquish the pride wrapped around his independence.

When such people become Christians, watch how their drive will often cause them to strive for teaching, counseling, or leadership positions in the church or parachurch organizations. In some cases, it's just their natural drive that's surfacing. But in many others, the safest place to hide in a room where people are asking questions or discussing relationships is to be the one leading the discussion.

## SPARKS CAN FLY WHEN EAST MEETS WEST

What happens when someone who grows up in a home that stresses separateness to an extreme meets someone who comes from a home just as committed to belonging? Oftentimes, it's called marriage!

It's sometimes said that two twenty-year-olds marry to make

one forty-year-old. That was almost too true for Joan and Norm. When Joan looked at Norm, his independence and ability to make decisions apart from his family seemed terrific. She came from a home where the family members were so tied together that she had never felt any freedom of choice in any decision she ever made. In Norm she saw the independence she longed for.

Norm was just as taken with Joan. He couldn't believe how close her family was. She was carrying a full load of classes at school and working part-time, and she still made time to call her mother two or three times every day. Norm hadn't even bothered to call home at Thanksgiving. But then no one from home had tried to call him either.

In Joan, Norm saw a side of himself he knew was lacking. If anyone could make him feel complete and acceptable, she had to be the expert on belonging. The reverse was true for Joan. She saw in Norm the embodiment of strength to help her stand apart from her family. He would supply the courage she had never been able to muster to make the change. In her eyes, he was an Olympic medalist or an All-American in the field of separateness.

But a funny thing happened on the way home from the altar. What was so stimulating in their courtship became killing in their marriage. Norm spent almost every waking moment badgering Joan to meet his needs for acceptance. He kept looking for more and more depth in their relationship, more and more touching and physical closeness, and grew impatient and irritable if they weren't actively involved in Bible study, marriage group, or something else that would help them "become intimate."

On the other hand, Joan had already had twenty years of overinvolvement with her family, and she reacted to Norm's calls for closeness by drawing away. For the first time in her young life she was on her own. Even the thought of getting deeply intimate with Norm was emotionally like going back inside a windowless classroom to study state government after getting to run outside on a beautiful spring day.

Instead of the strength she bargained for, Joan saw only Norm's emotional weakness and vulnerability. Instead of the warmth that had enraptured him, Norm thought he had been duped into marrying a defiant, uncaring, independent Joan.

Both Norm and Joan got all they were looking for in a marriage partner—and less. Going into marriage with their private lives tilted to one extreme or the other left little middle ground on which to build a lasting marriage. It was only after they began to individually balance their lives and to understand what unhealthy extremes they had reached that Norm had the freedom to let go of his stranglehold on her and give her room to grow, while Joan was able to draw closer to her husband.

People have always been fascinated by extremes. That's part of what pushed them to explore the polar regions and outer space. However, maintaining a healthy marriage or raising children is a different matter. Homes shifted to an extreme may be interesting to visit, but they instill low value in those who live there. Whether belonging is taken to an extreme or separateness is way out of balance, children go from such homes only half-prepared to be successful in relationships.

## A BIBLICAL BALANCE POINT

Where do we go to find an example of someone who balanced separateness and belonging in intimate relationships? We can look at the Master Lover and Equipper, for Jesus' relationship with the disciples pictures just such a balance.

Think of all the times and ways He communicated to the disciples before His death, resurrection, and ascension that they were secure in His love for them. In conversations with the disciples, standing near or in private times with them alone, He built in an unmistakable sense of attachment to each of His own with statements like these:

> *Do not worry, saying, "What shall we eat?" or "What shall we drink?" or "What shall we wear?" . . . But seek first the kingdom of God and His righteousness, and all these things shall be added to you (Matthew 6:31, 33).*

> *My sheep hear My voice, and I know them . . . I give them eternal life, and they shall never perish; neither shall anyone snatch them out of My hand (John 10:27–28).*

> *Let not your heart be troubled; you believe in God, believe also in Me. . . . I go to prepare a place for you. And if I go and prepare a place for you, I will come again and receive you to Myself (John 14:1–3).*

> *And I will pray the Father, and He will give you another Helper, that He may abide with you forever, . . . He dwells*

*with you and will be in you. I will not leave you orphans (John 14:16–18).*

The disciples would always be able to rest in their Savior's love, yet they were also given wings and the encouragement to carry a message of hope beyond the confines of their company. In fact, they were sent out time and again to carry the message of their King.

*And He called the twelve to Him, and began to send them out two by two (Mark 6:7).*

*Behold, I send you out as sheep in the midst of wolves (Matthew 10:16).*

Even on His last night with the disciples, Jesus comforted them with His love. Yet He also made it clear that they would have His Spirit, though not His physical presence, to guide them after that night. He said, "I tell you the truth. It is to your advantage that I go away; for if I do not go away, the Helper will not come to you; but if I depart, I will send Him to you" (John 16:7).

The disciples knew they were secure in their relationship with Christ, but they also knew it was natural and right to leave the mountaintop and go into the trenches with hurting people. Isn't it interesting how both aspects combined to mold the disciples into a force that changed the world? If they had been given a sense of belonging through the security of their relationship with Him but had never been encouraged to go out from their spiritual family, you wouldn't be reading a Christian book today. On the other hand, they would never have been able to stand fast and face the hardships they did in spreading the gospel without knowing they were eternally secure in God's love.

How does all this relate to parents' trying to honor their children by building worth and value into their lives? For three years, our Lord blended a message of love and acceptance with the encouragement to His disciples to take their faith to others outside their immediate circle. For parents, much the same task exists today.

Build in a strong sense of belonging, and your children will go away from home emotionally secure and less susceptible to peer pressure. Balance it by easing them into healthy independence, and you've given them both warmth and wings.

# Chapter Eight

## Providing a Healthy Balance in Our Homes: Part 2

*W*hat marks a home as a place where belonging takes root and grows? How can you provide a healthy separateness for your children without pushing them out of the nest too soon? In this chapter, we'll look at both aspects of keeping a home in balance, beginning with a look at belonging. When it comes to helping a child feel he belongs, we've found five marks that surface time and again as we interview families all across the country.

### BUILDING BELONGING IN A CHILD'S LIFE

#### 1. We Build Belonging By Expressing Praise and Appreciation.

Praising others or receiving their praise has a number of incredible by-products, including feelings of acceptance and belonging. Researchers have found this to be true even when people knew the nice things being said about them *weren't true*.

One study was conducted using two groups of clothing salesclerks. The two groups carried the same items, but their approaches to customers were very different. One group of clerks would speak only when spoken to and even then kept conversation to a minimum. The other salesmen did their best to make pleasing comments: "Is this dress for your sister?" to a young matron shopping with her nineteen-year-old daughter, or "I hope you know you're looking great today!"

Do you know what they found after interviewing shoppers and looking at sales in the two groups? Even when people knew they were being buttered up or unjustly flattered, they tended to think more highly of and buy more from the salesmen who unjustly praised them! They also said they would rather frequent the store where they were complimented, even if it was only flattery.[1]

Within a family, think how much greater the effect of legitimate praise can have on your loved ones. Children who grow up hearing words of thanks and appreciation often feel special and part of the group. One family we know has made this principle into an art—literally.

There's a tradition in the Keefer family that is everybody's favorite. Three months before Christmas, each person reaches into a hat and pulls out the name of some other family member. On the big day, handmade artistic creations that represent something special about the recipients are exchanged. From stick figures to oil paintings, each year some new art form takes shape. After Christmas, these artworks go into the Keefer Museum of Very Valuable People (better known as the wall in Dad's workshop).

This tradition was started by Mr. Keefer. For years he struggled with being able to express words of love and approval to his children. He knew he should, but he didn't find it easy to do. So, he spent hours in his workshop making special presents for each child. In giving his handmade gifts and telling each child the significance of the gift, he learned to more freely express his love and appreciation to his children.

What began as a liability in being able to express appreciation only through handmade gifts has been turned into a meaningful tradition. Each Christmas each child receives a special present and hears a story about his or her special value in front of the rest of the family.

Expressing genuine appreciation for your children is one way you build feelings of belonging into their lives. It can take so little time, yet it helps your children leave home feeling loved.

## 2. We Build Belonging through Listening.

In study after study, the healthiest families are those who score high in the area of listening. In fact, listening may be one of the healthiest things we can do.

In a study at Johns Hopkins Medical School, cardiac patients are being taught the life-saving skill of how to listen to others![2] The medical researchers have found that a common denominator in many who suffered a heart attack was an inability or unwillingness to actively listen to others.

While using a machine that continuously monitored a person's blood pressure, they noticed an unusual happening. Every time a patient spoke to someone else—without exception—his blood pressure went up. Whenever a person took the time to listen to someone else, however, *his heartbeat and blood pressure went down.*

In some patients, even though their words sounded calm when they were talking, blood pressure climbed up into the danger zone for heart attacks. It may be hard to believe, but some patients actually talked so much and listened so little that it was a life-and-death problem![3]

We're not saying that listening to your children is a matter of life and death (even though the Scriptures do tell us that 'life and death are in the power of the tongue'),[4] but it *is* emotionally and physically healthy for them and you. It also deepens their sense of belonging.

Joe Bayly was a godly man who recently went home to be with the Lord. During his lifetime, he and his wife had the burden of seeing three of their sons die due to accident or illness. In his excellent book *The Last Thing We Talk About,* Joe gave an example of the way that simply listening to people can bond us to them.

> *After the death of our second son, I can remember two visits from people quite vividly.*
>
> *One person came into the room, loudly talking about how "special" we were to God because this had happened to us and how God must have known in advance that we had the strength to handle this tragedy. He recited several Bible verses and then went out as loudly as he had come in. I felt unmoved, almost angry and glad he had gone.*

> *Then another friend came in. He just came over and sat down beside me. He took my hand. He listened. He prayed briefly, and he left quietly. I was moved. I was comforted. I wished he hadn't had to leave.[5]*

Most of us are far better lecturers than we are listeners. Even when we do listen, it's often just a pause between bursts of what's really important—what *we* have to say! Yet if children are to know that they are important, we need to show them by listening to them.

Be aware of this. The "Smalley-Trent Axiom of Communication" states, "The opportunity to listen to your children is directly proportional to the interest of the television program you are watching or book you are reading." In other words, the more interesting the program or the more exciting the plot of the book, the more likely that that will be the very time your children want to talk!

We know you can't drop everything every time your children want to share something with you. But if you close the door to communication too many times, before long you won't have to worry about shutting it at all. They will quit sharing with you even when you plead with them to talk to you.

I (John) remember a comment my mother would make repeatedly to her kids during our teen-age years. Because of her health problems, she would often have to go to bed quite early. But nearly every night, before retiring she would say, "Just wake me up if you boys want to talk about something. I can always go back to sleep, but I can't always talk with you."

Do you know what my twin brother and I used to do almost every weekend after getting home from our dates or a ball game in high school? You guessed it. We'd walk into our mother's room, flop down on the bed on either side of her, wake her up, and sometimes talk for hours about our dates, problems, dreams, goals, or life in general.

During a period of time in our teen-age years when many parents would love to be able to know what their children were thinking and doing, Mother knew many things in detail, largely because she built a sense of belonging in our lives by having an open-door policy when it came to listening.

### 3. We Build Belonging By Providing a Well-Defined Purpose for the Home.

Have you ever seen a business that's struggling? In many cases, such companies are guided by yesterday's actions or today's crisis instead of a clear purpose or plan. Employees can sense when a business is pointed in the right direction or when its leadership is simply navigating by the seat of its pants.

The same thing is true with a team. Our good friend Norm Evans, a former member of two of the Miami Dolphins' Super Bowl teams, gave us some valuable insight into winning teams and winning families. Much of what Norm taught us we see consistently in healthy families across America.

Norm told us the story of what it was like when Don Shula took over as the Dolphins' head coach. The year before Shula came, the team had 2 wins and 10 losses and was a struggling expansion franchise. But at the first team meeting he had with his players, the new coach told them, "Men, our goal for the year is to be 10–2."

Some team members chuckled to themselves, but Shula went on to explain how this could take place. "We're going to practice four times a day, every day, to get ready for the games on Sunday. Not only that, but you'll learn everything there is to know about the player across from you by the end of the week. You'll have a plan and will have practiced that plan until you're 100 percent ready for the game on Sunday."

Their record that year was 10–2, and the next year they were 13–0 and won the Super Bowl. Don Shula is now the winningest active head coach in the NFL for good reason. He has a clear purpose behind his methods and a plan for his team, and they practice it.

What's important to a successful business or sports team is also important in a close-knit home. As a family, we (the Smalleys) sat down with each of our children and set up a plan in our home that included three basics: honoring God, honoring each other, and honoring His creation. Then every night for three years while they were in grade school, we talked for a few minutes at the dinner table about how each of us was doing individually and as a family in these three areas.

As Norma and I recall the things that have positively affected our children, those three years of having a clear plan and practicing it each night have been a significant factor in helping each child mature and in keeping us together as a close-knit team. Not every football team reaches the Super Bowl, and not every family is a "Super Bowl" family. But we want at least to win more than we lose! And to do so, we all need a family plan we can practice daily in our homes.

God's Word is the blueprint for a successful life and family. Putting His Word into a practical plan of action parents can follow (in this case, understanding and applying seven aspects of honoring loved ones) is one of our main ministry goals.[6]

Children can sense whether there's a clear purpose or plan in their home or there's simply a collection of rules that are unrelated and unclear. Having a plan and practicing it can be an important way to encourage healthy independence in children. But for now, let's look at a fourth way in which we can build belonging in our children.

## 4. We Build Belonging By Making Sure Each Person Feels a Shared Burden for the Others.

Principles that surround our spiritual family can also enrich our natural family. In a church struggling with divisions and a lack of unity, the apostle Paul offered a word picture that illustrates the importance of family unity. Likening different Christians to different parts of the body, he said, "And if one member [like a hand or an eye] suffers, all the members suffer with it; or if one member is honored, all the members rejoice with it" (1 Corinthians 12:26).

One thing that stands out in the healthiest families we see is this type of shared burden for one another. If Daughter Jane is hurting, everyone comes alongside her to provide encouragement and support. If Son David is given a promotion at work, the success is shared with everyone.

How can parents build a sense of unity in their families, especially when they have healthy, average kids who by nature would rather fight with one another than eat? One thing I (Gary) have found that has drawn us into unity as a family more than any other is experiencing a trial together. Again, I'm not advocating *creating* trials. The book of James tells us that trials will come naturally. In our home, all we need to do is plan a family get-together, and something is bound to go wrong and draw us into unity as a result. Let me explain what I mean.

Several years ago, when the children were still in grade school, we decided to load up our mobile home and head to Colorado for a vacation. The trip proved to be uneventful until one particularly steep grade. Suddenly, as I looked down on the dash, I could see the temperature reading was "Hot!"

The kids looked forward to any reason for a stop, so as soon as I pulled the mobile home over to the side of the road, they jumped out and started running all over the place. As if it weren't enough that we were afraid they would run out into the highway and get hit, our older son, Greg, had the great idea of drop-kicking a can of oil that he found.

As if guided by a NASA radar system, the half-full can of oil flew high in the air and landed directly on the head of our younger son, Michael. He was drenched with oil from head to toe and got a big bump on his head.

I think you can picture the scene. The car is overheated. Greg is hiding because he knows he's in big trouble. Norma and our daughter, Kari, are crying because some of the oil got in Mike's eyes and they're afraid he'll go blind. Mike is crying because he's mad at Greg and because he can't see him to get revenge. I'm looking for some water to wash off the oil—and then it begins to rain!

As we all huddled in the mobile home, waiting for the car to cool down so we could take Mike to a doctor, no one said how great a family time it was or how unified we felt as a family. But once the trial was over (with no permanent damage to anything except the oil can), we've looked back on this near catastrophe a hundred times and laughed about it. As painful as they are when they happen, trials shared together can bond us and help us raise the value of our children.

## 5. We Build Belonging By Being Willing to Admit What the "Wise" Readily Acknowledge.

Of all the practical truths in the book of Proverbs, there are two simple instructions that can specifically help a parent build a sense of belonging in a child and raise his self-worth as a result: (1) the humble receive honor (Proverb 15:33) and (2) only the wise seek advice and correction for their ways (Proverb 1:7).

One of the hardest things for many parents to do is to admit to a child when they have made a mistake. For other parents, being open to receive legitimate correction from a child is even more difficult. In the Scriptures, however, the humble readily admit that they don't "know it all." They are open, teachable, willing to be corrected. You may think that saying "I'm sorry" or "I don't know" lowers your children's respect for you, but it does just the opposite. Children and others are drawn to people who are willing to admit they make mistakes and have flaws.

Dr. Charles Swindoll is one of our favorite pastors and Bible teachers, and we're not alone. His books and "Insight for Living" radio ministry have deeply affected thousands of men and women across the country, challenging them to grow deeper in the Christian life. What makes his ministry so effective? While there are certainly a number of good theological reasons, we believe it's because he's willing to be very honest and vulnerable about his successes and failures. It's hard to listen to someone who puts himself three levels above us. It's easy to relate to and be challenged by someone like Chuck Swindoll who lets us know he shares our struggles and has hurt where we hurt. The same things ring true for a parent.

It's humbling to say "I'm sorry" to your children, but it helps them to realize that you're honest with your weaknesses and that you have the feet of clay they see anyway! Early in life, children don't see many flaws in their parents. In most cases, until they are well into grade school, they look at parents as larger than life and often without fault. Yet the day will come when they begin to see your imperfections. And when they do, if you try to hide them or deny them, you lose ground in their eyes and teach them to deny problem areas in their lives. Being dishonest in this way can lower your children's self-worth, not raise it. By humbling yourself and even seeking correction, you can reverse that trend. Here's one example of how this has worked in my (Gary's) home.

Recently, my daughter Kari asked me to read several chapters of Proverbs with her that she had been studying in her Bible class in college. She had already marked up many of the verses, and as we read the chapters verse by verse, we stopped frequently and asked, "How do these verses match up with the way we're living our lives today?"

The first five verses we read instructed us that God wants us to search diligently and enthusiastically for His truth, even more than seeking after silver and gold. The next few verses spelled out specific attitudes and actions for those who would gain the skill of right living.

As we talked and evaluated our daily actions, Kari read one verse and mentioned that it was an area I needed to work on. I could tell after she said it that she didn't know whether she should have said it. She looked at me to see if I was upset or defensive and if she was in trouble! When she saw that I was open to correction, however—especially from my daughter—it helped her be that much more open and accepting of things she could work on in her own life.

After that time together, we both felt our love for each other grow stronger. We each had grown in our respect for the other because we could admit we don't "know it all" and we stand in need of correction at times like everyone else.

Add a willingness to receive correction to each of the other four ways to build belonging in children, and you have five key ingredients to raise your children's self-worth. And when children feel they truly belong, they are far better prepared to develop the second element you need to keep in balance in your home, which is a healthy separateness and independence.

## PROVIDING HEALTHY SEPARATENESS

### 1. Ease Them into Independence.

The key to encouraging a healthy sense of separateness in children is easing them into independence. One noted family physician believes this begins way back when we're weaning them.

The Hebrew word for *weaned* is *gamal*, which means "to ripen."[7] The term implies a state of readiness. Weaning should mean not a loss of or a detachment from a relationship, but a state in which a child feels so full and so right that he or she is ready to take on other relationships. Listen to what Dr. William Sears has to say about children who are rushed into relationships and responsibilities before they're ready to handle them.

*Weaning before his time of spiritual readiness may leave a*
*child unfulfilled and not feeling right. A child who is weaned*

> *from any childhood relationships before his time, and is hurried into other relationships may perhaps rebel both inwardly and outwardly and show what I call, "diseases of unreadiness."*[8]

What are these "diseases"? Negative behaviors like out-of-balance aggressiveness, violent tantrums, and severe mood swings, to name a few. These are not the occasional tantrums or pouting of nearly any child; these are repeated negative patterns and behaviors from a hurried child.

In our experience with parents and children, we've observed that children of any age who are hurried into taking on too much independence too soon struggle in their relationships. Sometimes the death of a parent or a divorce forces a child to grow up "overnight." But if there is any way possible to do it, small steps toward independence are always the best.

## 2. Provide Children with Choices Appropriate to Their Ages.

David Elkind wrote a best-selling book titled *The Hurried Child*. He may have sold so many copies because so many "hurried children" ran out and bought it!

We live in an instant society today. Many people get upset if their hamburger and shake aren't ready by the time they drive the four car-lengths from the clown to the pickup window! The same thing holds true of many children.

In an incredibly complicated society, parents often expect their children to make sophisticated judgments without preparing them with wise counsel. Children didn't invent expensive designer jeans for four-year-olds, but parents buy them by the droves. It's not unusual for five- and six-year-old children to come to school wearing make-up because their parents are in a hurry for them to grow up. But is it healthy?

Just like you, we've walked by the mall and watched five- and six-year-olds walk out of R-rated movies with their parents. Their moms and dads expect them to handle the fastballs thrown at them in such films without an error.

For every parent who feels his child can handle R-rated movies or literature, we can give one hundred examples of children who could not and were hurt by them. Biblically, we see no reason why even a "mature" teen-ager or adult should view such material. At the very least, watching such films can lower a person's self-worth, and at worst, it can give them permission to dishonor God and act out dishonoring practices they have viewed or read about. Remember the biblical term "to wean"? It means we allow someone to ripen and mature before we expose him to decisions and responsibilities that require real discernment and judgment.

A tremendous privilege I (Gary) had in life was getting to spend a great deal of time with Corrie ten Boom in her later years. She is the one who encouraged me to use "word pictures" and "objects" every time I speak, and that's become a trademark of our ministry today. Her faith was forged in a loving Christian home and then tested and found true in a German concentration camp during World War II.

Corrie told me a story that she also recounted in her inspiring autobiography, *The Hiding Place*. When she was a little girl of six, riding on a train with her father, she looked out on a pastoral setting and saw cattle in the process of breeding. Out of curiosity, Corrie asked her father, "What are those animals doing?"

"Corrie," her father said, "everything has a proper time. When it's the right time for you to know, we'll have a talk, the two of us." That was all Corrie needed to know at the time, and a few years later, when the time was ripe, they did have that talk.

Building healthy separateness into children doesn't come at the expense of their losing their innocence. We know of one set of parents who let a college-aged boy (known to have a terrible reputation) take their thirteen-year-old daughter on an overnight camping trip with several non-Christian couples. Unfortunately, we then watched them regret their lack of courage to say no when she became pregnant out of wedlock. While permissiveness may prevail in some circles, it has nothing to do with the courage parents need to have to withhold things from their children until they are ready.

Understanding a child's readiness to accept choices and responsibilities is a key to helping him gain a healthy sense of separateness.

## 3. Set Goals for Their Going—and Practice and Review Those Goals.

Let's ask a few questions. What goals do you have for your child's "going"? What character traits would you like him or her to leave home with? How often do you sit down and talk about character strengths or areas that need to be developed with your child? What view of God and others is she carrying away from home every day?

Many of you are familiar with the verse that tells you to "train up a child in the way he should go, / And when he is old he will not depart from it" (Proverb 22:6). While the section referring to the child's remembering his early training often gets top billing, it's actually telling you to have a goal for the child's going! (Train him up in the way he should *go*.)

Each day you have a child in your home is a day you capture or lose in preparing him to go. Getting your child ready to leave home is a high calling. The character traits and degree of responsibility you see surfacing in your child today will be essentially what you see magnified in his life five years from now, or ten. This is also true of how successful he feels at standing apart from you and on his own two feet.

In a marriage, one aspect of genuine love involves preparing for the future, even for a time when one partner is no longer with the family. That's why you spend time setting up IRA's and pensions, making out a will and picking guardians for your children, and why both a husband and a wife should know about the family finances and how to handle them. The same care that goes into preparing for your own future should go into preparing your children for their future.

Like an unprepared widow who feels lost and directionless at the death of her spouse, a child whose parents set no goals for his going can be left just as unprepared to leave home. You need to ask yourself questions that can help you get him ready to go. These include questions like the following.

What can I teach my child about finances today that can help him feel capable to handle his own finances later? How about starting his own checking and savings accounts and making sure he learns the importance of tithing? It's also important to teach him today that being faithful with a little is God's criterion for being faithful with much. Also, look for everyday opportunities to build responsibility in this area. For example, if a child leaves his bicycle unlocked and it's stolen, instead of your buying him a new one, have him save his own money to replace it.

What can I do today to teach my child to make wise decisions? How about reading through Proverbs with him over the course of a summer or a school year and seeing how these wise principles stack up in everyday life. While you're reading it with him, you can take the time to point out specific verses that confirm right choices he has made in the past and help him analyze and learn from his mistakes in the present.

> **Like an unprepared widow who feels lost and directionless at the death of her spouse, a child whose parents set no goals for his going can be left just as unprepared to leave home.**

How can I learn to strengthen and develop his view of God before he leaves home? Many parents delegate what the child learns about the Lord to the church or a Christian school. Although these can be tremendous places of learning and spiritual encouragement, the knowledge he picks up can remain "head" knowledge instead of "heart" knowledge unless a parent sets spiritual goals at home. You should take the lead in helping your child learn to understand and apply the Scriptures. If he sees no crossover between what he learns at church and what occurs in his home, the Bible can become just another textbook relegated to a dusty bookshelf in years to come.

Developing and practicing a plan for his "going" in each of these major areas and others should begin when a child is in diapers. And it should continue each day that he's under your care. Getting a child ready to leave home in a healthy way involves more than giving him a pep talk before his high-school graduation and handing him a tuition check for college.

Parents who set no goals for their children's going actually dishonor them and leave them unprepared to face the challenges of real life. Parents who take time to develop a specific plan in this area honor their children by helping them become better prepared for their future. Even so, without a much-needed step, setting goals for when children leave home may not be enough.

*A Much-Needed Step in Setting Goals for Their Going.* Setting goals for their going is one way you can honor your children. However, to make sure these goals move from your mind and into their lives, don't forget a key ingredient, which is to be sure you *review* your plan periodically.

It is said in business that people do what you "inspect," not what you "expect." There is some truth to this when it comes to setting goals for your children's going as well. At the very least, we encourage parents to sit down together near each child's birthday each year and ask themselves how they are doing at implementing their goals for that child's going. They can ask questions like these: What have we seen in our child this year that reflects his increased love for and knowledge of God? How responsible has he been in carrying out chores or taking care of pets around the house? At school and at home, is he developing the ability to get along with others? How faithful has he been in giving to the Lord and managing his allowance or the money he's earned? Then plan a time to sit down with that child and praise him for his accomplishments, as well as to work together to set next year's goals.

Setting goals for your child's going and reviewing them each year (along with how well you did at encouraging and supporting those goals) is a tremendous way to ease a child into independence. If you need further help in setting a specific plan, we recommend two excellent books that go into detail in this area.[9]

It takes time to sit down with your child and set goals, but it certainly beats the alternative. If you aim at nothing in helping a child leave home in a healthy way, you're likely to hit it every time.

## 4. Promote Landmark Ages and Accomplishments.

Is there a "Hall of Honor" in your home? There should be. It doesn't have to be a hallway. A faded scrapbook will do just as nicely. Whether it's pictures you hang on the wall or ticket stubs you keep in a scrapbook, however, making special note of landmark accomplishments in your children's lives is a tremendous encouragement to them. Things to be honored are having their first dance recital; playing their first soccer game; graduating from grade school, high school, college, or trade school; turning a certain age; or winning a certain award. Making mention of milestones in children's lives frees them to go on to new and more difficult stages instead of freezing them in the uncertainty of their abilities.

We saw this very thing take place with a young woman we met on a plane recently. Betty looked every inch a cadet when we sat down next to her. In the course of a casual conversation, we discovered that she was flying home after graduating from one of the nation's military academies and receiving her pilot's wings.

"That must have been a tremendous time for you!" we said.

"It was. Well, it should have been," said Betty as she looked down at her lap. When we gently pressed her for further comment, she sighed and said, "All my life I've waited for my father to say he was proud of me. I knew in my heart it would happen yesterday. I just knew it. But it didn't. I know he's proud of me, but I would have given anything to hear it from him. I guess I'll just have to work as hard as I can to be a good pilot. Maybe then he'll say it."

Can you sense the search this poor girl is on? By failing to recognize significant milestones in children's growth and achievements, parents fail to give them a sense of accomplishment. Perhaps because he had never heard words of encouragement growing up, this father failed to pass them along to his daughter. And because of it, another person searches for a healthy feeling of separateness, an inner sense of completion that says, "I've finally accomplished something worthwhile. I finally stood on my own and did something I'm proud of and my parents are proud of."

Keith Hernandez is one of baseball's top players. He is a lifetime .300 hitter who has won numerous Golden Glove awards for excellence in fielding. He's won a batting championship for having the highest average, the Most Valuable Player award in his league, and even the World Series. Yet with all his accomplishments, he has missed out on something crucially important to him—his father's acceptance and recognition that what he has accomplished is valuable. Listen to what he had to say in a very candid interview about his relationship with his father: "One day Keith asked his father, 'Dad, I have a lifetime .300 batting average. What more do you want?' His father replied, 'But someday you're going to look back and say, "I could have done more." ' "[10]

Gordon MacDonald, in his outstanding book *Ordering Your Private World*, points out that hurried adults and hurried children never "close the loop" on anything.[11] What he means is that they can never do anything well enough to prove to themselves or to their parents that they are finished with it. They always have to run faster, jump higher, try harder, all in an attempt to hear words of approval and acceptance. And even when they do hear them from parents, they rarely believe they can stop their frantic efforts.

In contrast to those who never feel a sense of recognition for milestone events or ages, we know of one family where just the opposite is true. Hank is a Christian education director who has world-class children. Each of his three daughters could be a poster child for someone who has grown up with a genuine sense of belonging and also developed a healthy sense of separateness from the family. What's this man's secret? When we asked each of the now-grown girls to tell us one thing their father did to instill a healthy sense of separateness in their lives, they all said the same thing: "my sixteen candle date with my father."

What is a "sixteen candle date"? Simply something a wise father did to mark a milestone in each daughter's life. And the only thing each girl had to "accomplish" before she spent this special time with Dad was to grow older. When each daughter turned sixteen (and for two or three years before), Dad would mention little things about a special night out for the two of them. And while Old Testament parents marked a child's coming of age with a special ceremony of blessing, this father used an evening out to mark a special coming of age in his daughter's life.

From walking up to the door with a corsage in his hand, to going out for a special dinner at a fine restaurant, to presenting a handwritten wish list and a prayer list for this daughter and her family in years to come, he made it an evening none of the girls would ever forget. One daughter told us,

> *After my sixteen candle dinner with my father, I felt for the first time like I was really growing up. We talked about some of the responsibilities like dating and driving I had ahead of me, and it really helped me realize it was time to grow up.*

Make special mention of milestones in your children's growth and maturity, things they have reached by age or their best efforts, and you honor them by giving them a sense of accomplishment (closing the loop). This track record of acknowledged successes is something they can build on throughout their lives in serving the Lord and their families.

Your children may be eleven, eighteen, twenty-four, or forty-two, but you can still have a "sixteen candle date" with them. It's not the age that matters. Rather, what you say to them really makes the impact.

## THE BLESSING OF A BALANCED HOME

We've looked at five ways to build a strong sense of belonging in our homes, and four ways in which we can ease our children into independence. Each aspect of a balanced home goes a long way toward making children feel valuable and secure, raising their self-worth as a result.

Honoring our own parents, helping our children find value in troubled times, discovering our own parenting strengths and style, and now uncovering the importance of keeping the home in balance—these four aspects of honor can help us develop a game plan for a winning family. They become even stronger when we add a fifth aspect of honor that was brought home to me when I (Gary) was a young boy.

As a child, I "fell into" one of the most fearful experiences of my life. Today, I realize it was only God's grace that helped me make it out alive. Looking back on that horror-filled afternoon, I can see more clearly than ever why it's crucial for parents to establish and maintain clearly defined boundaries, protective fences if you will, for their children. We'll talk about these in the next chapters.

# Chapter Nine

## Establishing Loving Boundaries:
## Part 1

**W**ho would have thought that ignoring a boundary would nearly lead to death? Certainly not my friend Jim and I (Gary). But that's exactly what happened. As young boys growing up in the state of Washington, Jim and I heard over and over from his mother, "Don't go near that area around Boulder Flats." Boulder Flats had been the bed of a local river until a major flood had changed its course. Now it was several acres of various sized river rocks that had been fenced in by the park service.

Well, you know how curious boys can be. Not only was I curious, but coming from a home where there were no boundaries, I felt that fences were something to disrupt my life, not protect it.

It was a beautiful late summer morning, and Jim and I had been hiking through the nearby woods. Lunch time was right around the corner, so we (or maybe I'd better say *I*) decided we should take a short cut home—right through Boulder Flats. After all, if we skipped across the rocks, we could cut a half-hour off our walk back into town and be at the bridge that crossed the river in no time. From there, we'd be home for lunch before you knew it. For ten-year-old boys, hunger can make a short cut sound mighty tempting!

The barbed wire fence was old and feeling the effects of time, and who reads those Keep Out signs anyway? Pulling apart the

barbed wire in one particularly shaky section, I let Jim in, and
then he held the wires so I could get through.

We scrambled out onto the rocks and started jumping across
them. We were making great time and doing just fine. At least
that's what we thought. It wasn't until we were in the middle of
the riverbed that we realized we were in trouble. Serious trouble.

When we jumped onto a big rock halfway across the dry
stream, all around us the quiet morning air was suddenly shattered by the hissing and piercing sounds of rattlesnakes. As we
held on to each other, we could see that we had landed right in
the middle of a snake pit. Squirming in and out of the smaller
rocks around us were dozens of rattlesnakes. Small snakes and
large snakes as thick as your fist lay coiled or moved around and
under the rocks. For what seemed like hours, we clung to that
rock yelling for help at the top of our lungs and trying not to lose
our footing.

The day went by, and no help came. As the afternoon sun
dipped lower toward the hills, we decided that if we were ever to
get free of the snakes, we had no choice but to try to continue
across the river bottom.

Near the rock where we stood were several pieces of driftwood,
relics of a time when water ran freely down this once mighty
river. But there would be no chance of water washing away the
snakes now, nor of our getting help from anyone who might have
happened along. We were over a mile from the nearest house, and
besides, everybody knew to avoid Boulder Flats! Picking up two
long pieces of driftwood, we began the terrible journey across the
riverbed.

There's no way I can convey to you the horror of the next hour
and what it was like to gather up all our courage and jump from
one large rock to another, knowing that if we slipped and fell to
the ground, snakes would strike us before we could get back up
to safety. At times, we used our driftwood sticks to beat at the
rattlers from our perches. At one point, we used the sticks to lift
up baby rattlesnakes and throw them out of the way.

Crying, praying, hoping, losing hope, we made our way across
the riverbed. Finally, after an hour and a lifetime, we jumped
from the last rock down onto the sand and ran up the river bank
to safety.

Days later, when we had regained the emotional strength to
think clearly about what had happened that horrible afternoon,

we could remember over twenty snakes we had killed and dozens of others we had struck at with our sticks or tossed out of the way. We told our story to the park service, so a number of men and a small bulldozer went to Boulder Flats. They said they captured or killed over three hundred snakes—some of them trophy length!

Ignoring a boundary had nearly cost us our lives. Jim and I had been more than fortunate. The Lord had protected us from certain death had we fallen amidst all the snakes. The lessons I learned that terrible afternoon have taught me something very important about healthy families, particularly about parents who don't realize what's at stake with their children.

Every day, we see parents who fail to put up adequate boundaries for their children, and as a result their sons and daughters walk right into their own Boulder Flats. Although theirs may not contain rattlesnakes, these children face emotional and spiritual problems that are just as deadly because they received little supervision or were allowed to ignore warning signs, or their parents never took the time to put up the signs in the first place.

How can you put up healthy boundaries for your children that can protect them from the many "Boulder Flats" experiences of life? Why *should* you provide boundaries for your children? What kinds of boundaries are most important? In the pages that follow, let's learn more about how healthy boundaries build children's sense of worth and how you can best set up protective fences for them.

## PROVIDING HEALTHY BOUNDARIES FOR CHILDREN

When we write about family boundaries, we're referring to protective "fences" put around a child for his security, support, and accountability. They give a child a sense of these things as he clearly sees limits on acceptable and unacceptable behavior. They also provide much-needed accountability when it comes to opening his life to positive people and experiences while closing the door to negative ones.

There was a time when parents didn't need to be reminded to provide boundaries for their children, but our permissive society seems to have changed all that. While we most certainly live in an age of grace, *tolerance* in many homes has become another word for *license*.

Unfortunately, the children in those "limit-less" homes are suffering the most. Here are just a few examples of situations we've seen personally or have read about this past year where parents have failed to provide healthy boundaries (protective fences) for their children.

- *Wanting to be liked and considered "in" by their teenager's friends, the parents provided an open bar at their daughter's party. Later that night, beyond the legal level of intoxication, a boy from the party sneaks out his parents' car, and he and another friend are killed in an automobile accident.*
- *A religion teacher at a major southwestern university says in an ethics class, "When my daughter turned sixteen, I put her on the pill. High school is a time for experimenting, and I wanted her to feel free to experiment."*
- *A nine-year-old is left alone to baby-sit his two younger sisters. A fire breaks out in the home, and all three children are killed while the mother is at her bowling league.*
- *A father sits in our office, crying because he has just found out his sixteen-year-old daughter is on drugs and pregnant from an immoral relationship with a twenty-six-year-old divorced man. He tells us, "We didn't want her to date him, but what could we say?"*
- *Even though they know their neighbor is actively involved in a popular cult that stresses "family values," they let those neighbors take their children to their church, where the kids become "enlightened." Now the children will have nothing to do with their parents' church or with them—unless they, too, join this cult.*

Extreme examples? Perhaps. But every day we see children who are growing up outside protective boundaries and who are left alone to steer their lives on an unmarked road. We realize that some parents provide too many and too firm boundaries for their children, and we'll address them later. However, we have found that parents who provide virtually no boundaries prevail. By their failure to have the courage and genuine love to set up and enforce clear boundaries, they can dishonor children and greatly lower their sense of significance and security.

Because of this, before we look specifically at the kinds of boundaries to set up, let's look at two reasons in this chapter (and two additional reasons in the next) why protective fences around children's behavior are essential, not optional.

## THE IMPORTANCE OF PROVIDING PROTECTIVE BOUNDARIES

### Boundaries Help Children Know They Are Loved.

One major way God communicates to His children that they are loved is by setting up a protective boundary around them and *disciplining* them if they go outside the fence of His Word.

> *"My son do not despise the chastening* [discipline] *of the* LORD. . . . *For whom the* LORD *loves He chastens."* [*He chases them back inside His fence.*]
> *God deals with you as with sons; for what son is there whom a father does not chasten? But if you are without chastening . . . you are illegitimate and not sons (Hebrews 12:5–8).*

In our study of the Scriptures, we can't find a single example of God's loving someone where He didn't discipline him when he walked outside the perimeter of His Word. God loved Adam and Eve and provided a perfect environment for them to live in. Yet when they moved outside God's boundaries in the Garden, they were disciplined.[1]

Abraham lied, and he was disciplined.[2] Sarah laughed at the wrong time, and she was disciplined.[3] Moses may have faced up to the greatest leader of his day and taken God's people right out from under the Pharaoh's nose, but he was disciplined when he moved outside of God's limits and struck the rock twice.[4]

We could add Samson, Saul, David, Solomon, Peter, and others whom we will one day see in heaven, people who experienced God's love and, because they were loved, were disciplined when they erred. It doesn't mean that none of these saints were forgiven. What it does mean is that there were boundaries set up for their actions.

The word *discipline* comes from the Aramaic root "to bind."[5] When we discipline someone, we rope or bind him in. The New Testament word carries a word picture as well. It was used of young athletes who were taught to compete in a game by "having to stay within the lines."[6]

Do we mean to say that people who are "bound" and are made to "stay within the lines" feel loved? Before you toss aside this book, give us a minute to explain. Limits or boundaries do indeed give a person a feeling of security and safety. A study of young children showed just that.[7]

**Security Means Staying Behind Protective Fences.** Two groups of early grade-school children were studied during recess at several different schools over a long period of time. The schools had the same playground equipment, the same length of time for the children to play, and the same ratio of teachers to students. What was different between the two groups? One group was playing in a fenced playground, while the other group's playground had no fence and lay in a large, open field.

When the study was over, which group showed more cooperative play, had fewer playground fights, and exhibited lower levels of anxiety? Which group used more space on the playground and had better attitudes toward school work following recess? The kids who played in the wide open spaces? Wrong. The children with the boundaries of a fence were far and away happier and better adjusted. Why?

Children with clear boundaries feel a security that other children do not. Many of the youngsters in the fenced-in playground would run right up to and along the fence, feeling free to test their limits but also feeling secure behind them. The children in the group with nothing but open space stayed inside a smaller area on their playground than the children with the fenced-in boundaries.

Living without clear, protective boundaries can cause real problems. That is part of the reason God has given us such clear boundaries in His Word.

**A Necessary Element of Genuine Love: Discipline.** If we are God's children and we step outside the protective fences He sets up, we're asking to be disciplined. We all need discipline, the encouragement to get back inside His protective fences, if we want to grow and mature. Being disciplined is a clear demonstration that God loves us.

Genuine love (agape love) means committing ourselves willfully and sacrificially to another's best interests.[8] Christ demonstrated this when He died for us on the cross. Even in that act, God's love was poured out in discipline on His only Son, as Christ bore our sins that resulted from our willfully stepping outside the fence of His Word.

If love and discipline are inseparable, two things follow: first, *genuine love involves self-discipline.* If we have no boundaries for our actions and attitudes (like worry, anger, tone of voice, following through on promises, etc.), no guidelines to direct us or ropes to bind us to what is right, we have no healthy, balanced love to pass on to our children.

Second, *if we genuinely love and want the best for our children, we will discipline them.* From an early age, most children seem to understand that love and discipline can and do go together. Children may never ask for a spanking, but frequently, children who break a rule or do something wrong feel the need to be disciplined. They need to know that there are limits that are enforced and that aren't going to change on an hourly basis.

My (Gary's) little niece was playing one time with a crystal dish that normally sat on the living room table. Tammie knew the dish was off limits. Nonetheless, when she held it up to the light to get a prism effect and see all the pretty colors of refracted light, she accidentally dropped the dish, and it smashed into little pieces.

Tammie's mother was in the other end of the house in the kitchen, getting dinner ready. When she looked up, in came Tammie with her head hanging low and dragging her daddy's special drafting ruler (the family "Board of Education"). "Mommy, you're going to have to spank me," she said. And she went on to explain the whole story to her mother.

"You're right, Tammie," her mother said. "You know we've talked to you about not handling that dish and what would happen if you broke it." Then she gave her a swat on the bottom with the ruler. What her mother didn't know was that Tammie had a pencil in the back pocket of her jeans. When she got the swat, the ruler broke.

The spanking over, her mother hugged her and told her she loved her. Feeling better because she had been loved and disciplined, Tammie went back to playing around the house.

Lest you think Tammie is ready for sainthood, her mother told her she needed to tell her father about the spanking when he got home from work. When he walked in the door, do you know what her first words were? "Daddy, Daddy, Mommy broke your ruler!"

Children might not like discipline, but it tells them that they are valuable enough to have somebody set limits for them. This was something Karl never felt.

**Withhold Boundaries and We Withhold Genuine Love.** Karl was one of the saddest cases we've seen in counseling. It wasn't that he was treated that badly in his home. It's just that he was treated indifferently. It was almost as if he were an insignificant vapor not worth bothering about.

Karl grew up in a "blended" family. When Karl's mother died, his father married a woman with three other children fairly close to Karl's age. Karl's stepmother wasn't intentionally cruel to him, but she did do something that was very unloving. She never disciplined him or set boundaries for him.

Her children had to turn off the television set at night to study, but Karl could stay up until midnight if he wanted. Let one of her children fail a test or get a bad conduct report from a class, and the thunder clouds would fill the air. If something similar happened to Karl, however, not a cloud would appear. It wasn't that this mother was leaving all of Karl's discipline to his father. When push came to shove, in comparison to "her children," she simply didn't think he was worth taking the time to correct. Her natural children or even her television shows were more important than her stepson.

Karl's stepmother provided hot meals and material things for him, but she didn't give him the most important thing he needed, a feeling of being genuinely loved and highly valued. Even though she occasionally told him she loved him, he never for a minute believed it. How could he? Every day he saw loving limits placed on his stepbrothers and stepsister and only a paper-thin permissiveness applied to him. Karl wanted to feel like a son. But all he got out of his stepmother's actions was a feeling that he was an illegitimate, unwanted child. We're convinced that many moms and dads simply don't realize that boundaries communicate such high value to their children, or that the lack of limits communicates such low value.

## Boundaries Protect Children from Jumping Too Far Ahead.

I (Gary) can remember another time when I learned something boundaries could do for me. They could protect me from jumping too far ahead of myself.

Nearby the home where I grew up was a huge lumberyard where my father once worked. One day I went with him to the mill to watch the sawing machinery in action and to see all the timber being prepared for cutting.

I can remember my father's saying to me before he went in to talk to the shop foreman, "Gary, you can wander around all you like until I get back, but stay out of the sawdust pit. When I get through with the foreman, I'll show you that myself." Of course, as soon as he disappeared, the sawdust pit was the very first place I headed.

Stretched out before me was a beautiful sight. Like freshly fallen, unspoiled snow, a layer of sawdust lay over the top of a pit some twenty yards wide and over fifty yards long. Talk about a temptation! I took one quick look around to make sure my father wasn't in sight and then set off in my brand-new canvas tennis shoes to put my footprints across the length of that pit.

I was having the time of my life plowing up the sawdust until I had run about a third of the way across the pit. All of a sudden I realized my feet were burning! What I didn't know before I jumped into the sawdust was that I was running on top of a burning pit. Sawdust covered the top four inches, but beneath was a smoldering, red-hot fire! Turning around as fast as I could, I broke the land speed record getting back to safety. But even so, my new tennis shoes were ruined, and my feet were badly burned. I had jumped ahead of my father's promise, and my blistered feet reminded me of that fact.

Providing boundaries can keep a child from running too far ahead in life and burning himself in the process. In a very real sense, providing boundaries today can secure a child's tomorrow. Take the area of dating, for example.

It's becoming almost old-fashioned for parents to provide healthy boundaries for the kind of person a child can date and the time to come home from that date. Old-fashioned or not, however, you can protect a child's future. In addition, when you talk to your children about God's view of sexual standards in dating, and when you give them the added help of setting boundaries in this area, you can guide them away from the smoldering consequences of jumping ahead of God's plan for sexual intimacy.

Sexual intimacy outside of marriage is much like that sawdust pit. It may look safe and inviting. Yet the further someone goes, the greater the chances of getting badly burned. As a child, I had no idea what I was running into. All I knew was that it looked like something exciting to do. Even though something may look very exciting and appealing to your children, one of the privileges you have as a loving leader in your home is to point out the pain they cannot see that may lie right under the surface.

We once heard a definition of sin that went this way: "Sin is doing the right thing at the wrong time." That's not too bad a definition. When our Lord was tempted in the wilderness, there was nothing wrong with His turning stones into loaves of bread. After all, only a few weeks later He took a few loaves and fishes and fed several thousand people. It wasn't even wrong for Him to throw Himself down from the temple and let His angels catch Him. After all, they exist to be at His service (Hebrews 1:14) and certainly would have caught Him if He called.

What was wrong in each temptation was the timing. For Christ to do the right thing outside the boundary of God's perfect time would have been sin. Even today, many believers can be deceived into taking a good thing and choosing to do it at the wrong time. There is nothing wrong with sexual intimacy, for example, yet outside of God's right timing in marriage, it can lead to years of hurt in exchange for only a few moments of pleasure (Proverb 6:20ff.).

Perhaps your child wants to rush ahead and be sixteen years old when he or she is really eight. Don't lose hope. Wise parents make, communicate, and *stick by* healthy boundaries that can save their children many fiery hurts associated with emotional sawdust pits.

As we've been reminded in this chapter, setting up protective fences helps a child feel secure and loved and also provides a way to protect him from running too far ahead of what's right. In the next chapter we'll look at two additional by-products of setting healthy boundaries: adding productive days to our children's lives and helping them understand that there are biblical absolutes in an ever-changing world.

# Chapter Ten

## *Establishing Loving Boundaries: Part 2*

*B*y this point in the book, we're sure that many of you are wondering how I (Gary) ever made it through my childhood days alive. But, something else I experienced as a child taught me another benefit of stable, protective boundaries. If I had learned this lesson earlier, it could have saved me from having the worst nightmare I'd ever experienced.

As a young boy, I (Gary) had been fishing on a beautiful lake in the Northwest. It was foresting country, and at many places along the lake, logs lay alongside each other in the water where they would soon be floated down to the mill. At one place on the lake, a good distance from where I stood, logs had been tied together to make a walking path out to a small island. From everything I'd heard from the old-timers around the lake, it was the perfect place to fish.

As I began the long walk toward the manmade bridge, I started thinking about the "natural" bridge right in front of me. Those logs stretched right out to the island, and they were so many and so thick that it would be no trick at all to get right to that great fishing spot and save the walk to the manmade bridge! Why waste time walking all the way to where the logs were tied together? I had a walkway right in front of me.

Chuckling to myself over the brilliance of my discovery, I ran on top of the logs out toward the island. Everything went well at first. The logs were so thick that there was very little give in them. Unfortunately, what I couldn't tell from the shore was that the logs got increasingly smaller in diameter as I got closer to the island. When I began, I could step on a log, and it would go down only a few inches. As the logs got smaller with each step I took, I sank lower and lower into the water until that last fateful step.

Even though the logs were still thickly bunched together, they had become so skinny that when I put my foot down, it slid right between the wet logs and suddenly I was underwater with a major problem. My fall had forced the logs apart momentarily, but just as quickly they moved right back together. As I fought my way up for air, the logs had formed a wooden roof above me that I didn't have the strength to pull apart.

Thrashing around underwater, desperately looking for the smallest opening, I found a crack between two logs and forced my arm and head out of the water, gasping for breath. As I crawled out on top of the logs, which barely held me afloat, I was wet, frightened, angry, exhausted, and embarrassed. I had also lost all my fishing gear—and nearly my life. What had looked like a tremendous short cut had turned into a long, life-threatening ordeal! For weeks I woke up in the middle of the night, fighting my way out of the covers as I dreamed I wasn't able to find a way through the logs to the surface.

Something I've seen many times since that experience is that cutting corners is often a good way to add time and energy to any project. In fact, another "Smalley-Trent Axiom of Life" is "It almost always takes twice as long to get out of something as it did to get into it!"

What does all this have to do with building self-worth and honoring children? Parents who want to see their children's sense of value go up need to set boundaries for short cuts that can damage their lives. These include corners they can be tempted to cut to gain a friend, win a promotion, or get out of a spanking.

## BOUNDARIES ADD PRODUCTIVE DAYS
## TO CHILDREN'S LIVES

When you establish clear boundaries for short cuts your children are tempted to take, you add days of peace and productivity to their lives. How is this possible? Let's look at a common short cut many people take in life and see how much work and anxiety it can cause and how much joy it can rob. That short cut is lying.

While stumping along the political trail one year, Abraham Lincoln was asked by a reporter why he always made it a habit to tell the truth. "There is a very good reason why I strive to tell the truth," Lincoln replied. "It means I don't have as much to remember!"[1]

Have you ever lied to someone or a group of people and had a hard time keeping your story straight? One problem with lying is that it gives you so little rest! It may have saved you from a spanking, kept you from losing face, or gained you favor in someone's eyes, but the lack of peace it leaves in your life can eventually turn on you.

The Bible puts it this way: "A false witness will not go unpunished, / And he who speaks lies will not escape."[2] Lying is like having a severely twisted ankle. As long as you walk slowly and carefully, you can often hide your lack of support. However, there's always the fear that you'll twist a conversation too far or put too much pressure on your alibi and fall flat on your face.

Establishing boundaries for lying honors your children and shows them you are serious about loving them. Why? Because it helps them experience the freedom of telling the truth and keeps them within protective fences.

## A Short Cut to Disaster

If you let little white lies go, your children can begin the descent into darkness. As their lies mount, they can experience the trauma of lying awake at night, knowing in the back of their minds that this may be the day their lies are discovered.

Duke Tully bore such a burden. For over twenty years, Duke was the editor of the largest newspaper in a major Sun Belt city. To newspaper opponents or to anyone else in the state who dared attack him or the paper, the Duke was as fierce a foe as John Wayne ever hoped to be. He was almost as tough on his friends and coworkers.

But hey, this was the Duke, a decorated combat pilot who flew missions in World War II, Korea, and Vietnam. No wonder he was so hard-nosed. One look at the combat pictures and decorations on the walls in his office would tell you why.

Just stand around him at those Veteran's Day functions, look at the decorations on his uniform, and listen to him swap war stories with the best of them. You could take it to the bank, old Duke was as much at home with men he knew like Joe Foss, World War II flying ace and Medal of Honor winner, as he was with any of his editors on the paper.

The only problem was that Duke Tully was never in the service. He never served during any war, never flew a combat mission.

It all began as a simple little lie about being in the service so that he could impress some people, but he kept adding embellishments to the story. It may have started out as flying combat missions in World War II, but then there was also Korea. And, oh yes, did we mention Vietnam?

Eventually, to back up his story and protect himself from questioning eyes, Duke had to purchase a uniform and get pictures made of himself beside various planes. And always, always, there had to be that gnawing feeling inside his stomach as he lay awake at night trying to remember what he said, when he had said it, and to whom.

Can you imagine the nights this man must have had, knowing that ultimately liars can't escape from all their words? Would you want *your* child to go through the humiliation and public ridicule this man has faced since the true facts of his story came out? Not indicating boundaries for your own words or your children's speech could lead you to a similar fate sooner than you think.

Lying isn't the only short cut children are tempted to take. A similar thing happens with other self-control issues such as studying. We can't tell you how many young men and women we've known who never had a protective fence around weeknights in grade school and high school when they had homework due. Then in their first year of college, the students awoke to a shattering reality when they began to flunk out of school. Because they never had a boundary set for their school evenings as they were growing up, they didn't know the first thing about how to study or how to set study times, and their grades and failing slips reflected it.

When you establish legitimate, healthy boundaries for areas of hurt into which your children can stray, you honor them by saving them twice the work and time of trying to get themselves out of something you should have put a protective fence around in the first place.

## BOUNDARIES HELP CHILDREN UNDERSTAND
## THAT THERE ARE ABSOLUTES

At the time we're writing this book, a popular television commercial pictures a large bull walking freely in a number of different locations. On an ocean beach, in the middle of a city, out in the wheat fields of the Midwest—like the five-hundred-pound canary, it goes anywhere it wants. And all the time, in the background a chorus sings "We know no boundaries." This commercial is supposed to demonstrate to investors what financial freedom is all about.

Unfortunately, for families who know no boundaries, the lack of limits demonstrates to children the absence of biblical absolutes. What do we mean by an "absence of absolutes"?

People without an absolute standard are ultimately left without a lasting value system. What is "right" today almost certainly won't be "right" in the future. (Would any of us alive in 1957 have imagined that "gay rights" activists would control entire political structures in certain cities as they do today?) Erwin Lutzer, in his excellent little book *The Necessity of Ethical Absolutes*,[3] points out that as a result of the uncertainty that goes along with situational ethics and our society's ever-changing values, people lose the ability to say no. Inadequate absolutes soon lead a person to inadequate morals.

Our trying to base absolutes on culture, situational ethics, or emotions is like a spider trying to build a web on the hands of a clock. Each tick of the clock pulls at the inadequate structure that's been set up hurriedly and will soon tear it apart, leaving the spider forever mending holes and always shifting positions.

Children who grow up in homes without consistent boundaries fall prey to the same problems a society faces when it leaves the protective fence provided by God's absolute, authoritative Word: inadequate identity and decisions based on feelings or glands, not what's lasting or right. Let's allow Todd's story to illustrate how such a home can undermine a child's self-worth and destroy his future.

### Cut Adrift from an Absolute Anchor

Todd's parents were so concerned about not disciplining him for the wrong things that they rarely disciplined him at all. They loved to brag at parties that they had "never laid a hand" on their son to correct him. After all, they grew up in a permissive society and an even more permissive church. As far as his liberated parents were concerned, there were no commandments in Scripture for "our age," rather, just "meaningful suggestions." As a result, clear boundaries for questionable practices were placed in the file marked "nonexistent."

Because Todd grew up knowing no boundaries, nothing anyone said to correct or instruct him ever carried much weight. Why should it? For Todd, if even God's Word was up for grabs, anything a teacher or coach or boss had to say to him carried as much weight as the air used to convey the words.

Children learn the basis of right and wrong in their homes. And if nothing was wrong, Todd assumed that meant that anything he felt like doing must be right. This included hitting, swearing, lying, and stealing from his friends.

Growing up without boundaries can become addictive. Like a horse that hasn't been bridled and ridden in months and then has a bit forced into its mouth and a saddle slapped on its back, a child who runs into the inescapable boundaries of life when he or she has rarely experienced them before will rebel.

Todd fought and kicked against anything and anyone who tried to put a protective fence around his actions. What made the story even sadder was that Todd's parents stood back and watched all this happening to him, never once having the courage or the genuine love to step in and help him or to admit they were a part of the problem.

With all the anger and restlessness that had developed in Todd's life, and with almost no controls on that anger from his parents, Todd became a textbook liar and a junior-grade criminal (sociopath). He would lie to and defy his parents to their faces, and he was allowed to dishonor them at every step. Every time he got away with dishonoring Mom and Dad by his actions and attitudes, he grew to believe he shouldn't suffer any negative consequences for dishonoring others. After all, anything goes.

As we mentioned earlier, when we dishonor our parents, we lower our own value because we're so much like them. Feeling out of control and insecure, Todd acted out how much he disliked himself. With no boundaries to corral his negative feelings and his mounting anger, his frustrations began to explode whenever he was at school or around his rapidly diminishing group of friends.

When his teacher tried to do something about his aggressive behavior and unwillingness to do his homework, she was met with back talk, anger, and glaring eyes. When his Little League coach benched him for swearing and throwing his bat when he struck out, he quit the team. A few years later, when his boss at the grocery store asked him to stay and work an extra hour, Todd refused and lost his job.

And what about God? What *about* Him? The last person Todd wanted anything to do with was Someone who calls on people to give up their lives and live His way. Besides, from what his parents had taught him, he couldn't believe God's words anyway.

Todd was angry with everyone except his parents, he thought. They never got in his way like all those other people. What he didn't realize was that the anger he spewed out on others stemmed from the original frustrations he felt toward Mom and Dad. He liked the way they let him "do his thing" by putting lewd posters in his room and smoking dope in the house, but he wasn't discerning enough to know how much they were hurting him by doing so. He couldn't see it at the time, but his parents were doing him incredible harm by ignoring biblical absolutes.

Even when they were confronted with this truth months later, his parents refused to acknowledge their part in his anger or their weakness in being unwilling to confront him. If only once they had stood up to him, perhaps they could have begun to reverse a terrible downward slide.

Why does the lack of boundaries cause such angry behavior in children? In some ways, it's very much like what happens to men during war.

## Casualties Too Close to Home

High levels of frustration and anger are a common denominator for men who have been in combat, even long after the battles are over. In talking with a number of Vietnam veterans, one researcher noted that the lack of safe boundaries overseas or at home lay at the heart of many men's complaints.[4]

War produces casualties of many types, and among them are soldiers who carry around tremendous anger because of living in a place without safe boundaries. Homes without the safe boundaries set up by loving parents produce casualties of their own—children like Todd.

Go without getting a healthy night's rest for a week, and watch how irritable and easily frustrated you become. Go without boundaries for years, and watch how deep and uncontrollable your anger becomes.

Like the children on the playground without a fence, Todd learned through his unnamed anxieties never to drop his guard. As a result of constantly feeling insecure and unprotected by his parents, Todd's deep-rooted anger brought him to the place where he couldn't care less what happened to himself or others. And because he demanded too much too soon and felt he was beyond any "absolute" rules, he was arrested at age sixteen—for selling drugs to two nine-year-olds.

In a world where everything is relative, Todd and many children like him are handed a road map with no north and south markings and left to wander into terrible places of self-destruction without a compass with a "true" north. They need clear boundaries that are marked off by biblical absolutes.

Before we go on to talk about what kinds of boundaries are best and how to set them up, we need to issue one vital caution. Most children have a natural mind-set that can make your setting and sticking with boundaries very difficult.

## ANYTHING BUT A WARM RESPONSE

According to the Scriptures, the wise man loves you when you correct him, and he'll meet you with thanks and appreciation. What about those who aren't so wise, however? Unfortunately, you can't expect such a warm response from the unwise. A fool's reaction to correction is anger, and sometimes active hostility (Proverbs 9:7–8).

What does this have to do with children and establishing boundaries for them? There is another verse that says, "Foolishness is bound up in the heart of a child" (Proverb 22:15). That verse helps you get the whole picture. By nature, children (like adults) have to grow into maturity and wisdom. It isn't a "given"; it's earned by learning the skill of living God's way.

When you honor your children by providing loving boundaries

for them, in the long run they'll become more enjoyable for you and for others to live with. However, there will probably be times when they'll become angry with you for suggesting legitimate restrictions for them.

When a child builds up all his fury and declares that he's going to attend that certain concert, watch that show, stay up until 4:30 A.M. on a school night, or spend the night with the guys in their fort, many parents fail to follow through on maintaining boundaries, even those that will protect a child from major hurts. The unfortunate thing is that the lower a parent's self-worth and personal value, the more insecure he'll be and the more difficulty he may have in dealing with his child's anger at legitimate restrictions. Sometimes we honor someone by disciplining him, yet many insecure parents have great difficulty with this kind of tough love.

## An Effective Barrier to Setting Up
### Protective Boundaries

Every parent loses his heart to that little boy or girl who looks up at him with a smile from the crib, sits in his lap, or flashes him that award-winning grin. However, when a person has never been loved or felt valuable himself, his child's love can mean more than normal parental attachment. It can also make up for years of past hurts.

When a child is angry with you, particularly when you establish boundaries for his actions, he often wants to have nothing to do with you for a short period of time. For an insecure parent, having to face a child's anger toward him, even for a few hours, can be too burning a pain to take. Cut off from the love he's received from that child, he's reminded too much of the years he's spent feeling alone and unwanted. Even in a home in which one parent tries to be more firm with the child to make up for the other parent who is not, watch how the insecure parent sabotages any attempt to discipline that "poor little lamb"—the same child who just broke the neighbor's chair by jumping up and down on it.

Watching their children relax and even smile when they give in to them can be a tremendous relief to some parents. It's almost as if they go underwater when their children become angry with them and they're finally able to come up for air! Children quickly learn how dependent their parents can become on their good graces, and they can hold their parents hostage by withholding their love when they want to avoid a rule.

Children, even very young children, can pound on boundaries with incredible force to see if the limits are real. But with some parents, like Jericho of old, all their children have to do is march around them seven times with their arms crossed and "shout with a great shout" (Joshua 6:5), and the parents' walls come tumbling down.

When children beat down their parents' boundaries, they learn that they are the ones who set the limits in the home, and the injustice and the illogic of that can cause havoc for both parents and children.

## Times of Testing in Single-Parent Homes

Single parents in particular typically go through a tremendous time of testing, especially if it's the dad who has moved out. For many children, Dad's "no" may be more frightening and harder to get around than Mom's, and Mom's natural sensitivity and relational skill make her vulnerable to attacks on the boundaries she sets up.

So single moms, expect to have your boundaries tested. When one parent leaves, a great amount of the children's security leaves, too, no matter how bad your "ex" may have been. Insecure children will often push against protective fences to make sure they really exist. Your children may try to make you think that you've become an unloving troll overnight in keeping them inside protective fences, but the clouds will begin to pass once they feel secure in your boundaries. If you give in to their testing demands, you'll have any number of days to regret your decision.

It's not nice to have someone "hate" you for a few hours or even for a few days, and it's tempting to give in. But one way you honor and eventually lead your children to wisdom is by holding fast to what's right instead of caving in because of their frowns. I (John) saw this illuminated in the loving actions of my aunt.

## LOOKING BACK ON LOVING BOUNDARIES

During my seventh-grade year, my mother had a long convalescence after several major surgeries. Because of all the help we had with our extended family back in Indiana, she spent her time recuperating in the Midwest while my aunt came out to Arizona to keep watch over us three boys.

Aunt Dovie is small in stature, and when we had been with her at family gatherings, she had always seemed as gentle as a lamb. What we didn't know was that she was made of pure steel when it came to setting and keeping loving boundaries. Her strength didn't come overnight. It came from raising children of her own and being a model servant to the rest of the family for decades. For over seventy years now, her personal resources and faith in God have made her the person we all turn to in our family when we're in need of help.

Although we wouldn't admit it, we boys needed help. With our mother gone away to recuperate, we felt like the class that's just found out they're going to have a substitute! As a single parent, my mother did a tremendous job of making us toe the line. Send us little, gentle Aunt Dovie, and we were overjoyed. It would be wall-to-wall parties and staying up all night! But then we began to find out that her gentle spirit didn't mean she would give in on what was best for us and right in God's sight.

I'll be honest with you. There were times when she disciplined me and I became incredibly angry with her. (For instance, there was the time I sneaked out my window late one night to meet with a group of low-lifes who had dropped out of school, and I forgot to put the screen back on the window. "The screen? Oh, well, uh, you see, Aunt Dovie, the wind must have blown it off!")

My aunt never yelled at me. She didn't have to. Holding the screen in her hand and waiting for my answer, she only had to look at me with those steady eyes and uncompromising words that asked for the truth, and I felt burning conviction inside. Yet like many foolish adolescents (and adults), I felt only anger when she corrected me, not the conviction of the wise.

Even as a seventh-grader, I was taller than Aunt Dovie by several inches. I can remember looking down on her as she gently talked to me about being truthful and the importance of having positive friends. No matter how softly she spoke, her words would pound inside my head like a screaming lecture, and I would walk away when she was finished and slam the door behind me.

"The nerve of this woman," I would say to myself or shout out loud to the air. "Nobody died and left her queen! Who does she think she is, anyway, all five feet of her, trying to stop me from ruining my life?"

"Who does she think she is. . . ." Over the years, as I've looked back at that crucial time in my early adolescent years, I know who she was: an angel from heaven. Aunt Dovie cared enough to stand in the gap between a foolish adolescent boy who was reaching out to the wrong side and the evil that would have loved to draw him in. She cared enough to stand up to my anger, sarcasm, and disrespect for her for well over a year and never back down or stop loving me.

I know for a fact that I wouldn't be the man I am today if my Aunt Dovie hadn't loved me when I was so hard to love. Time and again my childhood foolishness came to the surface, and I fought with her. But her courage and her commitment to what was right and what would honor God and me pulled both of us through until my mother got back on her feet.

Deep down inside, even in the midst of my rebellion, I wanted someone to love me enough to correct me. It wasn't until several years later, however, that I had enough wisdom to understand how much she had loved me and to thank her for it. Today, years older and a little wiser, if I were to begin a list of people who have truly loved me over the years, I'd put Aunt Dovie and a few others like her near the top of the list.

We've looked at four reasons we should provide protective boundaries and one caution that could sidetrack us from doing so if our own self-worth is low. Now we're ready to focus on the kinds of boundaries that work best and how we can set them up.

# Chapter Eleven

## Establishing Loving Boundaries: Part 3

*E*arl and Judy had finally built their dream house away from the sprawling city, the never-ending traffic, and the increasing pollution. It was nestled at the base of a mountain some thirty-five miles north of Phoenix, and the unspoiled southwestern desert came right up to their doorstep.

The desert has its own beauty: numerous shades of brown laced with the khaki green of native trees and cacti, rocks of volcanic black and milk-white quartz, lavender sunrises, and golden, sun-splashed sunsets. But the desert also has its own danger, something Earl and Judy never took seriously.

It had taken every available dollar the couple had—and more—to complete their home. Trying to cut costs, they decided one thing they could skimp on was the fence they wanted put around the back yard. Even though the few neighbors near them had concrete block or tall, chain-link fences around the area where children and pets would play, Earl and Judy decided that for the time being, a small wooden-rail fence would do just as well.

It was late in the afternoon on a beautiful spring day, and soon Earl would be driving down their gravel driveway after working in the city. Judy was at the sink, finishing her preparations for dinner, and the children had just come inside from playing in the back yard. That's when she heard their little dog, Muffin, barking hysterically near the side of the house.

Instantly, Judy looked up from the sink and out the window that gave her a clear view of the yard. What she saw was terrible. Four coyotes had jumped through the wooden fence and were attacking Muffin.

Before she could get the back door open, the battle was over. As she stepped outside, she saw the coyotes dragging the still form of the family pet under the fence. Crying and yelling, she could only watch as they disappeared into the desert. Through her tears, she was thankful that her two young children had not been in the back yard as well.

Because our children are more precious than our "Muffins," we continually urge parents to get involved and take seriously the need to set up positive, protective boundaries for children. We've encouraged you to put up protective fences against things and people that can rush in like coyotes and damage your children emotionally or physically, or sneak in and destroy their self-worth.

What types of fences do the best job of protecting children and of raising their value? Do children have any say in the boundaries that are set up? Can boundaries provide security but still allow freedom for positive development?

We can find some of the answers in the very hand that holds this book or the eyes that read it. The Lord has provided a picture of well-functioning boundaries right in the human body.

## PUMPING IN GOOD AND PUSHING OUT BAD

Every inch of the body is made up of millions and millions of cells, each of which can teach us something about positive boundaries. Although this is obviously an oversimplified explanation,[1] let's zoom in and focus on just one cell.

Like every other cell in the body, the one we've selected has a boundary (cell membrane) around it. We could picture that boundary as a fence that runs all the way around it. All along this fence are a number of gates (actually, little pump mechanisms). Picture each gate with a little guard watching over it who is responsible for opening and closing the gate.

Some of these gates only open in, letting in good things the cell needs such as essential nutrients and antibodies to fight disease.

Others only open out and are used for removing bad things that have somehow gotten inside the cell. These would include certain waste by-products of cell function and toxic substances that may have slipped in under the fence or gotten inside the cell through an unmanned or malfunctioning gate.

In a healthy cell, the little guards stay on duty day and night to carry out their specific functions. However, should disease or injury affect the cell, the fence around it can begin to deteriorate. When this happens, the little guards can be affected and fail to properly operate their gates. As a result, many gates that should be opening for needed nutrients stay closed, and other gates are left closed that should be opening to expel destructive elements that have accumulated. Ultimately, when a cell's protective fence breaks down, it signals the destruction of the cell.

As parents, we can learn about setting boundaries from looking at that cell. First, *the absence of boundaries almost ensures the presence of problems.* As we've observed in the last few chapters, a child can be much more easily carried away or infected with problems from peer pressure to petty thievery when there is no protective fence around him or her.

Second, *every fence we put around a child should have two different gates in it.* One is to let in positive words, experiences, and people, and the other is to remove or keep out as many bad experiences and agents as possible.

Isn't it interesting how God designed within each healthy cell both types of gates? Good things need to come in, but the expectation is that there will also be bad things that need to be removed. For parents, these two functions of "manning the gates" for children are just as important as setting up protective boundaries in the first place.

If you haven't asked yourself the question yet, consider it now: "How involved and faithful a guard am I in 'manning the gates' for my children?" The answer can determine much of how secure and stable is their future.

The book of Proverbs calls us to guard our spiritual lives by keeping out wrong and keeping diligent watch, for the good God will bring:

> *Blessed is the man who listens to me,*
> *Watching daily at my gates,*
> *Waiting at the posts of my doors.*

> *For whoever finds me finds life,*
> *And obtains favor from the* LORD.
>                          *(Proverbs 8:34–35)*

[2]Parents who watch over the gates of their children's lives are also a blessing to their children. But now you may ask, "How many boundaries should I set up around my children, and how do I know what to let in or put out?"

We've discovered that the healthiest homes aren't necessarily those that have the most rigid or the greatest number of boundaries. Neither are they the ones that have so many gates left open that every experience is allowed to wash over their children unchecked.

Rather, the ones that cause the greatest growth in their children's self-worth are those that base their boundaries on four simple questions that help to keep a home in balance. These four questions are ones that each of us, young or old, is continually answering as we interact with others, and the results of our answers either raise or lower our self-worth.[2]

## FOUR QUESTIONS THAT HELP SHAPE POSITIVE BOUNDARIES

### Question #1: "Who Am I?"

Every parent needs to set up a protective fence around the question each child will eventually ask, "Who am I?" Nearly every week, we see the damage done to a child who left home not knowing the answer to this question.

Boys and girls (some of them now adults) who didn't grow up inside the safety of loving parental and biblical boundaries often leave home without a positive sense of identity. As a result, their search to find an answer to this question often leads them to try damaging and devaluing solutions. Time after time, they find unfulfilling answers in alcoholism, immorality, workaholism, and broken relationships.

We need to know who we are if we're to stand on our own or relate successfully to others. Like individuals living in a house of mirrors, we'll be left to wander the halls gazing at distorted images of ourselves if we can't picture who we are. Talk to one person or group, and we're terrific. Talk to another, and we're rejected without a second thought. Gaining a realistic, positive sense of identity can unlock the door and release us from the prison of having each group we're in or every Hollywood personality on television determine our character, values, and self-worth.

One reason Jesus was able to face persecution, trial, and the peer pressure to set Himself up as Rome's king or set Himself down as a blasphemer was His knowledge of who He was (John 8:58; 16:5–13). Your children need to know their identity if they are to have the confidence to face their future and stand strong. One way you can guide them toward a positive understanding of themselves is to teach them who they are *not*.

***Show Them the Danger of the Inflated Self.*** From the earliest times, we human beings have had the tendency to answer the question of self-identity by saying we're something we're not.[3] Let's illustrate this by looking at some examples of everyday people.

Several studies have found that people tend to accept more responsibility for their successes than their failures, for their good deeds than their bad.[4] If their team wins, it's because of their superior athletic skills or cheering; if they lose, it's because of the crummy officiating. When they know which is the highest mountain in North America when asked in a Trivial Pursuit game, it's their brilliance that comes up with the answer; when they fail at the next question, it's because "nobody" knows the capital of Tibet.

In the excellent article "The Inflated Self," David Myers pointed out that one common manifestation of low self-worth is *inflated* self-worth.[5] He built a strong case that pride is every bit as big a problem as low self-worth, and we agree.

Pride can certainly cloud the issue of self-identity. It can mask a deep sense of low self-worth as an imperfect person fights to "claim" an exalted identity he really doesn't feel inside.

Pride has pushed people to set themselves up as God's equal to gain a fleeting feeling of power and a sense that their lives have meaning. No matter how high we jump, however, we can never escape our feet of clay that pull us back to the ground.

Thankfully, Christians have an advantage in answering the question "Who am I?" because they can openly admit they are fallen and in need of a Savior. They don't need to wait centuries to evolve into a higher moral form (have morals risen in the years since you were born?), nor do they need to pass themselves off as "little gods," as one popular cult teaches (never truly believing such a claim in their heart of hearts when they see sin and error deep inside).

We can answer the question "Who am I?" and help our children answer it by understanding our fallen nature and the liberating freedom of being able to throw ourselves on God's grace. Doing so frees us from having to play God and gives us the power and acceptance we're struggling to get. This freedom is found in who we are in God's eyes.

***Teach Them Their Identity in Christ.*** By teaching your children who God says they are, you honor them and help them leave home with high worth. His Word says that His children are deeply loved,[6] highly treasured,[7] of great worth,[8] only a little lower than the angels,[9] secure in His love,[10] His own special people,[11] made in His image,[12] of more value than the birds of the air,[13] and so important that God gave up His only Son to reclaim them from darkness.[14]

Every day, by teaching God's Word to your children and living it out before them, by having them listen to Christian music and allowing them to be with His people at church and at socials, you can build in positive words and thoughts that give them a secure identity in Christ. We'll take an entire chapter to highlight this point later,[15] but when children know how God views them, that can be the greatest single factor in building up their self-worth.

***Give Them a Name to Live Up to—and Protect That Name.*** Who they are in Christ and who they are not apart from Him are two important areas around which you can build protective fences. Children also need to know how highly you view them to truly answer the question "Who am I?" And a good place to begin is with their own names.

## DRAWING STRENGTH FROM THEIR NAME: ONE WAY TO LET GOOD THINGS IN

Letting a child know why you named her what you did can be a tremendous encouragement to her, especially if that name has biblical or some other special significance behind it. For example, each of us has a daughter named Kari. In Greek, *Kari* means "love from a pure heart."

For Gary and Norma's daughter, who is now in college and a delight to her parents, being told the meaning of her name when she was young has given her extra encouragement throughout the years to develop a pure, loving heart. For John and Cindy's infant daughter (who by the way was named after Gary's daughter), the name represents her parents' prayer for her and their commitment to raise her in an environment that reflects the virtues of her name.

In the Scriptures, a person's name always had great significance.[16] That's why God took special care in giving people names or in changing them. For example, in Peter's case, being called the Rock was a vivid reminder of his commission, of all he could become, and of how others would depend on him following the Resurrection (Matthew 16:18).

In addition to the attachment it can build between parent and child, there's another significant thing about naming a person: very often, children live up to the names they are called. And in that light, may we ask you a difficult question? Aside from their given names, what "names" are your children growing up with? Are they anything like the one a man in the restaurant booth next to us had for his son?

"Stump. That's what we call him," the burly man in the cap told us. "Oh, his name's really Billy, but just look at that neck. Show them your neck, Billy. Can you see that? He doesn't even have a neck! That's why we call him Stump. Come on, Stump. Show them your neck. Ha! Ha! Ha!"

This father never saw the way his preschool son hung his little head, never noticed the look of defeat and hurt that registered on his wife's face. But then again, she had to live with her own special name: "Cupcake—because she looks like a cupcake! Ha! Ha! Ha!"

Derogatory names can brutalize a child (or adult) and blast away at his self-worth. Some children have heard such names so often that they grow up thinking their name is "Stupid," "Clumsy," "Pudgy," or "Four Eyes" instead of Matt, Lisa, James, or Jill. Leave a negative label on a child too long, even if it's only in fun, and it can leave him feeling as if two all-pro linebackers have just smashed into him at full speed.

However, the opposite is true as well. Helping a child see the value in the names you give and call him can build worth and self-esteem in his life. I (Gary) recently witnessed the positive effects of my son's finding out more about his namesake. At the time of this writing, Greg is eighteen years old and a freshman in college. One of his assignments was to research his family tree. He had old photos and letters from relatives that I didn't even know he had kept.

Buried deep in his closet was a letter I had written Greg when he was first learning to read. It was a letter talking about why we had given him his name and who we had named him after. The letter was actually a detailed account of Cardinal Hildebrand, the eleventh-century clergyman who later became Pope Gregory VII. Through a relative who is a diligent historian, I had discovered that we were related to this saint of old on my mother's side, her name being Emily Hildebrand. As I had read about this man's life while I was in seminary, many of his qualities and character traits had impressed me. He was more than a church leader; he had a personal, vibrant relationship with Christ.

As I looked over Greg's shoulder while he reviewed the letter, he looked up at me and said, "Dad, is this really our relative and the person I was named after?" From the way he asked the question and commented on what he had learned, I could tell he read with honor about his namesake.

Taking time to point out the special significance of your children's names and being sure the pet names or nicknames you give them are helpful and not hurtful can open the gate to good things and help them answer the question "Who am I?"

A second way you can help them answer the question is to put *outside* the fence those words, people, or attitudes that tell them they are anything less than what God says they are. Take Karen, for example.

## GUARDING THEIR NAME: PUTTING BAD THINGS OUT

The vast majority of elementary school teachers are dedicated, caring professionals who build up children's self-worth. In fact, for many children in first grade, their teacher is the one they love the most after their parents and the one who sets the tone for their future expectations of school. In Karen's case, however, the teacher didn't inspire love. Mrs. Williams was a harsh, insensitive woman who evoked fear in her students with her frequent, angry outbursts.

Karen's parents had seen her excited and enthusiastic in her kindergarten class, but now they saw their daughter doing poorly in first grade. It wasn't that the material being taught was too difficult. Having been in a special reading camp over the summer, Karen was far ahead of many children in her class in writing and learning to read. But Karen was complaining of being sick more than ever before and was wanting to miss school with every complaint.

After searching for what could be affecting her so badly, her parents discovered the source of the problem. Angry words had robbed her of a positive identity and feelings of self-worth.

Karen was hearing two messages in her little life. One message at home and at church was that she was deeply loved and special to God and her parents. The other message was the one she received from her schoolteacher, who felt she was a bother and a pain. Her teacher had a pet name for her: "Miss Busybody."

From Karen's first day in school, her teacher had decided to make her an example to the other students to let them all know "who was boss." Being a talkative little girl, Karen was visiting with a classmate when the school bell rang, commencing class. The moment the bell sounded, an eraser flew across the room, hitting Karen in the back of the head. The flying eraser was followed by a barrage of angry words designed to put the "fear of Mrs. Williams" in her and the rest of the children. Needless to say, it worked.

Karen was a very sensitive child. In the days and weeks that followed, she had more and more difficulty in handling Mrs. Williams's angry outbursts. Some of the children would try to stand up to her or simply ignore her, but Karen could do neither. Sometimes her teacher could just look at her with those angry eyes when she walked by her desk, and Karen would begin to cry. Then she would get a lecture for being a "spoiled brat" and too emotionally immature for first grade.

Whether it was not lining up properly after recess or not putting away the paints as she should, Karen found the person she looked to for encouragement and support slamming emotional doors in her face almost daily. "No wonder you haven't gotten your assignments done, Miss Busybody," Mrs. Williams would typically say. "You can talk, but you can't do the homework!"

Like many children, Karen was too embarrassed and too loyal to her teacher to talk with her parents about what was happening at school.[17] Attempts by her mother and father to find out what was wrong were unsuccessful. At the first parent-teacher meeting, Karen's parents made a special point to talk to her teacher about Karen's behavior, and they found Mrs. Williams to be very pleasant. They were assured it was simply "the adjustment of a new school" that was affecting their daughter, and they went away puzzled, thinking the problem must lie with Karen.

However, as problems continued to mount, Karen's mother approached a young teacher's aide in the class, and she admitted and explained how dreadfully Karen was being treated in class. After an emotional confrontation between the principal, Mrs. Williams, the teacher's aide, and Karen's parents, Karen was transferred to another class, where they saw an almost instant improvement in her attitude and school work. As a result of the investigation the principal started after this meeting, the next year Mrs. Williams was transferred to an administrative position in the district away from any direct involvement with children.

If Karen's parents hadn't been sensitive enough to check the gates and monitor the words and names others repeatedly spoke to her as well as their own, little Karen would have been left with a confusing answer to the question "Who am I?"

Unfortunately, there's something within all of us (our fallen nature) that tends to throw out the positives we hear and put on the negatives. That's why monitoring the messages coming into our children's lives from outside sources can be every bit as important as being mindful of the messages we put in.

As important as it is to provide a healthy boundary for the question of self-identity, it is equally important to put up a fence around a second question, "Whom do I want to please?" As we'll show in the next chapter, children who can answer this in a healthy way gain confidence and self-worth by leaps and bounds.

# Chapter Twelve

## Establishing Loving Boundaries:
## Part 4

$M$y (John's) grandfather taught me a tremendous lesson about how loving boundaries can honor a child and help him feel tremendously valuable. That's because he taught me the importance of answering correctly the next question that should shape the boundaries we set up.

### Question #2: "Whom Do I Want to Please?"

When I was in third grade, I was part of a gang of neighborhood kids who constantly roamed the streets, alleys, orange groves, and desert areas near our homes on our bicycles. I knew my mother's rules: we could ride our bikes anywhere we wanted, but we had to be home before the streetlights came on. Unfortunately for my brothers and me, there was a streetlight directly in front of our house that didn't allow for any "fudge factor" in being home on time.

One afternoon, I knew it was about time to start heading home, but I decided to listen to one of my friends instead. He said, "Forget about going home now! We can make it to Camelback Mountain and back by dark with time to spare. No problem." It took only milliseconds for me to make up my mind, put my friend's words above my mother's and grandparents', and head for the hills—right into a real problem.

In those days, there were mainly dirt roads on the mountain and many more cacti than houses. We loved the area because of the hills and bumps that became launching pads for us on our bicycles.

As I took one particularly thrilling jump, I lost control of my bike and smashed it right into a cholla cactus near the path. Although I survived the crash without being covered with thorns, the same thing couldn't be said about my front tire. It was flat as a pancake, and I was on foot, far from home.

Needless to say, the streetlight in front of my house was glowing in the dark like an evil eye by the time I walked up with my bicycle. I knew that the excuse of a flat tire wouldn't get me out of trouble this time, and sure enough, I was sent back to my grandfather's room for a spanking.

After the spanking was over, I was moping around in the kitchen when my grandmother told me to get my grandfather for dinner. "No way!" I said. But with one look and the threat of another spanking, I slunk down the hall to knock on his door.

As I came up to his room, the door was slightly ajar. In our house, it was a rule that we knocked on a door before entering someone's room. Because it was already partly open, however, I slowly pushed it the rest of the way and saw my grandfather sitting on his bed, crying.

"Grandfather, what's wrong?" I said.

As he looked up from the bed with tears streaming down his face, he motioned for me to come over to him. He wrapped his arms around me. "John," he said, "I love you boys so much. I want you to grow up to be the kind of men I'd be proud of. I hate to have to spank you, but you need to learn to respect what your mother says. Please listen to her and make me proud of you."

Both my grandfather and I stood there crying and hugging each other. It was the first time in all my young life I had heard my grandfather say he loved me, much less that it wasn't easy for him to spank us. I was so moved by knowing that the boundaries he enforced in my life were for my own good that I didn't want to do anything to hurt him again for the rest of my life—and I'm sure I succeeded for at least a week!

Even though I didn't shape up overnight, there was a dramatic decrease in the number of spankings I received after that day. I knew too much about my grandfather's heart and his love for me to want to hurt him again. I also knew he was right in wanting me to follow my mother's rules instead of a friend's ill-founded advice.

Less than a year later, my grandfather died while we were all at home, but his words and those few moments in his room remain as vivid in my memory as if they happened yesterday. So, too, can be your words of love that call a child to please God and his parents before other people in his life.

## PLEASING OTHERS CAN COME AT TOO GREAT A PRICE

Not marking out boundaries for whom your children try to please or what they'll do to gain someone else's approval leaves them wide open to attack. Children who have the deepest needs for acceptance often go to the greatest lengths to receive it. Pleasing others no matter what the price proves most costly to themselves.

Parents who sense an unmet need for acceptance in a child's life or who have a son or daughter who has a natural bent to be a "people pleaser" have a special responsibility to provide helpful boundaries for them. What happens if they don't? Just look at Saul in the Old Testament. By wanting to please the wrong people, he ended up destroying the most precious relationships he had, those with his son and the Lord.

### Above Pleasing People

Saul never learned an important lesson parents should teach their children. First and foremost, we are to please God by honoring His Word. There's a very good reason for relying on God's Word as a light to our paths. Whatever God says we should do with our lives keeps us inside the fence where we are safe and secure. Every time we disobey God's Word or listen to another's voice (even our own) that contradicts the Lord's, we've stepped outside the fence and are on the path toward a forbidding wilderness.

Twice, Saul forgot whom he should be most concerned with pleasing, and each time it took him outside the protective fence of God's security. One time, to be successful in battle, Saul was specifically ordered by Samuel to stay put and wait for him to offer sacrifices (1 Samuel 13:8ff.). However, when his troops began to grumble and some began to desert, Saul caved in to peer pressure and offered the sacrifices himself. Another time, he was ordered to destroy an incredibly wicked, diseased city and its inhabitants and animals, but he listened to the people instead and left the best of the spoils intact for his soldiers (1 Samuel 15:12ff.).

Trying to please other people instead of God can land us in hot water. It certainly did for Saul. It damaged his relationship with his son, Jonathan,[1] and it crushed his relationship with the Lord. Samuel put it this way: "Because you have rejected the word of the LORD, / He also has rejected you from being king" (1 Samuel 15:23).

How can you help your children answer the question "Whom do I want to please?" and have them put God's name and your name at the top of the list? How can you help them have a fighting chance to face the often overpowering words *peer pressure?* We know this is going to sound trite, but sometimes what works best is getting back to the basics—actively loving them and helping them see how much they are loved by God.

---

**The worse your relationship is with your children, the lower the fence against peer pressure that you provide for them.**

---

When Paul wanted the Corinthian believers to shape up and quit trying to please the immoral crowd in their city, he pointed out how much their heavenly Father loved them: "You were bought at a price." (Literally, he told them, "You have been bought with honor."[2]) "Therefore glorify God in your body" (1 Corinthians 6:20).

If you want your children to think of you when it comes to whom they should please, you must major in loving them. Your best defense against peer pressure later in the kids' lives is building a great relationship with them when they're young. The worse your relationship is with your children, the lower the fence against peer pressure that you provide for them. However, when children know they are loved, they can be encouraged to stay within the limits of your words and please you and their Lord first.

There are two other questions that can give you specific help in setting up positive, protective boundaries.

### Questions #3 and #4: "What Should I Accomplish?" and "Where Am I in Accomplishing My Goals?"

Do you know the most important goals your children have today and how to help them reach those goals? Do you know what type of people they are attracted to as friends, and have you helped them set their dating standards? Are your children taking responsibility for or accomplishing tasks today that can give them a positive sense of their abilities in the future? If you don't help your children identify what they should accomplish and then help them reach goals that are important to them, you leave them without a protective fence. To put it another way, if you don't help your children set their schedules or make decisions on what is truly important, *someone else will.*

From celebrities on TV to negative influences at school, there is no lack of people who will set a direction children should follow, even if it differs from what you know is the way they should go. Children like to accomplish things and become proficient at some undertaking. If you simply turn your head instead of getting to know their likes and goals, they may become all-state drug takers instead of all-state band members.

When you set a boundary for what your child accomplishes, you should keep a loving balance between the child's real abilities and what you might envision or want for him. Sammy's father never took his son's feelings into consideration when he set goals for his life, and his actions nearly destroyed his son.

### When Goals Become Burdens

Sammy was larger than many boys his age in grade school and exceptionally gifted in sports, but he didn't like competitive sports at all. That dislike grew into a definite hatred as his father had him down at the local park every night, throwing a football to him or hitting him grounders to develop his talents. After all, with all Sammy's talent, his father was raising his own retirement plan if his son one day got into the pros.

Sammy made it as far as a ward in a psychiatric hospital. Along the way he picked up all-state honors in high-school football and a full scholarship to a major college, but during his junior year he cracked emotionally under the conflicting pressures within himself and never played a down of football again.

Exaggerated expectations can cripple a child. You should make every effort to help him set realistic goals he can try to reach. Recently, I did this very thing with my (Gary's) son Michael.

Inspired by many of the pro athletes he's met in the conferences John and I speak at, Mike decided last year he wanted to be a football player. This past spring, long before he tried out for the football team, Mike let me know in a number of ways that his goal was to make first string.

So one afternoon we sat down together for almost four hours and drew out a conditioning and skill-building plan as Mike had watched me do with his brother, Greg. All I did was ask Mike some questions like these: "How well do you want to do on the team?" "What do you think is your best skill today? Running? Passing? Kicking?" "How much time would you be willing to put into developing the skills that need strengthening? A half-hour a day? An hour a week? Once a month?" "Do you want me to ask you once a week how you're doing with your running and passing? Once a month?"

Mike wanted to improve several areas over the spring and summer. These things gave him a goal he could shoot for and a positive feeling that he was organized in his efforts and not simply shooting in the dark. We came up with a plan of exercises and practice drills that was designed to help him get in better shape and improve his passing and running skills.

That's an example of how I helped him figure out what he should accomplish. By taking a goal in his life and working with him to set up a plan to reach it, I was establishing a positive boundary so that other things wouldn't crowd out his goal. Then I helped him evaluate where he was in accomplishing that goal.

## Taking Time to Inspect Their Efforts

If you do it in a loving way, a child feels special when you inspect what she does. What parent hasn't taken his child to the swimming pool when the child is learning to go off the diving board and heard one hundred times, "Watch me!" as she goes off the end? However, if you're too critical in your appraisal of her abilities, you can drive her away and make her efforts seem like bondage, not a building time. A child who knows you care enough about her to ask the hard questions in a loving way tackles a task feeling loved, and her self-worth is raised in the process.

Mike and I decided together that I should ask him once a week during the off-season how he was doing at meeting his goals. We also decided together what penalty, if any, he wanted me to impose if he didn't do what he agreed to do. Finally, we put everything we talked about in the form of a short contract that we both signed.[3] He knew in advance when I'd ask him about his goals, and he was involved in setting up any discipline there would be if he didn't meet them.

Norma and I have done the same kinds of things with Kari concerning the type of person she wants to date, with Greg on the vocation he wants to choose, and with each of the children concerning their spiritual goals and ministry aspirations.

Leaving a child without any boundaries for what he could or should accomplish with the gifts God has given him can lead to ruin for the child. We can't tell you how many adults have lamented the fact that their parents never took the time to help them be really successful in at least one area of their lives, and that has always been a discouraging factor for them. Others have discovered the truth in the old adage "an idle mind is the devil's workshop."

By setting up helpful fences around a child, you can help him gain a sense of success he can carry with him to adulthood. Building loving boundaries gives you a chance to be involved in his life in a positive way as you teach him responsibility and show him what goals are really important.

## WHO'S MANNING THE GATES?

As we close this discussion of the importance of establishing boundaries and the types that are most helpful in honoring children and attaching high value to them, we'd like to ask, Who's manning the gates of the fences that surround your children?

Your goal should be to teach your children responsibility and the ability to self-monitor those things that should come into their lives and those things that should be removed. Yet for those of you who are still in the process of teaching your children about making wise choices and decisions, you risk having a mess if you let them man the gates. That's not to knock your children, but simply to point out the reality of what happens when they make decisions about things in which you should be involved. Leave a child in charge of the gates that enter or leave his world, and he may follow a junk food diet or fall prey to the lure of drugs.

Until children can establish a value system for themselves that reflects God's view of life, they are in danger of being controlled by their emotions or their glands. Loving them enough to set up protective boundaries gives them the gift of honor. Teach them to honor God's boundaries in their lives as well, and you do the best you can to build and protect their self-worth.

We've now looked at several ways in which you can raise your children's value. Next we'll consider an aspect of honor that can stretch across thousands of miles and through decades of time, namely, building positive loyalties.

# Chapter Thirteen

## *Building Positive Loyalties: Part 1*

Children are incredibly loyal. I (John) learned this firsthand when my brother and I decided to quit kindergarten after the first day.

Growing up in a home with three boys, we learned nursery rhymes that had undergone certain editorial changes. In particular, we were taught that little boys were made of "sugar and spice and everything nice" and little girls were made of "snips and snails and puppydog tails." This didn't present a problem at home, but it caused major problems at kindergarten.

Like all children with older brothers or sisters, my twin brother and I had longed for the day we would get to attend school. However, we had no more than sat down on our first morning of kindergarten than the teacher began reading a nursery rhyme. When she read that little boys were made of all manner of disgusting things, our hands shot up. The teacher had the nursery rhyme all wrong! Then, as if it weren't enough that the teacher didn't know how to recite nursery rhymes correctly, the entire class had it wrong, too! We were fit to be tied, and we stormed out of the room when class was over.

"We're never going back to kindergarten," we announced with firm resolve when we got home that afternoon. We went to great lengths to question the intelligence of that teacher and every child at that "dumb" school. Who cared how the rhyme was actually written? We were loyal to our family's way of doing things, and we *knew* how it should be read.

Now that we've grown up, it's easy to see how "childish" we were in clinging unquestioningly to what we were taught. The only problem is that when it comes to family loyalties, many of us never grow up. Like a cookie-cutter pattern, traits and actions often get passed down without question from generation to generation. Take children who are abused, for example.

Children who grow up experiencing terrible abuses often repeat the very same patterns they endured. In fact, one study noted that over 90 percent of parents who abused their children were themselves abused when they were young.[1]

Whether it's something cute, such as misquoting a nursery rhyme, or something crushing, such as experiencing the trauma of abuse, we all have a deep inner drive that calls us to be loyal to parental patterns and repeat what we've learned at home. Family loyalties are those positive or negative patterns, attitudes, or actions that we saw in the family as we were growing up, and by habit, compulsion, or choice, we're consciously or unconsciously repeating them today.

## BRINGING TO LIGHT INVISIBLE LINES OF LOYALTY

Family loyalties are the cords from our past that pull on us to put into practice what we have seen repeated by our parents or other close family members. They are the bottom-line ways of living what we "caught" by watching our parents on a daily basis, not necessarily what we were "taught" by their words.

A nonnegotiable parents need to understand is that *lines of loyalty are set up in every home.* The only option they have is whether their results will be beneficial or destructive.

Positive loyalties are those patterns and deeply ingrained ways of thinking and acting that call people back to God's light should they stray; they are the bonds that continue to link a child and her parents in their old age—even if there is no inheritance at stake. Positive loyalties are the patterns that, in spite of all the fighting and squabbling when children are young, draw siblings back together with a special love as they grow older.

Negative loyalties are those hurtful parental patterns that have just as much sway over a person. They're manifested in people like the alcoholic son who swore to himself and to God that he would never take to drinking like his dad; the daughter who, just like her mother, marries for the fourth time and has as her unwritten motto, When the going gets tough, get another partner; the man who, like his father, can never quite seem to be convinced "beyond a reasonable doubt" that there is a God he will answer to one day.

Lines of loyalty in a family act like invisible fibers that can be incredibly strong, strands that stretch across thousands of miles and through decades of time. As we'll discuss in the next few chapters, there's both a positive side and a dark side to family loyalties.

We'd like to offer you four ways to enrich your children's lives by building positive loyalties. Understanding and applying the elements of God's loyal-love is a great place to start and a great way to honor your loved ones.

## BUILDING POSITIVE FAMILY LOYALTIES

What exactly do we mean when we use the word *loyalty?* When you think of loyalty, you may picture your faithful dog, a couple celebrating their fiftieth wedding anniversary, or even the Royal Mounted Police. My (John's) first thought when I hear this word is of my older brother, Joe.

Joe is the embodiment of a perfect older brother. Always there when you need him, always interested in what you're doing, always the first one there and the last one to leave on moving day, always ready to listen to you or give his advice, and most of all, he's simply always there.

I have absolutely no doubt that if I had a flat tire in New York in the middle of the night and called Joe at his home in San Diego to ask him to give me a hand, he'd be on the next plane if he thought I needed him. That's the way he is. He's proved it over and over throughout the years by his committed love and his steadfast ways.

Joe's loyal-love for his brothers is a small reflection of God's loyal-love for us. One of the greatest benefits of being a Christian is knowing that God's love holds on to us—no matter what. Joe's love is a small picture of God's carving out an unchanging commitment to His children. C. S. Lewis once put it this way:

> *The great thing to remember is that, though our feelings come and go, His love for us does not. It is not wearied by our sins, or our indifference; and therefore, it is quite relentless in its determination that we shall be cured of those sins, at whatever cost to us, at whatever cost to Him.*[2]

In the Scriptures, we can see the positive side of God's commitment to love us in the concept of His loyal-love for His children. Translated in many places as "lovingkindness," the Hebrew word *hesed* speaks of lasting bonds of kindness or loyalty.[3]

Wrapped around this key concept are the twin ideas of love and loyalty.[4] This love speaks specifically of being tender and merciful, and this commitment is pictured as steadfast and unconditional. Let's look closer at these two elements of God's love for His children. In doing so, we can get a picture of the way positive lines of loyalty are developed.

## THE ELEMENTS OF GOD'S LOYAL-LOVE

### 1. Tenderness Is a Key to Providing Positive Loyalty Bonds.

There's a powerful principle at work throughout the Scriptures. We can catch a glimpse of it when we read:

> *A soft answer turns away wrath,*
> *But a harsh word stirs up anger.*
> *(Proverb 15:1)*
>
> *By long forbearance a ruler is persuaded,*
> *And a gentle tongue breaks a bone.*
> *(Proverb 25:15)*

A soft or gentle answer can stand up to a heated argument. Persistently making gentle requests can break the backbone of the most insensitive ruler. These verses are pointing to what needs to take place in our families.

*When it comes to setting down healthy lines of loyalty, we honor our children when we bring gentleness and tenderness into our homes.* In many places in the Bible, the word *loyal-love* is translated "tenderness, mercy, and lovingkindness."[5] When God bound Himself to His people, He did so with gentle bonds of affection and caring. This is important because children who grow up with loads of tender loving care can't help carrying into later life the stamp, "I'm valuable."

Have you ever had a treasured family heirloom that rated special attention and protection? Jimmy's parents did. In fact, their house was filled with antiques and art treasures that made nearly every room off limits to a healthy, growing boy.

**Of Less Value than a Vase.** Jimmy was constantly criticized for touching this or picking up that. His normal boyish curiosity became such a test of wills that his parents would tie him in the family room with a length of rope to keep him from getting into trouble or breaking something.

Eventually, Jimmy seemed to get better about being around the costly treasures. Whether it was the repeated lectures he received or, more likely, the repeated spankings, he seemed resigned to the fact that the house was filled with things that he shouldn't go near.

To be sure, Jimmy seemed to become increasingly withdrawn and tense, but at least he was showing some respect for his parents' precious possessions—that is, until one tragic day.

Jimmy's parents drove down to the neighborhood store one afternoon when he was in fourth grade. When they came home, they were greeted with a shocking sight. Little Jimmy had gone into his bedroom and put on his new pair of cowboy boots. Then with systematic persistence, he had gone through every room in the house, kicking and smashing to pieces every "precious" item he could get his hands on.

Little Jimmy knew that there were items in his house that rated special attention, and he also knew that he wasn't one of them. Every day he walked among vases and pictures that called out to him with mocking voices, "We're more valuable than you are. We're handled more gently than you!" That knowledge had simmered within him until it boiled over and resulted in his aggressive behavior. At nine years of age, Jimmy began what would turn into six years of psychiatric treatment at two different hospitals to deal with his problems, problems that were a reflection of how little he was valued by his parents.

Children need to know that they are valuable treasures to parents. This is at the heart of our definition of honor. One effective way parents can communicate honor is to handle them with tenderness.

**Priceless Treasures in Our Home** The next time you get angry with your children, try thinking of them as precious antique vases. How likely would you be to pick up a priceless vase in your living room and shake it around? The value you attach to it would make you check your behavior. The same thing should be true of your living treasures.

Are there things inside or outside your house that your children see you polishing, mowing, pruning, playing with, or spending time over that appear to be more valuable than they are? We know of one young woman who is convinced that her mother cares more for her pet poodle than she does for her. Why? Because of the difference in her mother's facial expressions and tone of voice. With the poodle, she is soft and tender. With her daughter, her face becomes strict and expressionless, and her words have a cold chill of disapproval.

How tender are you with your children? Does your tone of voice reflect the value you want to communicate to them? Do you touch them and tell them how special they are to you? Do you respond in gentleness to them when they're hurting? Are you willing to ask your spouse or a close family friend to express an opinion about how well you're doing in this area?

Children remember acts of tenderness with striking clarity. Unfortunately, they are just as good at remembering angry words and insensitive actions. Fathers in particular need to understand how damaging angry words can be. One research study concluded that a hostile, angry father leaves the greatest emotional scars on a child's life.[6]

It doesn't take an elaborate birthday party or a European vacation to convince a child he is special. Providing him with a gentle hug or a soft, loving tone of voice can do wonders toward building his self-worth.

No parent is perfect. There will be times when you'll speak out in anger. There will be other times when you'll discipline them with only punishment, not principle, in mind. But if you'll demonstrate tenderness on a *consistent basis,* you'll see positive lines of loyalty attach to your children's lives. We recommend actions like these:

- Gently admit to your children when you know you've been wrong to them. This goes a long way toward building self-worth.
- Take time to squeeze their arm or give them a hug.
- Watch or soften your tone of voice, if necessary, when they make a mistake.
- Listen carefully; don't lecture.
- Cry with them about something they hurt over.
- Write them a letter that expresses your love and commitment.
- Pray with them about a past or upcoming trying event.

Treating children with tenderness doesn't mean that you wrap them in cotton. Neither does it mean that righteousness goes out the window and permissiveness comes in. There will be times when you'll have to discipline them firmly, and other times when you'll have to let them learn life's hard lessons for themselves. But children will go away from home feeling valuable if they're treated consistently with tender care. And they'll find themselves treating others with the value they themselves received.

## 2. A Covenant of Love Is a Second Key to Providing Positive Lines of Loyalty.

Have you ever watched a television documentary on a mountain-climbing expedition? One thing you'll always spot is a length of rope that links the climbers together. Although it may get in the way at times and become a burden during the climb, you'll notice that none of the climbers is about to take it off. That bond can become a life line should they slip and fall.

Children need consistent lines of loyal-love from you to give them the security and courage to launch out in life. The knowledge that there's always a life line of love if they need it can make all the difference. How can you provide this? By patterning your love after the second element of God's loyal-love.

We've already seen that tenderness is a key way God builds in positive loyalties. Another aspect of His loyal-love is that it is linked with a covenant He makes with us. The original meaning of the Old Testament word *covenant* is to "bind" or "tie together."[7] *When God wanted to communicate how highly He valued His children, He did so by binding Himself to them in the form of a contract or covenant.* "Therefore know that the LORD your God, He is God, the faithful God who keeps covenant and mercy for a thousand generations" (Deuteronomy 7:9).

The security that comes with knowing we are lovingly tied to our heavenly Father, even when we stumble and fall, is a tremendous gift. And it is nearly as important for us to feel the same way about our parents' love for us. For one thing, knowing we are forever bound in love to our parents can free us from the constant burden of having to prove we're acceptable and the fear that we're not.

***Climbing without a Life Line.*** An interesting study examined the effects of parenting on a number of top-level executives.[8] The men and women were divided into two study groups that were later compared with each other.

One group was comprised of "Type A" individuals. They were men and women who were consumed with time pressures, or "hurry sickness." They were very competitive, had an intense need to accumulate more and more material possessions, and recorded high levels of hostility and aggression.

The second group contained "Type B" individuals. These people exhibited the opposite of "Type A" traits. They would often take time to relax, were basically content with the levels attained in their personal, business, and financial lives, and had little hostility or anger.

Two crystal-clear results surfaced in this study. First, "Type A" men and women scored at the top of the charts in feeling insecure about themselves. Even when they were surrounded by impressive business and personal accomplishments—often much more significant than those accomplished by people in the "B" group—they had a deep, inner fear that they would lose it all.

Where did such a fear come from? From the second major finding in the study: "Type A" men and women were at the bottom in viewing themselves as having received unconditional acceptance and high self-esteem from their parents.

The connection is not to be overlooked. Leave a person to climb the mountains of life without the life line of unconditional acceptance, and watch the problems mount. For many, getting to the top of one mountain peak only causes them to look up and see another, higher pinnacle they must climb. And if they don't burn out emotionally in the struggle, they are four times more likely to crumble physically through coronary artery disease.[9]

Not long ago we watched a national evening news broadcast profile the world's greatest woman triathlete. When she was asked what motivated her to swim several miles, ride a bicycle race of up to one hundred miles, and then run a full twenty-six-mile marathon—all without stopping—her reply was a window to her heart. She said, "I guess I am just one of those people who never grew up feeling very valuable. Even though it's difficult, when I go out and win a race, I guess I feel better about myself... at least for a while."[10]

We see more and more adults today who are out on the track of life trying just as hard to raise that "perfect" child, gain that next promotion, get that book accepted by a publisher, or drive that certain car to work. Most are missing the second element of God's loyal-love, a strong sense of being secure in the love of someone special. That someone special ought to be Mom or Dad.

Children get an incredible sense of security from knowing that they are tied to parents who are committed to their best interests for life. When the time comes that their feet are pulled out from under them and they are sent tumbling headlong, having a life line of loyal-love to break their fall and pull them to a place of safety is better than owning gold.

You can begin today to build feelings of security into your children by actions such as these:

- Take a few minutes each evening to ask them how their day went. (Usually, you'll get more information from your daughter than your son, but it's equally important to ask both.)
- Attend their games, concerts, and open houses.
- Demonstrate love for your spouse in front of the children.
- Put down in writing or record on a cassette ten reasons you're proud of each child, and share them in a special time together.

- Commend them on their effort, even when they lose a game or do poorly on an exam.
- Give them a plaque that's inscribed with your lifetime commitment to your spouse and your children.

## LEAVING CHILDREN WITH LOVING-KINDNESS

Children who are willing to risk new challenges and relationships know intuitively that there are lines of security to catch them if they fall. To be able to leave home in a healthy way, they need the reassurance that only unconditional love brings.

Just how much impact do acts of loving-kindness, actions that display God's loyal-love, have on children? Even small acts of tenderness and kindness can leave lasting memories that affirm the value of individuals. General Dwight Eisenhower learned this in the war-torn streets of London.

During World War II, London took a terrible beating at the hands of the German Luftwaffe. Nearly every night, the sirens would wail, and spotlights would pierce the black sky trying to find the German bombers. Before the planes returned to their bases in France, dozens more English men, women, and children would be dead, injured, or homeless. Many orphans roamed the streets months after the air raids stopped.

One day, in preparing for the invasion of France on D-day, General Eisenhower decided to walk to his headquarters instead of having his staff car drive him the few blocks. As he passed a bakery along the way, he noticed two young, poorly dressed boys with their noses pressed up against the window. The delicious smells of fresh bread and pastries floated out of the shop and wrapped themselves around anyone who walked by. The general could see the object of their attention—chocolate donuts.

While a few members of his staff looked on with skepticism, Ike stopped and had his orderly purchase a dozen donuts. The general bent down and gently placed a sack with a half-dozen donuts in each child's hands. Understandably, a look of disbelief swept over their faces. Looking up at the commander of the Allied forces, one of the young boys asked in a halting voice, "Mister, are you God?"

Our Lord knew that tenderness and kindness leave lasting bonds on His loved one's hearts. That's why He will remember even a cup of water we give to others in His name (Matthew 10:42). That's also why the Psalms are filled with praise for a God who is merciful and forgives our sins, and the gospels are filled with the story of a Savior who loved us all the way to the cross while we were yet sinners.[11]

# Chapter Fourteen

## Building Positive Loyalties: Part 2

We've looked at two ways to build positive loyalties in children's lives, strands that can provide loving support and a life line for them to rely on. In this chapter, we'll consider two more crucial ways in which nurturing positive loyalties can honor children and help them increase their sense of self-worth.

### 3. The Freedom to Question Is a Third Key to Providing Positive Loyalty Bonds.

We've been intrigued by the finding that some of the healthiest homes are those where children are allowed the freedom to ask questions—even of Mom and Dad. That may not sit well with some parents whose favorite line is, "Because I *told* you so, that's why!" However, being able to disagree *constructively* can give children a sense of confidence, competence, and independence and increase their love and respect for their parents.

In one major study, elementary-school boys and girls were asked to agree or disagree with the statement, "Children should never question the thinking of their parents." Researchers discovered that students who scored high on feelings of personal worth *disagreed* 5 to 1 with the statement, while 90 percent of the students who felt of little value *agreed* by the same margin.[1]

One family expert writes,

> *We find that the healthy family is notable for the high level of activity of its individual members, strong-minded parents dealing with independent, assertive children, stricter enforcement of more stringent demands and greater possibilities for open dissent and disagreement.*
>
> *This picture brings to mind firm convictions, frequent and possibly strong exchanges and people who are capable and ready to assume leadership and who will not be treated casually or disrespectfully.*[2]

When I (Gary) first read this statement, I thought someone had been listening in on some of the dinner conversations around our kitchen table! From the time our children were young, we've given them the freedom to ask us straightforward questions, and they've taken the opportunity to do so, just as Mike did the other day.

During the winter months when people across the country are shivering from the cold, those of us who live in Arizona enjoy sunny, warm, near-perfect weather. Something else we get to enjoy is the number of relatives and friends who come out to bask in the perfect weather with us.

Recently, we received the news that an old family friend would be coming out to visit us for several weeks. As we talked about it around the dinner table one night, I said, "Nancy can stay in your room, Mike, and you can sleep on the couch in the family room." This seemed like a perfectly good arrangement to me, and I really wasn't bringing up the subject for debate. But I noticed that Mike became quiet and began to look down at his plate.

"What's the matter?" I asked.

Mike looked at me and said, "Dad, the last three times we've had people stay with us, they've stayed in my room, not Greg's or Kari's. Why am I always the one who has to give up my room? Is it because I'm the youngest?"

There are a number of "typical" responses a parent (or I) could have made, such as:

> *I can't believe how selfish you are, Mike! Do you want me to call Nancy and tell her that you can't stand her and you want her to sleep on the couch?*

*or*

*You're not a lawyer, young man. I won't stand for being cross-examined in my own home! You're sleeping on the couch, or you can sleep in the garage!*

Thankfully, I didn't use either response. Because Norma and I have encouraged the children to ask questions throughout their growing-up years, we took the time as a family to talk about where Nancy should stay.

With a few well-chosen words, I could have lectured Mike about "doing what he was told" and closed his spirit in the process.[3] But by honoring his question as honest and valid, we grew closer together as a family. The result was that we took turns sleeping on the couch.

For some reason, questions can be threatening. This is particularly true when they come from our children. Perhaps this is because questions can demonstrate our fallibility in a flash or threaten to expose the fact that we're not perfect decision makers. Yet the more healthy the relationship, the more willing people are to ask and answer even difficult questions.

We see this frequently in troubled marriages. Many times a husband and wife have learned the hard way what *not* to talk about simply by asking questions. Others have received only icy stares from their mates when they uttered the off-limits question "Why?"

Having the security to allow your children to ask questions can go a long way toward building value into their lives. For some children, never allowing them to question you can teach them to drive their true feelings underground, cause them to have feelings of anger, lead them to challenge you on everything, or encourage them to develop manipulative tendencies. Others can stay tied up emotionally in cold steel chains, afraid or unwilling to challenge or change something you have said, even if it proves to be unbiblical or wrong.

We want to be sure we're communicating clearly the kinds of questions we're talking about. We're not talking about putting up with whining over regular chores ("Mom, I took the trash out once *last* week") or debating moral issues when God is crystal clear in His Word. There are and should be nonnegotiables in every household.[4]

However, for some parents, allowing their children to ask legitimate questions is equivalent to someone's turning the Ten Commandments into the Ten Suggestions. "This is my house, and this is the way my family does things. Period." No questions asked, no questions allowed. And that's unfortunate, not to mention unbiblical. As one person said about his father, "He may have not been right all the time, but he was never wrong!"

Our heavenly Father has always given His children the right to ask the hard questions and has felt free to ask them Himself. (Remember the hard questions He put to Adam and Eve in the Garden and to Cain?)[5] One reason He inspires such loyalty in those who love Him is that He's secure in His identity and can let us ask our most difficult questions.

Listen to the psalmist's penetrating words:

> *O God, why have You cast us off forever?*
> *Why does Your anger smoke against*
> *    the sheep of Your pasture?*
> . . . . . . . . . . . . . . . . . . . . . . . . . . . . . . . . . . . . .
> *O God, how long will the adversary reproach?*
> *Will the enemy blaspheme Your name forever?*
> *Why do You withdraw Your hand,*
> *    even Your right hand?*
> *Take it out of Your bosom*
> *    and destroy them.*
>
> (Psalm 74:1, 10–11)

Then listen to our Lord's words: "My God, My God, why have You forsaken Me?" (Matthew 27:46).

The more freedom you give your children to be open and honest with you, the higher you build their worth. When children ask a legitimate question and you give them the stock answer from Parenting 101, "Because I said so, that's good enough," you can leave them with more than their original question. You can also leave them with

*a)* a feeling their question was stupid
*b)* anger over being denied access to your reasoning process
*c)* the conclusion that you are too busy with "important" things to take the time to explain something to your "unimportant" children
*d)* all of the above

In all likelihood, the lower a parent's self-worth, the more difficulty he's going to have with questions from his children. Such a parent has too much to prove to himself and too much fear of looking bad to handle the "hot potato" questions a grade-schooler can raise about staying up past her normal bedtime or a junior-high girl can ask about sex.

Instead of laying down lines of loyalty based on how loud you can yell, build greater security into your children by allowing them to ask legitimate questions. If your kids are of high enough value to deserve being honored, they should be given the opportunity to ask questions.

## TWO STEPS BACKWARD, ONE BIG STEP FORWARD

### 4. Understanding Our Own Lines of Loyalty Is a Fourth Key to Providing Positive Loyalty Bonds.

The fourth key to providing positive lines of loyalty for children comes about as we take the time to reflect on and understand the lines of loyalty that are still present with our own parents. Understandably, this isn't always easy to do.

Some of us may pretend to be like the emperor with the invisible clothes. No matter how much we may protest that we're unaffected by our parents or past, the stark reality lays naked before others who know us well. Take Bill, for example.

Bill grew up with his mother and sister in a single-parent home. Although they were a very loving family, something happened once a month that has affected Bill all his life—bill-paying time. As in many single-parent homes, finances were very tight for Bill's family. And each month as his mother sat down to pay the bills, a black cloud would seem to settle over the household. Whether it was the "dumb" electric bill or the "dumb" charge card balance that set her off, for two days the kids knew it was best to spend time at their friends' houses and stay out of Mom's way.

Can you guess what's a major problem in Bill's home now that he's grown up and gotten married? You're right—paying bills. Even though Bill has a high-paying job and a fairly frugal lifestyle, he makes life miserable for everyone in the household at the end of the month.

All that is not to say that we bring only negative lines of loyalty into our later relationships, however. Sarah is an example of someone who remains loyal to a helpful family pattern her parents set down for her. Sarah grew up in a home where the welcome mat was always out for missionaries home on furlough or others in need. Three times when Sarah was young, her parents brought in unwed mothers and loved and counseled them through their pregnancies and deliveries.

Today, Sarah possesses a sensitivity and willingness to care for others that's beautiful to see. Sacrificing some personal comfort and needs in order to help others was second nature as she was growing up, and she has carried that tendency into her adult married life.

All of us enter into marriage carrying some of our past, which also affects our roles as parents. Successful husbands and wives, fathers and mothers, take the time to bring these powerful factors to light.

Several years ago, I (John) interviewed for an associate pastor position at a growing, vibrant church. Interviews are often like courtships, and I wasn't sure if I would get the "real scoop" during my visit or an unrealistic picture of what was happening. However, all my fears were dispelled in the first meeting I had with the search committee and the associate pastor who would become my supervisor. The pastor volunteered these words of advice: "John, like any church, we've got a few skeletons in the closet. However, the thing that makes this church different is that we can open the door and talk about them."

The same thing needs to take place in our families. It doesn't do any good to leave positives *or* negatives buried in the closets of our minds. To be free to build value into our children, we must be aware of the factors pulling on us from the past.

To help you discern some of these lines of loyalty in your own life, take the time to finish the following statements before you go on.

## Growing Up in My Family

A. In my family, the way we handled money was to . . .

The way I handle money today is to . . .

B. In my family, the place our spiritual life held . . .

Today my spiritual life is . . .

C. In my family, the kind of job my father/mother had . . .

The kind of job I have now is . . .

D. In my family, the way we were disciplined as children was . . .

The way I discipline my children is . . .

E. In my family, in regard to hospitality, you could say that we were . . .

For me today, hospitality is . . .

F. In my family, when it came to expressing affectionate words and hugs, we . . .

My comfort in being affectionate with my spouse and family today is . . .

G. In my family, anger was . . .

The way I handle my anger with my spouse and children is . . .

H. In my family, when it came to honesty, . . .

When it comes to honesty in my personal life, . . .

I. In my family, . . . was sometimes carried to an extreme.

In my own life, I tend to carry . . . to an extreme.

J. In my home when I was growing up, we moved seldom ____ never ____ often ____ .

My family has changed houses seldom ____
never ____ often ____.

---

In many cases, we can give thanks for the things we repeat from the past. But like Bill, if we become aware of emotional storm clouds that spring up only because it "always used to rain that way in our family," we do ourselves and our children a favor to honestly confront our family "traditions."

In the book of Proverbs, Solomon wrote, "The wisdom of the prudent is to understand his way, / But the folly of fools is deceit."[6] Giving thought to how lines of loyalty from our past still affect us is certainly wise, because it can help us be open to God's Spirit and build value into our children.

We've looked at four ways we can build positive lines of loyalty into our children. These practices can call forth their affection for a lifetime and give them security and support even after we're gone.

By applying each factor, a parent goes a long way toward building positive loyalties into his children. On the other hand, the "casual observer" type of parent runs the risk of seeing his children gravitate toward the dark side of family loyalties. That's a place as cold and lifeless as the dark side of the moon, where dishonor and low self-worth dwell. Let's enter the front door and look at five different homes where dishonor and low self-worth dominate.

# Chapter Fifteen

## Understanding the Dark Side of
## Family Loyalties: Part 1

*I*t would be wonderful if every child grew up in a home where positive lines of loyalty and God's loyal-love abounded. Unfortunately, that isn't always the case. As difficult as it may be to admit, we need to realize that there is a darker side to family loyalties as well.

In the last two chapters, we looked at actions parents can take today to build positive habits and characteristics that children will have a natural tendency to repeat tomorrow. Negative loyalties take shape in much the same way. With their big, perceptive eyes, children can pick up negative patterns from parents every bit as quickly as positive ones. Some of these bonds can inhibit their ability to develop a healthy self-concept, rob them of joy in the present, and chain them to devaluing patterns from the past. Left untouched and unexplored, these hurtful patterns will be seen again and again, passed down from parent to child.

Sound like too strong a statement? It's been true for generations. "I, the LORD your God, am a jealous God, visiting the iniquity of the fathers on the children to the third and fourth generations of those who hate Me."[1] Ever since Jesus died on the cross, Christians have been freed from the demands of this verse, and God gives us freedom to choose patterns that lead to life. Yet many people never experience freedom from past wrongs. Instead, they hold on to negative patterns with incredible loyalty from generation to generation. They're like people who have an inheritance of a million dollars in the bank, but choose to stand in a poverty line and never write a check against their bulging bank account.

In this chapter and the following one, we depict five homes that tend to produce strong negative lines of loyalty, gripping bonds that we see people struggling with almost on a daily basis. By taking an honest look at these patterns, you can see if any of them are a part of your parenting style—or a part of your past—and take steps to cope with them. Each can wrap around a child and pull him away from feeling valuable. Each dishonors a child and can damage his self-worth. If not brought into the open and dealt with, each has the power to chain a child to a hurtful pattern for a lifetime.

We also offer some practical help and hope to those who may have struggled with negative loyalty bonds for years. Although God's Word can cut even the strongest negative bond, it is far better never to have gone through such an experience.

Confronting negative lines of loyalty isn't easy. These dishonoring practices are powerful, and it's difficult to break free from them. As a way of illustrating their impact, let's look in on a practice that can shed some light on the task before us.

## PULLING AGAINST CHAINS FROM THE PAST

From the time we were young, most of us have been told that elephants never forget. Maybe this old adage started because of a particular training method used in India. When a baby elephant has been weaned from its mother, it is driven away from her and chained to a heavy stake. Until the animal's spirit is broken, it will be given neither food nor water.

Elephants are extremely bright, persistent animals, and there is much evidence to suggest that in some ways, they, indeed, never forget. For days many of these young animals will pull against the stake that holds them, rubbing the tethered leg raw in the process. However, we're told that one morning when the trainer wakes up, the struggle is over.

As if the animal has made some final decision, it no longer pulls at the stake, and it never will again. That's why at a circus, you'll often see huge elephants tethered with a rope around their ankles. In an instant, these grown animals could snap their feeble bonds, yet they stay in their place as if secured by heavy chains. Many elephants will rock back and forth as they stand (many do this continuously), but they will never again risk the pain involved in pulling away from what hurt them in the past.

All too often we've seen a similar reaction to negative family loyalties. Growing up in a dishonoring home, many children will initially pull away from painful practices in their homes. Often they make statements like these: "There's no way I'm going to do what my parents did with me when I grow up" or "Things are going to be different when I get out on my own and have my own family" or "I can hardly wait to leave this house!"

However, as they grow older, many of these same people stay chained to the very things they want so desperately not to repeat. After years of struggling, many become so emotionally tired and raw that they quit trying to change those patterns and let the chains from the past confine them.

If you find yourself in any of the examples that follow, please don't lose hope. While relief may not come overnight, we'll show how Christ can remove your chains from the past. With His power you are more than able to break free from them and make sure you don't pass them on to your children.[2]

When you have the courage to bring into His light negative lines of loyalty that have long remained in the shadows, you open yourself to genuine change. Just like your spiritual growth, freedom from these bonds usually comes through days and weeks of gaining understanding of your situation and making daily decisions to believe what God has said.

## 1. THE DESIGNATED SCAPEGOAT

For the Old Testament Jews, a special ceremony took place every year on the Day of Atonement. Unfortunately, that ceremony reflects what happens in many homes today.

The ceremony worked like this: two goats were chosen by lots, one to be sacrificed, and the other to become a scapegoat. Sacrificing an animal was a familiar part of Old Testament law. But what was the purpose of the scapegoat?

Aaron, the high priest, would gather all the people together and lay his hands on the goat's head. In doing so, he was giving them a symbolic picture that all the sins of the nation had been transferred to the animal.[3] The goat was then driven outside the camp and forced into the wilderness to die.

When Jesus was led outside the city to be crucified and the Father placed our sins upon Him, He became our scapegoat and our lamb of sacrifice.[4] For Israel of old as well as for Christians today, having a scapegoat pictured a meaningful, even glorious event.

Today, because of Christ's death on the cross, the sacrificial system is no longer needed, but unknowingly, some families carry it on anyway. These homes have adopted a scapegoat in the family, someone who shoulders all the blame for an unhealthy family's problems.

Just like the scapegoats of old, children who grow up bearing the brunt of all their family's problems are often discarded and driven away from those they love. Instead of severing the bonds between parent and child, this binds these children tighter to a negative picture of themselves. This type of home scores near-perfect marks in lowering a child's value. Just like Gretta. She was the scapegoat in her family.

Gretta was born during the early days of World War II, and from her first few days of life, she was unjustly labeled as being the cause of every problem in her household. The last of four children, Gretta developed a terrible skin condition shortly after she was born that caused lesions and boils to cover most of her body.

Not only that, but Gretta also had a terrible respiratory problem that made it hard for her to sleep longer than a few hours at a time and caused her to wake up coughing and choking. She would cry for hours at a time when she was young, and her mother soon was overwhelmed by all the care she required night and day.

Today, many men help with their children, but that wasn't the case in Gretta's era. Because of all the noise around the house from the other children and the stress his wife was under because of Gretta, the father simply spent more and more time away from home.

As the war grew in intensity in Europe and it looked as though the United States would be drawn in, Gretta's father decided he would enlist in the army. Even though he had a minor medical condition that could have kept him out of the service if he chose, he jokingly told his wife that he could still send her a paycheck, but he wouldn't have to listen to Gretta cry and fuss day and night!

After that, things became more and more strained between Gretta and her mother. These problems came to a head on Gretta's second birthday. That was the day the notice came from the War Department announcing that her father had been killed in the battle of Palermo in Italy.

Gretta's mother took the news terribly hard. As a way of dealing with the hurt, she began blaming Gretta for all their problems. None of the other children caused her such grief—only Gretta. None of the others demanded so much time—only Gretta. None of the other children gobbled up so much of the precious money for doctor bills—only Gretta. It wasn't because of Gretta's sisters or brothers that her husband had enlisted and now lay dead on a battlefield—it was Gretta's fault.

A year later, Gretta's mother remarried. However, things didn't improve for Gretta. As time went by, the poor girl grew up feeling she was the sole reason for all the problems in her family.

Her brothers and sisters picked up on their mother's negative attitude toward Gretta and shunned her, blaming her for the fact that their natural father would never return. The stepfather resented the constant medical attention Gretta required to help with her respiratory problems, and he gave her nothing but scorn and contempt. But the things her mother said to her hurt the most.

Gretta's mother had lived an immoral life before she was married. Although she had never been a religious person before her husband's death, she suddenly became interested in the Bible as a way of dealing with the guilt and anger she felt. However, instead of finding help or solace or a personal relationship with Christ, her understanding became twisted, and she found another weapon to use against Gretta. In an emotional outburst one day, Gretta's mother screamed at her, "God gave you to me as punishment for all my sins and all the wrongs I've done!"

While you might think that Gretta would have grown up and moved away without any bonds of attachment to her mother, just the opposite was true. She was attached all right, but it was to a negative image of herself that took years to correct.

## Singled Out for Shame

Children who become the scapegoat of the family long for the love and acceptance they never received. Often they act out their low self-worth with outbursts of anger or rebellion. They know deep inside the injustice of being singled out and pushed away from the family, and their intense frustrations can find their way out as behavior problems in school, defiance of authority, and flagrant immorality.

Each of these things was true in Gretta's life and is common in others like her. It's almost as if the person who is labeled the scapegoat makes the unhealthy decision to act out the low worth the family attributes to him or her and thus justify the label.

Gretta acted in this very way. She hated the negative attention she received for her angry temper and rebelliousness, but at least she got some attention when her behavior was bad! To a daughter starved for acceptance, even being the family scapegoat gave her some identity in her home. And now that years have passed and Gretta has her own family, her feelings of low self-worth have kept her from feeling genuinely loved by her husband and have made her far more critical of her children than she wants and needs to be.

Although Gretta's case is dramatic, having a scapegoat in a family is a much too common occurrence. As another example, take Mark, who became the scapegoat in a "blended" family. His new mother was so afraid he would "corrupt" her two sons that he was labeled as a troublemaker and held at arm's length for years. Always knowing he wasn't accepted, he still longed to have a relationship with his "brothers." Mark grew up feeling terrible that he was such a bad person, even when he knew deep inside he was not.

Consider Sara, whose marriage would carry on to the third generation the family tradition of having a scapegoat. In her great-grandmother's home as well as her grandmother's home, one of the daughters had married outside the family's faith and had been cut off as a result. Now as Sara tried to explain to her parents about her new Christian faith, she, too, was branded a family failure and told to stay away. In each generation that cast out a scapegoat, all the other members of the family would link up even tighter, unwilling for the love of their daughter or sister to penetrate their ranks.

In order to give you hope if you've been the family scapegoat, we'll see later on how Gretta, Mark, and Sara were able to break these negative bonds and be free from many of the negative effects of their hurtful past. However, before we do, let's look in on another home that can tie up children with negative lines of loyalty. This one binds them with imprisoning obligations.

## 2. IMPRISONING OBLIGATIONS

Label a child as the family scapegoat, and watch how tightly bound he becomes to a negative picture of himself. Smother a child with imprisoning obligations, and a similar thing happens. Children from this type of dishonoring home often become so tightly tied to unrealistic expectations that they are rarely able to travel very far in life on their own. This was true for Wayne, a man who had a dream of moving across the country and starting a business of his own but who faced the reality that negative bonds would only let him go across the street. Tragically, this darker side of family loyalties led him to dishonor and devalue his wife and daughter as well.

Wayne was an only child who grew up on the outskirts of a rural town. His father was gone frequently on business trips and seldom had any time for him when he was at home. However, his mother's attitude toward him was quite different. Because her husband was emotionally distant and traveled so often, she made her son the center of her life. For many years, this was a perfectly good arrangement for Wayne, and his mother became his constant companion and his closest friend.

Wayne often dreamed of leaving the small town he lived in and going to the "big city," and he would frequently tell his mother about this dream. Then when he began to mature, a curious thing happened. While his mother had always been the picture of good health before, her condition now started to deteriorate. She was continually fighting off one ailment or another. And though nothing specific could be diagnosed, her frail condition required ever more attention from her son.

With a brave little smile, his mother would look up from her bed and say to Wayne, "I just don't know what I'd do without you. You're the only thing that makes life worth living for me." Then she would add with a sigh, "But I know you'll need to move on one of these days, and I know I'll get along somehow."

"You're the only thing that makes life worth living for me." Her words were only too true. Wayne *was* her life. Through her manipulative words and actions, she began to lay down strand after strand of negative loyalty bonds. Whether it was reminding him of all the hours she had played with him as a child or how "little time she had left," strands of guilt, like reinforced steel wires, were wrapped around the lines of loyalty that held her son.

At age twenty-six, Wayne married without his mother's consent. In fact, he marched right into his mother's room and told her that he was finished living his life for her. He and his girlfriend would marry and move to the big city.

Up until the wedding, Wayne felt great about confronting his mother and taking a stand. But almost immediately after the ceremony, he began paying the price. Right after the wedding, his mother fell into a physical collapse, and he had to end his honeymoon three days early and rush back to be with her.

At her bedside, Wayne pleaded with his mother to forgive him for being gone when she needed him so much. The only promises that consoled her were that he would look for a job nearby and that he and his new wife would move into the small house across the street. Of course, he also promised he would visit or call her at least twice a day.

For years, Wayne refused to test his limits and pull again on the chains of negative loyalty that bound him. Often, his anger would surface at having to be over at his mother's house all the time or at having to drop everything to attend to an "emergency" that would turn out to be just another opportunity to have her son over. Yet every time, Wayne swallowed his angry feelings when the shadow of guilt passed over him. After all, he had confronted his mother once before, and his actions "brought on a condition." If he dared to do it again, he feared it might be fatal to her.

In a free country, Wayne was in gripping bondage. Unaware of and unwilling to deal with his misplaced loyalties, he was a prisoner to the negative family bonds that chained him.

## The Ripple Effect of Imprisoning Obligations

Wayne certainly suffered over the years, but his wife, Susan, probably did even more. The standing invitation for Wayne to come over to his mother's house didn't include his wife. Many evenings Susan would prepare a nice meal for her husband, only to see him drive in from work and walk across to his mother's for dinner, all without coming into the house to speak to her. Even when Susan was with her husband and her mother-in-law, they often talked around her or about her as though she were a child or wasn't in the room.

The more rigidly a person is tied to his parents, the more difficult it is for him to enter into a full commitment to another person in marriage. And Wayne's loyalty to his mother was so strong that he made no effort to commit himself to his wife. Each time he chose his mother over his wife, Susan's value as a person and as a marriage partner went further down. After ten years of marriage, her self-worth was so low that she consistently had thoughts about taking her life. That's when we first met Susan.

In counseling, Wayne spoke about his mother's illnesses and about how trying to meet her need for attention and affection was like trying to fill a cup with a hole in the bottom. Susan's eyes filled with tears, and she said, "How about me, Wayne? I know your mother has needs, but I'm thirsty, too."

Susan suffered in silence for years, never telling a friend or family member her hurt and disappointment, and that in itself is often a negative form of loyalty. It's often the dark side of family loyalties that keeps a child from telling a teacher or friend that he has been abused or that keeps a wife or husband from crying out for help. It's also the darker side of loyalties that makes it so difficult to treat many alcoholics. Getting each member of the family (particularly the nondrinking husband or wife) to quit protecting the person who is drinking and confront him with the truth is like pulling teeth. Misguided loyalty may "protect" a person for a season, but all too often it prevents a cure.

As we have seen, positive loyalty is crucial to marriage and family relationships and involves doing what is best for the other person, even if that means discipline or confrontation. Yet negative loyalty bonds bind a person to his problems rather than free him from them.

Susan was unwilling to risk her shaky relationship with her husband for no relationship at all. She never spoke with her mother-in-law about the treatment she received, and even though she argued with her husband continually, she was careful to push only so far. With all the buried emotions she felt, she began to experience many symptoms of poor health, just like her mother-in-law. And at long last, she was beginning to get some of Wayne's attention.

These two people experienced two different types of imprisoning obligations. Each shows a different aspect of the darker side of family loyalties, but thankfully, they don't have to be lifelong patterns. As we'll see in a later chapter, when Wayne learned who the Source of Life is and how honoring Him could change his life, positive things began happening in his family that would eventually break those crippling bonds.

In Wayne's home, a dishonoring parent played on the natural tendency a child has to be lovingly loyal to his parents. How tragic it was for her that in looking for life in her son, she missed out on knowing the only true Source of Life, and she nearly ruined her son's life and marriage as well.

For Wayne and for many people we see in counseling today, growing up with imprisoning obligations can cause them to develop a negative sense of loyalty. Afraid of losing that "special place" they have with their parents, they accept calling them four times a day, dropping everything to take them shopping, or making sure every vacation and family outing includes them. Making a decision on their own becomes unthinkable; acting on their own becomes unforgivable.

Naturally, there will be times when legitimate health concerns or life adjustments cause us to bind together and spend vast quantities of time or effort in helping a needy parent. As we mentioned earlier, trials like these *build* positive, valuing lines of loyalty between parent and child. It's only when the "illness" or demands on a child come from contrived sicknesses or unquenchable, selfish needs of a problem parent that this second dishonoring home lowers a child's worth.[5]

If you grew up in a home with imprisoning obligations, you don't need any further explanations. You've already felt the twisting and tightening of these bonds and the gripping prison they can become. If you haven't been raised in such a home, you should be thankful. Also be aware that in your own home, laying down imprisoning obligations has the possibility of greatly dishonoring a child for years to come.

The family scapegoat and the prisoner of unyielding obligations can develop incredibly strong negative attachments to the past and to parents. Before we look at how to break such hurtful bonds, we need to examine three other homes that can produce strong negative loyalty bonds.

# Chapter Sixteen

## *Understanding the Dark Side of Family Loyalties: Part 2*

*I*magine standing with your arms stretched out and two of the biggest members of the Dallas Cowboys football team trying to pull you in opposite directions! That's how many children feel who get pulled in two different directions by their parents. It also represents a third home in which negative loyalty bonds wrap around a child. Children who are *caught in the middle of a parental power struggle* have a hard time escaping from these patterns to move on to more healthy ways of life.

### 3. CAUGHT IN THE MIDDLE

Jim felt this way. From the time he was born until his parents finally divorced, they fought battle after battle. For a number of years, Jim was such a joy to them that they kept their eyes off their problems with each other and focused most of their attention on him. And talk about attention! Even though an only child does tend to get more time with his parents, Jim was off the charts when it came to being smothered with affection. The only problem came when his parents decided to divorce, and twelve-year-old Jim was expected to choose sides.

All the love and attention Jim had received built a deep love and loyalty for both parents. You can imagine his confusion at being asked to sever relationships with one parent if he wanted to maintain the acceptance of the other. As charges and countercharges were fought out between his parents at home and in court, Jim didn't know where to turn. And neither do many other children who get caught in the middle. A child like Sharon, for example.

Sharon's mother was always open to new things. Unfortunately, that led her to accept the teachings of a cult that's popular today. As a teen-ager, Sharon was torn between staying in her father's church or embracing her mother's newfound religion. Choosing one path meant rejecting the other; not choosing at all still left her out in the cold. After agonizing days, Sharon decided to remain with her father in her home church. In turn, her mother bristled with anger and cut off contact with Sharon until she, too, became "enlightened."

Putting children in the position of having to make choices like saying yes to one parent and no to the other brings to light negative bonds of loyalty. All too often, parents pull on these lines, trying to move their children over to their side of an argument.

In the Scriptures, Jonathan must have felt pulled in this way in his intimate friendship with David. Protect David, and go against his father. If he sided with his father, he might see his best friend killed. In fact, Jonathan's father, Saul, became so angry when he sensed his son was more loyal to David that he hurled his spear at David and tried to pin him to the wall! (See 1 Samuel 19:1-10.)

Putting a child in the middle of a power struggle is unfair, and it also lowers his sense of self-worth. Parents who truly want to raise the value of their children will keep from making their children's loyalty a tool for defending their own position.

## 4. ALL GROWN UP . . . AND STILL A CHILD

Did you ever sneak into the attic or basement and try on some of your father's or mother's clothes when you were young? Most of us enjoyed dressing up like "Mom or Dad." It made us feel special and "just like them." There's a kind of home where the play-acting becomes real and a child is forced to take over as the parent in the household. Basically, the child is told, "Pass over childhood and go directly to adulthood." When she does, negative lines of loyalty can pull her away from developing into the person she could be. This happened to Martha.

Martha's mother was an alcoholic. It made little difference that Martha was only nine years old when her mother's drinking began to incapacitate her. For several years she had already been "mother" to her poor little sisters and brothers.

Because of her mother's irresponsibility and inability to care for the children, parental responsibilities fell on Martha's shoulders. Martha, not her mother, would take care of the cooking, cleaning, and doing the laundry. She would sneak into the living room when her mother had passed out and steal money from her purse so she and the little ones could eat.

Years went by, and Martha learned how to be a mother. However, she never had the chance to learn how to be a child and how to let someone else take some responsibility. Forced to become a parent to her brothers and sisters, she developed extremely deep bonds of loyalty to them.

There's nothing wrong with close ties between siblings, of course. Martha and her brothers and sisters have a special closeness because of all they suffered together. But Martha developed intense lines of loyalty that shifted to the darker side. Like many "parentified" children, she continued to feel incredibly responsible for her siblings long after they were grown up, and she failed to develop as a person because of it.

At age thirty-nine, Martha still carries on the role of the parent in her home, only now her "baby" is her mother. Martha's brothers and sisters never discussed who would take care of Mother when she got older or the alcohol made her too confused and disabled to live alone. They simply assumed that Martha would be the one to do so. After all, Martha had always been the one to "take care of people and things" in the family. "She must enjoy it," they concluded.

Martha has never married, and she constantly checks on her brothers and sisters and their families. Although they're always glad to see her, they grow tired of her need to be so closely involved in the intimate details of their lives. But negative lines of loyalty keep Martha duty bound to play out a role she should never have been given.

For a number of children, being in a single-parent home or a home where they are forced to grow up fast can build a certain strength and character into them. However, saddle children with the responsibility of being full-time parents when they should be full-time children, and watch the problems begin and their self-worth drop.

## 5. CHOOSE YOU THIS DAY

The fifth type of home that lowers the worth of children demands perhaps the greatest loyalty from them and offers the least in return. It's a home where children are expected to choose their parents' way over and above God's way. Sometimes this kind of negative loyalty becomes only too clear when children seek to replace it. That's exactly what Mark found to be true with his family.

Mark came from a family that truly was a dynasty. His grandfather had followed two simple principles for making money. The first was to find out where people were going and get there first. He had done this by purchasing several farms in what was once a sleepy valley in southern California, and his foresight had netted him millions.

The second principle was to "do unto others before they do you in." Mark's grandfather and his father based their business on cutthroat corporate politics. Stand in their way on a business deal, and get mowed down. Cheat if you could, but be sure you were so good at it that you wouldn't get caught. This also included cheating on income taxes and buying off zoning decisions whenever they could. Whatever it took to be "successful," the end justified the means.

With their own employees, Mark's father and grandfather made sure they kept a "professional distance" from even the most senior executives in the firm. Keeping everyone at arm's length made it easier to fire whomever they wanted whenever they wanted with the desired effect of putting the "fear of God" into the ones who remained.

Mark was the heir apparent to the family business. And as in many wealthy families, his childhood and adolescent life was a grooming time to prepare him for future responsibilities. Mark lived out his family script to perfection—right up until the end of high school, when he attended a church youth retreat and became a Christian.

As the only believer in the family, Mark began to question

things that he had never questioned before. Why had that vice president been fired when he was only two years away from retirement? Why did his father have so many "secret" meetings when it was time to invest his personal and company profits? Why did he continue to get "that look" when he first met people who had worked with his father on a business deal?

Unlike his father, Mark developed an interest in things apart from the family business, particularly spiritual things. While he was at home, he became involved in the leadership of his church youth group. In college, he began a discipleship program with the Navigators, and within a year he was leading a group.

Both in the many comments he received from those he worked with and discipled and in his own heart, Mark felt called to the ministry. He talked at length with his pastor and spent hours in prayer by himself. With graduation only a year away, Mark made the decision to send in his application to seminary rather than law school.

When Mark spoke to his father about his change in plans, he found out about family loyalties in a hurry. With all the commotion he caused, Mark felt branded and disloyal. Invisible obligations and expectations that had been hiding in the shadows suddenly came to light and swirled around him. Whether it was a disturbing card from his mother or his uncle flying out from Boston to try to "talk some sense" in him, doing what had once seemed so right now became a family battlefield.

In the book of Matthew, Jesus made several strong statements about discipleship: "Do not think that I came to bring peace on earth. . . . For I have come to 'set a man against his father, a daughter against her mother, and a daughter-in-law against her mother-in-law'" (Matthew 10:34–35). Particularly in homes where negative lines of loyalty pull a child away from a relationship with Christ, Jesus brings a sword to cut these lines, not peace to compromise with them. Yet such statements are hard to accept.

Trying to discern the Lord's will in the midst of such family pressure was the most difficult and confusing thing Mark had ever done. After several months of intense pressure from home, he gave up trying to understand what God might be telling him. Regardless of what God's best might be, Mark refused to question a strongly held family pattern. Instead of maintaining his convictions despite the cost, he slowly broke his ties with the Navigators and pulled away from his church.

## All-Too-Common Choices

Before you pick up stones to hurl at Mark, take a long look at your own life. Does your lack of spiritual growth keep you in step with how your parents viewed spiritual things? Is that uncontrolled temper you struggle with a reflection of something you once saw in your father? Can that tendency to overspend, even when it puts a strain on your marriage, call to mind patterns you've seen in the past? Does that tendency to fudge a little— when you should be totally honest—trace its roots to what you saw in your parents? Could your discomfort with being warm and huggy with your children, even when you know they need it, stem from your missing out on being touched?

Your relationship with your parents can leave many positive marks on your life, but there can also be strong negative lines of loyalty. And if you're to be free to build love and value into your children or to see it in your own life, you must recognize these factors.

Today, Mark's marriage is in trouble, and he struggles in his relationship with his sons. And Mark, not his father, is the one the government is investigating for improper business dealings. In the midst of counseling, Mark traces the incredible hostility, guilt, and shame he carries inside and his struggles in his spiritual life back to one primary factor. His life has been controlled by unbending negative family loyalties.

In many homes, the choice to honor God or give precedence to unbiblical family rules is put squarely on the table. Such homes reverberate with statements like these: "Who cares about the problems it causes, in *this* home the *men* in the family drink!" "Pay no attention to your wife's (or husband's) need to spend time with her family. There are too many important family gatherings on our side of the family to spend time with them. And besides, we have to think about what's best for the children—and you know who can buy them the nicest presents." In other homes, the choice is more subtly placed on the table, yet it's every bit as prevalent.

Some families automatically turn their back on the one who

picks up the card marked "Live Life God's Way." Try to explain to some parents or family members why being a Christian can bring about changes in lifestyle, and the chasm between the two sides opens wider.

Up to this point, we've tried to illustrate five homes that tend to wrap strong lines of loyalty around children and pull them back from becoming all they could be. These five homes dishonor children rather than build honor into their lives. Is there a way to break free from these negative loyalties and replace them with the positive one we looked at previously?

For each of the people we used as an illustration, the answer is yes. Each of them went through the difficult process of identifying negative loyalties in their lives and replacing them with life-lines of security and support.

## TURNING FAMILY WRONGS AROUND

Why is it so hard to turn family wrongs around and so easy to repeat a past pattern? As we've looked in the Scriptures and talked with couples and families across the country, we've found at least three things that often interact and keep people in bondage, leading them to repeat the past.

### 1. Bondage Can Feel So Familiar.

For many people, even for the nation of Israel, negative experiences lay down strong lines of negative loyalty. Not only that, but the fear of giving up familiar bonds is greater than the faith a person has to have when he's free.

For hundreds of years before Moses led God's people out of Egypt, the nation had suffered in captivity. Just give them a taste of freedom, and watch how appreciative they would be, right? Wrong! Three days after Moses miraculously parted the Red Sea, the people began to complain that the only water they had to drink was bitter (See Exodus 15:23–24.) (as if the God who parted the sea couldn't supply a glass of water when they needed it). A few days later, the people said to Moses, "Oh, that we had died by the hand of the LORD in the land of Egypt, when we sat by the pots of meat and when we ate bread to the full! For you have brought us out into this wilderness to kill this whole assembly with hunger" (Exodus 16:3).

Just a few weeks out of slavery, and already Egypt wasn't looking so bad. Almost overnight, negative lines of loyalty began their pull to bring Israel back into bondage. Even when God supplied manna for them to eat, they complained again, saying, "We remember the fish which we ate freely in Egypt, the cucumbers, the melons, the leeks, the onions, and the garlic; but now our whole being is dried up; there is nothing at all except this manna" (Numbers 11:5–6). For some reason, bondage can look different once we are free. We may have cried and groaned under our burden, but when we leave our familiar cell, it may not look so bad.

Perhaps each of us has experienced something similar to what the Israelites felt. Did you ever have a dating relationship where there were problems galore and very few positive things to commend it? On the night you broke up with that person, do you remember saying, "Boy, what did I ever see in him (or her)?" A few weeks or months later, however, do you remember looking back and saying to yourself, "Maybe that dating relationship really wasn't so bad after all. I wonder if we should get back together?"

Ever since the Garden of Eden, men and women have had a tendency to lean back into bondage and fear going down a new path on their own. We may be miserable in our present situations, but at least it's a familiar misery. Our shoes may be filled with holes and unable to keep out the cold, but "My, are they comfortable."

It takes courage to work at freeing ourselves from past patterns. It takes courage to look honestly at our parents and how they raised us. It takes courage to admit past mistakes and to confront wrong in the family without dishonoring our parents or siblings in the process. It takes only complacency to remain where we are.[1]

## 2. Fear = Procrastination.

Why do so many people put off confronting wrongs or making long overdue changes? A second reason is that just like the Roman governor Felix, they become afraid of change and let that fear keep conviction at arm's length.

Felix was a Roman ruler who lived an immoral life. At one point, he had his brother killed so he could marry his sister-in-law.[2] But Felix is best known for being one of the world's great procrastinators. He had the opportunity to have the apostle Paul point out areas he needed to change in his life, yet fear closed the door to genuine change, and procrastination sneaked in the window and made itself at home. "Felix . . . sent for Paul and heard him concerning the faith in Christ. Now as he reasoned about righteousness, self-control, and the judgment to come, Felix was afraid and answered, 'Go away for now; when I have a convenient time I will call for you' " (Acts 24:24–25).

Perhaps there's been something that convicted you in reading the Scriptures, this book, or another Christian book. Some of you may have realized for the first time that your life is being held in check by negative lines of loyalty. You may have seen yourself in one of the homes we illustrated, and you may not have had the courage to confront your past or stop dishonoring your parents. Perhaps you've seen something you've done with your children that lowers their self-worth and ties them up in knots, yet you put off changing your behavior. What can head off any attempt at needed change? *Fear.*

Jim really wanted to talk to his father about problems in the past, but he was afraid of the reaction he would get. Martha knew that she shouldn't yell at her brothers and sisters, but facing that problem in her life might make her face others as well, and she was afraid of what she would find. Gretta was tired of being the scapegoat in her family, but fear kept her from bringing her hurt out into the open. It's never easy to go through the process of uncovering negative lines of loyalty. It goes against our very make-up.

***Painful Memories.*** An interesting study conducted a few years ago sought to understand how the brain stores memories of past events. Through electrical stimulation, the researchers activated certain areas of the brain that they thought might "hold" memories. To their delight, many experimental subjects recalled memories with striking clarity, even if the events had occurred years earlier. As the experiment progressed, however, an unexpected side effect developed. When the subjects recalled a particular event, they also experienced many of the feelings associated with the memory. So painful were some of the feelings that several of the experimental subjects refused to continue with the research.[3]

Many people fear bringing up the past because their memories bring back feelings that are too painful. Yet only when negative patterns and lines of loyalty are revealed and dealt with honestly can they lose their powerful effect.

## 3. More of the Same Doesn't Bring Change.

Some of you may have difficulty breaking negative lines of loyalty because you've grown too accustomed to the pain or because fear of change rears its head and you put things on hold—again. Although these are two frequent reasons for not following through with needed changes, many people repeat a past hurtful pattern because deep inside they think it will go away on its own. They know there must be happiness in there somewhere, and it will come one day if they continue to do things the "old-fashioned way." Even if they've spent a lifetime casting into the same spot and never catching a fish, that trophy catch must be in there somewhere.

Imagine watching someone sitting in front of a television set, anxiously waiting for the programs to begin. He's been waiting for days to catch a glimpse of the shows. But as you look over to the set he's staring at, you notice there's no picture. The set isn't even plugged in to an electrical outlet!

When you mention this to the person, he replies, "Don't bother me with that. I was watching this television one time, and it worked perfectly. I'm sure it's just warming up."

How does this relate to people who put off change in their lives? There is a principle we see very often in counseling that many people put into practice in their homes: people are convinced that *more of the same will eventually bring change.* Many people want change, but they don't want to do anything to bring it about. Like the man who waited anxiously for the television set to go on, they feel that just wanting and waiting to change will eventually bring needed changes to life.

Challenging a person to change his behavior makes great motivational sense. Unquestionably, that's why many spiritual life and marriage seminars exist. People pay top dollar to get motivated to change, but rarely is there any accountability following the cheerleading session, and few needed changes take place. (That's a major reason why we stress small group follow-up so much if you attend any of our seminars.)

The fact is that *more of the same does not bring change.* If you sit tight and let a parent manipulate you, the negative bonds can continue to hurt your parent and you for a lifetime.[4]

The tremendous pastor of our home church is Darryl DelHousaye, and he frequently issues us this challenge in his sermons: "Scripturally, the stronger person always initiates the peace." You need to be the strong one in dealing with problems. Not doing so is like having a broken watch and waiting for it to repair itself. It can keep you operating on the wrong time for years.

If you're motivated to change and are willing to give up the familiarity of your bonds and the fear of doing something new, how can you begin to change? By making sure you're plugged in to the Source of Life where you can receive the inner power you need to change even the most destructive patterns from the past.

## KNOWING WHAT TO PLUG IN TO AND WHEN WE'RE UNPLUGGED

Let's go back to an example we used in the previous chapter. While we'll be using this one woman's story to illustrate our points, what we told her is also what we explained to each person whose story we mentioned in this chapter.

Gretta was the young woman who suffered terribly as the scapegoat of her family. She was hated by her mother and rejected by her brothers and sisters. She wanted to change things in her home, and later in her own life and family as well. She would cry herself to sleep at times, wanting so much for things to change. How could she possibly deal with all the hurts she experienced and break free of the negative bonds that held her?

As we began counseling with Gretta, we discovered that in many ways, her desires in life were the same as anyone else's. She longed for others to highly value her. She wanted inner happiness, calm, and contentment. Yet because of her negative home situation, she received only anger, bitterness, and defeat.

It was as if Gretta's life were a lamp with a single cord. She wanted desperately to see her life lit up with positive feelings and a warm inner calm. She wanted the joy of knowing she was accepted unconditionally by her mother and loved by her brothers and sisters. Yet every time she tried plugging her life in to her natural family, the bulb remained dark, or even worse, she received terrible shocks.

Do you know what can happen when something that should reward you turns around and shocks you? For some people, it can cause enough despair to lead to suicide.

## Pushing a Painful Lever

Years ago, there was a classic study done on some mice who were each placed in an experimental box.[5] On one end of the box was a bar that would drop a food pellet when it was pressed. Being curious and active little animals, these mice weren't in their boxes very long before they accidentally pushed or stood on the bars and a food pellet came out. It didn't take very long after that before the mice were pressing their bars like crazy whenever they were in the mood for food.

But then the researchers did something to the metal bar in each box. They attached wires to each bar that were connected at the other end to a large battery. Every time a mouse touched his bar, he would receive a terrible shock along with a pellet of food.

Smarting and confused, the mice would usually push the bar a second time and sometimes a third, each time receiving the painful shock. What do you think happened after that? Even when their hunger threatened their lives, most of them would die in the box, unwilling to be shocked again. And did you know the really tragic thing about this study? After the third shock, the researchers had turned off the battery. There was no longer a shock when the mouse pressed the bar! He could have pressed it and received all the food he needed, but he wouldn't face the potential pain of pushing it again.

Over the years, Gretta had been shocked so many times by her family that she also felt like giving up. The very people who should have given her love and acceptance had given her only pain and hurt, and she thought seriously about taking her own life.

Gretta didn't attempt suicide, but she was so tired of darkness and being shocked, and so desirous of light in her life, that she tried plugging in to anything that she thought might bring her power and warmth. She tried lighting her life by plugging it in to friends, dating, school, jobs, houses, even drugs and alcohol. And every time she plugged in to any of those sources, they, too, left her trapped in darkness and afraid she would never see the light she longed for.

Do you know someone like Gretta? Has a dishonoring home left that person searching for the light of love and peace and full of the darkness of fear and despair? We hope he or she can discover what Gretta did. There is really only one place where any of us can plug in to find the satisfaction in life we so desperately need.

## Plugging in to the Source of Life

When Gretta finally discovered that she needed to plug in to the Source of Life, Jesus Christ, for the first time she saw her life light up. In His love she found unconditional acceptance (Romans 8:38–39; John 10:1ff.; Hebrews 13:5). In His power she found the strength to be joyful in spite of her circumstances (Philippians 4:11–14; 1 Peter 1:6–9). In His hand she found a spiritual family at a church that loved her unconditionally, and from Him she received the peace she had never before found (John 14:6; 1 John 5:1ff.).

Perhaps you need to consider what your life is plugged in to. Many people try to carry around dozens of cords and plug them in to the Lord and many other things, but God has designed us with one cord and only one place where we can plug in and find lasting life and power—Himself.

Gretta left our office one afternoon after making the most significant decision anyone can make. For the first time, she plugged her life in to the Source of Life. For the next year and a half, Gretta made a daily decision to look only to the Lord to light up her life. As we mentioned earlier, it takes thirty days of doing something consistently before it becomes a habit. Gretta didn't give up, and soon she found that the first thing she did in the morning and the last thing she did at night was to say to herself, "Time to plug in to what God says about me and unplug from the disappointing sources I'm plugged in to, to bring light into my life!"

Whenever she found herself angry with her husband or impatient with her children, she took time to realize that she was really plugged in to them, trying to use them for fulfillment, and they were frustrating or shocking her. Most important, whenever she thought back to her family background and her light began to dim, she would unplug her worth from the past and plug it in to what her heavenly Father had to say about her.

This concept is so important that I (Gary) have taken an entire book titled *Joy That Lasts*[6] to talk about it. If you're struggling through problems or a past like one of the homes we've pictured, we would encourage you to take things a step further and practice plugging in to a personal relationship with God and unplugging from unfulfilling expectations placed on people or things.

## Persisting to the End

For Gretta, it took a year and a half of consistently making the decision to plug in to God and unplug from others before she began to feel released from her past hurts. But that's not the end of the story.

At fifty-one years of age, Gretta began calling her eighty-six-year-old mother and telling her for the first time in years that she loved her. Because she was no longer dependent on her mother to light up her life, she was free to love without any expectations. The result was that she began to feel compassion for her mother instead of hate, and she discovered things she had never known about her mother's past. For one thing, she was shocked to discover that her mother had come from a home where there was almost constant sexual abuse. Instead of dishonoring her mother (and lowering her own worth as a result), Gretta made a decision to honor and value her.

"No wonder she was never able to love me," Gretta told us after discovering her mother's past. And with that admission, years of hurt and darkness began to be replaced by a love for the Lord, for her family, and even for herself that she had never known before. When God lights up our lives and fills us with love, it's a gift we can share freely with others, not the artificial light that comes only when people "earn" our love.

All the people we mentioned in this chapter and the last— Wayne with his imprisoning obligations, Jim with the way he was pulled to love one parent and not the other, Mark whose family loyalties cut him off from serving the Lord, and Gretta—first confronted their reasons for not changing and then began plugging in to the Source of Life. When their lives were lit up by being consistently plugged in to Christ, they were able to see the negative lines of loyalty that had held them down for so long. Then they had the freedom to receive God's love and the inner power to deal with the effects of their past.

While it didn't happen overnight and they also had to learn to find value in their trials,[7] they are freer today than they've been in years. Their freedom comes from being plugged in to the only permanent source of love, joy, and peace.

The six aspects of honor we've discussed so far have the potential to make lasting, positive changes in our children's self-worth—that is, if the seventh aspect of honor is laid on top of all the others. In this final aspect, we go to the power source we need to balance and blend each element together and see it make a lasting change in our own lives.

# Chapter Seventeen

## Offering Honor to God

*E*very day, parents are in the process of teaching their children to honor or dishonor God, even if they never use religious words. That was certainly the case in Don's home. His parents thought that part of being educated included a healthy dose of skepticism and the intellectual questions about a "Supreme Being" that were taught at upper crust schools.

Don's parents were never very interested in formal religion, and they often criticized "religious fanatics" who believed in God and the Bible. After all, as his father would often say, "We Spencers are successful without having to rely on emotional crutches."

If the truth be known, Don's parents were never very interested in *anything* they couldn't put in their bank account or flaunt at the club, including Don. How did Don know this? By the hours of consistent time Mom and Dad devoted to gaining wealth and prestige, and the minutes of inconsistent time they spent trying to teach him he was valuable to them.

There was always another land deal his father had to save or another Junior League function his mom had to attend that kept them from meeting the lonely boy's deepest needs. It wasn't that Don didn't have inner longings or questions about God. Like most children, he sensed there was a Creator and Lord of creation by looking at nature (Romans 1:20) and by talking with several of his friends who came from Christian homes.

As the years went by, Don developed a thirst for God apart from any encouragement from his parents. The only problem stemmed from where he chose to quench that thirst. Like many boys and girls who grow up with a deep longing for God but are stiff-armed in approaching Him by their parents, Don was so parched and dry that he was willing to drink at any well, even one filled with poisoned water.

At age seventeen, Don became deeply entrenched in a nation-wide cult that preaches family, love, and acceptance yet demands bondage and unquestioning allegiance. While it may not sound like much of a bargain, Don was eager to forfeit his parents and his future to join such a cult. After all, he told us, *it was the first place where he felt truly valuable to someone.*

Like Don's parents, many moms and dads are simply not aware of the powerful influence they have on their children's spiritual lives. Yet for those who want to have a positive spiritual impact on their children, we're excited to illustrate how the concepts we've been talking about throughout this book can become avenues for your children to raise their value of God.

## LEADING CHILDREN TO THE SOURCE OF HONOR

For several chapters we've looked at how on a horizontal level, we can and should provide honor to our loved ones. However, for us to be able to love and value others as we should—and to teach them to do so—we must begin by making sure our vertical relationship with God is growing and developing.

The Lord is the source of honor, the One from whom it flows. Plugging into Him provides us with the power source we need to love our children or others. In fact, we are capable of loving others because we are first loved by Him (1 John 4:10–11, 19, 21). We have the power to treat others as valuable treasures because He treats us that way (Ephesians 1:18–19). We have a model for giving our loved ones a special position in our lives because of the place of honor we're allowed to share in His family (1 John 3:1).

Not only do the Scriptures give us principles and guidelines for motivating our children to honor God and others, but they also give us real life models we can follow.

Children love stories, and the Bible is full of examples of men and women who honored their relationship with God as their most priceless treasure and because they did, honored their loved ones. We can share with our children stories of people like Ruth, who honored her mother-in-law and stayed with her in her time of need (even when she could have legally abandoned her mother). (See Ruth 1:1ff.) The Old Testament saints who honored their children by providing a special blessing for them (Genesis 49:1ff), or even James and later each of the disciples made the ultimate sacrifice to put their faith in the Lord before their very lives.

However, of all the great examples of faith, the ultimate example of someone who gave high value to people—even to those who did not deserve His attention—is our Lord Himself. He gives us the motivation to serve and honor others.

Traveling through a crowded city street, He stopped to call down an insignificant Zacchaeus from a tree and confront a woman with a hemorrhage, who reached out in faith to touch Him for healing. Before the Last Supper, Jesus laid aside His position of honor at the Passover meal to wash the disciples' feet. I (Gary) have experienced someone washing my feet only once, but it was one of the most humbling and honoring experiences of my life.

At the cross, Christ honored His mother by placing her in the care of His beloved friend, He took the time to meet the dying request of a common criminal, and He even prayed for the forgiveness of those who nailed Him to the tree.

Because our heavenly Father made the decision to honor us—to count us of great value—through His Son's death on the cross, He opened wide the door for us to experience eternal life. On our own, none of us merits that life, nor God's grace or favor, but on the basis of Christ's sacrifice, we are no longer enemies but actually beloved friends. C. S. Lewis once put it this way:

> *To please God . . . to be a real ingredient in the divine happiness . . . to be loved by God, not merely pitied, but delighted in as an artist delights in his work or a father in a son—it seems impossible, a weight or burden of glory which our thoughts can hardly sustain. But so it is.*[1]

Each of the major sections of this book speak specifically about honoring our children or loved ones, but each can also apply to our learning to honor God.

---

- **We obey His word, gaining life and making our days pleasant by giving honor to our parents (Deuteronomy 17:6).**
- **When we acknowledge God has a special plan for our lives, even in the midst of trials, we honor Him and learn to depend on Him as our source of life.**
- **Understanding our strengths as parents can make us better vessels to serve our children and others.**
- **Like the disciples of old, we, too, can find a helpful balance between nestling close to Him (belonging) and going out to serve others (separateness).**
- **Spending time in God's Word can alert us to the boundaries He has put up around things and people that should or should not enter our lives.**
- **Looking to His loyal-love as a model, we have the basis for building positive loyalties into our own and our children's lives.**

---

Each aspect of honor needs to be filtered through our relationship with the Lord and can be used to draw us closer to Him. By understanding and applying the three major aspects of the definition of honor, we can see our children's spiritual lives blossom and develop.

## DRAWING GOLD FROM THE DEFINITION OF HONOR

A picture is indeed worth a thousand words for teaching children lessons in right living. That's true of the three word pictures we can use with our children to illustrate what it means for them (or us) to dishonor or honor God.

## 1. Learning a "Weighty" Lesson on Dishonoring Others

As we saw in chapter 2, the word picture behind *dishonor* is a "vapor" or "steam." How can a word picture like this help a child understand a concept like dishonoring someone? One creative parent used it to illustrate to her daughter what it meant to dishonor God's Word by hurting a friend.

Jammie was a nine-year-old who was already quite a people pleaser. That's why she was swayed so much by her friends' opinions on who to invite to her slumber party. Jammie had a cousin her age who lived nearby. The girls were the same age and for years had been close friends and playmates. However, in the last few years they had drifted apart. Jammie was attractive and was becoming popular at school, while her cousin had long struggled with a weight problem and was not well liked by others.

Jammie mentioned to her friends at school that she was going to invite her cousin. "No," they said emphatically, "she's too fat and ugly!" Rather than stand her ground and defend her cousin or insist she be a part of the party, Jammie joined in with their giggles and decided not to invite her after all.

When Jammie's mother asked her if she was going to invite her cousin, Jammie tried to change the subject and ignore the question. Finally she lied and said her cousin was "busy" and couldn't attend. After the party, however, quite by accident, Jammie's mother found out her niece had not been busy and was deeply hurt at being overlooked by her former best friend.

As a Christian parent, Jammie's mother was concerned about her daughter's actions. As a wise mother as well, she used the experience to teach her daughter the difference between honoring and dishonoring words and actions. Having learned the literal meaning behind dishonoring someone, she decided to demonstrate it to her daughter in a creative and convicting way.

That winter evening, when it was time for Jammie's bath, her mother went in with her and took along an extremely heavy paperweight from the study. "Jammie, do you know what it means to dishonor someone?" she asked. When Jammie said she really didn't know, her mother told her to try to grab hold of the steam that was coming out of the faucet as they filled the tub with warm water.

"How much do you think that steam weighs, Jammie?" her mother asked.

"Not very much!" her daughter said with a giggle as she tried to grab handfuls of steam from the air.

Then handing Jammie the paperweight, her mother asked, "How much do you think this weighs?"

"Tons!" said Jammie as she struggled to hold up the paperweight with both hands.

Then her mother explained that what she had just illustrated was like what Jammie had done to her cousin. "Jammie, when you dishonor someone, you treat her like a vapor, like she's only as heavy as that steam coming up from the tub. But when you honor someone, you treat her as if she's important and carries a lot of weight like Dad's paperweight.

"Honey, did you realize that by not inviting your cousin to your slumber party, and by lying to me, you treated both of us as though we had as little weight as the steam you tried to catch? Not only that, but God's Word also tells us we're to love those who may not be so lovable, and especially that we're not to lie. When you hurt your cousin and lied to me, you also treated God as if He didn't weigh anything either. Is that what you wanted to do by your actions?"

As her mother's words dawned on her, Jammie's smile turned into tears of conviction. For the first time she understood how her dishonoring actions had affected her cousin and her mother and had even dishonored God. After a good cry during her bath, Jammie asked her mom to forgive her, and she prayed and asked God to forgive her, also. Perhaps hardest of all, she then went into the kitchen, called her cousin, and asked to be forgiven.

In the Scriptures we read, "You who make your boast in the law, do you dishonor God through breaking the law?"[2] Like Jammie, when we disobey God's Word and treat it like a vapor, we dishonor Him. The lower our value of the Scriptures, the easier it will be for us to treat His rock-solid words as sifting sand and brush them aside whenever it's convenient to do so.

## 2. Going in Search of a Priceless Treasure

As we're sure you remember, one word picture behind the concept of honor is to view someone as a special treasure, and another is to give him a highly respected position in our lives. When we use these analogies, the door is wide open to teaching our children practical lessons in loving God.

At the time we're writing this chapter, stores are gearing up for the mobs of people who will be looking for bargains between Thanksgiving and Christmas. To use this analogy of shopping, if our lives were like a department store, what price would we put on the Lord?

Chuck Swindoll has an exceptional book of layman's theology that we highly recommend, *Growing Deep in the Seasons of Life*.[3] In it is a convicting chapter titled "Mary's Little Lamb." At the close of that chapter, he tells the story of a major department store chain that had a cuddly, washable, plastic "baby Jesus" for sale. It came complete with artificial straw and was distributed to all their stores nationwide. The dolls, however, proved to be a sales flop. One store manager became worried at the backlog of "Jesus" dolls and had a sign made up: "JESUS, MARKED DOWN 50%. GET HIM WHILE YOU CAN!"

What a beautiful description of the way the people *of* the world look at our Lord! They put Him in plastic; they mark Him down; they try to manipulate Him to gain riches (as Felix and others in the Scriptures have done for centuries).[4]

However, putting the story of this doll aside, what kind of price tag would you put on Jesus in your home? Do your actions and attitudes toward Him convey that He's on discount special and not of great value in your life?

***Let Them Catch Your Passion*** The best way to convey to children that the Lord is of great value is to illustrate it by the way you live. Children are God's little spies. They know what you treasure without your telling them. You may tell them they're important, but if you can't take your eyes off the TV set long enough to make eye contact with them when they're talking to you, they know what's more valuable to you. You may tell them your relationship with Christ is first in your life, yet you say grace at meals only when company comes or consistently skip church to watch the game. Your value system is showing, and you can be sure that they're watching.

The best way to teach children to value God, then, is to develop a passion for knowing Him. For parents who may be struggling in this area (and most of us do at times), we recommend two exceptional books that can help them get back into God's Word and into valuing God and others.[5] For parents who are already doing a good job of attaching high value to God, we have a practical suggestion to help children learn to count the Lord as a special treasure.

It's one thing to take an element that's already beautiful, like gold, and shape a precious ring or necklace out of it. It's quite another thing, however, to take something that appears worthless and bring beauty and value out of *it*. Throughout the Scriptures, there are examples of humble people and things that God has taken and transformed into valuable creations. That's what one father tried to communicate to his children.

Recently, the children had lost their only remaining grandparent, and their father wanted to be sure they understood what a loving, powerful God they had even in the midst of their loss. This was important because one son in particular was having a very difficult time "liking" God and attaching any value to Him after the loss of his grandmother (the same way adults often react to a loss).

As we've already mentioned, seeing God's presence and the value that can be gained in trials is a tremendous way for children to continue to attach value to God. However, spinning off the definition of honor he had learned, this father wanted to give them a living example of how God could take tragedy and turn it into triumph. So on a Saturday morning, he gathered the children together and had each of them plant a sweet pea seed in his or her own little container of potting soil. While they were all having fun planting and watering, he explained to them what the Scriptures say about the resurrection of the dead, that our bodies are "sown in dishonor" and "raised in glory" (1 Corinthians 15:43).

He told them that the seeds they were planting would die, but that one day soon they would bring forth fruit or a flower—and the same thing would be true for their grandmother. Her physical body had died and been placed in the ground, but one day God will raise it up, imperishable, in a new and beautiful form as glorious as any flower.

As he explained this to the children, the son who was struggling seemed to let the words bounce off him, and he remained angry and sullen—until the first sprouts of green shot up from his planting. That's when the truth of his father's words sank in.

Instead of continuing to be angry with God because he lost his grandmother, he had a new reason and hope for what had scared him the most about the funeral—watching his grandmother's casket being lowered into the ground.

Having a picture of a scriptural truth growing in front of him gave this young boy a new way to honor God by seeing His incredible power to bring life. Instead of "marking down" God's value in that home, a wise parent used a teachable moment to raise his children's value of God.

Growing seeds together isn't the only way to teach children about God's value in their lives. A parent could study with them what it means to say Jesus is our Good Shepherd or read them stories in the Scriptures that speak of His unchanging love for us (John 10:11–15; 15:9–10). Simply talking about the Cross can be a graphic way to illustrate to children how valuable they are to God, and it can raise their view of Jesus at the same time.

Thus far, we've looked at how children can see their value of God raised when they learn what it means to dishonor Him and how Jesus remains a priceless treasure even during times of trial. There's also a third aspect of the definition of honor that can give you some handles on teaching your children to highly value God.

### 3. Uncovering the Place of Honor (or Dishonor) God Plays in a Child's Life

There's one method you can use to evaluate the place God holds in your children's lives and raise it higher if need be. If your sons or daughters are in grade school or older, you can ask them what they consider to be the most valuable things in their lives. You may be surprised at the answers. Grant was when he asked his junior-high-aged son this question, yet it gave him a starting place to help his son raise his sense of value of God.

Grant's son had a real problem going to Sunday school and would skip it nine times out of ten. When Grant asked his son what was most important in his life, he found out that the boy's relationship with God was in sixth place—just behind television.

Grant could have reacted at this point, but instead he asked his son another question: "On a one to ten scale, with ten being of tremendous value to you—something you really treasure like that autographed poster in your room—where would you rate your sense of value for God?"

"About a four, I guess," answered his son.

Instead of getting angry and lecturing him, Grant asked, "Son, what would it take to move that four up higher toward a ten?"

Without a moment's hesitation, his son answered, "I always feel so stupid when I'm in Sunday school class. Everybody knows all the verses and where to find them, and I get embarrassed and hate it when they call on me."

Being embarrassed when you're a junior-higher is almost the same as being disbarred if you're an attorney! His fear of the other children's finding out how little he knew of the Scriptures was at the heart of what was holding him back from going to class.

Grant met with his son each week and went through the verses and lessons the junior-high class was studying. After several months of consistently studying the Bible together, Grant's son was going regularly to the junior-high class, and Grant felt he had never been closer to his son than in the times they spent together studying God's Word.

Before we end our look at the concept of honor, we'd like to offer one final story that we feel captures the heart of much of what we've wanted to say. It's an example of the tremendous impact one family member can have on the rest of his family by putting what he learned about honor into action.

# Chapter Eighteen

## Honoring Others in Action

We've explained and illustrated the biblical concept of honor and shown practical ways a parent can put this concept to work in his home. But when all is said and done, does it really work? Does honoring God, honoring others, and raising our own value in Him really cause the changes we've talked about in this book?

As we close our discussion of this life-changing concept, we'd like to share a beautiful story of a man who grew up feeling the brutal effects of being dishonored, but who excitedly told us of a miraculous change that took place in his life and his family's as he learned to honor God, himself, and others.

### LIVING IN DISHONOR—CHOOSING TO GIVE HONOR

Denny was the oldest of five children in an alcoholic home. As any child knows who grows up in such a home, there are all kinds of drinkers. Some become passive and sleep away their lives in a stupor. Others become violent and use the alcohol to rationalize their deep hostility. Unfortunately for Denny and his sisters, their father was a combination of the two. As long as their father was in his withdrawn mood, Denny and his sisters were safe. But when he sobered up just enough to regain his senses, his anger wouldn't be appeased until someone had been hurt.

For Denny's sisters, that hurt came in the form of physical and sexual abuse. For him, it came at the cost of repeated beatings and verbal assaults. Like a thief who doesn't care what he steals or from whom he steals it, this father stole five children's innocence and trust and replaced it with shattered lives and broken futures.

As the years went by, Denny and his sisters followed the script we've already seen a number of times in this book. Being made to feel valueless, they acted out their emptiness in ways that damaged themselves and others. Two of Denny's sisters became prostitutes, another a practicing lesbian. And what of Denny? As in Harry Chapin's powerful song "Cat's in the Cradle," Denny's life echoed the pain-wrapped words, "I'm gonna be like you, Dad. You know I'm gonna be like you."

By the time he was in high school, Denny was a borderline alcoholic. He hated school and fought with students and teachers alike, but he found a positive release in football—that is, if you can call his excuse for legitimized brutality positive.

Denny loved football not for the clean sport of it, but for the opportunity it gave him to see how far he could go in hitting below the belt. He mastered the cheap shot and gloated over the players he had "taken out" with a knee injury or blind-sided with an illegal block. If he hadn't been big like his father and so filled with anger at all of life, he probably would never have been as good an athlete as he was. However, much to his and his parents' surprise, he was offered a scholarship at a major out-of-state university.

When Denny left his home at eighteen, he never expected to go back. Luckily, his father was in stupor the day he left; there was no way he wanted to see him. Not that Denny was afraid of him anymore. During his sophomore year in high school, he had become so big and strong through weightlifting and playing football that he was able to beat his father brutally one night when his dad tried to "get physical" with his mother. Never again had his father tried to lift a hand against him or his mother, but Denny often egged him on to try to get one more chance to pulverize him.

Denny's life seemed similar to Cinderella's life. On game nights in college, he felt on top of the world in his football uniform. But when the stadium lights dimmed, so did any value he had as a person. Then came the knee injury in his junior year that ended his college career and his pro aspirations, and Denny had nothing in life to live for or give him hope.

Denny had married his high-school sweetheart their third year in college, but when he realized his sports career was over, he began drinking heavily again. After six months of his abusive behavior, his wife left him and school to return home to her parents. At the end of his final semester of college, he received his diploma in physical education and the notice from his wife's lawyer that his divorce had gone through. Denny would go through one more marriage and five years of increasing alcoholism before he hit rock bottom—and found the one door through which he could get back on his feet.

An old-high-school teammate who had moved to the city where Denny lived was the only person to keep in touch with him on a regular basis. And this man's life had a peace and joy that came from knowing the Source of Life, Jesus Christ. For nearly six years, this friend had invited Denny to church and had shared his faith with him at a ball game or over breakfast. At life's lowest ebb, Denny broke down on an Easter Day and went to church with his friend for the first time. "After all," he rationalized, "it's the thing to do on Easter." The last time Denny had been in a church (besides his first wedding) was when he was required to attend church as a young boy to play on their softball team.

While it was the last thing he expected, that morning Denny heard the simple plan of salvation explained, and he gave what was left of his shattered life over to the Savior. Over the next several years, God did a number of miraculous things in Denny's life. The first and biggest step was his being convinced of his need to deal with his drinking problem. After many months of wrestling with the decision, he began attending a Christian chapter of AA (Alcoholics Anonymous).

Then the Lord brought a most special gift into Denny's life, a Christian widow who loved him in spite of all his imperfections and his terrible past. As the years went by, their marriage was blessed with several children whom he loved beyond his wildest expectations.

Once Denny had made the decision to honor God, to place Him as the highest value in his life, honoring others came as a second step. He had never given his former wives the honor due them, but now he spent time listening to his wife and working at being sensitive to her needs. Where once he had all the potential of building negative lines of loyalty into his children, now he worked hard at providing the elements that build positive loyalties.

For several years Denny worked hard at treasuring his wife and children and giving them a special place in his life. But there was still one aspect of honor he needed to face. He had never made contact with his father in all those years, and he knew one day he would have to deal with that issue. At age thirty-five, prompted by several men in a small group Bible study who encouraged him to try to make things right with his father, he called him for the first time in over fifteen years. Alone in his office, he picked up the phone and dialed his father's number. When his father answered, Denny said, "Dad, this is your son Denny. And I just wanted you to know that I love you." Before he could say any more, his father hung up.

When he was forty, Denny became convicted again of his need to try to set things right, and he called and began the conversation with the same words as before: "Dad, I love you." For the second time, his father hung up as soon as he heard his son's words.

Two years later, Denny was at a special week-long Christian conference as a guest of one of the businessmen he called on in his work. He met a young couple who seemed extremely warm and friendly. Although he rarely let down his guard, they seemed to be genuinely interested in his life. Before he realized it, he was sharing a little of his struggle with his father.

The next morning as he went down to breakfast, Denny saw the young couple in the lobby, only they looked so worn out and tired that he walked over to them to see what was wrong. "Nothing's wrong," the couple said. "It's just that we've been up all night praying for you, Denny. We really feel that your relationship with your father is still crippling your life, especially your relationship with your wife. We think you need to try to contact him one more time."

Denny was almost shaking as he went to find his wife, and the two of them went up to their hotel room. He got the operator to place the call, and his father picked up the phone. "Dad," he began, "I want you to know I love you." Without a moment's hesitation, his father hung up for the *third* time.

Denny was stunned. He didn't know whether to cry or to get angry. He sat on the bed in silence until his wife demanded that he call his father back, this time insisting that he not hang up. Grudgingly, Denny did what his wife requested, and he rang his father again. "Dad, don't hang up on me," he said. "I want you to know that I love you, and I want you to know why."

For the next twenty minutes or so, he explained to his father how much his own life had changed, and how he could forgive and honor his dad now because of all he had been forgiven. His father listened, mostly in silence, and at the end of the call he felt great about what he had said. He had no idea, however, what response to expect from his father.

Several months passed. One day his mother called him at the office. "Denny, you'd better get back here. I don't think your father has long to live," she said. Immediately, he made plane reservations and began working with his secretary to cancel his appointments for the next few days. Then his mother called back.

"Never mind about coming back," she said. "We can't find your father. He's disappeared!"

A few hours later, Denny found out where his father had gone. His mother called him back and told him, "Your father called me, and he has checked himself into an alcohol rehabilitation clinic. *He wanted me to tell you that he wants you to come out before he dies to talk to him about spiritual things, and he wants to be sober when you talk to him."*

Denny did go back, and he had the overwhelming joy of leading his father to Christ. He went with his father to the house of one of his sisters who lived in the same city as their parents. Denny's sister took a dozen steps back when they showed up at her door. She let them inside, and as they sat together on the couch, her father asked her forgiveness and reached over and touched her on the shoulder. As soon as her father touched her, she doubled over into the fetal position and started screaming. She got up, ran out of the house, and screamed that he should never, ever come back.

A few days later, Denny's father received a letter from that daughter. Listen to a few lines from her letter:

> *Father, your coming to see me was an outrage! There is no way you can come and preach forgiveness to me after all the scars I bear from you. For years, you have been all I have thought about. My every word, each decision I have made. You have been responsible for me becoming a prostitute.*

*You are responsible for my marriage that broke up. You are the reason I have had an operation so I can never have children—I'm afraid of what I'd do to them. You ask me to forgive you? You are not to be forgiven. You are to be conquered. If it takes me the rest of my life, I'll bury your memory. Don't ever call or come to see me again.*

In a few months, Denny's father died, but not before he was able to talk to each of the other children and ask for and receive their forgiveness. The one unforgiving daughter did come to the funeral; she told Denny she wouldn't have missed that day for anything in the world.

## THE GIFT OF HONOR

We chose this story to end the book for several reasons. From the moment Denny told us his story, we felt it was a beautiful example of each principle of honor. When it came to someone feeling of as little value as a mist, Denny had been dishonored all his life. Yet when it came to demonstrating the power of God when we give the gift of honor, he also stood out like a light.

Denny made a decision to honor others, beginning with his relationship with God, and by doing so he found a heart and desire for His Word and the power to take the next step. Alcoholics Anonymous and his Christian friends at church gave him a basis for breaking with the past and setting up a strong family.

As he gave honor to his wife and children, they had more security and love than he ever dreamed of or felt as a child. And when he made the decision to give honor to his father, with all the pain and heartache involved, it was as though he found the last missing piece of his own self-worth. At long last, he was free from many fears from the past and able to be at peace in the present.

Of all the joy in Denny's story, we appreciate its reality the most. While his days are brighter now and filled with God's light, in his family is a sister who has made totally opposite choices based on her past. His sister's life has been controlled for years because she's made a decision out of her hurt to treat others with as little value as she herself received. She devalues God and explains away the changes in her father and in Denny's life. She dishonors her father's memory with a passion, and she remains in emotional and spiritual chains. Denny has already seen treasure after treasure from his trials in the past; his sister thinks he is mentally ill for even thinking such thoughts.

So, we've come to the fork in the road. It's been our joy to walk with you as we've all learned more about the concept of honor. But we can walk with you no further. Real life begins when you close this book and look up into the eyes of your children, your spouse, your Lord, or even that parent far away whose face never disappears.

We know for a fact that God is worthy to receive "glory, and honor and power" (Revelation 4:11). We also know that because we are made in His image, we are called on to "honor all people" (1 Peter 2:17).

Our prayer for you is that you'll not take the easy road of forgetfulness and procrastination, but that you'll take the narrow, steeper path that leads to building value into your loved ones' lives. It is in that journey that you'll learn for yourself and be able to teach your children to truly honor God, self, and others.

Gary Smalley

John Trent

# Notes

## Chapter 1

1. J. S. Brown, "Responses and Reaction to Motivation," *Journal of Comparative Physiological Psychology* 41 (1978): 450–65.
2. While there are any number of good books in print on parenting, some of our favorites are Charles R. Swindoll, *You and Your Child* (Nashville: Thomas Nelson, 1977); James Dobson, *Hide or Seek* (New Jersey: Revell, 1974); Henry Brandt, *I Want To Enjoy My Children* (Grand Rapids: Zondervan, 1975); Paul Meier, *Christian Child-Rearing and Personality Development* (Grand Rapids: Baker, 1977); Gordon MacDonald, *The Effective Father* (Wheaton: Tyndale, 1977); and Richard Allen, *Common Sense Discipline* (Ft. Worth: Sweet Publishing, 1986).
3. Lloyd Wright, "Correlates of Reported Drinking Problems among Male and Female College Students," *Journal of Alcohol and Drug Education* 28, no. 3 (1983): 48.
4. Thomas Darwin, "Parental Influences of Adolescent Self-Esteem," *Journal of Early Adolescence* 4, no. 3 (1984): 259–74.
5. Jane B. Burka and Lenora M. Yuen, *Procrastination: Why You Do It, What to Do About It* (Reading, Mass.: Addison-Wesley, 1983). This is a secular book with secular conclusions, but we found its exploration into the reasons why we procrastinate interesting and helpful.
6. Maxine Kingston, *The Woman Warrior* (New York: Knopf, 1976).
7. Frank Minirth, Paul Meier, and Bill Brewer et al., *The Workaholic and His Family* (Grand Rapids: Baker, 1981).

8. Joanna Norrell, "Parent-Adolescent Interaction: Influences on Depression and Mood Cycles," *Dissertation Abstracts International* 45, no. 4-A (1984): 1067.

9. James Juggins, "Parents as Change Agents with Low Self-Concept Elementary School-Age Children," *Dissertation Abstracts International* 43, no. 1-B (1983): 3385.

10. Edward McCraye, "Childhood Family Antecedents of Dependency and Self-Criticism: Implications for Depression," *Journal of Abnormal Psychology* 93, no. 1 (1983): 3.

11. Steven Ambrose, "Cognitive-Behavioral Parent Training for Abusive and Neglectful Parents," *Dissertation Abstracts International* 44 (1985): 2544.

12. Kim Openshaw, "Parental Influences of Adolescent Self-Esteem," *Journal of Early Adolescence* 4, no. 3 (1984): 239–41.

13. J. R. Heiman, "A Psychophysiological Exploration of Sexual Arousal Patterns in Females and Males," *Psychophysiology* 14, no. 3 (1977): 2266–74.

14. Jeff Hollowell, "The Relationship Between Self-Concept of Academic Ability and Discrepancy in Perceived Feedback Regarding Achievement," *Dissertation Abstracts International* 45, no. 1-A (1985): 125.

15. J. B. Rotter, "Generalized Expectancies for Internal Vs. External Control of Reinforcement," *Psychological Monographs* 80 (1981): 609.

16. T. Dawler, "Susceptibility to Heart Disease and Social Structure," *Studies in Cardiovascular Disease* 30 (1982): 671–76.

17. W. H. Masters and V. E. Johnson, *Human Sexual Inadequacy* (Boston: Little, Brown & Co., 1970).

18. Sue Evans, "Failure to Thrive: A Study of 45 Children and Their Families," *Journal of the American Academy of Child Psychology* 11 (1982): 440–57.

19. Sheldon Robinson, "Attempted Suicide During Adolescence: Elements of Self-Concept and Identification with a Rejecting Parent," *Dissertation Abstracts International* 44, no. 11-B (1984): 3539.

20. Robert Pandia, "Psychosocial Correlates of Alcohol and Drug Use of Adolescent Students and Adolescents in Treatment," *Journal of Studies on Alcohol* 44, no. 6 (1983): 950.

21. Elma VanLuven, "Effects of Parent-Child Dyads on Self-Image and Mate Selection," *Dissertation Abstracts International* 42 (1984): 1067.

22. Frank Minirth and Paul Meier, *Happiness Is a Choice* (Grand Rapids: Baker, 1978).

23. David Stoop, *Living with a Perfectionist* (Nashville: Thomas Nelson, 1987). An important book we feel will have a tremendous impact on people with low self-worth.

24. Lee Courtland, "Predicting Career Choice Attitudes," *Vocational Guidance Quarterly* 32, no. 3 (1984): 177.
25. Minirth and Meier, *Happiness Is a Choice*, 149.
26. N. J. Anastasiow, "Success in School and Boys' Sex-role Patterns," *Child Development* 36 (1978): 1053–66.
27. H. B. Biller, "Father Absence and the Personality Development of the Male Child," *Developmental Psychology* 11 (1978): 181–201.
28. Brian Lucas, "Identity Status, Parent-Adolescent Relationships, and Participation in Marginal Religious Groups," *Dissertation Abstracts International* 43, no. 12-B (1984): 4131.
29. J. V. Mitchell, "Goal-Setting Behavior as a Function of Self-Acceptance, Over- and Under-Achievement and Related Personality Variables," *Journal of Educational Psychology* 50 (1970): 93–104. As part of our research for this book, we did a computer search at Arizona State University, and for the years 1980 through 1986, the data base pulled up 12,432 studies directly related to the study of self-concept.
30. Matthew 22:37, 39.
31. Proverbs 24:33–34.

## Chapter 2

1. William F. Arndt and R. Wilbur Gingrich, eds., *A Greek-English Lexicon of the New Testament and Other Early Christian Literature* (Chicago: University of Chicago Press, 1957), 119.
2. Ibid., 120.
3. Ibid.
4. Things like coming home late without calling, failing a course, talking back, and so on.
5. See also Proverbs 3:9; John 5:23.
6. Arndt and Gingrich, *Lexicon*, 825.
7. Gerhard Kittel and Gerhard Friedrich, eds., *Theological Dictionary of the New Testament* (Grand Rapids: Eerdmans, 1972), 170.
8. In the book of Ezekiel, the word *honor* is used to stand for "treasures" of silver and gold that were stolen from the people. See also Numbers 22:17, 37.
9. R. Laird Harris, *Theological Workbook of the Old Testament, Volume 1* (Chicago: Moody Press, 1980), 426.
10. For a very challenging look at how God's glory should motivate us to honor and praise, see John Piper's *Desiring God: Meditations of a Christian Hedonist* (Portland: Multnomah Press, 1986). Don't be thrown off by the subtitle. It's an excellent book for those who want to learn more about worshiping God.
11. The same thing is true in a marriage. Time after time in counseling, we see a couple where one or both parties have "no feelings whatso-

ever" for the other person. But if they'll treat each other like a priceless treasure, within a few weeks, very often their positive feelings for each other will come back! Just by getting couples to act on this one fact, we've seen the Lord restore relationships that looked beyond repair.

12. Kittel and Friedrich, *Theological Dictionary*, 171.

13. J. H. Moulton and George Milligan, *The Vocabulary of the Greek Testament: Illustrated from the Papyri and Other Non-Literary Sources* (Grand Rapids: Eerdmans, 1974), 635.

14. A. D. Noch, "Studies in the Graeco-Roman Beliefs of the Empire," *Harvard Studies in Classical Philology* 41 (1958): 252.

15. Hebrews 3 and 5.

16. H. G. Liddell and Robert Scott, *An Intermediate Greek-English Lexicon* (Oxford: Oxford University Press, 1975), 808.

17. Psalms 63:6; 77:11.

## Chapter 3

1. Deuteronomy 5:16.

2. E. Hooker, "The Adjustment of the Male Overt Homosexual," *Journal of Projective Techniques* 27 (1967): 18–21; C. A. Trip, *The Homosexual Matrix* (New York: McGraw-Hill, 1975); and many other findings.

3. William S. Appleton, *Fathers and Daughters* (New York: Berkley Books, 1984), 171.

4. C. S. Lewis once wrote of God's masculine characteristics, "In comparison to God, everyone is feminine." "Notes on the Way," *Time and Tide* 29 (1948): 14.

5. Deuteronomy 5:16.

6. To our doctor or nurse friends, please don't scream as you read this. We've tried to explain this complicated process very simply and draw a practical application from it.

7. Neil R. Carlson, *Physiology of Behavior* (Boston: Allyn & Bacon, 1977), 11.

8. By the way, as short-distance joggers, we can verify that this is a wise decision for anyone being chased by a dog.

9. John M. Davis, "Models of Affective Disorders Due To Stress," *Neuropsychopharmacology* 6 (1984): 192.

10. Albert A. Kurtland, "Biochemical and Emotional Interaction in the Etiology of Cancer," *Psychiatric Research Review* 35 (1978): 25.

11. Psalm 119:105.

12. Adapted from Matthew 6:21.

13. Gary Smalley and John Trent, *The Blessing* (Nashville: Thomas Nelson, 1986), 219ff.

14. Our thanks to Tim Kimmel at Generation Ministries for explaining

this concept to us as part of his excellent upcoming book, *Finding Rest in a Restless World*.

15. Marshall Goodman, "Divorce Takes Its Toll," *USA Today*, September 14, 1986.
16. Ibid.

**Chapter 4**

1. Hebrews 12:5ff.; James 1:2.
2. For a challenging look at the need to honestly confront problems rather than try to avoid them, see M. Scott Peck, *The Road Less Traveled* (New York: Simon & Schuster, 1978).
3. Romans 5:3; Hebrews 12:10ff.; James 1.
4. Arndt and Gingrich, *Lexicon*, 157.
5. Matthew 18:6.
6. Matthew 22:36–40; Romans 8:28; 1 Timothy 1:5.
7. Genesis 37–50.
8. Genesis 50:20, italics added.
9. Isaiah 61:3.
10. Psalm 119:105.
11. Since we saw him on television, David's inspiring story has come out in book form: David Rover, *Welcome Home, Davie* (Waco: Word Books, 1986).
12. Ibid.

**Chapter 5**

1. William Shakespeare, *Romeo and Juliet*, Act II, Scene 2, Line 1.
2. Gary Collins, *How to Be A People Helper* (Santa Ana, Calif.: Vision House, 1976), 33.
3. 1 Samuel 19:1ff.
4. 2 Samuel 1:12ff.
5. 2 Samuel 6:16.
6. 2 Samuel 15:1ff.
7. 2 Samuel 11:1ff.
8. See chapters 9 through 12 on establishing loving boundaries for children.
9. Evert F. Harrison, ed., *Baker's Dictionary of Theology* (Grand Rapids: Baker, 1960), 257.
10. C. S. Lewis, *The Problem of Pain* (New York: MacMillan, 1946), 69.

**Chapter 6**

1. Matthew 15:1ff.; Mark 7:5ff.; Luke 5:30–32.
2. Matthew 16:21–23; John 18:10; Matthew 26:69–75.
3. Proverb 10:19.
4. Isaiah 50:7.

5. Luke 7:34.
6. Proverbs 2:1–9; 9:8ff.

**Chapter 8**

1. M. Rands, "Implicit Theories of Relationships," *Journal of Personality and Social Psychology* 37 (1979): 645–61.
2. James J. Lynch, *The Language of the Heart* (New York: Basic Books, 1985).
3. Ibid., 225.
4. Proverbs 18:21.
5. Joe Bayly, *The Last Thing We Talk About* (Chicago: Cook, 1973).
6. Our missions statement for *Today's Family* is based on the greatest commandment; our goal is to motivate people to highly value God and others and to see their own value in Christ.
7. William Sears, "Your Responsive Baby," *Family Life Today*, 12, no. 4 (1986): 30.
8. Ibid., 30.
9. Carol Kuykendall, *Learning to Let Go* (Grand Rapids: Zondervan, 1985); Gary Smalley, *The Key to Your Child's Heart* (Waco, Tex.: Word, 1984).
10. Guy Mecklin, "Always Up to Bat," *Sports Illustrated*, October 1986.
11. Gordon McDonald, *Ordering Your Private World* (Nashville: Thomas Nelson, 1985).

**Chapter 9**

1. Genesis 3:1ff.
2. Genesis 12:20.
3. Genesis 18:13.
4. Numbers 20:11–12.
5. Francis Brown, S. R. Driver, and Charles A. Briggs, *A Hebrew and English Lexicon of the Old Testament* (Oxford: Clarendon Press, 1974), 407.
6. Arndt and Gingrich, *Lexicon*, 247.
7. R. W. White, "Self-Concept and School Adjustment," *Personnel and Guidance Journal* 46 (1976): 478–81.
8. Kittel and Friedrich, *Theological Dictionary*, 49.

**Chapter 10**

1. Elton Trueblood, *Abraham Lincoln: Theologian of American Anguish* (New York: Harper & Row, 1971), 171.
2. Proverb 19:5.
3. Erwin W. Lutzer, *The Necessity of Ethical Absolutes* (Grand Rapids: Zondervan, 1981).
4. William Lewis, *Coming Home* (New York: Harper and Row, 1986), 211.

### Chapter 11

1. Our special thanks to Dr. Jeffrey M. Trent, associate professor at the University of Arizona Medical School, for his help in explaining this concept to us.
2. Our thanks to Rev. John Werhaus who first illustrated to us the importance of asking and answering these four questions.
3. Isaiah 14 and Ezekiel 28 both speak of Satan's fall because he claimed a position he didn't hold. Others have followed his lead down through the years.
4. David G. Myers, "The Inflated Self," *The Christian Century* 18 (1974): 1226–30.
5. Ibid.
6. John 3:16.
7. Deuteronomy 7:6.
8. Matthew 13:46.
9. Psalm 8:5.
10. Romans 8:37–39.
11. 1 Peter 2:9.
12. Genesis 1:27.
13. Matthew 6:26.
14. Ephesians 2:4–5.
15. See chapter 17 on offering honor to God.
16. Hans Walter Wolff, *Anthropology of the Old Testament* (Philadelphia: Fortress Press, 1974), 23.
17. See chapters 15 and 16 on the dark side of loyalties.

### Chapter 12

1. 1 Samuel 14:24ff.
2. Arndt and Gingrich, *Lexicon*, 825.
3. For more information on setting up contracts with your children, see Gary's book, *The Key to Your Child's Heart*, "Balancing Loving Support Through Contracts," 77ff.

### Chapter 13

1. D. J. Owens, "The Social Structure of Violence in Childhood," *Aggressive Behavior* 12 (1975): 68.
2. Clyde S. Kilby, ed., *An Anthology of C. S. Lewis: A Mind Awake* (New York: Harcourt, Brace & World, 1968), 73.
3. Brown, Driver, and Briggs, *Hebrew Lexicon*, 137.
4. Norman H. Smaith,*The Distinctive Ideas of the Old Testament* (London: Epworth Press, 1964), 118.
5. William L. Holladay, *A Concise Hebrew and Aramaic Lexicon of the Old Testament* (Grand Rapids: Eerdmans, 1971), 113.
6. See Appleton, *Fathers and Daughters*, 81.

7. Brown, Driver, and Briggs, *Hebrew Lexicon*, 137.
8. James Tramill, "The Relationship Between Type A and Type B Behavior Patterns and Level of Self-Worth," *Psychological Record* 35 (1985): 323–27.
9. D. C. Glass, "Behavior Patterns and Stress Management," *American Journal of Medicine* 108 (1981): 55–59.
10. NBC Evening News, September 11, 1986.
11. Romans 5:6ff.

**Chapter 14**

1. S. A. Coopersmith, "A Method for Determining Types of Self-Esteem," *Journal of Abnormal and Social Psychology* 59 (1967): 459.
2. Ibid.
3. On opening and closing a child's spirit, see Gary's *The Key to Your Child's Heart*, "How to Overcome the Major Destroyer of Families," 1ff.
4. See chapters 9 through 12 on establishing loving boundaries.
5. Genesis 3:9–13; 4:6–12.
6. Proverb 14:8.

**Chapter 15**

1. Exodus 20:5.
2. Romans 8:37.
3. Levitcus 16.
4. Alfred Edershime, *The Life and Times of Jesus the Messiah, Part One* (Grand Rapids: Eerdmans, 1972), 103.
5. For a chilling look at such a parent, see M. Scott Peck, *People of the Lie* (New York: Simon & Schuster, 1983).

**Chapter 16**

1. James Dobson, *Love Must Be Tough*; (Waco: Word Books, 1983).
2. Acts 24:25.
3. Wilder Penfield, *The Mystery of the Mind* (Princeton: Princeton University Press, 1977), 148.
4. Dobson, *Love Must Be Tough*.
5. K. E. Moyer, "Kinds of Aggression and Their Physiological Basis," *Communications in Behavioral Biology* 2 (1968): 65–87.
6. Gary Smalley, *Joy That Lasts* (Grand Rapids: Zondervan, 1986).
7. See chapters 4 and 5 on finding value in troubled times.

**Chapter 17**

1. C. S. Lewis, *The Weight of Glory* (Grand Rapids: Eerdmans, 1949), 10.
2. Romans 2:23.

3. Charles Swindoll, *Growing Deep in the Seasons of Life* (Portland: Multnomah Press, 1985).
4. Acts 24:25–26.
5. Gordon MacDonald's book, *Restoring Your Spiritual Passion*, and Swindoll's book on *Growing Deep in the Seasons of Life*.